Communications in Computer and Information Science

2696

Series Editors

Gang Li, *School of Information Technology, Deakin University, Burwood, VIC, Australia*

Joaquim Filipe, *Polytechnic Institute of Setúbal, Setúbal, Portugal*

Zhiwei Xu, *Chinese Academy of Sciences, Beijing, China*

Rationale

The CCIS series is devoted to the publication of proceedings of computer science conferences. Its aim is to efficiently disseminate original research results in informatics in printed and electronic form. While the focus is on publication of peer-reviewed full papers presenting mature work, inclusion of reviewed short papers reporting on work in progress is welcome, too. Besides globally relevant meetings with internationally representative program committees guaranteeing a strict peer-reviewing and paper selection process, conferences run by societies or of high regional or national relevance are also considered for publication.

Topics

The topical scope of CCIS spans the entire spectrum of informatics ranging from foundational topics in the theory of computing to information and communications science and technology and a broad variety of interdisciplinary application fields.

Information for Volume Editors and Authors

Publication in CCIS is free of charge. No royalties are paid, however, we offer registered conference participants temporary free access to the online version of the conference proceedings on SpringerLink (http://link.springer.com) by means of an http referrer from the conference website and/or a number of complimentary printed copies, as specified in the official acceptance email of the event.

CCIS proceedings can be published in time for distribution at conferences or as post-proceedings, and delivered in the form of printed books and/or electronically as USBs and/or e-content licenses for accessing proceedings at SpringerLink. Furthermore, CCIS proceedings are included in the CCIS electronic book series hosted in the SpringerLink digital library at http://link.springer.com/bookseries/7899. Conferences publishing in CCIS are allowed to use Online Conference Service (OCS) for managing the whole proceedings lifecycle (from submission and reviewing to preparing for publication) free of charge.

Publication process

The language of publication is exclusively English. Authors publishing in CCIS have to sign the Springer CCIS copyright transfer form, however, they are free to use their material published in CCIS for substantially changed, more elaborate subsequent publications elsewhere. For the preparation of the camera-ready papers/files, authors have to strictly adhere to the Springer CCIS Authors' Instructions and are strongly encouraged to use the CCIS LaTeX style files or templates.

Abstracting/Indexing

CCIS is abstracted/indexed in DBLP, Google Scholar, EI-Compendex, Mathematical Reviews, SCImago, Scopus. CCIS volumes are also submitted for the inclusion in ISI Proceedings.

How to start

To start the evaluation of your proposal for inclusion in the CCIS series, please send an e-mail to ccis@springer.com

Cristian Tommasino · Cristiano Russo ·
Michele Bernardini
Editors

Artificial Intelligence for Biomedical Data

First International Workshop, AIBio 2025
Held in Conjunction with the European Conference on
Artificial Intelligence, ECAI 2025
Bologna, Italy, October 25–26, 2025
Proceedings

 Springer

Editors
Cristian Tommasino [ID]
University of Naples Federico II
Naples, Italy

Cristiano Russo [ID]
University of Naples Federico II
Naples, Italy

Michele Bernardini [ID]
eCampus University
Novedrate, Italy

ISSN 1865-0929   ISSN 1865-0937 (electronic)
Communications in Computer and Information Science
ISBN 978-3-032-17215-0   ISBN 978-3-032-17216-7 (eBook)
https://doi.org/10.1007/978-3-032-17216-7

Preface

We are pleased to present the proceedings of the 1st Workshop on Artificial Intelligence for Biomedical Data (AIBio 2025), held in conjunction with the 28th European Conference on Artificial Intelligence (ECAI 2025) on 25–26 October 2025 in Bologna, Italy.

AIBio was conceived as an interdisciplinary forum for presenting and discussing cutting-edge research at the intersection of Artificial Intelligence (AI) and biomedical data science, addressing challenges related to disease prediction, multimodal data integration, data generation, image analysis, and clinical validation.

Biomedical data is inherently complex, characterized by heterogeneity, high dimensionality, and scalability constraints, all of which pose significant challenges to extracting meaningful insights. AI provides powerful and innovative tools to overcome these difficulties, enabling advances in disease diagnostics, personalized treatment strategies, and overall healthcare efficiency.

Three distinguished keynote speakers enriched the workshop with forward-looking perspectives on biomedical AI. Francesco Martino highlighted how adopting interoperability standards such as DICOM can unlock the potential of AI in digital pathology by improving data accessibility, integration, and collaboration. Soumick Chatterjee presented unsupervised and self-supervised AI approaches capable of linking morphology to genetics across imaging scales—from histology to cardiac MRI, without the need for manual annotation. Federico Cabitza proposed a multidimensional framework for evaluating clinical AI models, emphasising metrics that capture data reliability, case similarity, and clinical utility, thus moving beyond traditional accuracy-based assessments.

The breadth of biomedical AI research is reflected in this volume, which includes contributions on medical imaging analysis, multimodal learning, federated learning, explainable AI, predictive medicine, synthetic data generation, and ethical and regulatory considerations in AI-driven healthcare. By embracing these diverse domains, AIBio 2025 fostered discussions that not only showcased technical innovations but also explored broader issues such as model interpretability, fairness, data governance, legal constraints, and the open challenges that will shape the future of biomedical AI.

All submitted papers underwent a double-blind peer-review process, with each manuscript evaluated by at least three independent reviewers and, on average, four papers assigned to each reviewer. The workshop received 29 submissions, of which 12 full papers and 5 short papers were accepted. Of the 18 accepted papers, 17 were presented orally at the workshop; only one paper was marked as a no-show due to the absence of the presenting author. Contributions co-authored by Program Committee members were managed independently to avoid conflicts of interest. Furthermore, keynote speakers were invited to submit a paper based on their talks. After an additional double-blind peer-review process, four such papers (3 short and 1 regular) were accepted for publication in these proceedings.

November 2025

Michele Bernardini
Mariachiara Di Cosmo
Cristiano Russo

Organization

General Chair

Cristian Tommasino	University of Naples Federico II, Italy

Program Committee Chairs

Michele Bernardini	eCampus University, Italy
Mariachiara Di Cosmo	School of Advanced Studies Sant'Anna, Italy
Cristiano Russo	University of Naples Federico II, Italy

Organizing Committee Members

Francesco Ciompi	Radboud University Medical Center, Netherlands
Pietro Liò	University of Cambridge, UK
Francesco Merolla	University of Molise, Italy
Sara Moccia	University of Chieti, Italy
Antonio Maria Rinaldi	University of Naples Federico II, Italy
Luca Romeo	University of Macerata, Italy

Program Committee

Domenico Amalfitano	University of Naples Federico II, Italy
Miriam Angeloni	Friedrich-Alexander-Universität Erlangen-Nürnberg, Germany
Domenico Benfenati	University of Naples Federico II, Italy
Daniele Berardini	Italian Institute of Technology, Italy
Francesco Casadei	IRCCS Institute of Neurological Sciences of Bologna, Italy
Michele Ceccarelli	University of Miami, USA / University of Naples Federico II, Italy
Angela Crispino	University of Naples Federico II, Italy
Giovanni Maria De Filippis	University of Naples Federico II, Italy
Maria Chiara Fiorentino	Polytechnic University of Marche, Italy
Reet Ghosh	University of Calgary, Canada

Marko Harasic	Fraunhofer-Institut FOKUS, Germany
Deeptanshu Jha	Alexandria Technology, USA
Nadieh Khalili	Radboud University Medical Center, Netherlands
George Klioumis	Technical University of Crete, Greece
Lucia Migliorelli	Polytechnic University of Marche, Italy
Temitayo Olugbade	University College London, UK
Erasmo Purificato	European Commission Joint Research Centre, Italy
Dario Righelli	University of Naples Federico II, Italy
Francesco Russo	IEOS, Italy
Pierpaolo Vendittelli	Radboud University Medical Center, Netherlands
Jiguang Wang	Hong Kong University of Science and Technology, China

Contents

AI for Desease

Data Generation and Augmentation

Multimodal Techniques

Image Segmentation

Keynote Papers

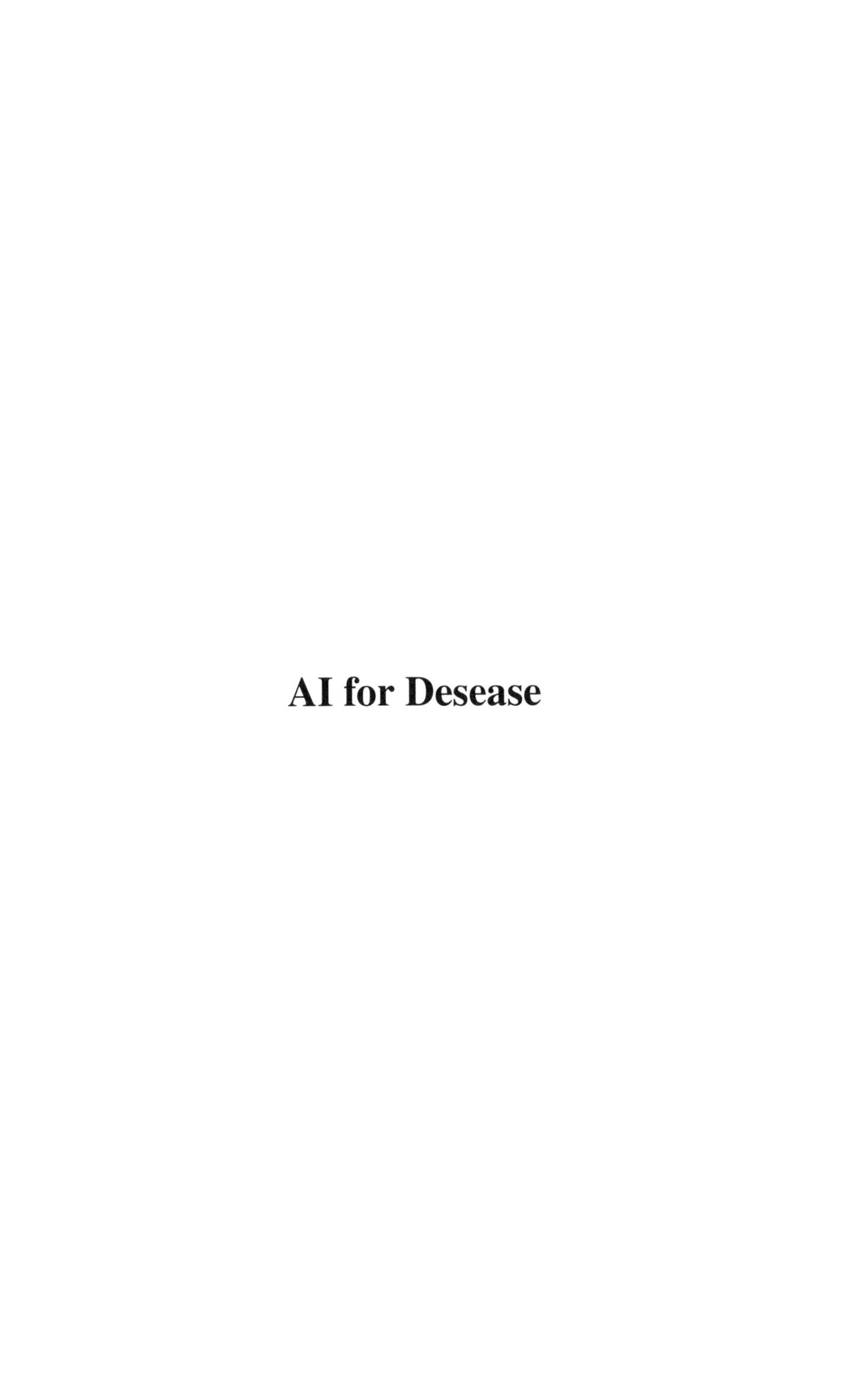

AI for Desease

Improving Early Sepsis Onset Prediction Through Federated Learning

Christoph Düsing$^{(\boxtimes)}$ and Philipp Cimiano

CITEC, Bielefeld University, Bielefeld, Germany
`cduesing@techfak.uni-bielefeld.de`

Abstract. Early and accurate prediction of sepsis onset remains a major challenge in intensive care, where timely detection and subsequent intervention can significantly improve patient outcomes. While machine learning models have shown promise in this domain, their success is often limited by the amount and diversity of training data available to individual hospitals and *Intensive Care Units* (ICUs). *Federated Learning* (FL) addresses this issue by enabling collaborative model training across institutions without requiring data sharing, thus preserving patient privacy. In this work, we propose a federated, attention-enhanced Long Short-Term Memory model for sepsis onset prediction, trained on multicentric ICU data. Unlike existing approaches that rely on fixed prediction windows, our model supports variable prediction horizons, enabling both short- and long-term forecasting in a single unified model. During analysis, we put particular emphasis on the improvements through our approach in terms of early sepsis detection, i.e., predictions with large prediction windows by conducting an in-depth temporal analysis. Our results prove that using FL does not merely improve overall prediction performance (with performance approaching that of a centralized model), but is particularly beneficial for early sepsis onset prediction. Finally, we show that our choice of employing a variable prediction window rather than a fixed window does not hurt performance significantly but reduces computational, communicational, and organizational overhead.

Keywords: Federated Learning · Sepsis Onset Prediction · Recurrent Neural Network

1 Introduction

In recent years, *Clinical Decision Support Systems* (CDSSs) have seen increasing demand, particularly due to the growing adoption of *Electronic Health Records* (EHRs) and the need for tools to assist in timely and adequate therapy. In this context, various *Machine Learning* (ML) techniques have facilitated remarkable improvements in CDSS quality, with applications ranging from diagnosis to prognosis and treatment recommendation [23]. These systems are particularly valuable in intensive care settings, where critically ill patients benefit the most from real-time recommendations. Among the most critical and time-sensitive conditions encountered in *Intensive Care Units* (ICUs) is sepsis, a life-threatening response to an infection that requires timely identification and intervention [21].

C. Tommasino et al. (Eds.): AIBIO 2025, CCIS 2696, pp. 3–16, 2026.
https://doi.org/10.1007/978-3-032-17216-7_1

While the improvements in the quality of CDSSs through ML – and *Deep Learning* (DL) in particular – are impressive, they come at the cost of requiring large and diverse amounts of EHRs to learn from. Unfortunately, in the context of sepsis, it has been shown that average U.S. hospitals do not possess sufficient volumes of EHRs to reliably train such models [3,4]. This raises concerns regarding the ability of smaller hospitals to benefit from these technologies, especially when data centralization is restricted due to privacy concerns.

To address this limitation and avoid direct data sharing among institutions, *Federated Learning* (FL) has emerged as a promising paradigm [5]. FL enables multiple institutions to collaboratively train a shared model while keeping patient data private [9,10]. This makes FL particularly well-suited for the healthcare domain, where data privacy regulations such as the *Health Insurance Portability and Accountability Act* (HIPAA) and the *General Data Protection Regulation* (GDPR) strictly limit data sharing across institutional boundaries.

FL has already demonstrated success in various medical applications beyond sepsis, including kidney injury prediction [18], ICU mortality prediction [11], and drug discovery [15]. These studies demonstrate that FL can be effectively applied in settings where data privacy is a major concern. In the specific context of sepsis, prior work includes the deployment of FL for therapy recommendation [3,4] and for sepsis onset prediction with fixed prediction windows sizes [16].

While the existing body of work shows that the application of FL in the medical domain is not novel per se and has demonstrated promising results – particularly in sepsis prediction and therapy support – we argue that our study advances beyond these existing approaches. Specifically, the novelty and contributions of our work are as follows:

1. **Variable Prediction Windows:** Unlike most existing models that rely on fixed prediction horizons (e.g., [11,16]), we propose an attention-enhanced *Long Short-Term Memory* (LSTM) model, which supports a variable prediction window (25h to 1h predictions). This enables both short-term predictions of sepsis onset at the time of admission as well as long-term forecasts, increasing the model's flexibility and practical utility while reducing the overhead associated with maintaining multiple specialized models [6].

2. **Improved Early Prediction Through FL:** Although early identification is critical, prior research has largely overlooked the specific challenge of early sepsis prediction [25]. To this end, we provide an in-depth analysis demonstrating that FL does not merely improve prediction performance uniformly across time but is particularly effective at enhancing early sepsis detection. Our results show that FL provides more significant improvements as the prediction horizon increases, thus allowing for earlier interventions and potentially better clinical outcomes.

3. **Focus on Multi-Centric Settings:** Unlike previous approaches that often conduct mono-centric analyses, our study highlights the utility of FL in a multi-ICU setting. This is especially important in clinical research, where multi-centric studies are widely considered the gold standard for achieving reliable and generalizable results [25].

2   Related Work

Sepsis onset prediction has been previously studied to some extent due to its critical importance in improving patient outcomes, especially in intensive care settings [14]. Such early warning systems can help physicians identify deteriorating patients and enable more timely interventions, potentially reducing mortality.

Initial efforts in sepsis prediction often employed classical ML models such as *RandomForests* [1]. For instance, Zhou et al. [25] proposed a model that utilizes this technique alongside unbalanced data processing to predict early sepsis in a clinical context. Similarly, Rajendran et al. [18] used a *Multi-Layer Perceptron*, while Pan et al. [16] developed an ensemble-based approach for sepsis prediction. While these models can effectively capture patterns in tabular patient data, they are less suitable for modeling temporal dependencies inherent in most EHRs. This limitation is especially relevant in sepsis care, where recognizing dynamic and temporal changes – such as trends in vital signs or lab values – is essential for timely intervention. For example, the widely adopted *Sepsis-3* definition [21] considers sepsis as a rise of 2 or more points in the *Sequential Organ Failure Assessment* (SOFA) score, regardless of its absolute value, proving the importance of tracking trends over time.

To better capture the temporal nature of patient data, more recent approaches have leveraged *Recurrent Neural Networks* (RNNs), particularly LSTM networks [7]. Svenson et al. [22], for example, deployed LSTMs to predict deteriorating conditions in sepsis patients. Similarly, Scherpf et al. [20] and Zhang et al. [24] applied RNN-based models to forecast sepsis onset directly from multivariate time-series data. Other works have expanded on this with more advanced architectures such an attention-based models for predicting sepsis mortality [13].

More recently, such time-series-based models have been extended to the FL setting. As discussed earlier, FL enables multiple institutions to collaboratively train a shared model without exchanging raw patient data, thereby preserving privacy in compliance with regulations like HIPAA and GDPR [10]. Technically, FL involves multiple rounds of training, where each round consists of: (1) distributing a global model to all participating clients; (2) clients locally updating the model using their private data; and (3) aggregating these local updates on a central server to produce a new global model [9,10]. Following this paradigm, Mondrejevski et al. introduced *FLICU*, a federated LSTM-based model designed for ICU mortality prediction across multiple hospitals without data centralization [12]. Building on this foundation, they later applied a similar framework to predict sepsis onset [11]. However, both models employ a fixed *prediction window* – i.e., they are trained to forecast sepsis a pre-determined number of hours in advance. To compare performance across different prediction windows, some studies train multiple separate models with different prediction windows (e.g., 3h, 6h, or 12h) [6,11,19,20]. The general consensus across these studies is that predictive accuracy tends to decline as the prediction window increases.

Despite their contributions, two key limitations remain across the majority of these studies. First, they rely exclusively on fixed prediction windows, limiting the flexibility and practical deployment of models. Some attempt to address this by training multiple separate models for different prediction horizons, but this adds substantial overhead. Second, although many works observe that performance declines for longer prediction windows, they do not conduct in-depth analyses of whether FL or alternative strategies can mitigate this degradation. In particular, no comprehensive evaluation has been provided to assess if FL contributes more effectively to early detection compared to local models.

3   Methodology

Our approach aims to enhance early sepsis prediction using FL to collaboratively train an LSTM model. This model processes sequences of patient features to predict whether a patient is likely to develop sepsis during their ICU stay – without requiring data centralization. Beyond maintaining privacy, FL reduces regulatory burdens compared to alternatives such as shared data spaces, which require exchanging sensitive patient data across institutions. We begin by describing the dataset acquisition steps for this study. We then introduce the prediction model and detail how it is trained across multiple ICUs in a federated manner. Finally, we outline the evaluation strategy used to assess the model performance.

3.1   Data Acquisition

This study is based on the publicly available *MIMIC-IV* dataset [8], which contains de-identified EHRs of ICU patients admitted to the *Beth Israel Deaconess Medical Center* and was chosen for its public availability, which facilitates reproducibility and broader adoption. The dataset includes admissions from seven ICUs: *Medical ICU* (MICU), *Medical/Surgical ICU* (MICU/SICU), *Surgical ICU* (SICU), *Trauma SICU* (TSICU), *Coronary Care Unit* (CCU), *Cardiac Vascular ICU* (CVICU), and *Neuro SICU* (NSICU).

Patient Inclusion. To ensure data quality and consistency, we applied the following patient inclusion criteria, inspired by prior work [12]:

– Only the first ICU stay per patient is considered.
– Patients with ICU stays shorter than 30 h are excluded to ensure a sufficient observation window.
– Patients admitted to the *Neonatal* or *Pediatric* ICUs are excluded.

After applying these criteria, the final dataset comprises 28,610 patients. Each patient is then assigned to the ICU they were initially admitted to, resulting in a naturally partitioned dataset for FL, where each ICU resembles a client. Among other things, the number of patients per ICU are outlined in Table 2.

Data Pre-processing. The selection of features was guided by prior studies on sepsis onset prediction and therapy recommendation [3,4,11]. In total, we selected 26 clinically relevant features, grouped into four categories: *general, vital signs, diagnoses,* and *therapies.* These are detailed in Table 1.

Then, all features are aggregated into 1-hour time windows following ICU admission to balance temporal resolution with data sparsity. If multiple values for a feature occur within the same hour, the most recent measurement is retained.

Table 1. Feature Selection for Sepsis Onset Prediction

Category	Features
General Features	Gender, Ethnicity, Age, Height, Weight
Vital Features	Platelet, Leukocytes, PO2, FiO2, Lactate, Creatinine, Bilirubin, Glasgow-Coma-Scale, C-reactive protein, Diastolic Pressure, Systolic Pressure, Mean Blood Pressure, Respiratory Rate, Temperature, SpO2, Urine Output, Glucose, Heart Rate
Diagnosis Features	Diabetes, SOFA
Therapy Features	Mechanical Ventilation

Missing values within a patient's time-series are imputed via linear interpolation, while features entirely missing for a patient are replaced with the global mean to provide a neutral value when no patient-specific information is available.

We collect data for the first 30 h of each patient's ICU stay. This time frame is motivated by previous findings suggesting that clinical patterns up to 20–30 hours before sepsis onset are relevant to its prediction [24]. This results in multivariate time-series with 30 hourly measurements for each of the 26 features.

Subsequently, sepsis labels are assigned following the *Sepsis-3* definition [21]. Accordingly, each patient is labeled as positive if they developed sepsis within the first 30 h of ICU admission.

This pre-processing results in seven federated datasets $\mathcal{D}_{\mathrm{ICU}}$, one per ICU, as listed in Table 2. To support subsequent model development and evaluation, each ICU further splits its local dataset $\mathcal{D}_{\mathrm{ICU}}$ into a training set $\mathcal{D}_{\mathrm{ICU}}^{\mathrm{Train}}$ (80%) and a test set $\mathcal{D}_{\mathrm{ICU}}^{\mathrm{Test}}$ (20%). Among other things, Fig. 1 provides a conceptual illustration of the data structure used for each client in the federated setup.

3.2   Sepsis Onset Prediction Model

In this subsection, we describe the architecture of our sepsis onset prediction model, the organization of data into time-series windows for training, and the configuration used to enable FL across participating ICUs.

Data Windowing. To enable the prediction of sepsis onset, patient data is structured into multiple overlapping 6-hour input windows. This design choice is motivated by prior research demonstrating that predictions on patients' outcomes typically require at least 4 h of observational data to achieve reliable performance [17]. Additionally, input windows of 5 to 6 h have been shown to be particularly effective for early sepsis detection tasks [11].

Following this approach, the initial window spans from the time of admission ($t = 0$) to hour 5 ($t = 5$), with the corresponding label indicating whether the patient develops sepsis by hour 30 ($t = 30$). This yields a prediction window of 25 h. A sliding-window approach is then applied, where each subsequent window is shifted forward by one hour. For example, the next sample includes data from $t = 1$ to $t = 6$ and aims to predict sepsis occurrence within the subsequent 24 h.

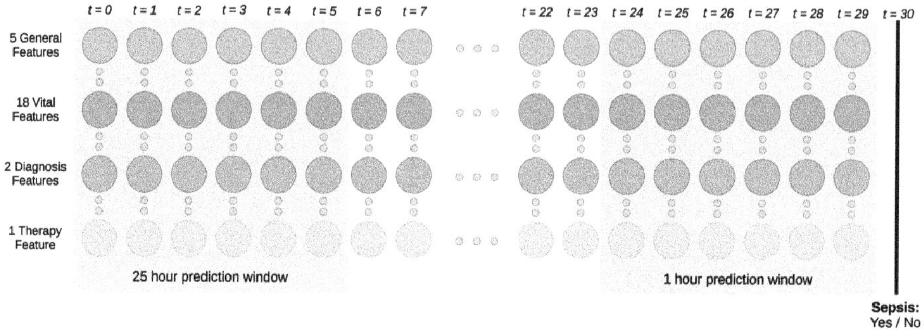

Fig. 1. Time-Series Data and Sliding-Window Approach.

This process continues until the prediction window reduces to one hour, resulting in a dataset with varying prediction horizons.

Figure 1 illustrates this sliding-window mechanism and its alignment with the binary sepsis labels. This multi-horizon setup allows the model to learn from a spectrum of early-warning intervals, enhancing its ability to detect patterns indicating future sepsis onset. As a result, the model gains greater generalizability and is better suited for real-time clinical deployment, where predictions must adapt dynamically to the evolving state of a patient's condition.

Prediction Model. To leverage the temporal structure of the data and due to its proven effectiveness in clinical prediction tasks, we follow previous work and deploy a deep LSTM-based model for our sepsis onset prediction.

Our model builds on architectures proposed in prior FL studies (e.g., [12]) and is enhanced with an attention mechanism [13], which allows the model to assign higher weights to clinically relevant time steps, capturing long-range dependencies. More precisely, the model's input layer is followed by a self-attention layer, then three LSTM layers with 16 units each. Each LSTM layer includes batch normalization and a dropout rate of 0.2 to prevent overfitting. A subsequent linear layer reduces the dimensionality to 8 units, again followed by batch normalization and dropout. Finally, a single linear output neuron provides a binary prediction indicating the likelihood of sepsis onset.

Federated Training. To train this model across institutions without centralizing data, we rely on the *Federated Averaging* (FedAvg) algorithm [10]. FedAvg is the most widely used aggregation strategy in FL, particularly in healthcare applications [4]. It aggregates local model updates from each hospital by computing a weighted average of their parameters, where weights correspond to the size of each hospital's local dataset [9].

The federated training proceeds as follows: the central server initializes the global model and sends it to all participating ICUs. Each ICU then trains the model locally on its own data for three epochs and returns the updated model to the server. After receiving updates from all ICUs, the server aggregates them to form a new global model. This process is repeated for a total of 50 rounds, enabling the model to learn across all ICUs while preserving data privacy.

3.3 Model Evaluation

Model evaluation is conducted on two levels: an ICU-specific evaluation and an overall aggregated evaluation. The ICU-specific evaluation utilizes each ICU's held-out test set $\mathcal{D}_{\text{ICU}}^{\text{Test}}$ to assess the extent to which each hospital benefits from the FL approach, particularly in terms of early and accurate sepsis onset prediction. The overall evaluation, by contrast, aggregates all clients' test sets into a unified dataset $\mathcal{D}^{\text{Test}}$ and serves to quantify the global predictive capabilities of the model across institutions.

To contextualize the effectiveness of the proposed FL model, we compare three distinct evaluation settings during our analyses, namely *Local*, *Federated*, and *Central*:

- **Local:** The proposed LSTM model is trained independently at each ICU using only its local training set $\mathcal{D}_{\text{ICU}}^{\text{Train}}$.
- **Federated:** The proposed FL-based model is trained collaboratively across hospitals without sharing raw data, as described in the previous subsection.
- **Central:** The model is trained centrally on the aggregated training data $\mathcal{D}^{\text{Train}}$ from all ICUs, serving as a theoretical gold standard. Much like FL, it leverages all available data, but unlike FL, it does so without requiring frequent model aggregation, thus providing an upper bound on achievable performance in the absence of data privacy constraints.

To compare the performance across these evaluation settings, we utilize four different metrics: the *F1-Score*, the *Area Under the Curve (AUC)*, and two use-case-specific metrics designed to capture clinical advantages in FL settings, namely the *Federated Improvement Ratio (FIR)* and the *Early Detection Advantage (EDA)*. The former two metrics are standard and can be applied independently to each of the three evaluation settings. In contrast, *FIR* and *EDA* are designed specifically for the use-case at hand to compare the federated and local settings in order to quantify potential improvements gained through FL. These metrics are defined and motivated as follows:

- **F1-Score:** The F1-Score balances the trade-off between precision and recall, providing a single value that captures both aspects of prediction quality. It is computed as:
$$\text{F1-Score} = \frac{2 \cdot TP}{2 \cdot TP + FP + FN}, \tag{1}$$
where TP, FP, and FN denote *True Positives*, *False Positives*, and *False Negatives*, respectively. This metric is especially useful as both false alarms and missed detections carry significant consequences in the clinical setting.
- **AUC:** *AUC* measures the model's ability to distinguish between sepsis and non-sepsis cases across all classification thresholds. It is widely used in healthcare due to its robustness to threshold selection and its interpretability in terms of discriminative ability. It is defined as:
$$AUC = \int_0^1 TPR(FPR^{-1}(x))dx, \tag{2}$$

where TPR and FPR denote the *True Positive Rate* and *False Positive Rate*, respectively. We follow common implementations and rely on the trapezoidal rule to compute a practical approximation of the AUC from discrete data points. Higher AUC values indicate better overall performance across varying decision boundaries.

- **FIR:** FIR is intended to quantify the improvement achieved by the federated model over the local baseline by comparing two sets: (1) sepsis cases correctly predicted by the federated model but missed by the local one, and (2) those correctly predicted by the local model but missed by the federated one. It is defined as:

$$FIR = \frac{TP_{\text{Federated}} \cap FN_{\text{Local}}}{TP_{\text{Local}} \cap FN_{\text{Federated}}}. \tag{3}$$

A ratio greater than 1 indicates that the federated model captures more true sepsis cases than it misses in comparison to the local baseline, highlighting a net diagnostic gain through the use of FL.

- **EDA:** EDA captures the temporal benefit of the federated model by computing, for each correctly identified sepsis case, how many hours earlier the prediction was made compared to the local model. It is defined as:

$$EDA = \frac{1}{|\mathcal{D}^{\text{Test}}_{\text{Sepsis}}|} \sum_{d \in \mathcal{D}^{\text{Test}}_{\text{Sepsis}}} \left(t^{(d)}_{\text{Local}} - t^{(d)}_{\text{Federated}} \right), \tag{4}$$

where $\mathcal{D}^{\text{Test}}_{\text{Sepsis}}$ is the subset of test data with sepsis onset, and $t^{(d)}_{\text{Local}}$, $t^{(d)}_{\text{Federated}}$ denote the earliest correct prediction time of sepsis onset by the local and federated models for case d, respectively. A positive EDA indicates that the federated model recognizes sepsis onset earlier.

All evaluations are performed using 5-fold cross-validation, balancing reliability and computational cost. For each metric, we report the mean and standard deviation across folds to reflect both average performance and variability.

4   Demonstration and Evaluation

During model evaluation, we focus on three aspects: (1) the performance of the FL model compared to both local and central baselines, (2) a deeper temporal analysis of sepsis prediction quality, and (3) a comparison with fixed-prediction-window models in terms of performance and overhead.

4.1   Federated Model Performance Comparison

Baseline Comparison. We begin our evaluation by comparing the federated model to two baselines: a model trained locally at each ICU and a centralized data model. Table 2 shows the performance in terms of $F1$-Score and AUC across all seven ICUs and the overall setting. The federated model consistently outperforms the local baselines across all ICUs. In some cases, it even surpasses the

Table 2. Performance Comparison of FL With Local Baselines and Central Gold Standard (Improvements Over Local Baselines Bold and Underlined)

	Model Training	MICU/ SICU	TSICU	CVICU	MICU	NSICU	SICU	CCU	Overall
	Number of Patients	5,499	6,056	3,460	4,379	3,507	3,998	1,711	28,610
F1-Score	Local	0.7261 ±0.01	0.7680 ±0.01	0.8167 ±0.04	0.7574 ±0.01	0.5890 ±0.05	0.7251 ±0.02	0.7551 ±0.01	0.7522 ±0.03
	Federated	**0.7791** ±0.02	**0.7953** ±0.02	**0.8482** ±0.01	**0.7811** ±0.01	**0.6389** ±0.04	**0.7803** ±0.01	**0.7745** ±0.01	**0.8002** ±0.03
	Central	0.7741 ±0.01	0.7876 ±0.02	0.8793 ±0.02	0.7816 ±0.02	0.7056 ±0.03	0.7439 ±0.01	0.7904 ±0.01	0.8127 ±0.03
AUC	Local	0.7221 ±0.01	0.7706 ±0.01	0.8334 ±0.04	0.7855 ±0.02	0.6136 ±0.04	0.7315 ±0.02	0.7568 ±0.02	0.7613 ±0.03
	Federated	**0.7907** ±0.01	**0.7799** ±0.02	**0.8478** ±0.03	**0.8087** ±0.01	**0.6340** ±0.04	**0.7689** ±0.02	**0.7925** ±0.01	**0.8057** ±0.04
	Central	0.7779 ±0.01	0.7926 ±0.01	0.8830 ±0.02	0.7813 ±0.02	0.7179 ±0.03	0.7699 ±0.02	0.7967 ±0.01	0.8195 ±0.03

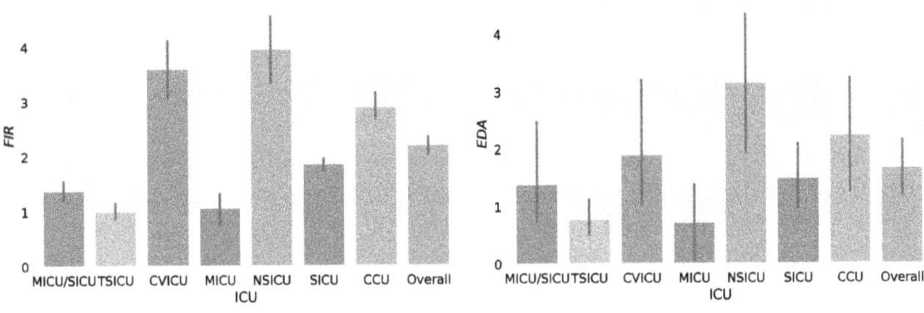

(a) Federated Improvement Ratio   (b) Early Detection Advantage

Fig. 2. ICU-wise Comparison of Improvements Through FL.

centralized model, though these differences are not statistically significant. Gains in $F1$-Score over local models range from modest to substantial, particularly in clients with more limited data. These results highlight the benefit of collaborative training across institutions, where FL compensates for local data scarcity or bias. Importantly, the federated model achieves an overall $AUC = 0.8057$, exceeding the clinically relevant threshold of 0.8 commonly cited for sepsis prediction models [2].

Given the strong correlation between $F1$-Score and AUC observed in Table 2, subsequent analyses report only $F1$-Scores for clarity.

Federated Improvement Analysis. To further quantify the benefit of FL, Fig. 2(a) shows the FIR, which captures the relative change in correct sepsis detection compared to the local model. It shows that all ICUs except TSICU

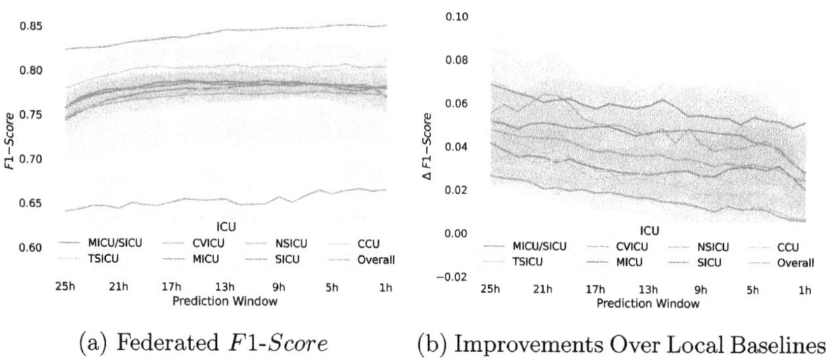

(a) Federated F1-Score   (b) Improvements Over Local Baselines

Fig. 3. Performance and Improvements Over Local Baselines Over Time.

exhibit $FIR > 1$, indicating that the federated model identifies more sepsis cases than it misses relative to local models. CVICU, NSICU, and CCU achieve particularly strong gains with FIR values above 3, whereas ICUs such as MICU/SICU show modest improvements. On average, the federated model correctly identifies twice as many sepsis cases missed by local models as vice versa.

Early Detection Advantage. To complement our performance comparison, we assess whether the federated model enables earlier sepsis detection. Figure 2(b) plots the average number of hours sepsis is detected earlier using the FL model compared to local baselines. All clients exhibit $EDA > 0$, confirming the benefit of FL in accelerating detection. The average improvement is close to 2 h. Notably, NSICU shows the largest lead time gain (over 3 h), followed by CVICU and CCU (around 2 h). The remaining ICUs experience gains between 0.7 and 1.5 h.

Overall, the federated model improves both detection accuracy and timeliness compared to local models and achieves performance close to a centralized gold standard – all while preserving data privacy. This confirms the viability of FL for clinical prediction tasks across diverse hospital environments.

4.2 Temporal Evaluation of Prediction Performance

Predictive Performance. Figure 3(a) plots the F1-Score for each client for the different prediction windows (from 25h to 1h). In line with existing studies on the subject [6,11,19,20], we find that the prediction performance is better for short-term predictions, whereas long-term predictions are less accurate.

More specifically, we find that the performance for prediction windows smaller than 12h are mostly stable, where only few ICUs (e.g., CVICU and NSICU) improve when smaller prediction windows. For larger prediction windows, we observe a clear trend among all clients, where longer prediction horizons correlate with weaker performance in terms of F1-Score. For most ICUs as well as the overall performance, the F1-Score starts at about 0.75 for 25h predictions and increases to about 0.79 for predictions below 12h horizons.

Notable exceptions are CVICU, which has a significantly higher F1-Score starting at 0.82 and improving up to 0.85. Contrary, NSICU has significantly smaller scores, ranging from 0.64 to 0.67. These discrepancies are likely due to the fact that their data is dissimilar from the data held by the remaining ICUs, which turns out favorable for CVICU and unfavorable of NSICU.

Improvements over Baseline. While the previous finding on the temporal aspects of predictive performance mostly confirmed existing studies, Fig. 3(b) plots the improvements achieved through the use of FL over its local baselines. This is a novel perspective on the evaluation of models for sepsis onset prediction.

The results show an almost linear trend among most ICUs as well as overall. The plot shows that the improvements over the local baselines are the largest for large prediction windows and decrease for smaller prediction horizons. This is interesting as our previous analysis proved weaker performance for such prediction windows, indicating that the local models suffer even more significantly from long prediction windows. The plot shows that the improvements for 25h predictions range between 0.02 and 0.07. For short term predictions such as 1h, improvements decrease to about 0.01 to 0.06. Notably, the CVICU client, which we previously found to perform best among all prediction windows, offers the smallest improvements over the local baselines, indicating a particularly strong local baseline model. These findings are also supported by the previous Table 2, where CVICU has, in fact, the highest baseline F1-Score.

The combined findings from Fig. 3 show that while FL is also prone to deteriorating model performance for long-term predictions, we provide evidence that models trained federately are more resilient to these effects, indicated by the larger improvements over baselines for long-term predictions.

4.3 Comparison with Fixed Prediction Window

In earlier sections, we discussed the conceptual advantages of using a variable prediction window – namely, reduced computational and organizational overhead, as well as greater clinical flexibility. Here, we complement those arguments by empirically comparing our proposed model against dedicated models trained for fixed prediction windows in terms of performance and computational cost.

Predictive Performance. Table 3 compares the F1-Score of our variable-prediction-window model to three representative fixed-prediction-window models trained independently for the exemplary prediction windows of 25h, 15h, and 5h. While the fixed-window models show slightly higher scores in several cases, most differences fall within one standard deviation and are therefore not statistically significant. Notable exceptions include MICU/SICU and SICU, where two of the three fixed-window models significantly outperform the variable-window model. In contrast, for NSICU, our variable-prediction-window model achieves better performance in two of the three comparisons.

Computational Overhead. To quantify computational cost, we measured training time under identical conditions using the same hardware (NVIDIA Tesla V100 16GB). Average training time per round was comparable across settings – 109 s for our variable-window model versus a combined 115 s for the all

Table 3. F1-Score Improvements of Fixed-Prediction-Windows Over Variable-Prediction-Windows (Bold and Underlined if Exceeding Standard Deviation)

Prediction Window	MICU/ SICU	TSICU	CVICU	MICU	NSICU	SICU	CCU	Overall
25h	**0.0265**	0.0281	0.0091	0.0265	-0.0037	**0.0277**	0.0116	0.0203
	±0.02	±0.03	±0.03	±0.04	±0.05	±0.02	±0.02	±0.03
15h	**0.0286**	0.0268	-0.0119	0.0201	0.0059	0.0193	0.0160	0.0171
	±0.02	±0.03	±0.02	±0.02	±0.05	±0.02	±0.03	±0.02
5h	0.0293	0.0297	0.0115	**0.0275**	-0.0159	**0.0246**	0.0192	**0.0202**
	±0.03	±0.03	±0.02	±0.02	±0.06	±0.02	±0.03	±0.02

fixed-window models. This is expected since data size and model complexity are constant, and aggregation overhead is minimal. However, convergence behavior differs significantly. The variable-prediction-window model converged within an average of 5.3 rounds, while the fixed-prediction-window models required approximately 15.4 rounds on average – nearly three times as many. This difference is likely caused by the fact that each fixed-prediction-window model is trained on a smaller data subset, limiting generalization and convergence.

The previous comparison does not even account for some variable factors affecting the total overhead. For example, training multiple models instead of a single one using FL increases the communication overhead involved in the training, which scales linearly with the number of models. Furthermore, it disregards the substantial organizational overhead associated with maintaining and validating multiple specialized models in practice.

Taken together, these results suggest that our variable prediction window approach offers a substantially more efficient and scalable alternative, with only minimal, often statistically insignificant trade-offs in predictive performance. We argue that the computational and operational benefits far outweigh the marginal performance gains occasionally observed with dedicated fixed-window models.

5   Conclusion, Limitations, and Future Work

In this study, we present a FL approach for early sepsis onset prediction based on an attention-enhanced LSTM architecture. Our model is specifically designed to support variable prediction windows, allowing it to operate flexibly across a range of clinical scenarios, ranging from immediate risk assessment at ICU admission to long-term forecasts. Compared to existing approaches that rely on fixed prediction horizons [6,11], our model generalizes across multiple prediction windows in a single training process, reducing computational overhead without significant performance trade-offs.

Through extensive evaluation on the MIMIC-IV dataset, we demonstrate that the federated model consistently outperforms local baselines across all participating ICUs and performs competitively with a centrally trained upper-bound model. These findings validate that FL not only enables collaborative model development across institutions but also improves early detection of sepsis – a critical requirement for clinical decision support. In particular, we show that FL provides the greatest performance improvements in long-term predictions, where local models deteriorate in performance. This contributes a novel and clinically meaningful insight to the literature, addressing a gap in prior works that largely focused on short-term prediction accuracy.

Limitations. To start with the obvious, our experiments are conducted on a single dataset and task only. Although the MIMIC-IV dataset is well-established in the field of medical research, this limits the generalizability of our findings. Moreover, our FL setup assumes ideal conditions, ignoring practical aspects of FL application, such as issues with client dropout, client synchronization, and increased deployment complexity. Additionally, we did not include baselines other than the local and central training of the same LSTM model we train federately.

Future Work. In the future, we aim to focus on validating our approach in clinical settings and using external datasets to assess generalizability in real-world settings. We also plan to integrate techniques facilitating model explainability and transparency – an essential factor for clinical adoption. Lastly, we aim to explore and mitigate potential failure modes in FL settings, including issues arising from data imbalance, malicious participants, or unreliable clients, to further strengthen robustness and practical viability of our approach.

References

1. Breiman, L.: Random forests. Mach. Learn. **45**, 5–32 (2001)
2. Çorbacıoğlu, ŞK., Aksel, G.: Receiver operating characteristic curve analysis in diagnostic accuracy studies: a guide to interpreting the area under the curve value. Turk. J. Emerg. Med. **23**(4), 195 (2023)
3. Düsing, C., Cimiano, P.: Federated learning to improve counterfactual explanations for sepsis treatment prediction. In: International Conference on Artificial Intelligence in Medicine, pp. 86–96. Springer (2023)
4. Düsing, C., et al.: Integrating federated learning for improved counterfactual explanations in clinical decision support systems for sepsis therapy. Artif. Intell. Med. **157**, 102982 (2024)
5. Fang, M.L., Dhami, D.S., Kersting, K.: Dp-ctgan: differentially private medical data generation using ctgans. In: International Conference on AI in Medicine, pp. 178–188. Springer (2022)
6. Goh, K.H., et al.: Artificial intelligence in sepsis early prediction and diagnosis using unstructured data in healthcare. Nat. Commun. **12**(1), 711 (2021)
7. Hochreiter, S., Schmidhuber, J.: Long short-term memory. Neural Comput. **9**(8), 1735–1780 (1997)
8. Johnson, A., Bulgarelli, L., Pollard, T., Horng, S., Celi, L.A., Mark, R.: Mimic-iv (2022). https://doi.org/10.13026/rrgf-xw32
9. Kairouz, P., et al.: Advances and open problems in federated learning. Found. Trends® Mach. Learn. **14**(1–2), 1–210 (2021)

10. McMahan, B., Moore, E., Ramage, D., Hampson, S., y Arcas, B.A.: Communication-efficient learning of deep networks from decentralized data. In: Artificial Intelligence and Statistics, pp. 1273–1282. PMLR (2017)
11. Mondrejevski, L., Azzopardi, D., Miliou, I.: Predicting sepsis onset with deep federated learning. In: Joint European Conference on Machine Learning and Knowledge Discovery in Databases, pp. 73–86. Springer (2023)
12. Mondrejevski, L., Miliou, I., Montanino, A., Pitts, D., Hollmén, J., Papapetrou, P.: Flicu: a federated learning workflow for intensive care unit mortality prediction. In: 2022 IEEE 35th International Symposium on Computer-Based Medical Systems (CBMS), pp. 32–37. IEEE (2022)
13. Mondrejevski, L., Rugolon, F., Miliou, I., Papapetrou, P.: Masicu: a multimodal attention-based classifier for sepsis mortality prediction in the ICU. In: 2024 IEEE 37th International Symposium on Computer-Based Medical Systems (CBMS), pp. 326–331. IEEE (2024)
14. Moor, M., Rieck, B., Horn, M., Jutzeler, C.R., Borgwardt, K.: Early prediction of sepsis in the ICU using machine learning: a systematic review. Front. Med. **8**, 607952 (2021)
15. Oldenhof, M., et al.: Industry-scale orchestrated federated learning for drug discovery. In: Proceedings of the AAAI Conference on Artificial Intelligence, vol. 37, pp. 15576–15584 (2023)
16. Pan, W., Xu, Z., Rajendran, S., Wang, F.: An adaptive federated learning framework for clinical risk prediction with electronic health records from multiple hospitals. Patterns **5**(1) (2024)
17. Pattalung, T.N., Chaichulee, S.: Comparison of machine learning algorithms for mortality prediction in intensive care patients on multi-center critical care databases. In: Materials Science and Engineering, vol. 1163, p. 12027. IOP (2021)
18. Rajendran, S., Xu, Z., Pan, W., Ghosh, A., Wang, F.: Data heterogeneity in federated learning with electronic health records: case studies of risk prediction for acute kidney injury and sepsis diseases in critical care. PLOS Digit. Health **2**(3), e0000117 (2023)
19. Rosnati, M., Fortuin, V.: MGP-AttTCN: an interpretable machine learning model for the prediction of sepsis. PLoS ONE **16**(5), e0251248 (2021)
20. Scherpf, M., Gräßer, F., Malberg, H., Zaunseder, S.: Predicting sepsis with a recurrent neural network using the MIMIC III database. Comput. Biol. Med. **113**, 103395 (2019)
21. Singer, M., et al.: The third international consensus definitions for sepsis and septic shock (sepsis-3). JAMA **315**(8), 801–810 (2016)
22. Svenson, P., Haralabopoulos, G., Torres Torres, M.: Sepsis deterioration prediction using channelled long short-term memory networks. In: International Conference on Artificial Intelligence in Medicine, pp. 359–370. Springer (2020)
23. Tonekaboni, S., Joshi, S., McCradden, M.D., Goldenberg, A.: What clinicians want: contextualizing explainable machine learning for clinical end use. In: Machine Learning for Healthcare Conference, pp. 359–380. PMLR (2019)
24. Zhang, D., Yin, C., Hunold, K.M., Jiang, X., Caterino, J.M., Zhang, P.: An interpretable deep-learning model for early prediction of sepsis in the emergency department. Patterns **2**(2) (2021)
25. Zhou, L., Shao, M., Wang, C., Wang, Y.: An early sepsis prediction model utilizing machine learning and unbalanced data processing in a clinical context. Prev. Med. Rep. **45**, 102841 (2024)

Experimenting Federated AI Models for Hematological Diseases

Luciana Carota[1]([✉]) [iD], Francesco Casadei[2] [iD], Gianluca Asti[3] [iD],
Davide Piscia[4] [iD], Patricia A. Apellániz[5] [iD], Saverio D'Amico[3] [iD],
Riccardo Biondi[2] [iD], Claudia Sala[1] [iD], Nono S. C. Merleau[6] [iD],
Michel S. J. van Deventer[7] [iD], Raffaella Colombatti[8] [iD],
Elisabetta Mezzalira[8] [iD], María del Mar Mañú Pereira[9] [iD],
Sara Isabel Reidel[9] [iD], Stefano Polizzi[1] [iD], Sara Peluso[1,11] [iD], Cesare Rollo[10] [iD],
Tiziana Sanavia[10] [iD], Piero Fariselli[10] [iD], Juan Parras[5] [iD],
Alejandro Almodóvar[5] [iD], Santiago Zazo[5] [iD], Matteo Della Porta[3] [iD],
Federico Alvarez[5] [iD], Gastone Castellani[1,11] [iD], and Enrico Giampieri[1,11] [iD]

[1] Department of Medical and Surgical Sciences, University of Bologna, Bologna, Italy
luciana.carota@unibo.it
[2] IRCCS Istituto delle Scienze Neurologiche di Bologna, Bologna, Italy
[3] Humanitas Clinical and Research Center IRCCS, Milan, Italy
[4] Centro Nacional de Análisis Genómico, C/Baldiri Reixac 4, 08028 Barcelona, Spain
[5] Information Processing and Telecommunications Center, ETS Ingenieros de
Telecomunicación, Universidad Politécnica de Madrid, Madrid, Spain
[6] Max Planck Institute for Mathematics in the Sciences of Leipzig, Leipzig, Germany
[7] UMC Utrecht, Utrecht, The Netherlands
[8] Department of Women's and Children's Health, University of Padua, Padua, Italy
[9] Vall d'Hebron Research Institute, Barcelona, Spain
[10] Computational Biomedicine Unit Department of Medical Sciences, Turin, Italy
[11] IRCCS Azienda Ospedaliero - Universitaria di Bologna, Bologna, Italy

Abstract. Federated learning is an Artificial Intelligence framework that allows to train machine learning models in a distributed way, avoiding the sharing of sensitive data. This method is crucial, especially in healthcare applications, where patient privacy is an enormous concern. This study aims to demonstrate the effectiveness of federated learning in addressing real use-cases. In addition, the platform developed by the GenoMed4All consortium was tested against computational simulations. Two real use-cases were considered: a survival estimation task on a Myelodysplastic Syndrome cohort, and a classification task on a scarce Sickle Cell Disease dataset. Both cohorts were distributed in a federated learning scenario with 3 clients and a common test set. Federated learning came out to be crucial in improving the performance of local survival models, especially for nodes with the lower number of samples, which most benefit from federated aggregation. Despite the limited number of patients for the classification task, federated learning consistently improved model performance across multiple metrics beyond the F1 score, including comparisons between different sample distributions among the three clients. These results confirmed the effectiveness of federated learning in healthcare applications, especially for scarce datasets,

C. Tommasino et al. (Eds.): AIBIO 2025, CCIS 2696, pp. 17–30, 2026.
https://doi.org/10.1007/978-3-032-17216-7_2

for which this technique can represent a viable solution. Moreover, the results of the GenoMed4All platform are completely in agreement with the computer simulations, proving the reliability of the developed platform.

Keywords: Federated Learning · Hematology · GenoMed4All · Survival analysis · Classification

1   Introduction

In recent years, the development of Artificial Intelligence (AI) models has transformed healthcare research, contributing to improved diagnostics, prognostics, and therapeutic strategies [1,2]. However, training AI models typically requires large datasets, which are often not available within a single institution, especially for rare hematological diseases, where patient numbers are limited and spread across multiple centers. In addition, the sharing of sensitive clinical data between institutions is heavily restricted due to national and international privacy regulations.

Machine Learning (ML) and in particular Deep Learning (DL) models have shown promise in hematology for tasks such as automated cell classification, prediction of disease progression, and treatment response. Nevertheless, the application of DL to rare diseases is particularly challenging because of small sample sizes, high inter-patient variability, and heterogeneous data acquisition protocols. These limitations reduce model generalization and increase the risk of overfitting when using conventional centralized training approaches [3].

Federated Learning (FL), introduced by Google in 2016 [4], is a privacy-preserving framework that allows training AI models in a distributed way, avoiding sensitive data sharing. It consists of sharing and aggregating model parameters (or gradients) between the involved institutions, rather than data itself [5,6].

Among FL workflows, horizontal FL with a central aggregation server is the most widely adopted in healthcare [7,8]. In this framework, a central Manager Node (MN) collects model updates from multiple local Worker Nodes (WNs), aggregates them, and redistributes the updated global model. Each WN trains the shared model on its local data in a secure environment, ensuring that patient-level data never leave the institution. This setup is particularly suited for rare hematological diseases, where data sharing is restricted, and collaboration across multiple centers is essential to build robust predictive models.

The simplest federated aggregation strategy is called Federated Averaging (FedAvg) [6] and consists of a weighted average of the parameters of the local model:

$$W_{glob} = \sum_{k \in S_t} \gamma_k \cdot w_k \tag{1}$$

where S_t is the set of nodes available, γ_k is the ratio between the data volume of node k and the total amount of data, w_k are the model parameters of node k and

W_{glob} are the aggregated global model parameters. Other aggregation solutions can be used, spanning from small variations of FedAvg (e.g. using median instead of average) to more complicated algorithms (e.g. FedNova [9]).

The FL approach has enormous potential in healthcare applications, especially in hematology and rare diseases, where sensitive patient data and diverse datasets are crucial for advancing research and improving care [10,11]. Although it has been gaining attention in the medical field as an attractive privacy-enhanced alternative to traditional centralized training, the current landscape of FL in healthcare reveals a significant gap between research and real-world implementation [12]. Most FL studies are not suitable for clinical use due to methodological flaws, privacy concerns, limited generalization issues due to limited cohort sizes, and communication costs [13].

Only two recent parallel initiatives and platform efforts illustrate the feasibility of FL for hematology applications without sharing patient-level data. The BloodCounts! is a clinical data consortium that builds models on Full Blood Count (FBC) large-scale routine laboratory data distributed across multiple countries (UK, Netherlands, Gambia), demonstrating FL for population/global hematology analytics without centralizing raw data [14].

Differently, the GenoMed4All and Synthema consortia [15] have developed research platforms for rare diseases in hematology, enabling models built across multiple institutions using clinical and genomic data in the case of GenoMed4All, and multimodal data in the case of Synthema.

The horizontal FL framework described above was implemented through both a platform deployed by the GenoMed4All consortium (FL_Platform), and software simulation running on a single computer (FL_Local). Both simulations and platform allow to optimize the models training for the studied hematological use cases.

The main objective of this study is to demonstrate the effectiveness of FL in a real healthcare setting, investigating the feasibility and performance of FL models for two rare hematological diseases whose data are available on the GenoMed4All platform [16]. The two considered hematological use cases are a survival task performed in a cohort of patients with Myelodysplastic Syndrome, and a classification task applied to a small dataset of people with Sickle Cell Disease. The effectiveness of FL in scarce datasets was clearly demonstrated for SCD. This result is particularly interesting, as rare diseases are one of the main issues in healthcare and FL could represent a viable and robust solution to this problem.

In addition, the present study tested the FL platform developed by the GenoMed4All consortium. Two main aspects of the platform implementation were considered: usability and reliability. The first aspect was qualitatively evaluated according to the ease and flexibility in implementing the models. The second was assessed quantitatively by comparing the results from the platform with the results of software simulations.

2   Materials and Methods

2.1   Federated Frameworks: Platform and Simulations

The implementation of the FL setting is based on Flower [17], which is a Python library developed for the deployment of FL solutions. It is an object-oriented library and is compatible with the most popular ML solutions, such as Scikit-learn, TensorFlow, PyTorch, etc.

Flower allows to simulate FL experiments by deploying a virtual central server and virtual local nodes. The main entity of the setting is the FL model. It is a Python object characterized by five methods for data loading, parameter setting, parameter retrieval, data fit, and performance evaluation. The FL model returns the Flower strategy, which governs the aggregation at the server node, and a local learner used for training on the individual client nodes.

FL_Local and FL_Platform implementations are based on Flower and FL models stored in pickle files. Pickle package is the Python module used for object serialization and deserialization (i.e., converting Python objects to a byte stream and vice versa). The reliability of the platform was validated by comparing simulations and real experiments.

The FL platform developed by the GenoMed4All consortium includes the two main entities, an MN and several WNs. In the first experimental version of the GenoMed4All platform, the MN is located at Humanitas Research Hospital (ICH) in Milan, Italy, and five WNs were installed in different European institutions: ICH, Leipzig Institute for Advanced Mathematics (LPZ), University of Bologna (UNIBO), Polytechnic University of Madrid (UPM), and University of Utrecht (UTR).

In both hematological use cases, the two entire datasets were split on 3 nodes: ICH, LPZ, and UNIBO for the MDS dataset, and ICH, UNIBO, and UPM for the SCD cohort. The two compared use cases, one with a large dataset, and the other with few samples, use only three nodes out of the 5, since a basic configuration is a suitable starting point for first tests: scalability properties will be addressed in future research studies.

The main interface of an MN is a dashboard where a data science user can instantiate and run a new FL task by selecting the local datasets to use, the ML model to fit, the runtime library, and the number of local epochs. By a specific section of the dashboard, it is possible to upload a new FL model in pickle format, which must have the structure described above. Additional metrics can be shared back with the MN to monitor FL training, which is supported by the MLFlow library [18] and reported on the dashboard.

2.2   Hematological Use Cases

The FL platform test was conducted by exploiting two rare hematological use cases: a large Myelodysplastic Syndrome (MDS) cohort and a small Sickle Cell Disease (SCD) dataset. For both real use cases and compatibly with the ethical and legal requirements, the data were recorded on the platform omitting any codes enabling to trace patient identities.

MDS Use Case. MDS are a group of oncohematological disorders in which bone marrow stem cells do not mature and may eventually evolve into Acute Myeloid Leukemia [19]. MDS mainly affects elderly people, and the most common symptoms are fatigue, anemia, and frequent infections [20]. The MDS pathophysiology is a complex process that involves both cytogenetic alterations and genetic point mutations [21]. The most common MDS treatment consists of allogeneic stem-cell transplantation [20]. The main prognostic systems, which are the International Prognostic Scoring System (IPSS) [22] and its revised version (IPSS-R) [21], are based on hematological and clinical parameters, such as cytogenetic abnormalities, mutations and percentage of blasts in the bone marrow [23]. However, these indexes can fail in capturing important prognostic information.

The MDS cohort consists of 3152 samples, collected from the GenoMed4All and Synthema consortia. Only a sample is reported for each patient, with all the input features collected at the time of diagnosis. Humanitas Ethics Committee approved the study (ClinicalTrials.gov Identifier: NCT04889729). Written informed consent was obtained from each participant.

A total of 64 features, clinical, genomic and karyotype, were available. Laboratory and demographics features correspond to 6 continuous variables: hemoglobin, platelets, bone marrow biopsy (BMB), neutrophils, and age of diagnosis. Genomic and karyotype variables include point mutations and chromosomal structural variations, reported as binary variables. Time to event and censoring status information were also provided.

The entire cohort was artificially and randomly divided among 3 clients, named Node1, Node2 and Node3, with the following partition: 1524, 677, and 508 samples, respectively. A unique test dataset of 443 samples was used. The large size of the datasets prevents class imbalance and variability.

SCD Use Case. SCD is the most common group of inherited red blood cell disorders, resulting in the production of abnormal hemoglobin and causing red blood cells to become rigid and crescent-shaped, or sickled [18]. In spite of originating from a single point mutation, the disease is very unpredictable and has a very heterogeneous clinical phenotype, manifesting itself with recurrent painful vaso-occlusive crises, anemia, increased susceptibility to infections, and multi-organ damage, varying dramatically between individuals [24]. Silent Cerebral Infarction (SCI) is one of the most common neurological complications of SCD, resulting from chronic or acute cerebral ischemia due to sickled cells obstructing cerebral microvasculature, anemia-induced hypoxia, or endothelial dysfunction [25]. It refers to brain infarcts detectable on Magnetic Resonance Imaging (MRI) that occur without overt clinical symptoms, but are associated with long-term cognitive and neurodevelopmental impairments [26]. Early detection through predictive models implies interventions to reduce risk factors for closely monitored patients [27]. SCD laboratory data were analyzed in a federated context to classify the emergence of Silent Cerebral Infarction (SCI).

The small SCD cohort includes 65 samples enrolled at the Hospital of Padua. The cohort is characterised by a total of 19 input features, subdivided into 5 data types for each patient: presence or absence of SCI defined by MRI outcomes as the binary outcome to predict, hematological tests, physical parameters, a diagnosis that defines the SCD type and time intervals of the hematological and physical measurements from the observed SCI presence/absence. Clinical variables from hematological tests include: alanine aminotransferase (ALT), aspartate aminotransferase (AST), direct, indirect and total bilirubin, creatinine, ferritin, white blood cells (WBC), lactate dehydrogenase (LDH), and urea. Physical parameters include blood pressure, oxygen saturation, weight, height, and heart rate. The time intervals are different across patients. For each patient, the time intervals differed across the hematological variables, whereas the physical parameters were measured simultaneously. The 10 time intervals of hematological measurements and the unique time interval of physical measurements were not included as input features in the experiments, in order to prevent overfitting due to the high number of inputs relative to the limited number of patients. Instead, the mean and standard deviation of the 11 time intervals were included as input features for each patient, improving the model performance.

The 80% of the entire dataset (52 samples) was used for the training and distributed to the three clients (named Node1, Node2 and Node3) of 27, 15 and 10 samples, respectively. The remaining 20%, including 13 patients, was used to validate the performance in all training settings. The datasets show the following distributions of SCI presence/absence: the entire training set includes 21 SCI-positive and 31 SCI-negative patients; the test set includes 5 SCI-positive and 8 SCI-negative patients; Node1, Node2, and Node3 include 11, 7 and 3 SCI-positive, and 16, 8, and 7 SCI-negative patients, respectively. This data configuration was designed to limit variability among datasets to the number of patients and the overall shapes of the input feature distributions, reflecting the constraints imposed by the small sample sizes.

Pairwise Energy [28] and Maximum Mean Discrepancy (MMD) [29] tests were applied to compare distributions across the involved datasets and for each continuous input feature. Both tests produced low p-values ($p < 0.05$), even after correction for multiple comparisons, indicating that the null hypothesis of comparable distributions can be rejected with very high confidence, suggesting substantial differences in location, variability, or overall shape. To test results' generalization, two different distributions of patients across the three nodes were comparatively experimented by two distinct trials, called Trial1 and Trial2. The node sizes were preserved identical across the trials and the same proportion of presence/absence of SCI was maintained in each node. Trial1 was executed both on a single computer by FL_Local simulations, and on the platform by FL_Platform experiments to test result equivalence. Once that such an equivalence was demonstrated, the Trial1 and Trial2 were compared only by simulations to test the results' generalization.

Both MDS and SCD use cases underwent the same preprocessing steps. Non-binary features were normalized between 0 and 1. Then, ML models were trained on a 10-fold cross-validation (CV) framework to calculate a mean performance metric with its uncertainty. In each CV fold, a client dataset was split into a training and a validation dataset (85% and 15% of the total amount of local data, respectively) and the performance result was calculated by means of the common and shared unique dataset of test. The 10 CV-subsets were stratified to limit excessive variability.

2.3 Federated Models

Considering that complex algorithms may slow down federation mechanisms or, more seriously, leave technological faults undiscovered, simple ML models can be better candidates for the initial applications of the platform, even when using real data.

Considering the survival task, since MDS provides a large cohort of patients, the DeepSurv model [30] was chosen and implemented by PyTorch. The parameters of the DeepSurv neural network were set to the following values by a grid search based on the output performance: a dropout of 0.7, batch size of 512, learning rate of 0.01, ReLu activation function, batch normalization, and 100 training epochs. Adam optimization was chosen.

To classify the presence or absence of SCI, the federated Logistic Regression (LR) of Scikit-learn, with class balance, L2-penalty and optimization method L-BFGS [31], was applied to the SCD use case. Due to the small size of the dataset, the performance was not fully satisfactory in the centralized mode. However, the LR model was chosen because it meets the simplicity requirements for initial platform tests, focusing on the possibility to implement an advantageous federated algorithm rather than a final prediction goodness. Once federated aggregation is comparable to centralized performance and the platform is robust, larger SCD datasets and more complex models could be used for the same binary classification or more complex tasks.

2.4 Performance Evaluation of the Models

The main task for the MDS use case was the prediction of overall survival. The Harrell's C-index [32] is a goodness-of-fit metric suitable for survival models, since it accounts for censored events.

The SCI prediction for the SCD use case can be considered a classification of the presence or absence of an event, based on previously recorded measurements. The metrics commonly used to evaluate the performance of a classification model are the Accuracy, Precision, Recall, F1 score and the ROC-AUC score.

3   Results

3.1   MDS

The C-index curves for centralized, isolated and federated training for the MDS use case obtained for both FL_Local and FL_Platform are shown in Fig. 1a and Fig. 1b, respectively.

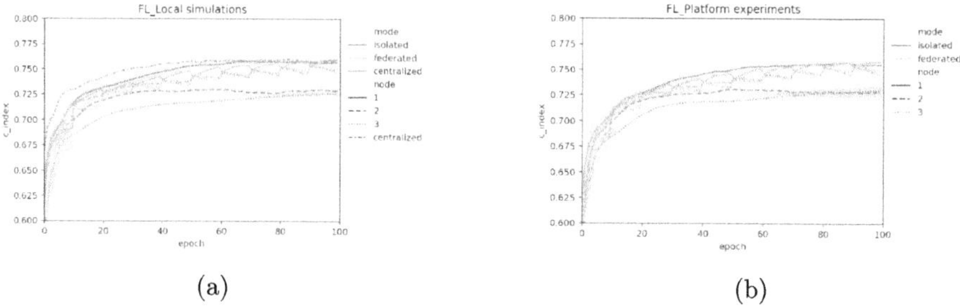

(a)   (b)

Fig. 1. Mean C-index of the DeepSurv model trained in the 10-fold CV versus each epoch for centralized (green), isolated (blue) and federated (orange) mode, for (a) FL_Local simulations and (b) FL_Platform experiments. Each mode was evaluated on the external common test dataset. The line-style defines the node type (Node1, Node2, Node3 or centralized) and the color the training setting (isolated, federated and centralized). In the federated mode, the parameters' aggregation occurs with a period of 10 epochs. (Color figure online)

Table 1. C-index of DeepSurv model for performances of FL_Local and FL_Platform settings.

Centralized FL_Local	Nodes	Pats	Isolated FL_Local	Isolated FL_Platform	Federated FL_Local	Federated FL_Platform
0.760 ± 0.001	Node1	1524	0.757 ± 0.001	0.755 ± 0.001	0.760 ± 0.001	0.758 ± 0.001
	Node2	677	0.729 ± 0.002	0.728 ± 0.004	0.747 ± 0.002	0.745 ± 0.002
	Node3	508	0.726 ± 0.001	0.730 ± 0.002	0.750 ± 0.001	0.749 ± 0.001

Each CV fold ran for 100 epochs, and the FedAvg aggregation occurred every 10 epochs. The estimates of the C-index are reported in Table 1. Each value has been computed as the mean of the final C-index evaluated at each epoch. The uncertainty has been estimated through the 95% confidence interval.

3.2   SCD

The mean F1 scores of the 10-fold cv versus each algorithm iteration are shown for both FL_Local and FL_Platform implementations for nodes in isolated and federated modes, in Fig. 2a and 2b, respectively. FL_Local results include also the centralized mode (green curve). Each trial runs for 40 epochs and FedAvg occurs every 2 training epochs.

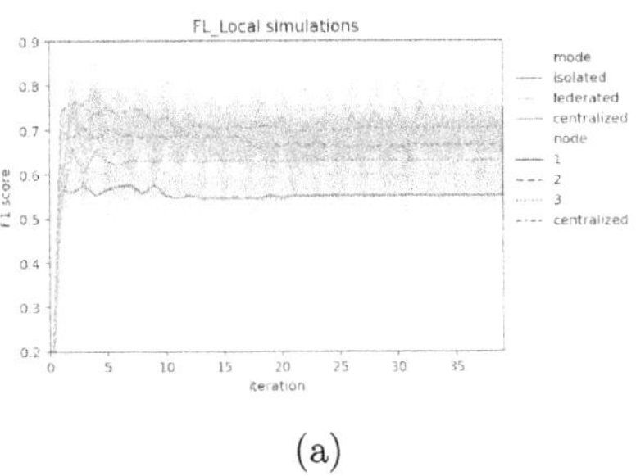
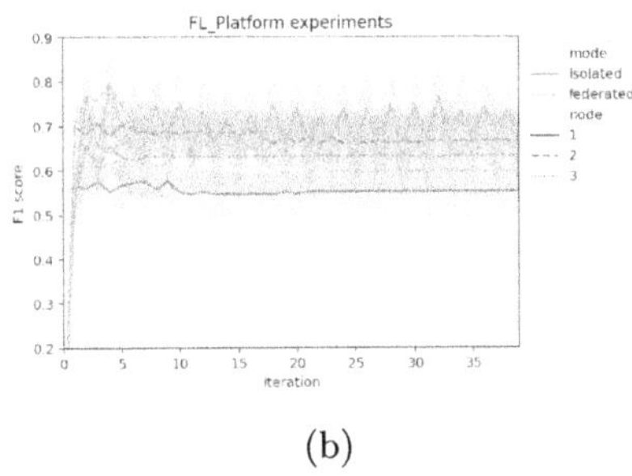

(a)   (b)

Fig. 2. Mean F1 score of of the LR model trained in the 10-fold CV versus each epoch for centralized (green), isolated (blue) and federated (orange) mode, for (a) FL_Local simulations and (b) FL_Platform experiments. Each mode was evaluated on the external common test dataset. The line-style defines the node type (Node1, Node2, Node3 or centralized) and the color the training setting (isolated, federated and centralized). In the federated mode, the parameters' aggregation occurs with a period of 2 epochs. (Color figure online)

Table 2. F1 score of LR model for performances of FL_Local and FL_Platform settings.

Centralized FL_Local	Nodes	Pats	Isolated FL_Local	Isolated FL_Platform	Federated FL_Local	Federated FL_Platform
0.70 ± 0.03	Node1	27	0.55 ± 0.03	0.55 ± 0.03	0.73 ± 0.03	0.73 ± 0.03
	Node2	15	0.67 ± 0.03	0.67 ± 0.03	0.73 ± 0.03	0.73 ± 0.03
	Node3	10	0.63 ± 0.05	0.63 ± 0.05	0.73 ± 0.03	0.73 ± 0.03

F1 score estimates are reported in Table 2 to compare the centralized performance, and FL_Local and FL_Platform performances for the 3 nodes in isolated and federated mode. Each value of F1 score was computed as the average of the 10 F1 scores at the last training epoch for each CV fold, where the federation shows its maximum performance during its asymptotic oscillatory behavior. The uncertainty has been estimated with a 95% confidence interval.

4   Discussion

4.1   MDS

From both Fig. 1a and Fig. 1b it is possible to notice the improvement due to federated aggregation. Even if centralized training still performs better with respect to the other two strategies, FL allowed to significantly improve the performance of local models in Node2 and Node3, while the performance of the DeepSurv model of Node1 is comparable to the isolated training case. As expected, FL enhances the performance of the less populated clients, which benefit from the sharing of weights from the more robust models.

Table 3. Comparative performances of LR model for 2 different patient distributions of the 3 nodes.

Score	Centralized	Node	Trial	Isolated	Federated
Accuracy	0.73 ± 0.02	Node1	1	0.63 ± 0.02	0.82 ± 0.02
		Node1	2	0.64 ± 0.04	0.83 ± 0.03
		Node2	1	0.68 ± 0.03	0.82 ± 0.02
		Node2	2	0.65 ± 0.03	0.83 ± 0.03
		Node3	1	0.77 ± 0.03	0.82 ± 0.02
		Node3	2	0.80 ± 0.03	0.83 ± 0.03
Precision	0.61 ± 0.02	Node1	1	0.55 ± 0.03	0.84 ± 0.04
		Node1	2	0.52 ± 0.02	0.81 ± 0.05
		Node2	1	0.55 ± 0.03	0.84 ± 0.04
		Node2	2	0.54 ± 0.03	0.81 ± 0.05
		Node3	1	0.80 ± 0.05	0.84 ± 0.04
		Node3	2	0.85 ± 0.06	0.81 ± 0.05
Recall	0.86 ± 0.06	Node1	1	0.60 ± 0.04	0.68 ± 0.05
		Node1	2	0.6 ± 0.1	0.78 ± 0.05
		Node2	1	0.84 ± 0.05	0.68 ± 0.05
		Node2	2	0.62 ± 0.06	0.78 ± 0.05
		Node3	1	0.52 ± 0.04	0.68 ± 0.05
		Node3	2	0.58 ± 0.04	0.78 ± 0.05
F1 score	0.70 ± 0.03	Node1	1	0.55 ± 0.03	0.73 ± 0.03
		Node1	2	0.54 ± 0.07	0.78 ± 0.03
		Node2	1	0.67 ± 0.03	0.73 ± 0.03
		Node2	2	0.57 ± 0.05	0.78 ± 0.03
		Node3	1	0.63 ± 0.05	0.73 ± 0.03
		Node3	2	0.69 ± 0.05	0.78 ± 0.03
ROC-AUC	0.81 ± 0.04	Node1	1	0.64 ± 0.03	0.85 ± 0.04
		Node1	2	0.70 ± 0.07	0.93 ± 0.02
		Node2	1	0.83 ± 0.03	0.85 ± 0.04
		Node2	2	0.77 ± 0.03	0.93 ± 0.02
		Node3	1	0.75 ± 0.05	0.73 ± 0.03
		Node3	2	0.85 ± 0.05	0.93 ± 0.02

Table 1 shows the performance for isolated and federated settings for both simulations and platform experiments. The Wilcoxon test rejected the hypothesis of significant differences between simulations and experiment (p value > 0.05). However, some slight differences can be noticed between the two performances. These could be due to the non-linearity and complexity of the DeepSurv architecture, which resulted in a slightly different weight update and loss computation after each training epoch. Nevertheless, the differences are within errors, and consequently the MDS results confirm the reliability of the GenoMed4All platform.

4.2 SCD

Despite the oscillations perhaps due to overfitting and caused by the small number of samples, the improved performance of the federated nodes is demonstrated by the results of Fig. 2. In contrast, a stable behavior is reached after 30 epochs for the three local models.

Deducing also from the Table 2, federated aggregation improves the performances of local models, allowing to achieve F1 scores of about 0.70, as centralized values show a mean F1 score of 0.69 ± 0.03. Isolated learning curves show relatively poor performance, especially for Node1 and Node3, whose mean F1 scores are about 0.57 and 0.59, respectively.

Finally, Table 2 shows the agreement between the FL_Local and FL_Platform approaches for this simple federated ML model, supporting the robustness of the GenoMed4All platform. Unlike the MDS use case, the simplicity of the model implies complete agreement between simulation and platform run, as the algorithm includes linear decision boundaries.

Due to the small datasets size, the overfitting leads to a rapid convergence of the model parameters for all modes (centralized, isolated, federated) by different trends. Particularly in the federated setting, performances assume a visible oscillatory behavior in FL curves, also for the model convergence. Upon a detailed study of the convergence behaviors, the two following trends emerge.

- In both centralized and isolated modes, F1 scores across the iterations differ for each CV-fold because the respective training datasets are slightly different, resulting in a nearly stable mean value when the model converges.
- In federated mode, the oscillatory behavior is determined by a shared F1 score for the aggregation step and different values for the next iteration. At the aggregation step, the measurement of the shared F1 score shows its maximum value, indicating that such an iteration is optimal to measure the asymptotic performance.

In Table 3 all the performance scores are reported for Trial1 and Trial2, corresponding to different patient distributions across the nodes. Federated aggregation with the FedAvg strategy improves the low performance of isolated nodes, caused by the extremely small number of available patients, reducing overfitting problems, with performance values that are comparable to, or in some cases exceed, those obtained with centralized training. The Wilcoxon test rejected the hypothesis of significant differences between Trial1 and Trial2 in federated mode (p value > 0.05), demonstrating that FL could lead to better generalization of results for small nodes.

These results clearly show that FL could be a robust and viable solution to improve performance in scenarios characterized by scarce datasets, as for rare diseases. Possible future research could involve larger SCD datasets and more complex models to better calculate the risk of different types of SCI based on clinical and physical features.

4.3   Limitations

It is important to notice that this study presents some limitations. The relatively small dataset size and/or the simplicity of the used models may not fully capture the complexity of real-world scenarios. Moreover, it would be interesting to implement aggregation strategies other than FedAvg, which could bring about improvements in use cases with small or heterogeneous datasets. Until now, only FedAvg was implemented in the GenoMed4All platform.

In addition, the FL platform itself deserves some improvements, especially in terms of usability. Working with files in pickle format could be complicated and cumbersome. The low flexibility of pickle files also causes the need for a different model for each scenario, corresponding to different input features. Increasing the number of nodes participating in the FL framework is another crucial aspect, since it would allow to better represent real-world scenarios and would demonstrate the utility of FL, especially in more complex and diverse settings.

5   Conclusion

The ultimate goal of using a robust FL platform would be to develop ML models for precision medicine, especially for rare diseases, where data is scarce and distributed between various institutions. This study validates federated AI models of two rare real hematological use cases for large and small datasets, respectively, demonstrating the performance improvement by the federated mode over the isolated mode, evidently for smaller nodes. In addition, FL proved to be a robust solution for application to rare diseases, where datasets are scarce. The performance comparison between local simulations and platform experiment validates also the technology of the GenoMed4All platform, opening the way to the expansion of the number of participant nodes.

References

1. Bajwa, J., Munir, U., Nori, A., Williams, B.: Artificial intelligence in healthcare: transforming the practice of medicine. Future Healthc. J. **8**(2), e188–e194 (2021). PMID: 34286183; PMCID: PMC8285156
2. Kandhare, P., Kurlekar, M., Deshpande, T., Pawar, A.: A review on revolutionizing healthcare technologies with AI and ML applications in pharmaceutical sciences. Drugs Drug Candidates **4**(1), 9 (2025)
3. Zhang, H., Sarvari, T.E., Kalra, A., Amjad, A.I., Adnan, N., Mazzone, E.: Deep learning applications in visual data for benign and malignant hematologic conditions: a systematic review and visual glossary. Haematologica **106**(6), 1623–1634 (2021)

4. Sheller, M.J., et al.: Federated learning in medicine: facilitating multi-institutional collaborations without sharing patient data. Sci. Rep. **10**, 12598 (2020)
5. Qi, P., Chiaro, D., Guzzo, A., Ianni, M., Fortino, G., Piccialli, F.: Model aggregation techniques in federated learning: a comprehensive survey. Future Gener. Comput. Syst. **150**, 272–293 (2024). ISSN 0167-739X
6. McMahan, B., Moore, E., Ramage, D., Hampson, S., Arcas, B.A.: Communication-efficient learning of deep networks from decentralized data. In: Artificial Intelligence and Statistics, 20th International Conference on Artificial Intelligence and Statistics, on Proceedings of Machine Learning Research (PMLR), vol. 54, pp. 1273–1282 (2017)
7. Aledhari, M., Razzak, R., Parizi, R.M., Saees, F.: Federated learning: a survey on enabling technologies, protocols, and applications. IEEE Access **8**, 40699–140725 (2020)
8. Qi, P., Chiaro, D., Guzzo, A., Ianni, M., Fortino, G., Piccialli, F.: Model aggregation techniques in federated learning: a comprehensive survey. Futur. Gener. Comput. Syst. **150**, 272–293 (2024)
9. Wang, J., Liu, Q., Liang, H., Joshi, G., Poor, V.: Tackling the objective inconsistency problem in heterogeneous federated optimization. Adv. Neural. Inf. Process. Syst. **33**, 7611–7623 (2020)
10. Sheller, M.J., Edwards, B., Reina, G.A., et al.: Federated learning in medicine: facilitating multi-institutional collaborations without sharing patient data. Sci. Rep. **10**, 12598 (2020)
11. Crowson, M.G., Moukheiber, D., Arévalo, A.R., Lam, B.D., Mantena, S., et al.: A systematic review of federated learning applications for biomedical data. PLOS Digit. Health **1**(5), e0000033 (2022)
12. Teo, Z.L., et al.: Federated machine learning in healthcare: a systematic review on clinical applications and technical architecture. Cell Rep Med. **5**(3), 101481 (2024)
13. Li, M., Xu, P., Hu, J., Tang, Z., Yang, G.: From Challenges and Pitfalls to Recommendations and Opportunities: Implementing Federated Learning in Healthcare, arXiv, eprint 2409.09727. https://arxiv.org/abs/2409.09727
14. Zhang, F., Roberts, M., Fernandez-Marques, J., Lane, N., et BloodCounts! Consortium: Announcing BloodCounts! and Flower Partnership. Flower AI. https://flower.ai/blog/2025-03-20-flower-bloodcounts-partnership/. Accessed 20 Mar 2025
15. Asti, G., D'Amico, S., Carota, L., Piscia, D., Casadei, F., Merleau, N.S.C., et al.: An artificial intelligence-based federated learning platform to boost precision medicine in rare hematological diseases: an initiative by genomed4all and synthema consortia [abstract]. Blood **144**(Supplement 1), 4989 (2024)
16. Cremonesi, F., et al.: The need for multimodal health data modeling: a practical approach for a federated-learning healthcare platform. J. Biomed. Inform. **141**, 104338 (2023)
17. Flower A Friendly Federated Learning Framework. http://flower.ai/. Accessed 02 May 2025
18. MLFlow. https://mlflow.org/docs/latest/index.html. Accessed 10 Mar 2025
19. Sekeres, M.A., Taylor, J.: Diagnosis and treatment of myelodysplastic syndromes: a review. J. Am. Med. Assoc. **328**(9), 872–880 (2022)
20. Adès, L., Itzykson, R., Fenaux, P.: Myelodysplastic syndromes. Lancet **383**, 2239–2252 (2014)
21. Greenberg, P., et al.: Revised international prognostic scoring system for myelodysplastic syndromes. Blood **120**(12), 2454–2465 (2012)
22. Greenberg, P., et al.: International scoring system for evaluating prognosis in myelodysplastic syndromes. Blood **89**(6), 2079–2088 (1997)

23. Chiereghin, C., et al.: The genetics of myelodysplastic syndromes: clinical relevance. Genes **12**(8), 1144 (2021)
24. Sickle cell anemia - Symptoms & causes - Mayo Clinic. https://bit.ly/3s0D1vE. Accessed 05 Apr 2025
25. DeBaun, M.R., Armstrong, F.D., McKinstry, R.C., Ware, R.E., Vichinsky, E., Kirkham, F.J.: Silent cerebral infarcts: a review on a prevalent and progressive cause of neurologic injury in sickle cell anemia. Blood **119**(20), 4587–4596 (2012)
26. Gupta, A., et al.: Silent brain infarction and risk of future stroke: a systematic review and meta-analysis. Stroke **47**(3), 719–25 (2016)
27. Estcourt, L.J., Kimber, C., Hopewell, S., Trivella, M., Doree, C., Abboud, M.R.: Interventions for preventing silent cerebral infarcts in people with sickle cell disease. Cochrane Database Syst. Rev. **4**(4), CD012389 (2020)
28. Aslan, B., Zech, G.: A new class of binning-free, multivariate goodness-of-fit tests: the energy tests, arXiv preprint hep-ex/0203010 (2002). https://arxiv.org/abs/hep-ex/0203010
29. Gretton, A., Borgwardt, K.M., Rasch, M.J., Schölkopf, B., Smola, A.J.: A kernel two-sample test. J. Mach. Learn. Res. **13**(25), 723–773 (2012). http://jmlr.org/papers/v13/gretton12a.html
30. Katzman, J.L., et al.: DeepSurv: personalized treatment recommender system using a Cox proportional hazards deep neural network. BMC Med. Res. Methodol. **18**, 1–12 (2018)
31. Liu, D.C., Nocedal, J.: On the limited memory BFGS method for large scale optimization. Math. Program. **45**, 503–528 (1989)
32. Harrell, F.E., Califf, R.M., Pryor, D.B., Lee, K.L., Rosati, R.A.: Evaluating the yield of medical tests. JAMA **247**(18), 2543–2546 (1982)
33. Opitz, J.: A closer look at classification evaluation metrics and a critical reflection of common evaluation practice. Trans. Assoc. Comput. Linguist. **12**, 82–836 (2024)

Hearing Impairment Assessment in Infants Through Explainable Computer Vision Analysis of Facial Features

Samuele Pe[1]([✉]) [iD], Anisa Visram[2] [iD], Iain Jackson[2] [iD], Michael Stone[2] [iD], Enea Parimbelli[1,3] [iD], Kevin Munro[2,4] [iD], and Arianna Dagliati[1] [iD]

[1] Department of Electrical, Computer and Biomedical Engineering, University of Pavia, Pavia, Italy
`samuele.pe01@universitadipavia.it`
[2] Manchester Centre for Audiology and Deafness, School of Health Sciences, University of Manchester, Manchester, UK
[3] Telfer School of Management, University of Ottawa, Ottawa, Canada
[4] Manchester Academic Health Science Centre, Manchester University Hospitals NHS Foundation Trust, Manchester, UK

Abstract. Hearing assessment in infants is complicated due to the lack of reliable behavioral responses. The BAMBINO (Behavioural Audiometry Measures in Babies: Innovation, Novelty and Optimisation) project explores the feasibility of automating hearing assessment in infants by leveraging facial behaviour analysis. This feasibility study investigates the potential of action units, head pose, and gaze direction to identify changes in behavioural response to suprathreshold sound stimuli in infants aged 7 to 24 months. Video recordings of 58 healthy infants were analysed using convolutional neural networks (1D-CNN and 2D-CNN), evaluated against human observers. Results indicate that head pose is the primary feature for classification, closely aligning with current clinical protocols, but facial expressions still provide additional insights. SignalGrad-CAM, was employed to interpret model decisions, revealing nuanced patterns such as subtle micro-expressions and subtle facial reactions that often preceded head turns. Post-hoc analyses regarding age and trial progression in the test set highlighted that infants aged 12–18 months were most responsive and performance declined in later trial stages, likely due to fatigue, highlighting the importance of selecting a proper session duration. Future work will address biases in the data, and subsequent phases of the BAMBINO project aim to extend this study to younger infants (3–7 months), including hearing-impaired populations.

Keywords: Visual Reinforcement Audiometry (VRA) · Behavioural Observation Audiometry (BOA) · CNN · SignalGrad-CAM

C. Tommasino et al. (Eds.): AIBIO 2025, CCIS 2696, pp. 31–38, 2026.
https://doi.org/10.1007/978-3-032-17216-7_3

1 Introduction

Hearing assessment in infants is challenging because of limited behavioural responses. Effective assessment during this critical developmental period is vital, as early detection and intervention significantly influence language acquisition and cognitive development. The BAMBINO (Behavioural Audiometry Measures in Babies: Innovation, Novelty and Optimisation, https://sites.manchester.ac.uk/bambino) project seeks to improve these diagnostics through innovative methodologies. Visual Reinforcement Audiometry (VRA) [1, 2], a behavioural test widely used in clinics to assess hearing in infants aged 7 to 24 months, leverages infants' natural tendency to turn their heads toward sound stimuli, using visual reinforcers like toys to condition and encourage this behaviour. While clinically valuable, VRA relies on subjective observer judgments, introducing bias when unblinded (as in typical clinical situations) and requiring significant clinician time. This study aims to mitigate these limitations by analysing facial behaviour with OpenFace 2.0 [3] – a tool that tracks facial landmarks and action units. Automated analysis of facial expressions, in addition to head-turning, could enable more objective, efficient, and scalable diagnostic approaches to assist clinicians' assessment of hearing. Furthermore, VRA is unsuitable for infants under seven months. At this stage, infants are yet to develop the muscle strength, control, and coordination to reliably respond with head turns. Consequently, infants aged 3 to 7 months are typically assessed using Behavioural Observation Audiometry (BOA) [1], where clinicians observe behavioural changes in response to suprathreshold sounds. The study has the potential to inform the design of new procedures and decision support systems (DSSs) for younger infants, leveraging mostly facial features for early, objective auditory assessments.

2 Materials and Methods

2.1 Data Collection and Preprocessing

The study involved 58 healthy, full-term infants aged 7 to 24 months who had passed newborn hearing screenings and had no reported hearing concerns. Experiments were conducted in a sound-treated room at the Clinical Research Facility (CRF) of the Royal Manchester Children's Hospital (Manchester, UK) to ensure a controlled acoustic environment. Infants sat on their caregiver's lap, facing a video camera that captured facial and behavioural responses. An experimenter played with toys near the camera to maintain the infant's attention. Auditory stimuli were delivered via a loudspeaker positioned 90 degrees to the infant's right, accompanied by a visual reinforcer – a toy in a box adjacent to the speaker. Initially, the reinforcer (illuminated and animated) was paired with the auditory signal to condition the child, while during the test phase, it was activated only after the child turned their head in response to the sound. Conditioning trials were excluded from the dataset. Trials were categorized as either stimulus trials, featuring an audible sound (70 dB SPL, 1 kHz warble tone), or control trials, with no sound. These were randomly presented in a 3:1 ratio and continued until the infant met a habituation criterion, defined as failing to respond in four out of five consecutive trials. Clinicians in a separate control room, blinded to trial type, initiated each trial when the infant was calm and facing forward. In stimulus trials, if the child turned their head within four seconds of the auditory stimulus, these clinicians recorded the response with a button press, activating the display of the reinforcer (with a 0.5-s delay).

The video recordings were preprocessed to ensure uniformity and compatibility for analysis. Videos were trimmed to a common starting point: the onset of the sound in the first conditioning trial. They were then exported at 720p resolution with a frame rate of 25 fps. Facial behaviour data, including action units (e.g., lip raising), head pose, and gaze orientation, were extracted using OpenFace 2.0 [3]. Sound presentations and observer judgments were synchronized and merged with OpenFace outputs using timestamps. The final dataset retained a 12-s window around each trial: 2 s before and 10 s after stimulus onset, capturing both anticipatory and reactive behaviours.

2.2 Classification Methods

This study aims to classify each multi-channel signal into one of two categories: stimulus trials, where a sound stimulus is provided to the child, and control trials. Data is divided through an inter-patient randomization process into training (41 children, 1571 signal instances), validation (8 children, 333 instances), and test sets (9 children, 387 instances). Despite the slight imbalance in the dataset, with the stimulus class being predominant (about 3:1 ratio), no additional preprocessing or data augmentation techniques are deemed necessary. The simplest approach to signal classification involves the use of 1D convolutional Neural Networks (CNNs). Figure 1 illustrates the proposed three-branched architecture for processing OpenFace data: gaze direction, head pose, and facial expression signals are independently processed through different convolutional layers, and the resulting embeddings are concatenated for the final classification via fully connected layers. Alternatively, multi-channel signals can be treated as 2-dimensional matrices, considering time as one dimension and the channels as the second: in this context, 2D CNNs show promise for signal processing, however, this comes at the cost of higher parameter counts, making them more challenging to optimize. The proposed 2D CNN architecture is equivalent to the 1D counterpart shown in Fig. 1.

After completely training the classification models, we employ a visual post-hoc explainability algorithm to generate saliency maps: Gradient-weighted Class Activation Mapping (Grad-CAM) [4], which was originally developed for image-based CNNs. Its output is a heatmap highlighting the areas of the input image that contribute most to the classification. This output is referred to as the Class Activation Map (CAM). Although primarily designed for images, Grad-CAM can be applied to signals through the SignalGrad-CAM Python package (GitHub: bmi-labmedinfo/signal_grad_cam). For 1D CNNs, the resulting CAM is a one-dimensional array that highlights the most important time intervals contributing to the signal classification. In the case of 2D convolutional networks, the CAM is a two-dimensional heatmap, with one axis representing time and the other representing the input channels: this allows for a more granular visualization of the time-varying importance of each specific channel in the signal. Given our network's three-branched architecture, SignalGrad-CAM can effectively assess the relative importance assigned to different OpenFace features (gaze direction, head pose, and facial expression).

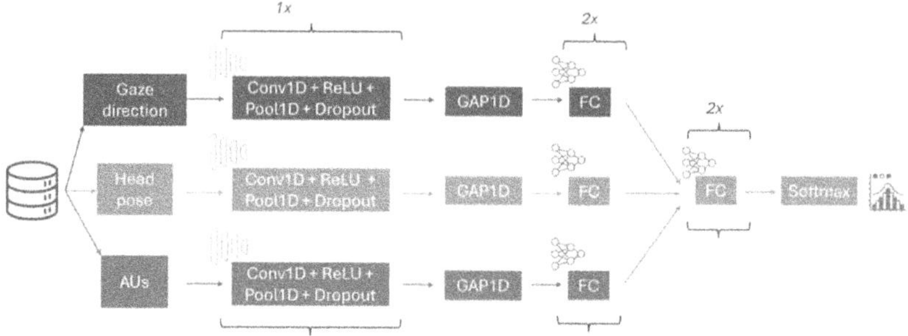

Fig. 1. Three-branched model architecture for 1D-CNN. "Conv", "pool", "GAP", and "FC" denote 1D-convolutional layers, 1D max-pooling layers, global average pooling operation, and fully connected layers, respectively. "AU" stands for action units.

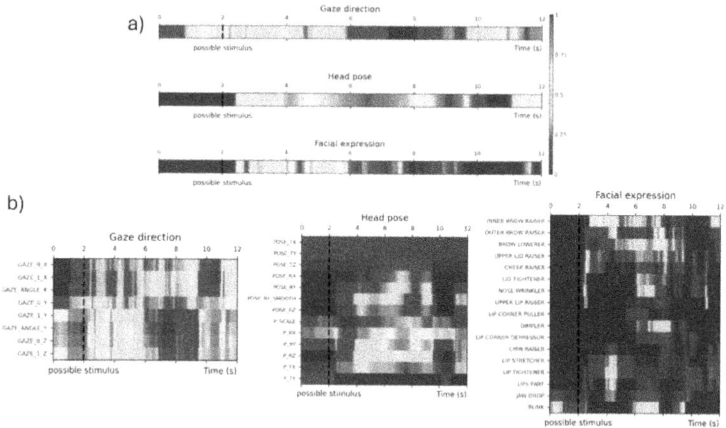

Fig. 2. Class Activation Maps for 1D-CNN (a) and 2D-CNN (b) for the "stimulus" class on a correctly classified positive example from the test set. The vertical dotted line marks the timestamp (2 s) at which the stimulus was provided.

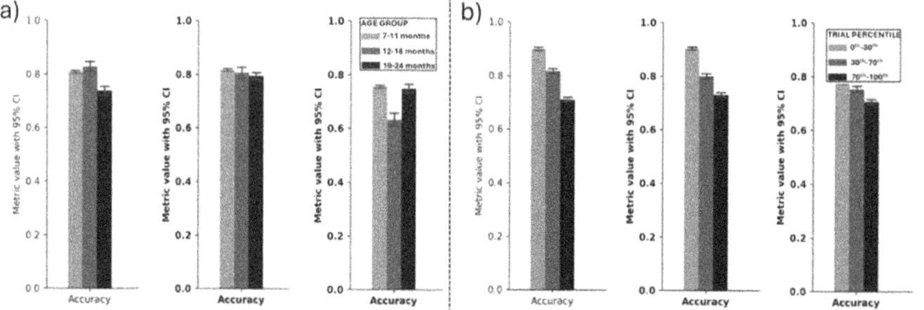

Fig. 3. Performance comparison of the classifiers across different data subgroups (represented by colour) in the test set: age groups (a) and trial progression groups (b). Each bar plot displays accuracy and 95% confidence intervals for clinicians' opinion (left triad), 1D-CNN (middle triad), and 2D-CNN (right triad).

2.3 Post-Hoc Analyses

We conduct further analyses to evaluate the influence of potential confounding factors on the classifiers' performance. Specifically, we examine how the accuracy of each classifier – whether human or ML-based – varies across different subgroups of the population, focusing on two key dimensions: age and trial progression. These factors are known to influence behavioural and cognitive responses in infants, potentially biasing the classification results. Given the rapid developmental changes in infants aged 7 to 24 months, it is natural to expect behavioural differences across age groups. Both literature [2] and clinical experience suggest that children in the middle of this age range (12–18 months) are generally the most responsive during VRA testing. Younger children (7–11 months) may struggle with attention span or head-turn responses, as their performance in VRA tends to improve with age. In contrast, older children (19–24 months) may require more complex tasks to sustain their engagement and hence tend to habituate (stop responding) more quickly. Given these considerations, we aim to investigate whether an age effect exists in terms of response magnitude in three groups: 7–11 months, 12–18 months, and 19–24 months. Another characteristic confounder is the trial progression effect. As noted, data collection is stopped if an infant displays clear signs of fatigue or boredom; however, it remains likely that a child's responsiveness diminishes over time. To study this, we perform subgroup analyses using trial timing information to bin the data in three groups according to percentiles: 0 to 30th, 30th to 70th, and 70th to 100th.

3 Results

3.1 Models' Performances

Table 1. Performance comparison of the models and the reference clinicians' evaluation in the test set. The best results for each statistic have been highlighted in bold.

Classifier	Accuracy	F1-score	Brier score
1D-CNN	**81.14%**	**87.35%**	**0.07**
2D-CNN	74.42%	83.25%	0.10
Clinicians	80.36%	85.44%	N/A

The CNN models were compared against clinicians' performance, serving as a proxy for a gold standard reference. As mentioned before, a clinician judged whether a response was present based solely on whether a head turn towards the reinforcer was observed within four seconds of the trial onset. Table 1 compares the classifiers' specific performances in terms of classification correctness (accuracy and F1-score) and model calibration (Brier score). In both scenarios, the 1D-CNN outperformed the other classifiers in classification correctness and model calibration. Although the 2D-CNN achieved very good results, the clinicians consistently outperformed it on the test set. Despite the superiority of the 1D-CNN model and aligning with the final aims of the BAMBINO project, we decided to further assess both models to better understand their potential: in fact, the 2D-CNN, combined with SignalGrad-CAM, is expected to provide a more nuanced evaluation of input channels compared with its 1D counterpart.

Class activation maps have been employed to analyse to which extent different input information – either gaze direction, head pose, or facial expression – contributed to the classification of stimulus trials. In each map, we see the time dimension – from 0 to 12 s – represented on the X scale and the time-varying feature importance, displayed with a "jet" colouring scheme (i.e., blue for less important parts and red for the most important ones). CAMs highlight a clear pattern that will be discussed with the aid of a representative sample from the test set: Fig. 2(a) presents three one-dimensional CAMs (corresponding to gaze direction, head pose, and facial features) for this sample. Most importance is retained by head pose data, suggesting that – like clinicians do – the model relies on children turning their heads to acknowledge the stimulus. Gaze data, instead, is attributed minimal importance and mostly in the final moments (after the head turn), which may correlate with the child focusing on the toy in the direction of the sound stimulus. The CAM for facial expression indicates that facial features also contribute – albeit scarcely – to the model's correct classification of this instance, particularly immediately after the stimulus: this hints at the possibility of the infant somatising emotions after acknowledging the stimulus. The advantage of using a 2D convolutional network, despite the increased model complexity, lies in SignalGrad-CAM's ability to output the importance of each channel over time in the form of a 2D heatmap. Figure 2(b) illustrates an example of the 2D output for a data instance in the test set. We see that spurious importance is given to gaze information only in the initial and final time steps (i.e., before or long after the stimulus has been provided). Certain importance is highlighted for head rotation along the X and Y axes (4 s after the sound is played), reaffirming the fundamental role of head turns in the classification. Although facial features are assigned relatively less importance, changes in importance patterns are observed following the stimulus. For instance, analysis of the action units reveals that the subject smiles right after the stimulus is played and raises their brows after a couple of seconds, providing additional context for the classification.

3.2 Post-Hoc Analyses Outcomes

Figure 3(a) illustrates how accuracy varies across age groups in the test set. We expected infants in the middle age group (12–18 months) to perform better than those in the other groups: we witnessed this phenomenon only for clinicians' opinion, with statistically significant differences ($\alpha = 0.05$). 1D- and 2D-CNN do not show the same behaviour. Another notable pattern is that, except for the worst-performing model (2D-CNN), the performance in the youngest age group (7–11 months) is better than in the oldest group (19–24 months), again with statistical significance ($\alpha = 0.05$). The infants' performance, and consequently the classifiers' capabilities, are also hypothesised to decrease as the experiment progresses, given that children might lose focus or become tired over time. The results for the test set Fig. 3(b) confirm this, showing decreasing accuracies with the experiment progression, with these differences being statistically significant ($\alpha = 0.05$).

4 Discussion and Conclusion

In this study, we explored two convolution-based networks for multi-channel OpenFace data classification to recognise sound stimuli acknowledgment in healthy infants aged 7 to 24 months. SignalGrad-CAM was employed to inspect the models and the relative importance of three feature groups: head pose, gaze direction, and facial expression (i.e., action units). Preliminary findings suggest promising potential for automating the Visual Reinforcement Audiometry assessment, a method used for diagnosing hearing impairment in infants, by utilising patient recordings captured with a simple RGB camera. The use of CAMs revealed that AI prioritises head-related features when making classifications, closely aligning with the approach of a human observer. Interestingly, while facial features are assigned less importance, they are not disregarded entirely, as the models demonstrated the ability to detect subtle facial reactions in children prior to head turns. This observation is particularly significant, as it highlights the potential capacity of machines not only to surpass human performance – e.g., see the superior results of the 1D-CNN model – but also to uncover patterns that may elude human perception. In the context of decision support system design, this capability offers valuable assistance to clinicians, enabling them to identify nuanced patterns that might otherwise go unnoticed. This advantage becomes even more critical in complex scenarios such as Behavioural Observation Audiometry, requiring clinicians to rely solely on behavioural changes, such as facial expressions, to indicate the perception of sound.

The influence of two confounding factors on model performance was also investigated: age and trial progression. Performance evaluations across different age groups in the test set revealed that the classification accuracy of blinded human observers was statistically superior in the middle age range (12–18 months). This suggests that children in this category gave the most consistent responses throughout the test session, in contrast with younger infants, who may still be developmentally young to perform the test optimally, and older infants, who are known to habituate more quickly. This result aligns with the considerations of previous works [2], but the same pattern cannot be witnessed in the CNN classifiers, presumably owing to their relatively smaller generalization power. Notably, models' results on younger children were generally better compared with the oldest ones (19–24 months), which likely indicates that the VRA test is less able to sustain the attention of older children. Finally, the analysis of trial progression revealed a statistically significant decline in performance over time. This degradation is likely due to fatigue or boredom affecting the infants' responses, emphasising the importance of optimising session duration in future studies.

This preliminary study presents some limitations. For example, the evaluation of CAMs Fig. 2 points out that a notable amount of importance is attributed to the final timesteps of the signals, long after the stimulus presentation. This phenomenon is particularly evident in CAMs for gaze direction. We hypothesise that this is linked to the introduction of the visual reinforcer, which may act as a source of bias in the classification of stimulus and control trials. While this preliminary phase focused primarily on evaluating the utility of facial features in the classification process – a focus that mitigates the impact of such biases on our conclusions – future analyses will address this issue. Specifically, signals will be cropped after the visual reinforcer presentation to eliminate potential confounding factors. Furthermore, this study exclusively involved healthy infants aged 7 to 24 months, so a first, natural extension of this work will focus on evaluating younger healthy infants (3–7 months): for this subsequent phase, we envision a similar data acquisition setup; however, considering the physical limitations of this age group (e.g., inability to sit upright and underdeveloped neck muscles), a BOA approach [1] – without visual reinforcers – will be adopted. The aim of this phase is to determine whether stimulus acknowledgment can be reliably recognised based solely on facial features. Lastly, the final phase of the BAMBINO project will involve children with and without hearing loss.

Acknowledgments. Samuele Pe is a PhD student enrolled in the National PhD program in Artificial Intelligence, XXXIX cycle, course on Health and life sciences, organized by Università Campus Bio-Medico di Roma. This work was supported by the Italian Ministry of Research, under the complementary actions to the NRRP "Fit4MedRob - Fit for Medical Robotics" Grant (# PNC0000007). Enea Parimbelli acknowledges funding support provided by the Italian project PRIN PNRR 2022 InXAID - Interaction with eXplainable Artificial Intelligence in (medical) Decision-making. CUP: H53D23008090001 funded by the European Union - Next Generation EU.

Disclosure of Interests. The authors have no competing interests to declare that are relevant to the content of this article.

References

1. Sabo, D.L.: The audiologic assessment of the young pediatric patient: the clinic. Trends Amplif. **4**, 51–60 (1999). https://doi.org/10.1177/108471389900400205
2. Visram, A.S., Jackson, I.R., Almufarrij, I., et al.: Optimisation of visual reinforcement audiometry: a scoping review. Int. J. Audiol. 1–11 (2024). https://doi.org/10.1080/14992027.2024.2397716
3. Baltrusaitis, T., Zadeh, A., Lim, Y.C., Morency, L.-P.: OpenFace 2.0: facial behavior analysis toolkit. In: 2018 13th IEEE International Conference on Automatic Face & Gesture Recognition (FG 2018), pp. 59–66 (2018). https://doi.org/10.1109/FG.2018.00019
4. Selvaraju, R.R., Cogswell, M., Das, A., et al.: Grad-CAM: visual explanations from deep networks via gradient-based localization. Int. J. Comput. Vis. **128**, 336–359 (2020). https://doi.org/10.1007/s11263-019-01228-7

Type 2 Diabetes Prediction from Multi-center Electronic Health Records in General Practice Using Machine Learning

Max Rerisi[1], Mariachiara Di Cosmo[2], Michele Bernardini[3(✉)], and Luca Romeo[4]

[1] Columbia Grammar and Preparatory School, New York City, NY 10025, USA
[2] The BioRobotics Institute, Sant'Anna School of Advanced Studies, Pisa, Italy
`mariachiara.dicosmo@santannapisa.it`
[3] Department of Theoretical and Applied Sciences, eCampus University, Novedrate, Italy
`michele.bernardini@uniecampus.it`
[4] Department of Economics and Law, University of Macerata, Macerata, Italy
`luca.romeo@unimc.it`

Abstract. Early prediction of Type 2 Diabetes Mellitus (T2DM) is crucial for effective prevention and management. While Machine Learning (ML) has shown promise on structured hospital data, little attention has been given to primary care data. This study investigates the performance of several state-of-the-art ML models (including Logistic Regression, SVM, KNN, Decision Tree, Random Forest, XGBoost) and the recent TabPFN foundation model on a novel real-world multi-center dataset (FIMMG-6GP) collected from six general practitioners (GPs). We evaluate models using two validation strategies: stratified Five-Fold cross-validation (5F-CV) to assess within-distribution performance, and Leave-One-GP-Out (L1GPO-CV) to capture cross-practice variability. XGBoost consistently outperformed all models in terms of AUC (93.70% in 5F-CV; 93.10% in L1GPO-CV) and sensitivity, while also providing clinically interpretable insights via SHAP analysis. In contrast, TabPFN achieved high overall scores but showed poor sensitivity in detecting T2DM cases. Our findings underscore the value of the proposed cross-practice evaluation in developing trustworthy ML-based decision support systems for real-world clinical settings, and particularly for primary care.

Keywords: Machine Learning · Decision Support System · Electronic Health Records · General Practice · Type 2 Diabetes

1   Introduction

Type 2 Diabetes Mellitus (T2DM) is a chronic metabolic condition affecting over 500 million individuals worldwide [3]. Early identification of T2DM is essential to limit long-term complications and reduce healthcare costs. General Practitioners

C. Tommasino et al. (Eds.): AIBIO 2025, CCIS 2696, pp. 39–46, 2026.
https://doi.org/10.1007/978-3-032-17216-7_4

(GPs), as the primary point of contact in the care pathway, play a key role in recognizing early signs and risk factors of T2DM. GPs collect rich longitudinal data stored in Electronic Health Records (EHRs), which can be leveraged to develop Machine Learning (ML) models for early diagnosis support. Despite the growing number of ML applications in clinical settings, most predictive models have been trained and evaluated on clean, hospital-based datasets[1] and their generalizability to heterogeneous, real-world primary care remains underexplored. In particular, EHRs from GPs are often characterized by sparsity, irregular spatiotemporal sampling, and inter-practice variability, which may introduce significant biases that can affect model transferability and generalization. Current literature covers a wide number of ML approaches for the prediction of T2DM onset [8], ranging from more interpretable tree-based models to more complex Deep Learning (DL) techniques, each offering a trade-off between predictive power and explainability. Leveraging demographic, clinical, and laboratory features, several state-of-the-art ML models—such as Logistic Regression (LR), K-Nearest Neighbors (KNN), Support Vector Machines (SVM), Decision Trees (DT), Random Forests (RF), and gradient-boosted decision trees—have been applied to structured EHR data for predicting the onset of T2DM, with varying degrees of predictive performance. Among these, eXtreme Gradient Boosting (XGB) has consistently demonstrated robust results across different patient cohorts, also when using selected subsets of relevant features [2,7,10]. More advanced models have been developed to handle EHRs common challenges, such as overfitting, model interpretability, and computational cost. For instance, authors in [1] introduced a sparse-balanced SVM tailored to a single GP's dataset. However, most of these approaches have been developed and validated on single-center EHRs [1] or on hospital-based datasets like MIMIC-III, limiting their applicability in multiple general medicine scenarios. Although some primary care multi-center EHR datasets exist - such as CPRD, PCORnet, THL Primary Care Register, THIN [2] - they are often underutilized due to limited research access. Moreover, existing studies typically assess model performance in the overall dataset, without discriminating its behavior in relation to different GPs or clinical practices. More recently, Hollmann et al. [5] introduced the Tabular Prior-data Fitted Network (TabPFN), a transformer-based foundation model, which has shown potential to outperform gradient-boosted trees in low-data regimes. However, its potential in primary care applications remains unexplored.

To address these gaps, we introduce a real-world multi-center EHR dataset collected from six Italian GPs, which reflects the heterogeneous and decentralized nature of everyday clinical practice. We investigate the performance of both standard ML models and the novel TabPFN architecture in predicting the onset of T2DM, with a particular focus on model reliability and clinical interpretability. In particular, we adopt a Leave-One-GP-Out cross-validation (L1GPO-CV)

---

[1] MIMIC-III.

[2] Clinical Practice Research Datalink (CPRD), National Patient-Centered Clinical Research Network (PCORnet), Finnish Primary Care Register, The Health Improvement Network (THIN).

strategy to simulate clinical-world conditions where models trained on certain practices must generalize to unseen ones. The proposed dataset and evaluation framework mirror the real-world challenges of integrating ML into clinical decision support systems. In this context, ML models must demonstrate robustness across heterogeneous care settings, account for inter-practice variability, and provide interpretable outputs to support informed medical decision-making.

2   Materials and Methods

2.1   Dataset

In this study, we used a real-world anonymized dataset, referred to as FIMMG-6GP, which includes structured EHR data collected from six GPs across a 15-year clinical history. The FIMMG-6GP dataset comprises a total of 13571 patients and 5029 predictors, spanning both categorical and numerical variables. These cover key domains such as demographics (#5 features), blood pressure (#6), pathologies (#2298), exam prescriptions (#1051), exam outcomes (#391), drugs (#1150), and exemptions (#128). Each GP contributes to the total cohort.

We preprocessed the FIMMG-6GP dataset by selecting a subset of features, retaining only those categorical with less than 99.5% zero values and those numerical with less than 99.5% missing values to reduce sparsity and discard features with limited informative value. This filtering step reduced the feature space to 414 predictors. All numerical variables were normalized to $[0, 1]$ by dividing each value by the maximum absolute value observed within its respective feature. Missing values in numerical fields were replaced with an out-of-range placeholder value (-999), to preserve the presence of missingness in the data while ensuring compatibility with models that do not natively handle missing values.

Table 1 summarizes the dataset statistics for each GP after preprocessing, including the number of patients, the proportion of control and T2DM cases, the average patient age with standard deviation, and the gender distribution.

Table 1. Descriptive statistics for each general practitioner (GP), including patient population, the number of non-diabetic (*Control*) and diabetic (*T2DM*) subjects (also in percentage over total population), the average age with standard deviation (Age ± SD), and the gender distribution (M = male, F = female).

GP	Tot	Control	T2DM (ratio)	Age ± SD	M	F
1	2870	2658	212 (7.39%)	53.59 ± 23.43	1469	1401
2	2145	1963	182 (8.49%)	56.89 ± 22.91	1016	1129
3	1814	1646	168 (9.26%)	54.17 ± 20.79	887	927
4	2019	1886	133 (6.59%)	50.74 ± 21.60	879	1140
5	2248	2099	149 (6.63%)	53.33 ± 22.90	1079	1169
6	2475	2237	238 (9.61%)	57.64 ± 23.70	1209	1266
All	13571	12489	1082 (7.97%)	54.46 ± 22.82	6539	7032

2.2   Models

To ensure reliability and interoperability, crucial in medical applications, we explored six well-established ML models: LR, SVM, KNN, DT, RF, and XGB. These models offer the advantage of being more explainable compared to complex DL architectures, making them well-suited to clinical decision support and enabling us to investigate how and why predictions may vary across different GPs, which is a central aspect of our analysis. Exploring both parametric (LR, SVM) and non-parametric (DT, RF, XGB) models, as well as the instance-based learner KNN, allows us to evaluate how model complexity, internal assumptions, and inductive bias can affect overall performance across GPs [6].

In addition, given the promising results on structured EHR data in [5], we also evaluate TabPFN on our dataset in inference mode to assess its out-of-the-box generalization capabilities. This choice aligns with TabPFN's intended use as a pre-trained foundation model, designed to provide strong performance in new classification tasks without additional training [5]. However, it lacks the interpretability of traditional ML models, as it does not offer explicit insights into feature importance, which is critical for clinical contexts.

2.3   Experimental Design

To assess model performance and its ability to generalize across GPs, we adopted and compared two cross-validation strategies:

- **Stratified 5-Fold Cross-Validation (5F-CV)**: This strategy evaluates performance within the overall dataset distribution. The dataset is randomly split into five folds while preserving class balance. At each iteration, one fold is used for testing and the remaining folds for training. Since all data originate from the same distribution and all GPs are present in each fold, this setting provides an optimistic estimate of performance under the assumption of independent and identically distributed (i.i.d.) data.
- **Leave-One-GP-Out Cross-Validation (L1GPO-CV)**: This strategy evaluates performance across different distributions. Patients are grouped by their GP, and at each iteration, the model is trained on data from five GPs and tested on the held-out GP. This simulates a real-world deployment scenario where a model is applied to an entirely unseen clinical practice, thus capturing inter-practice variability and potential distribution shifts.

This comparison is motivated by potential data variability across GPs, in terms of patient populations, data recording habits, or clinical practices. Hence, a model trained on one subset of GPs may not necessarily perform well on another, making it essential to evaluate both within-distribution and cross-GP.

To obtain an unbiased estimate of model performance and prevent overfitting, we adopted a nested cross-validation approach: for each outer fold (either in 5F-CV or L1GPO-CV), an inner stratified three-fold cross-validation is performed to optimize hyperparameters in terms of Area Under the Receiver Operator Characteristic Curve (AUC) score via grid search.

2.4 Evaluation Metrics

To evaluate model performance, we computed the main classification metrics: Accuracy (Acc), macro F1-score (F1), macro Precision (Prec), macro Recall (Rec), AUC, Area Under the Precision-Recall Curve (PRAUC), Specificity (Spec), and Sensitivity (Sens). For model interpretability, we employed SHAP (SHapley Additive exPlanations) values [9]. SHAP offers a theoretically grounded approach for estimating the marginal contribution of each feature to individual predictions, enabling a transparent assessment of feature relevance.

3 Results

Table 2 presents the performance metrics of all models using the 5F-CV strategy. The XGB model achieved the best overall performance, with AUC = 93.70%, PRAUC = 76.06% and Sens = 81.79%, highlighting its robustness in detecting the minority class. Notably, TabPFN showed high scores in terms of Acc = 96.18% and Prec = 95.18%, but limited effectiveness in detecting T2DM cases with Sens = 52.35%. All other models underperformed across most metrics.

Table 2. Predictive performance in percentage (%), reported as mean ± standard deviation for each model trained using a stratified Five-Fold cross-validation (5F-CV) strategy. Highest values are in bold.

Model	Acc	F1	Prec	Rec	AUC	PRAUC	Spec	Sens
LR	92.02 ± 0.01	47.92 ± 0.00	46.01 ± 0.01	50.00 ± 0.00	77.37 ± 0.91	18.35 ± 0.96	**100.00**	0
SVM	94.10 ± 0.21	71.69 ± 1.89	89.53 ± 3.05	65.90 ± 1.90	83.22 ± 1.71	52.02 ± 6.79	99.45	32.34
KNN	89.75 ± 0.53	62.62 ± 1.24	63.72 ± 1.33	61.85 ± 1.43	61.85 ± 1.43	33.94 ± 2.12	95.05	28.65
DT	95.68 ± 0.37	**82.75 ± 1.74**	89.99 ± 1.38	78.07 ± 1.94	90.05 ± 1.58	67.38 ± 1.62	99.03	57.11
RF	95.12 ± 0.68	81.64 ± 1.13	86.43 ± 4.37	78.52 ± 1.29	84.93 ± 2.96	68.60 ± 2.37	98.27	58.78
XGB	88.27 ± 0.60	72.99 ± 0.57	68.57 ± 0.51	**85.31 ± 1.29**	**93.70 ± 0.79**	**76.06 ± 2.70**	88.83	**81.79**
TabPFN	**95.82 ± 0.86**	81.59 ± 4.61	**95.28 ± 2.10**	75.14 ± 5.34	91.00 ± 3.25	70.84 ± 8.82	99.76	50.53

To assess generalization across different GPs, we evaluated model performance using the L1GPO-CV strategy. As shown in Table 4, XGB again achieved the best results with AUC = 93.10%, PRAUC = 74.94%, and Sens = 80.22% on average. All other models exhibited similar performance trends to those observed in the 5F-CV setting. Further analysis of the L1GPO-CV results is detailed in Table 4, which reports the performance of the XGB model across individual GPs. While AUC scores remained relatively stable across GPs, ranging from 89.92% to 96.99% ($\Delta = 7.07\%$), PRAUC values exhibited substantial variability (from 57.90% to 86.86%) with a much wider spread ($\Delta = 28.96\%$). This discrepancy highlights how the model's ability to rank positive cases varies substantially across practices. Specifically, GP1 recorded the lowest scores across most metrics, particularly in PRAUC = 57.90% and Rec = 78.75%, whereas GP2 consistently achieved the highest (PRAUC = 86.86 %, Rec = 89.99%). These results suggest notable differences in data collection procedures across GPs, potentially due to variability in data completeness, coding practices, or patient populations.

Table 3. Predictive performance in percentage (%), reported as mean ± standard deviation for each model trained using a stratified Five-Fold cross-validation (5F-CV) strategy. Highest values are in bold.

Model	Acc	F1	Prec	Rec	AUC	PRAUC	Spec	Sens
LR	92.02 ± 0.01	47.92 ± 0.00	46.01 ± 0.01	50.00 ± 0.00	77.37 ± 0.91	18.35 ± 0.96	**100.00**	0
SVM	94.10 ± 0.21	71.69 ± 1.89	89.53 ± 3.05	65.90 ± 1.90	83.22 ± 1.71	52.02 ± 6.79	99.45	32.34
KNN	89.75 ± 0.53	62.62 ± 1.24	63.72 ± 1.33	61.85 ± 1.43	61.85 ± 1.43	33.94 ± 2.12	95.05	28.65
DT	95.68 ± 0.37	**82.75 ± 1.74**	89.99 ± 1.38	78.07 ± 1.94	90.05 ± 1.58	67.38 ± 1.62	99.03	57.11
RF	95.12 ± 0.68	81.64 ± 1.13	86.43 ± 4.37	78.52 ± 1.29	84.93 ± 2.96	68.60 ± 2.37	98.27	58.78
XGB	88.27 ± 0.60	72.99 ± 0.57	68.57 ± 0.51	**85.31 ± 1.29**	**93.70 ± 0.79**	**76.06 ± 2.70**	88.83	**81.79**
TabPFN	**95.82 ± 0.86**	81.59 ± 4.61	**95.28 ± 2.10**	75.14 ± 5.34	91.00 ± 3.25	70.84 ± 8.82	99.76	50.53

Table 4. Predictive performance in percentage (%) reported by each GP for the XGB model using the L1GPO-CV strategy. Highest values are in bold.

Metric	XGB model					
	GP_1	GP_2	GP_3	GP_4	GP_5	GP_6
Acc	87.97	88.53	**92.61**	89.79	87.54	86.98
F1	69.37	75.47	**81.41**	72.03	69.55	73.83
Prec	65.71	70.55	**77.55**	67.52	65.39	69.66
Rec	78.75	**89.99**	87.37	83.70	84.28	85.48
AUC	89.92	**96.99**	94.79	92.04	92.24	92.61
PRAUC	57.90	**86.86**	82.81	70.63	73.05	78.41
Spec	89.51	88.23	**93.80**	90.72	88.04	87.34
Sens	67.92	**91.75**	80.95	76.69	80.53	83.61

Overall, the L1GPO-CV strategy provides a more realistic assessment of model generalizability across diverse clinical practices.

Regarding model interpretability, Fig. 1 shows the SHAP summary plots for XGB under both the 5F-CV and L1GPO-CV strategies. The most influential features are consistent across both settings, indicating stable model behavior. Estimated Glomerular Filtration Rate (eGFR) and age consistently emerge as the top predictors. This aligns with clinical literature, which identifies eGFR as an important early indicator for detecting the initial signs of diabetes [12]. Despite its potential for integrating heterogeneous feature types, TabPFN exhibited suboptimal performance on the minority class, limiting its current applicability to clinical tasks such as early T2DM detection. In contrast, XGB consistently achieved superior predictive performance, while also offering greater simplicity, interpretability and robustness across practices. These qualities make XGBoost a more reliable and clinically suitable choice for supporting early identification of T2DM in primary care settings.

4   Discussion

Our experimental findings reveal a substantial difference between random stratified sampling and partitioning based on real-world structures, such as the GP identifier. This gap is particularly evident in the larger standard deviations observed across AUC and PRAUC scores in the L1GPO-CV setting compared to

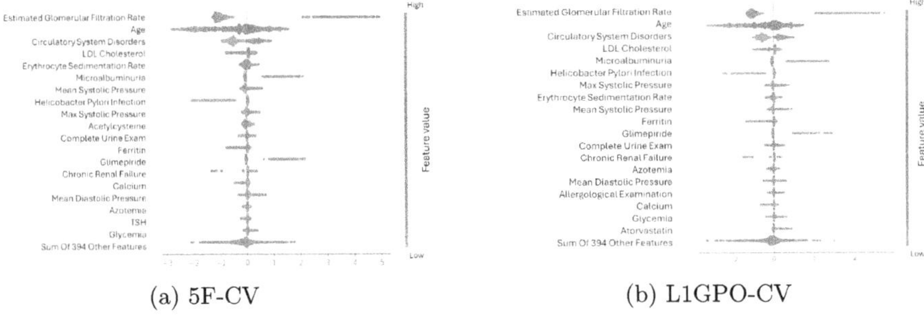

(a) 5F-CV   (b) L1GPO-CV

Fig. 1. SHAP value plots for XGB model in Stratified Five-Fold cross-validation (5F-CV) and Leave-One-GP-Out cross-validation (L1GPO-CV) strategies.

the stratified 5F-CV (see Table 2 and Table 3). While stratified 5F-CV assumes data homogeneity and offers an optimistic estimate of performance, the L1GPO-CV strategy exposes underlying distributional shifts arising from differences in data collection, coding practices, or patient populations that randomly sampled folds may not capture. This finding reinforces the notion that clinically relevant ML models must be capable of generalizing across practice-specific variability. Accordingly, cross-practice evaluation strategies such as L1GPO-CV are essential to uncover inter-practice biases and rigorously assess predictive models' robustness in heterogeneous primary care settings. Following this direction, another future work will focus on extending the experimental framework to include a broader set of GPs distributed across different national regions. The goal will be to develop a more generalized model capable of encapsulating regional variability in clinical practices, patient demographics, and data recording standards—thereby enhancing the model's generalizability across diverse clinical contexts.

Looking ahead, future developments should prioritize model transparency and trustworthiness to facilitate integration into clinical decision support systems. This step includes not only adopting explainable AI techniques [4] that provide interpretable insights into model predictions, but also uncovering the causal patterns that drive early T2DM prediction, thereby enabling more meaningful, actionable support for practitioners. Additionally, federated learning approaches [11] can enable collaborative model training across multiple GPs while preserving privacy and respecting data ownership, thereby improving generalizability and robustness across diverse primary care settings.

5   Conclusion

This study demonstrates the feasibility of applying ML for the early detection of T2DM by proposing the FIMMG-6GP dataset. Among all the models evaluated, XGB emerged as the most reliable, offering the optimal balance between predictive performance and clinical interpretability. Furthermore, adopting an L1GPO experimental strategy proved most effective in capturing and assessing inter-practice heterogeneity across GPs. In this context, the proposed approach demonstrated robustness across heterogeneous care settings, providing valuable insights to support informed medical decision-making. Overall, despite the existence of advanced methods, our findings emphasize the critical role of clinical collaboration in developing trustworthy, interpretable, and generalizable machine learning tools for primary care.

Disclosure of Interests. The authors have no competing interests to declare relevant to the content of this article.

References

1. Bernardini, M., Romeo, L., Misericordia, P., Frontoni, E.: Discovering the type 2 diabetes in electronic health records using the sparse balanced support vector machine. IEEE J. Biomed. Health Inf. (2019)
2. Deberneh, H.M., Kim, I.: Prediction of type 2 diabetes based on machine learning algorithm. Int. J. Environ. Res. Public Health **18**(6), 3317 (2021)
3. Galicia-Garcia, U., et al.: Pathophysiology of type 2 diabetes mellitus. Int. J. Mol. Sci. **21**(17), 6275 (2020)
4. Gomez, C., Smith, B.L., Zayas, A., Unberath, M., Canares, T.: Explainable AI decision support improves accuracy during telehealth strep throat screening. Commun. Med. **4**(1), 149 (2024)
5. Hollmann, N., et al.: Accurate predictions on small data with a tabular foundation model. Nature **637**(8045), 319–326 (2025)
6. Imam, F., Musilek, P., Reformat, M.Z.: Parametric and nonparametric machine learning techniques for increasing power system reliability: a review. Information **15**(1), 37 (2024)
7. Kopitar, L., Kocbek, P., Cilar, L., Sheikh, A., Stiglic, G.: Early detection of type 2 diabetes mellitus using machine learning-based prediction models. Sci. Rep. **10**(1), 11981 (2020)
8. Mohsen, F., Al-Absi, H.R., Yousri, N.A., El Hajj, N., Shah, Z.: A scoping review of artificial intelligence-based methods for diabetes risk prediction. NPJ Digital Med. **6**(1), 197 (2023)
9. Prendin, F., et al.: The importance of interpreting machine learning models for blood glucose prediction in diabetes: an analysis using shap. Sci. Rep. **13**(1), 16865 (2023)
10. Ravaut, M., et al.: Development and validation of a machine learning model using administrative health data to predict onset of type 2 diabetes. JAMA Netw. Open **4**(5), e2111315–e2111315 (2021)
11. Teo, Z.L., et al.: Federated machine learning in healthcare: a systematic review on clinical applications and technical architecture. Cell Rep. Med. **5**(2) (2024)
12. Wang, Y.: Implications of a family history of diabetes and rapid EGFR decline in patients with type 2 diabetes and biopsy-proven diabetic kidney disease. Front. Endocrinol. **10**, 855 (2019)

Self-Attention as a Predictor of EEG Anomalies

Natalia Koliou[1], Maria Sierra[2], Christoforos Romesis[1],
Stasinos Konstantopoulos[1]([✉]), and Luis Montesano[2]

[1] Institute of Informatics and Telecommunications, NCSR Demokritos,
Ag. Paraskevi, Greece
`konstant@iit.demokritos.gr`
[2] BitBrain, Zaragoza, Spain

Abstract. One of the main concerns when dealing with electroencephalographic signals (EEG) is assuring that clean data with a high signal-to-noise ratio is recorded. The relevant denoising methods tend to have a narrow scope of application as what is noise for one application might be useful signal for some other application and there no general-purpose approach (or even paradigm) that works best across domains and applications. Machine learning methods are often used for this task, by training Autoencoders and Transformers on reconstruction and prediction, and then assuming the reconstruction/prediction error as an indication of anomalies. These approaches only take into account the morphology of the stream, and are not aware of the different, often highly contextualized, aspects of artifacts.

In this article we explore the novel idea that we can create application-specific artifact detectors by training an attention-based deep neural network and then extracting from the attention layer information about what is ignored. This removes the most pressing challenge of artifact detection, namely that artifacts are vaguely defined and thus difficult to directly supervise, and allows application-specific artifact patterns to be extracted from non artifact-related supervision. We evaluated our method using electroencephalogram (EEG) signals on a sleep-stage labeling task. The performance of the proposed approach was compared against reconstruction/prediction error and against EEG-specific noise detection methods. The results indicate that the proposed method is a promising task-agnostic tool for anomaly detection in streaming data.

Keywords: Machine learning · Biomedical data · EEG · denoising

1 Introduction

One of the main concerns when dealing with electroencephalographic signals (EEG) is assuring that clean data with a high signal-to-noise ratio is recorded. The EEG signal amplitude is in the microvolts range, and it is easily contaminated with noise, known as artifacts, which need to be filtered from the neural processes to keep the valuable information needed for different applications.

C. Tommasino et al. (Eds.): AIBIO 2025, CCIS 2696, pp. 47–60, 2026.
https://doi.org/10.1007/978-3-032-17216-7_5

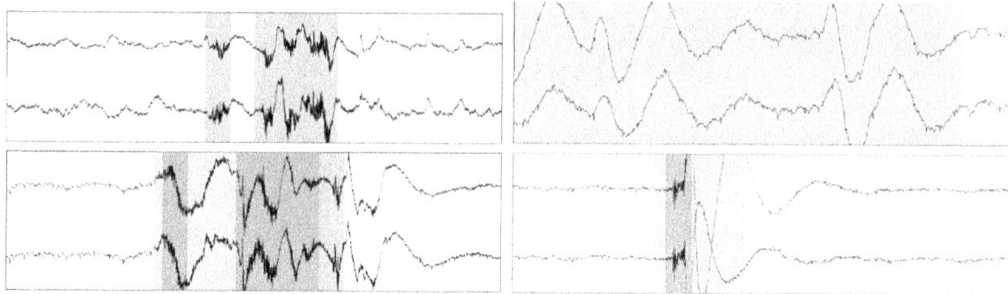

Fig. 1. Examples of the temporal visualization of EEG signals and coloring of noisy segments.

In this domain, an artifact is denoted as any component of the EEG signal not directly produced by human brain activity, making the system register noise that contaminates the neural EEG data. The ability to recognize these artifacts is the first step in removing them. EEG artifacts can be classified depending on their origin, which can be physiological or external to the human body (technical/non-physiological).

Figure 1 shows some examples of EEG signals contaminated with noise. In this figure, pink-colored areas are typical of low-frequency noise (0.2–4 Hz), which is mainly due to perspiration originating from small drops of sweat produced by the skin glands, which cause changes in the electrical baseline of the electrodes. Brown-colored and green-colored areas are typical of high-frequency noise (30–45 Hz) that may originate from electrical activity produced by the muscles when they are contracted, like, for example, muscle tension in the jaw or forehead that can take place when clenching or frowning, respectively. Orange-colored areas are typical of high-amplitude noise that may be due to temporary failures in contact between the EEG sensor and the scalp produced by touching the sensor or by spontaneous changes in electrode-skin contact.

As understood from the above, there is a variety of artifacts, both technical and physiological, each with different characteristics. Furthermore, and in particular regarding the physiological artifacts, what is noise for one application might be useful signal for some other application. It is well-known that there is no general-purpose approach (or even paradigm) that works best across domains and applications and performance depends on the use case and the nature of the encountered anomalies [7].

In the work described here, we present a method for automatically adapting a deep-learned anomaly detector to different domains. In other words, instead of aiming at a general-purpose anomaly detector (which is unatainable for the reasons explained above), we aim at a general-purpose way to train a case-specific anomaly detector without direct supervision. The core of the idea is that anomaly detection is a pre-processing step for some sequence processing task. We operate under the assumption that there is supervision for this downstream task, although there is no supervision for what constitutes an anomaly. We then make the following research hypothesis: *Anomalies are the parts of the sequence that have the property that ignoring them gives superior performance despite the fact that decisions are made from fewer datapoints.*

One can easily see how this maps directly to specific instances of anomalies. For example, assuming a sleep-stage classification task on EEG data, electrical activity produced by muscle contraction will have the same morphology regardless of the sleep stage and a successful classifier will learn to ignore it. *We aim to exploit the labelling available for a given task in order to train a general-purpose anomaly detector that can be ported to different tasks, less well-understood, tasks.*

Our contribution is the formulation of a methodology for leveraging the outputs of intermediate layers of deep neural networks in order to extract the level of significance the network places on the different parts of the sequence being learned. In the remainder of this article, we first provide the necessary background (Sect. 2) and then proceed to describe our methodology (Sect. 3), which we evaluate on an EEG dataset where we have supervision for both a downstream task (sleep stage prediction) *and* carefully curated anomaly annotations (Sect. 4). We then present and discuss the experimental results (Sect. 5) and conclude (Sect. 6).

2   Background

One of the main frameworks in sequence processing are *recurrent neural networks* where the sequence is presented to the network one token at a time and the network maintains a *hidden state* which distills the information needed from past tokens to provide a context for the processing of the current token. One of the most successful recurrent architectures is the *Long Short-Term Memory (LSTM)* where trainable *gates* control the flow of information to and from the hidden state [3]. This allows LSTM to capture long temporal dependencies in a low-dimensional state representation [2,4].

LSTMs are often combined with other techniques, such as convolution and encoder-decoder architectures. Encoder-decoder LSTMs, in particular, learn a compressed representation of the data. When training the decoder to reconstruct the original sequence back (which is known as *autoencoding*), the compressive encoding is trained to drop information that is not detrimental for the loss estimation. Anomalies (in the sense of patterns not encountered during training) can then be identified by higher reconstruction error [1,8]. Reconstruction error over autoencoding has been used extensively for anomaly detection in various architecture besides LSTM [10], and its limitations are well-understood: Autoencoders struggle with high-dimensional data, as it is up to the system designer to find the layer widths (effectively, the level of compression) that drop the correct amount of information. Further, Autoencoders are limited with the respect to the kind of information they drop: Since this decision is driven by a loss that compares the reconstructed sequences against the input sequence, a commonly occurring pattern will be retained even when it is an anomaly in a given context.

Besides recurrency, the other major approach to sequence-processing is the *Transformer* architecture. Transformers are Autoencoders based on the *self-attention* mechanism [9]. Unlike LSTMs and other recurrent architectures,

Transformers receive the complete sequence as input and model relationships across the entire sequence. This allows gradients to flow directly across the entire sequence, rather than being propagated step by step, making it easier to discover long-distance dependencies. At the core of the Transformer architecture lies the self-attention mechanism, which enables the model to assign different levels of importance to elements in the input sequence based on the value of *any other element in the sequence*. Specifically, Transformers learn three sets of weights which are applied to input of dimensionality d to get the *query (Q)* vector, the *key (K)* vector, and the *Value (V)* vector. The attention mechanism computes the *similarity score* QK^T which is a $d \times d$ matrix that determines the contribution of each element in the final representation of each other element. The similarity score is scaled and softmax'ed into a matrix of weights, which are applied to the value vector. This yields the representation softmax $\left(QK^T/\mathrm{sqrt}(d) \right) \cdot V$ where each element contains information aggregated from the entire sequence, improving the model's ability to detect long-range dependencies.

3   Research Methodology

3.1   Research Hypothesis

As discussed in the previous section, reconstruction and prediction errors are widely used as key indicators for anomaly detection in time-series data due to their intuitive appeal and straightforward implementation. However, these approaches do not take into account differences in the nature of what is considered an anomaly for each use case.

As we framed our work in a context where there is no anomaly supervision, it follows that it is also not possible to select training data that is not contaminated with anomalies. This means that the model may inadvertently learn to reconstruct anomalies. Additionally, reconstruction-based methods often struggle to detect contextual anomalies, where an observation may be anomalous only in specific temporal or multivariate contexts. For example, a high-temperature reading might be expected in the summer but anomalous in the winter, and reconstruction models may overlook such contextual nuances.

Similarly, prediction error, which measures deviations between predicted and actual values, can be susceptible to noise and non-stationarity in time-series data. In highly dynamic systems, normal variations may result in significant prediction errors, leading to false positives. Moreover, models relying on prediction error often assume that future patterns can be reliably forecasted based on past observations, an assumption that may not hold in volatile or chaotic systems.

On the other hand, the attention mechanism offers an alternative, currently unexplored, way to extract indications about what parts of the sequence are anomalies. The hypothesis is that noise or anomalies are the part of the equence that receives the least attention while performing a relevant task. The intuition is that neural networks will happily overfit the data when they are given enough parameters to do so. Such an overfitted network might not be good to actually perform the task, but is good at recognizing two ways in which a sub-sequence is

Table 1. Methods under comparison.

Acronym	Architecture	Detection
LSTM	LSTM Autoencoder	Reconstruction
C-LSTM	Convolutional LSTM Autoencoder	error
AE_err	Attention-based Autoencoder	
TP_err	Transformer Predictor	Prediction error
AE_att	Attention-based Autoencoder	Attention
TP_att	Transformer Predictor	
MNE	IIR filter	

anomalous: (a) it does not follow any pattern that was boosted (gradient-wise) by the training; (b) it follows a pattern that is inconsistent, it is sometimes associated with one class on the task and sometimes with an another, so it alternates between being boosted and penalized by the loss function, again resulting in low attention.

To investigate this hypothesis, we experimented with several methods for anomaly and noise detection ranging from attention-based methods to state-of-the-art machine learning approaches, as well as conventional anomaly detection methods. These are listed in Table 1 and described in more detail in the remainder of this section.

3.2   Reconstruction and Prediction Error

The *LSTM Autoencoder (LSTM)* uses a sequence-to-sequence architecture with LSTM layers for both encoding and decoding. The encoder compresses the input into a fixed-size latent representation by processing the input sequence and retaining the final hidden state of the LSTM. This is achieved using an LSTM layer, followed by a dropout layer for regularization, and a fully-connected layer for dimensionality reduction. The decoder then processes this compressed representation using the reverse architecture (FC, dropout, and LSTM) to reconstruct the original data.

In this architecture, fully connected (FC) layers process the final hidden state of the LSTM (the last timestep in the sequence) as a single, comprehensive representation of the entire input sequence. This output is then projected into a lower-dimensional latent space through a linear transformation. While this approach is computationally efficient, it assumes that the LSTM's final hidden state sufficiently captures all relevant temporal dependencies. As a result, it can struggle to retain fine-grained temporal details, especially for data like EEG signals, where localized patterns are crucial.

The *Convolutional LSTM Autoencoder (C-LSTM)* enhances feature extraction by combining LSTM layers with convolutional layers. The key difference between the LSTM and C-LSTM architectures lies in how dimensionality reduction is achieved in the encoder and decoder: the first uses fully connected

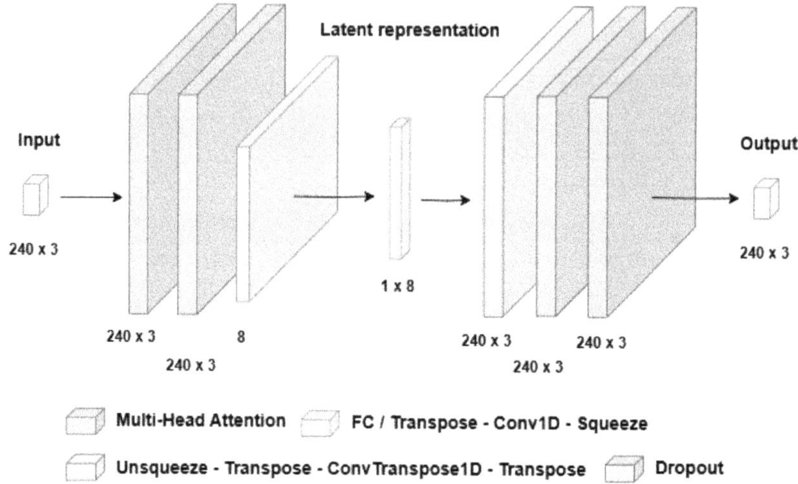

Fig. 2. AE_err/AE_att architecture.

(FC) layers, while the latter uses Conv1D layers. These operate directly on the sequence of hidden states produced by the LSTM. By applying a kernel across the temporal dimension, they extract localized patterns and dependencies within the sequence. This convolutional operation integrates information from multiple timesteps, creating a more nuanced and structured representation. After convolution, the output is reduced to a lower-dimensional latent space, where temporal features are preserved and compactly encoded. This method emphasizes localized temporal dynamics while reducing dimensionality.

The *Attention-based Autoencoder (AE_err)* combines convolutional layers with an attention mechanism to reconstruct the input data, again using the convolutional layers to capture local features while replacing LSTM with attention to capture long-term patterns. Fig. 2 illustrates this architecture. The input to the encoder consists of a sequence of 240 measurements from two simultaneous channels, along with a same-size sequence of time representation. The input data passes through the encoder and is compressed into a latent representation of size 1×8, where the first dimension represents a single compressed time step, and the second dimension corresponds to eight learned features. This is achieved by applying multi-head attention to the input data, followed by a dropout layer for regularization, and a convolutional layer for dimensionality reduction. The decoder then processes this compressed representation using the reverse architecture (transposed convolution, dropout, and attention) to reconstruct the original data, capturing both trends and amplitudes.

In all three autoencoding systems, anomaly detection is based on the assumption that the compressed latent representation preserves only recurring, periodic fluctuations and trends. Atypical spikes, often caused by noise, do not cause enough loss to be worth the space to represent them (in terms of nodes in

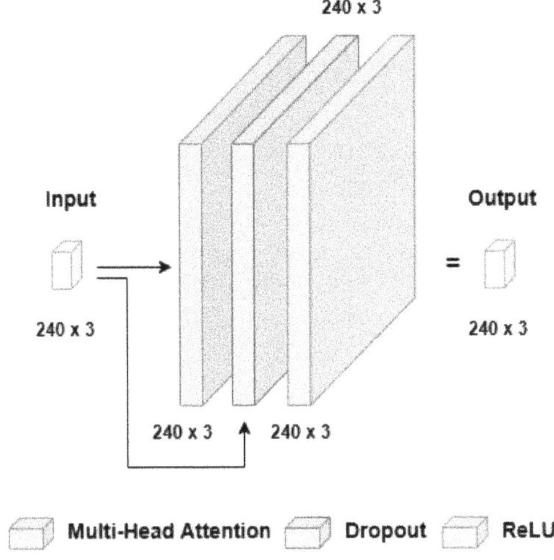

Fig. 3. TP_err/TP_att architecture.

the latent representation). Therefore, the level of anomaly is estimated as the reconstruction error, the difference between the original input sequence and the sequence decoded from the latent representation.

The *Transformer Predictor (TP_err)* method utilizes a Transformer that uses multi-head attention for time-series forecasting. It consists of a sequence-to-sequence architecture, with multi-head attention layers in both the encoder and decoder components. The encoder captures temporal dependencies in the input sequence, while the decoder predicts the next sequence based on these encoded features. Figure 3 illustrates this architecture. The input consists of a sequence of 240 measurements from two simultaneous channels, along with a same-size sequence of time representation. This data passes through the embedding layer, which applies multi-head attention to capture key temporal patterns. The output is then processed with dropout regularization and passed through a LeakyReLU activation function to introduce non-linearity.

The TP_err method estimates noise through prediction error, i.e. the difference between the model's predicted output and observed values. When the model predicts the next time step in the sequence, a significant difference between the predicted and actual values suggests that the input data may be noisy.

3.3   Attention-Based Detection

The exact same architectures as in AE_err and TP_err above are also used for the respective attention-based detection methods *Attention-based Autoencoder (AbAE_att)* and *Transformer Predictor (TP_att)*, except that now anomaly is estimated by the attention weights.

The key idea is that when a part of the sequence receives a low attention weight, it suggests that the information at that moment is likely noisy and, therefore, unimportant for the task.

3.4 Conventional Noise Detection

Alongside machine learning methods, conventional techniques provide a reliable alternative for detecting noise in time-series data and are commonly utilized. *Multinomial Noise Exponential filtering (MNE)* is a method used to remove unwanted frequencies from time-series data, typically EEG signals. It applies a bandpass filter to the data, allowing signals within a specific frequency range to pass through while reducing frequencies outside this range.

4 Experimental Setup

This study employs a case analysis to validate the efficacy of the proposed noise estimation methods. The focus is detecting noise within electroencephalographic (EEG) signals, recorded via headbands utilized during slumber to monitor various stages of the user's sleep cycle.

In this analysis, EEG signals collected from a headband with two EEG channels synchronized with medical-grade EEG devices are considered. The recorded signal frequency for each channel of the headband is 128 Hz. These signals are grouped into consecutive 30-second segments, and each segment is further annotated by three experts, into one of five sleep stages: Wake, N1, N2, N3, and REM. These stages correspond to specific brain activity patterns, such as slow eye movements, sleep spindles, and other characteristic waveforms. The goal of the current analysis is to detect the presence of noise, if any, at any of these segments. In total, 56 recordings were examined. Each recording refers to the EEG signals acquired by the headband of a user during a night-long sleep. These signals are grouped into 30-second consecutive segments.

As a ground-truth method to evaluate the results of the proposed noise estimation methods, the original estimation method used by BitBrain, the headband manufacturer, is considered. This method consists of task-specific algorithms to automatically estimate noise and evaluate the overall quality of EEG signals, identifying the artifacts in recordings made using their wearable textile headband. The dataset is publicly available [6].

4.1 Data Pre-processing

Data normalization is required for the machine learning methods to ensure robust model training and reliable outcomes. It is performed using statistics derived from the entire training dataset instead of relying on per-batch calculations. The median and *interquartile range (IQR)* are used instead of the mean and standard deviation, respectively, to improve robustness against outliers. The median measures central tendency and is resistant to extreme values, and IQR

Table 2. Absolute number and percentage of segments with artifacts in each channel and recording session.

RecID	A	B	C	D
HB1	0	57 (5%)	27 (3%)	9 (1%)
HB2	151 (14%)	56 (5%)	26 (3%)	9 (1%)

is a measure of statistical dispersion that represents the spread of the middle 50% of a dataset and reduces the influence of outliers by focusing on the range within which the central portion of the data lies.

MNE requires raw data that preserves the characteristics of the original signal, so no normalization is applied for these methods.

To train the machine learning models, the available recordings were randomly split into training (43 recordings), validation (3 recordings), and testing subsets (10 recordings). Among the testing recordings, six had zero or one noisy segments are not reported here as it makes little sense to compare methods on having identified a single datapoint.

Table 2 gives the absolute and relative noise density for the remaining four testing recordings, arranged in descending order. Specifically, the table gives the count of 30-second segments within which at least one artifact is annotated as noise in the ground-truth labeling. Note that recordings are *not* of equal length.

What is noteworthy is that Recording A has considerably different noise rates between the two channels. Since the signals from the two channels are heavily correlated, this presents an opportunity for the machine learning methods to demonstrate learning a comparative model that exploits the fact that the noisy parts of HB2 are not correlated to their corresponding parts in HB1. However this is a difficult theory to construct, since it requires 'discovering' correlation first.

4.2   Training Process and Hyper-Parameters

The implementations of the methods in Table 1 that we used in our experiments are publicly available. Our implementation of the machine learning methods have been reposited in Zenodo.[1] MNE is used as implemented and configured in the 'MNE Tools' Python package for exploring, visualizing, and analyzing human neurophysiological data.[2] MNE is a bandpass filter with pre-configured cut-offs specifically targeting EEG data.

To process the data with the *AE* and *TP* methods, we split each 30-second segment of EEG data (3840 samples per channel) into 16 smaller chunks of 240 samples each. This point is moot for *LSTM*, *C-LSTM*, and *MNE*.

---

[1] Cf. https://doi.org/10.5281/zenodo.14842198.
[2] Available from https://mne.tools and Pypi.

The Autoencoder methods are trained on sequence reconstruction. The Predictor methods are trained on predicting sleep stage. To balance the autoencoders' focus on both the amplitude and trends of the time-series data, we define a custom loss function, called *BlendedLoss*. This function combines the median and mean of the powered absolute differences between the predicted values ($\hat{x}$) and the target values (x):

$$\text{Loss} = (1 - b) \cdot \text{median}(|\hat{x} - x|^p) + b \cdot \text{mean}(|\hat{x} - x|^p)$$

where p is the power parameter that controls the sensitivity of the loss to differences and b the *blend factor* that controls the trade-off between learning the overall trend (median error) and closely following local patterns (mean error).

Revisiting our research hypothesis, we expect methods trained on predicting sleep stage to outperform methods trained on autoencoding since they have access to task-specific labels. More generally our methods are ordered as follows in terms of task-specific knowledge they have access to:

1. *MNE* is specifically, expertly designed to detect noise in EEG signals and has proven to be very effective on this task.
2. *AE_att* and *TP_att* implement our hypothesis that the attention mechanism can exploit supervision unrelated to anomaly detection to automatically extract task-specific knowledge of anomalies.
3. *LSTM, C-LSTM, AE_err* and *TP_err* are general-purpose autoencoders with minimal access to task-specific knowledge in the form of a task-specific loss function.

This ordering reflects our prior expectation regarding their relative performance. *None of the above (neither machine learning nor manual calibration) has ever had any access to noise annotations in the training data, but only to sleep-stage annotations.*

For the training configuration, we set the batch size to 512 and trained the models for a maximum of 1000 epochs with patience of 30 epochs, meaning that if the validation loss does not improve for 30 consecutive epochs, training will stop. We set the learning rate to 1e-4 and use the Adam optimizer to adjust the model weights. Additionally, we use *ReduceLROnPlateau* scheduling to reduce the learning rate if the validation loss plateaus.

5   Results and Discussion

We prepared three validation/testing setups. In the first setup validation and testing scores are calculated on the original 30-sec segments where each segments is annotated as 'noise' if it includes at least one sample marked as 'noise' in the ground-truth annotation. In the 5min and 10min-window setups segments evaluation was performed on 5min and 10min windows. If a method reports noise on any part of the window and the ground truth also annotates as noisy any part of the window, the window counts as a true positive. Obviously, these are easier tasks than the original 30-sec segmentation on two grounds: (a) Since any part of the window marks the window as noisy, longer windows give fewer instances but the same number of noisy instances; thus positives are less sparse and the task becomes less of a needle-in-a-haystack problem, and (b) learners have access to a longer context for the same number of input tokens, which we know to be an important factor in sequence processing [5].

Table 3 presents F-score, Precision, and Recall metrics for the evaluated methods on all three evaluation setups. Since all methods give a numerical estimation and not a binary decision, a threshold was established. The threshold was calculated on the training data, separately for each method, as the threshold that makes 1% of the training data come out as noise. This is the only piece of prior domain knowledge shared by all learners. F-score is calculated for $\beta = 2$, in order place more weight on recall than precision. This is due to the fact that the dataset is very unbalanced and noise instances are rare, even in the 10min-window setup. F-score is adapted accordingly to reflect that recall is harder to achieve than precision.

The first observation is that by comparing the three sub-tables we can immediately see that the three windows behave as expected, with results improving with longer windows. By comparing horizontally from right to left we also see that results improve as noise gets denser.[3] We cannot speculate on whether the top-to-bottom improvement is due to the longer context or due to denser positives. But either way, we have clear indications about how task difficulty scales across the table.

What is directly relevant for our hypothesis are the comparisons between (a) attention-based anomaly detection (AE_att and TP_att) against the error-based anomaly detection from the same models (AE_err and TP_err), and (b) models trained on the sleep stage task (TP) against autoencoded models (AE). TP_att generally outperforms all four TP/AE_err/att combinations, although autoencoding proved better on HB1-C (primarily LSTM and secondarily AE_att) with the gap becoming more pronounced on the denser setups. Although the conditions present in HB1-C are worth investigating, the results show that the ideas presented here are validated and promising.

What is also noteworthy is that TP_att outperforms MNE on HB2-A and HB2-B. Regarding HB2-A it is worth investigating whether the transformer has 'discovered' the lack of correlation between HB1-A and HB2-A on noisy segments. Regarding HB2-B, a possible explanation is that TP_att is more robust to noise density considerably above the hard-wired 1%: it suffers the unavoidable precision loss just as all methods, but it gets a comparatively higher F-score through perfect recall.

---

[3] Note that HB1-A is out-of-order in this respect, as it has no noise.

Table 3. F2-score ($\beta = 2$) on HB1 (left) and HB2 (right) for different segment lengths. When precision and recall not within three percentile points of the F2 score, they are also given in parenthesis. Empty cells where no segment was marked as noise.

(a) Evaluation on 30sec windows.

RecID	A	B	C	D	A	B	C	D
LSTM		**2%**			**2%**(6%,1%)	**4%**(7%,4%)	**4%**(3%,4%)	
C-LSTM			**4%**(11%,4%)					
AE_ATT		**4%**			**1%**(20%,1%)			
TP_ATT		**2%**			**15%**(13%,15%)	**10%**(5%,14%)	**4%**(2%,8%)	**3%**(1%,11%)
MNE					**2%**(40%,1%)			

(b) Evaluation on 5 min windows.

RecID	A	B	C	D	A	B	C	D
LSTM	**13%**(6%,18%)				**19%**(12%,22%)	**22%**(8%,38%)	**11%**(3%,35%)	
C-LSTM			**21%**(10%,30%)		**1%**(2%,1%)			**4%**(1%,11%)
AE_ERR	**16%**(27%,14%)				**4%**(10%,3%)			
AE_ATT	**9%**(3%,18%)		**10%**(3%,22%)		**7%**(18%,6%)			
TP_ATT	**14%**(6%,19%)				**42%**(14%,84%)	**26%**(7%,100%)	**16%**(4%,100%)	**5%**(1%,100%)
MNE			**96%**(82%,100%)		**15%**(38%,13%)			**14%**(100%,11%)

(c) Evaluation on 10 min windows.

RecID	A	B	C	D	A	B	C	D
LSTM	**19%**(7%,37%)		**5%**(2%,11%)		**28%**(12%,42%)	**25%**(7%,64%)	**9%**(2%,42%)	
C-LSTM			**34%**(11%,67%)		**1%**(1%,1%)			**21%**(5%,100%)
AE_ERR	**31%**(30%,32%)				**6%**(8%,5%)			
AE_ATT	**12%**(3%,35%)		**26%**(7%,89%)		**9%**(14%,9%)			
TP_ATT	**21%**(7%,39%)		**2%**		**41%**(13%,90%)	**22%**(5%,100%)	**14%**(3%,100%)	**5%**(1%,100%)
MNE			**96%**(82%,100%)		**25%**(35%,23%)			**96%**(82%,100%)

6   Conclusions and Future Work

This paper investigates the extraction of anomaly indicators from *intermediate* layers of a deep neural network trained on a sequence processing task. By removing the need to train on a sequence reconstruction/prediction task, we are free to train on whatever task-specific supervision is available. This alleviates the most pressing challenge of anomaly detection, namely that anomalies are vaguely defined and thus difficult to directly supervise, while simultaneously allowing task-specific knowledge to be extracted from whatever other (non anomaly-related) supervision might be available.

Our ideas are positively validated on EEG signals sourced from wearable sleep-monitoring devices. This dataset has the great advantage of having both task supervision (sleep stage detection) and noise supervision, both expertly annotated by the device manufacturer. Our current findings already indicate that the attention layer of a Transformer trained on the sleep stage task exhibits promising performance when used as an anomaly detector.

Subsequent steps will pursue two directions: exploring the current experimental setup at more depth and expanding the breadth of the results with diverse datasets and tasks. Regarding the first direction, we mostly plan to investigate how the components of the attention layer (Q, K, and V) interact in order to understand whether a subset of these components is more tightly fitted on recognizing patterns that should be ignored. Another investigation would be to understand if the performance on HB2-A really indicates that the Transformer has 'discovered' the lack of correlation between HB1-A and HB2-A on noisy segments or is incidental. Despite the inherent difficulty in trying to understand the inner workings of neural networks even for single-layer attention, as the field of *explainable machine learning* evolves the required tools are starting to materialize. Regarding the second direction, the most immediate goal is to jointly train on multiple tasks, which we expect to help the network distinguish between noisy segments and segments that happen to be irrelevant for a given task.

Acknowledgments. This research was co-funded by the European Union under GA no. 101135782 (MANOLO project). Views and opinions expressed are however those of the authors only and do not necessarily reflect those of the European Union or CNECT. Neither the European Union nor CNECT can be held responsible for them. AWS resources were provided by the National Infrastructures for Research and Technology GRNET and funded by the EU Recovery and Resiliency Facility.

Disclosure of Interests. The authors have no competing interests.

References

1. Basora, L., Olive, X., Dubot, T.: Recent advances in anomaly detection methods applied to aviation. Aerospace **6**(11) (2019). https://doi.org/10.3390/aerospace6110117
2. Duja, K.U., Khan, I.A., Alsuhaibani, M.: Video surveillance anomaly detection: a review on deep learning benchmarks. IEEE Access **12** (2024). https://doi.org/10.1109/ACCESS.2024.3491868

3. Hochreiter, S., Schmidhuber, J.: Long short-term memory. Neural Comput. **9**(8) (1997). https://doi.org/10.1162/neco.1997.9.8.1735
4. Hojjati, H., Ho, T.K.K., Armanfard, N.: Self-supervised anomaly detection in computer vision and beyond: a survey and outlook. Neural Netw. **172** (2024). https://doi.org/10.1016/j.neunet.2024.106106
5. Lee, M.-C., Lin, J.-C., Gran, E.G.: How far should we look back to achieve effective real-time time-series anomaly detection? In: Barolli, L., Woungang, I., Enokido, T. (eds.) AINA 2021. LNNS, vol. 225, pp. 136–148. Springer, Cham (2021). https://doi.org/10.1007/978-3-030-75100-5_13
6. López-Larraz, E., et al.: The Bitbrain open access sleep (BOAS) dataset. OpenNeuro (2025). https://doi.org/10.18112/openneuro.ds005555.v1.1.1
7. Mejri, N., Lopez-Fuentes, L., Roy, K., Chernakov, P., Ghorbel, E., Aouada, D.: Unsupervised anomaly detection in time-series: an extensive evaluation and analysis of state-of-the-art methods. Expert Syst. Appl. **256** (2024). https://doi.org/10.1016/j.eswa.2024.124922
8. Sgueglia, A., Di Sorbo, A., Visaggio, C.A., Canfora, G.: A systematic literature review of IoT time series anomaly detection solutions. Futur. Gener. Comput. Syst. **134**, 170–186 (2022). https://doi.org/10.1016/j.future.2022.04.005
9. Vaswani, A., et al.: Attention is all you need. In: Advances in Neural Information Processing Systems 30 (2017). http://papers.nips.cc/paper/7181-attention-is-all-you-need
10. Zamanzadeh Darban, Z., Webb, G.I., Pan, S., Aggarwal, C., Salehi, M.: Deep learning for time series anomaly detection: a survey. ACM Comput. Surv. **57**(1) (2024). https://doi.org/10.1145/3691338

Cross-Dataset Multivariate Time-Series Model for Parkinson's Diagnosis via Keyboard Dynamics

Arianna Francesconi[1]([⊠]) [iD], Donato Cappetta[2], Fabio Rebecchi[2], Paolo Soda[1,3] [iD], Valerio Guarrasi[1] [iD], and Rosa Sicilia[1] [iD]

[1] Unit of Artificial Intelligence and Computer Systems, Department of Engineering, Università Campus Bio-Medico di Roma, Rome, Italy
`arianna.francesconi@unicampus.it`
[2] Eustema S.p.A., Research and Development Centre, Naples, Italy
[3] Department of Radiation Sciences, Biomedical Engineering, Umeå University, Umeå, Sweden

Abstract. Parkinson's disease (PD) presents a growing global challenge, affecting over 10 million individuals, with prevalence expected to double by 2040. Early diagnosis remains difficult due to the late emergence of motor symptoms and limitations of traditional clinical assessments. In this study, we propose a novel pipeline that leverages keystroke dynamics as a non-invasive and scalable biomarker for remote PD screening and telemonitoring. Our methodology involves three main stages: (i) preprocessing of data from four distinct datasets, extracting four temporal signals and addressing class imbalance through the comparison of three methods; (ii) pre-training eight state-of-the-art deep-learning architectures on the two largest datasets, optimizing temporal windowing, stride, and other hyperparameters; (iii) fine-tuning on an intermediate-sized dataset and perform external validation on a fourth, independent cohort. Our results demonstrate that hybrid convolutional–recurrent and transformer-based models achieve strong external validation performance, with AUC-ROC scores exceeding 90% and F1-Score over 70%. Notably, a temporal convolutional model attains an AUC-ROC of 91.14% in external validation, outperforming existing methods that rely solely on internal validation. These findings underscore the potential of keystroke dynamics as a reliable digital biomarker for PD, offering a promising avenue for early detection and continuous monitoring.

Keywords: Imbalance · Deep Learning · Telemonitoring

1 Introduction

Parkinson's disease (PD) is one of the major challenges for global healthcare systems, with a growing impact in terms of both prevalence and socioeconomic

---

V. Guarrasi and R. Sicilia—Contributed equally to this work.

C. Tommasino et al. (Eds.): AIBIO 2025, CCIS 2696, pp. 61–74, 2026.
https://doi.org/10.1007/978-3-032-17216-7_6

costs. PD affects over 10 million people worldwide, with projections indicating a doubling of this population by 2040 [24]. The primary issue is late diagnosis, which limits the effectiveness of therapeutic interventions and exacerbates functional decline. Indeed, the hallmark motor symptoms (bradykinesia, rigidity, tremor) emerge only after a neural loss of at least 50% [1], resulting in unsatisfactory diagnostic accuracy in the early stages. The search for accessible, non-invasive, and scalable biomarkers has thus become a top priority.

In PD, subclinical motor signs can be detected early through abnormalities in motor sequencing and force stability; however, traditional neuropsychological tests and qualitative clinical rating scales present inherent limitations, including evaluator dependency, ceiling and floor effects, and low sensitivity to subtle fluctuations [1]. In this context, keyboard dynamics (KD) have emerged as promising digital biomarkers capable of translating manual dexterity tests (e.g., finger tapping) into passively collected data via everyday devices such as smartphones and keyboards [11,15]. The integration of artificial intelligence (AI), particularly deep learning (DL) models, with human-device interaction data represents a methodological breakthrough [10,22]. KD offers a rich space of kinetic features (e.g., key flight time and typing rhythm) that can be correlated with specific motor phenotypes such as arrhythmokinesia (irregular rhythm of movement) or movement heteroscedasticity (inconsistent speed across repetitions), leading to variability in keystroke timestamps. DL architectures such as convolutional neural networks (CNNs) and transformers, already validated in physiological signal analysis, have the potential to extract latent patterns from typing time series, thereby overcoming the limitations of traditional models based on handcrafted features [6]. However, their application to KD in PD remains limited and largely unexplored, particularly in cross-dataset validation scenarios that are critical for clinical deployment.

This work aims to explore the effectiveness of advanced DL models for PD detection through the analysis of KD, moving beyond proof-of-concept to a robust cross-dataset validation. We integrate data from multiple public datasets collected in different settings, including both *free-text* (self-generated content, e.g., emails) and *fixed-text* (standardized phrases) tasks, adopting a cross-dataset approach. Our study defines a replicable framework for patient stratification and real-time longitudinal telemonitoring, paving the way for accessible and personalized diagnostic tools. We advance the field of digital PD diagnosis through three main contributions:

- Extensive analysis of state-of-the-art DL architectures for multivariate time-series modeling of KD signals;
- Comparison of three strategies for handling data imbalance, including unbalanced dataset (baseline), random undersampling, and a novel ensemble-based method called IMBALMED [9], which creates multiple and complementary undersampled subsets to improve model diversity;
- Robust integration and validation on three public datasets using a pretraining followed by a fine-tuning strategy. Additionally, external validation

is performed on a smaller, independent fourth dataset to demonstrate the generalizability of the proposed framework.

The rest of this manuscript is organized as follows. Section 2 first introduces key concepts necessary to understand the application context of the proposed methodology. Then, it presents state-of-the-art studies on KD for PD detection. Section 3 presents our methodology and experimental setup. Section 4 reports and discusses the obtained results. Finally, Sect. 5 provides concluding remarks and future directions.

2   Related Work

The diagnosis of PD through the analysis of KD primarily focuses on four temporal signals: Hold Time (HT), the interval between pressing and releasing a key; Flight Time (FT), the time between releasing one key and pressing the next; Press-Press Time (PP), the duration between two consecutive key presses; and Release-Release Time (RR), the interval between two consecutive key releases. KD data can be collected in two distinct contexts: *in-the-clinic*, where data is acquired in controlled environments (e.g., laboratories or clinics), and *in-the-wild*, where it is derived from daily interactions with personal devices (e.g., keyboards or smartphones) in uncontrolled settings. In addition to being a highly imbalanced classification problem, since datasets typically contain fewer PD cases than controls, KD data introduce further challenges: they consist of multivariate, non-periodic time series, which complicates the application of standard balancing techniques. Time-domain oversampling or data augmentation methods often fail to preserve the temporal structure, whereas noise-based magnitude-domain augmentations risk altering meaningful motor patterns [17].

This section reviews studies that employ public KD datasets for PD diagnosis, categorizing them by learning approach (machine learning vs. deep learning) and highlighting if and how they address class imbalance. To the best of our knowledge, the first study to employ KD for PD detection was conducted by Giancardo et al. [11]. The authors introduced the public neuroQWERTY MIT-CSXPD dataset, consisting of 85 participants (42 with PD), whose data were collected *in-the-clinic* via a touchscreen keyboard. Participants performed a *free-text* task, typing spontaneously as they would at home. The study implemented an ensemble of 200 support vector regression models in a cross-validation setting, achieving an AUC-ROC of 79%. Subsequent research followed two main directions: traditional machine learning (ML) approaches and, more recently, DL methods. Among traditional ML approaches, Iakovakis et al. [15] used a public dataset (hereafter referred to as TyPD), which includes 33 participants (18 with PD), collected during a routine clinic visit using a smartphone-based *fixed-text* task. The authors developed a two-stage ML model based on low- and high-order statistical features, such as mean, standard deviation, skewness, and kurtosis, extracted from HT, FT, and normalized pressure signals. Despite the limited sample size, their method achieved an AUC-ROC of 92% using leave-one-patient-out cross-validation (LOPO). Milne et al. [19], using the neuroQWERTY

MIT-CSXPD dataset, proposed a univariate logistic regression model based on mean absolute consecutive difference, a dynamic feature derived from the HT signal, which reached an AUC-ROC of 85% under cross-validation. More recently, Roy et al. [22] explicitly addressed class imbalance by applying undersampling to both the neuroQWERTY MIT-CSXPD and Online English datasets. The latter, composed of 230 participants (100 with PD), was collected *in-the-wild* during a *fixed-text* task using keyboards and involving multiple sentences. The authors combined ensembles of ML models (i.e., SVM) and DL models (i.e., long short-term memory (LSTM [14])), extracting temporal features (i.e., mean, standard deviation, median, Q1, Q3) from HT, PP, and RR signals using sliding windows of 100 and 50 keystrokes for *free-* and *fixed-text* tasks, respectively. Their LOPO-based evaluation achieved an AUC-ROC of 85%.

Regarding DL approaches, Iakovakis et al. [16] employed the TyPD dataset in a study that implemented a 1D CNN with three convolutional layers, using input windows of 100 samples from HT and FT signals. Their model, evaluated with LOPO, achieved an AUC-ROC of 89%. Dhir et al. [6] focused on HT and FT signals from the Online English dataset. They segmented with sliding windows of 50 characters, and applied an LSTM network validated via a hold-out strategy, reaching an AUC-ROC of 73%. Bernardo et al. [3] used the Tappy dataset (103 participants, 57 with PD) along with the Synthetic Minority Oversampling Technique (SMOTE) for balancing. The Tappy data were collected *in-the-wild*, with participants using their personal computer keyboards to perform *free-text* typing over longitudinal periods. They proposed a pipeline that transformed time-series data into spectrograms via continuous wavelet transform. To address the imbalance, they applied SMOTE for oversampling in the image domain. Their model, based on a SqueezeNet architecture and hold-out validation, reported an accuracy of 90%, though the AUC-ROC was not specified.

The reviewed studies differ across datasets in terms of acquisition context (*in-the-wild* vs. *in-the-clinic*) and interaction device (keyboard vs. touchscreen). While such variability in training could foster generalization, most works rely on a single homogeneous dataset, limiting evaluation across heterogeneous sources or task settings. Although early results are encouraging, the field still faces several critical gaps, including the absence of approaches that are both effective and clinically scalable. First, few studies perform a comprehensive benchmarking of DL architectures specifically tailored to KD as time-series signals. Second, the problem of class imbalance is often overlooked or addressed through basic strategies. Third, even though some works explore typing on either keyboards or smartphones, very few attempt to integrate signals from both modalities, limiting the potential for widespread applicability. Lastly, most studies rely on single-dataset validation, with limited testing across heterogeneous data sources or task settings (e.g., *free-text* vs. *fixed-text*, *in-the-wild* vs. *in-the-clinic*). Our work addresses these limitations through a unified framework that integrates multivariate typing signals, compares state-of-the-art DL architectures and balancing methods, and validates the approach across diverse public datasets.

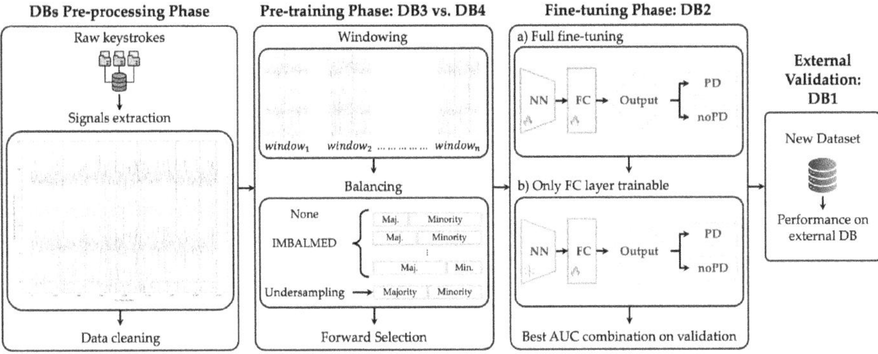

Fig. 1. Schematic representation of the proposed method, comprising four steps: dataset pre-processing, pre-training, fine-tuning, and external validation. In the NN (Neural Network) and FC (Fully Connected) blocks, weight freezing and updating are represented by ice and flame icons, respectively. Class balancing is illustrated with orange for the majority class ("Maj.") and light blue for the minority class ("Min."). In the IMBALMED [9] strategy, multiple sub-datasets with different class distributions are created.

3   Proposed Method and Experimental Setup

The proposed methodology, illustrated in Fig. 1, consists of four main phases: pre-processing, pre-training, fine-tuning, and external validation. The following subsection details the pre-processing step; pre-training is presented in Sect. 3.2, whilst fine-tuning and external validation are described in Sect. 3.3.

3.1   Datasets and Pre-processing

We employed four publicly available datasets, described in detail in Sect. 2: TyPD (33 samples), neuroQWERTY MIT-CSXPD (85), Tappy (103), and Online English (230), which we refer to as DB1 through DB4, respectively, in order of increasing sample size. We focused on handcrafted temporal signals (HT, FT, PP, RR) instead of raw key timestamps, as these features are well-established in the KD–PD literature, as discussed in the previous section, and facilitate cross-dataset comparability. Table 1 provides an overview of these datasets, including: the dataset identifier (ID) used in this work, the name and reference of the dataset (where the reference corresponds to the first paper that introduced and discussed the dataset), the number of participants with PD (#PD), the number of healthy controls (#HC), and the availability of four KD signals (HT, FT, PP, and RR). Each of them is marked as Derived (D) if computed from other signals or raw keystrokes, or Provided (P) if directly available in the original dataset. The last four columns indicate the average signal length per subject (in number of keystrokes) with the standard deviation, the average number of sessions per subject, the nature of the typing task (*Fixed-text* or *Free-text*), and the context of data acquisition (Clinic or Wild). The average signal length was computed by aggregating the lengths of individual acquisition sessions for each subject within a dataset.

Table 1. Summary of the four publicly available datasets used in this study, where 'ID' stands for dataset identifier, '#PD' is the number of PD participants, and '#HC' is the number of healthy controls. HT, FT, PP, and RR are the available KD signals marked as Derived (D) or Provided (P). The last four columns report average signal length (measured in keystrokes per subject) ($\pm$ SD), average sessions per subject, typing task (Fixed-text vs. Free-text), and acquisition context (Clinic vs. Wild).

ID	Dataset Name	#PD	#HC	HT	FT	PP	RR	Avg. Signal Length	Avg. # Sessions	Task	Context
DB1	TyPD [15]	18	15	D	D	D	D	60.18 $\pm$ 14.64	8.91	*Fixed-text*	Clinic
DB2	neuroQWERTY MIT-CSXPD [11]	42	43	D	D	D	D	1492.59 $\pm$ 644.76	1.36	*Free-text*	Clinic
DB3	Tappy [12]	57	46	P	P	P	D	210.74 $\pm$ 82.34	145.09	*Free-text*	Wild
DB4	Online English [6]	100	130	D	D	D	D	127.52 $\pm$ 22.15	14.57	*Fixed-text*	Wild

The pre-processing steps were tailored to each dataset, following methodologies adopted in the already cited studies in which they were introduced or analyzed. From each dataset, we extracted HT, FT, PP, and RR signals. For DB1 and DB4, both derived from *fixed-text* tasks, we applied the preprocessing methodology proposed by [15]: we enforced a minimum typing rate of 20 characters per minute per session to exclude recordings with irregular typing behavior. FT values exceeding 3 s were removed as outliers, whereas HT values were retained in their raw form, given their lower sensitivity to interruptions [15]. The PP and RR signals were computed from the original press and release timestamps of each key. In contrast, DB2 and DB3 are based on *free-text* tasks, and, in accordance with [3], no data cleaning was applied to preserve the natural typing rhythm of the users. However, a specific adjustment was necessary for DB3. This dataset, collected during the patients' daily activities, is organized on a monthly timescale, whereas all other datasets are structured daily. To harmonize the temporal resolution, we segmented the monthly data from DB3 into daily sessions. This segmentation was based not only on the date but also on the latency between consecutive keystrokes. When the time interval between two keystrokes exceeded 30 s, we considered this a discontinuity and treated it as the beginning of a new session. This threshold was chosen under the assumption that pauses longer than 30 s could lead to partial recovery from accumulated motor and cognitive fatigue, potentially disrupting the continuity of the typing pattern, which we aim to analyze through KD. Finally, given the high average signal lengths across datasets (as reported in Table 1), we applied on-the-fly windowing during pre-training (see Sect. 3.2) to enable the model to capture both local patterns within each signal and global dependencies across the multivariate sequences.

The pre-processed datasets were then used in different phases of our experimental pipeline according to their size and task characteristics. Specifically, the two largest datasets, DB3 (*free-text*) and DB4 (*fixed-text*), were independently used as pre-training sources to assess how task type affects generalization performance. Their resulting models were then fine-tuned on the medium-sized DB2 (*free-text*), allowing adaptation to a free-typing scenario. Finally, DB1, the smallest dataset based on a *fixed-text* task, was used for external validation, providing an independent evaluation of the framework's generalizability. This experimental setting enabled us to assess not only the model's robustness across datasets of varying sizes, but also its ability to generalize across different typing task modalities, reflecting heterogeneous real-world usage conditions.

3.2   Pre-training

We adopted a pre-training strategy and evaluated eight DL architectures from the tsai library [21], specifically designed for time series analysis. These models can be grouped into four main families: recurrent neural networks (RNNs), including Gated Recurrent Unit (GRU [5]) and LSTM; hybrid models that combine recurrent and convolutional components (RNN-CNN), namely GRU-Fully Convolutional Network (GRU-FCN) and LSTM-Fully Convolutional Network (LSTM-FCN) [18]; purely convolutional networks, such as Temporal Convolutional Network (TCN [2]) and Explainable Convolutional Network (XCM [8]); and transformer-based architectures, including Time-Series Transformer (TSiT) and Time-Series Transformer Plus (TSTPlus) [25].

To investigate the effect of early stopping, we trained all models for 50 epochs and compared three patience settings: no patience, a patience of 5, and a patience of 25. We also compared two different loss functions: binary cross-entropy and focal loss. The latter was included to address class imbalance, as it reduces the influence of dominant classes by focusing on challenging minority examples. Pre-training was conducted on the two largest datasets (DB3 and DB4), with each model trained independently. We did not merge DB3 and DB4 due to their task heterogeneity (*free-text* vs. *fixed-text*). Instead, we assessed them separately to analyze cross-context transferability. Hyperparameter optimization was conducted using a forward selection strategy: it was used as a simple grid-search-like strategy, where hyperparameters were optimized sequentially (first window size, then stride, etc.), fixing the best value from the previous step. For DB3, we explored window sizes of 90, 100, and 110 keystrokes; for DB4, we tested 40, 50, and 60, in accordance with [22]. For the stride parameter, we evaluated values of 1, half, and full window size. We tested batch sizes of 8, 16, and 32, and learning rates of 0.001, 0.0001, and 0.00001. We further compared two checkpointing strategies: last epoch vs. best validation. Finally, we examined the impact of different class balancing strategies: we compared no balancing, random under-sampling, and the IMBALMED strategy [9]. IMBALMED (multImodal enseMble via class BALancing diversity for iMbalancEd Data) is an ensemble-based method that leverages undersampling to generate multiple imbalanced subsets, each characterized by a different class distribution. For instance, in the first subset shown in Fig. 1, the minority class represents only about 20% of the data, but its proportion gradually increases across the subsets until it becomes the majority. This progressive diversification encourages the ensemble to learn from varying imbalance conditions, enhancing generalization. The method was previously shown to outperform other state-of-the-art balancing techniques on multimodal tabular data. Its strong performance and compatibility with KD, where undersampling is particularly effective (see Sect. 2), motivated its inclusion in our experimental setup.

We used a leave-20%-subjects-out cross-validation scheme (stratified by subject), which corresponds to a 10-fold partition but ensures subject-level separation, as some datasets contained multiple sessions per patient.

Performance was evaluated at the patient level by averaging predicted probabilities across windows and sessions and computing metrics on the aggregated outputs. The best-performing configuration for each model was selected based on validation performance for subsequent fine-tuning on a third dataset.

3.3 Fine-Tuning and External Validation

The second block of Fig. 1 corresponds to the fine-tuning phase: the best-performing hyperparameter configuration was identified for each model and balancing strategy, based on their validation AUC-ROC. The selected configuration was subsequently used to fine-tune the classifiers on DB2, the dataset chosen for this stage due to its intermediate size. A lower learning rate, set to an order of magnitude smaller than in pre-training, was used during fine-tuning to allow for more stable updates and to avoid disrupting the pre-trained representations. We also compared two weight-freezing strategies: no frozen layers, allowing full fine-tuning, and freezing all layers except for the final fully connected layer. The best-performing weight-freezing strategy on the validation set was then used in the external validation phase. All fine-tuning experiments were carried out using the same 10-fold cross-validation strategy presented in Sect. 3.2, aggregating the results across windows and sessions.

For external validation, we assessed the models' configurations that achieved the highest validation performance during fine-tuning. The entire DB1 dataset, the smallest one, was used as an independent test set to assess the generalizability of the proposed approach. This ensured that the most effective version of the model was tested on the independent DB1 dataset, providing a realistic estimate of out-of-distribution performance and supporting the assessment of model robustness in new clinical settings.

4 Results and Discussions

For all pre-training experiments, selecting the best validation weights, applying an early-stopping patience of 5, and using focal loss consistently outperformed their respective alternatives. Therefore, only the results under these optimized settings are reported in this section.

Table 2 summarizes the optimal hyperparameters selected on the validation set for each model across both DB3 and DB4, considering the three balancing strategies: Unbalanced, Undersample, and IMBALMED [9]. The table is organized in two parts: (a) reports the best window size (WS) and stride (ST); (b) shows the corresponding learning rate (LR) and batch size (BS) used during training. The optimal hyperparameters varied notably across model architectures and balancing strategies. IMBALMED generally enabled more flexible configurations, likely due to the regularizing effect introduced by the ensemble's diversity. Recurrent models often favored shorter WS, while transformers sometimes benefited from longer WS, though results were not consistent across datasets (Table 2). Lower learning rates were typically selected under the undersampling strategy, likely reflecting the reduced data volume and the need for more cautious updates. Overall, these findings highlight that hyperparameter tuning must be carefully adapted to both the specific model and the balancing method employed.

Table 3 reports the AUC-ROC scores for each model on DB3 and DB4 under the three balancing strategies. For each model, the highest AUC-ROC value is highlighted in bold. As evident from the results, any balancing method boosts AUC-ROC over the unbalanced baseline. In the smaller, *free-text* DB3, undersampling yields the largest gains (e.g., LSTM rises from 46% to 69%), likely by removing noisy majority samples. IMBALMED also improves performance but often trails undersampling on DB3 (e.g., GRU: 60% vs 65.9%), suggesting its diverse sub-dataset strategy could benefit from further tuning in this context. Conversely, on the larger *fixed-text* DB4, IMBALMED almost always outperforms undersampling, indicating that creating multiple unbalanced subsets better captures intra-class variability when extensive data are available. Hybrid RNN-CNN models consistently lead pure RNNs, demonstrating that augmenting temporal recurrence with convolutional filters uncovers complementary kinetic patterns. Pure convolutional networks perform moderately: XCM approaches hybrid performance on DB4 (71.55% vs top hybrids) but underperforms on DB3, showing they can still model temporal dependencies without recurrence. Attention-based models display the widest sensitivity to balancing: TSTPlus goes from 53.7% unbalanced to 67.3% under IMBALMED on DB4, implying they need further architectural or hyperparameter optimization to match more established RNN-CNN designs. Finally, absolute AUC-ROC values are higher on DB4 overall, reaffirming that larger *fixed-text* corpora yield more stable keystroke biomarkers for PD detection.

In Table 4, we report fine-tuning results for models pre-trained on DB3 and DB4, focusing exclusively on IMBALMED-balanced models, as this method led to higher AUC-ROC scores compared to undersampling for 6 out of 8 models (see Table 3). Since full fine-tuning consistently yielded the best validation AUC-ROC across all experiments, we report only results obtained using this approach. Alongside AUC-ROC, we also include the F1-Score for a more complete evaluation. The highest AUC-ROC score for each model is highlighted in

Table 2. Optimal window size (WS), stride (ST), learning rate (LR), and batch size (BS) for each model, dataset, and balancing method, as determined during the pre-training step.

(a) Window size (WS) and stride (ST)

Model	DB3						DB4					
	Unbal.		Under.		IMB.		Unbal.		Under.		IMB.	
	WS	ST	WS	ST	WS	ST	WS	ST	WS	ST	WS	ST
GRU	90	45	90	90	90	90	50	1	50	1	40	40
LSTM	100	50	90	45	90	45	40	20	60	60	60	1
GRU-FCN	90	45	100	100	90	90	60	60	40	40	40	1
LSTM-FCN	90	90	90	45	90	90	40	1	50	1	50	1
TCN	90	90	110	110	100	100	60	60	60	60	40	20
XCM	90	45	100	50	100	50	60	60	50	25	40	20
TSiT	90	90	90	90	100	100	40	40	40	20	60	60
TSTPlus	90	90	90	45	100	100	60	60	60	60	50	50

(b) Learning rate (LR) and batch size (BS)

Model	DB3						DB4					
	Unbal.		Under.		IMB.		Unbal.		Under.		IMB.	
	LR	BS	LR	BS	LR	BS	LR	BS	LR	BS	LR	BS
GRU	0.001	64	0.0001	8	0.001	32	0.001	16	0.0001	32	0.001	16
LSTM	0.01	32	0.0001	8	0.001	8	0.001	16	0.001	16	0.001	16
GRU-FCN	0.0001	32	0.001	16	0.001	32	0.001	16	0.001	16	0.001	16
LSTM-FCN	0.001	32	0.0001	8	0.001	32	0.001	16	0.001	16	0.001	16
TCN	0.0001	32	0.0001	8	0.001	64	0.001	16	0.001	64	0.001	16
XCM	0.001	64	0.00001	8	0.001	32	0.0001	32	0.001	16	0.001	16
TSiT	0.001	32	0.0001	16	0.01	32	0.001	16	0.001	16	0.001	16
TSTPlus	0.001	32	0.0001	8	0.001	32	0.00001	64	0.001	32	0.001	16

bold. As the results show, transferring from DB3 to DB2 yields modest AUC-ROC values, peaking at around 66%, whereas fine-tuning from the larger DB4 to DB2 produces substantially stronger performance, with top AUCs nearing 89%. Although DB3 and DB2 are both free-text datasets, this counterintuitive gap may be explained by two factors: the higher noise inherent in DB3, collected in uncontrolled daily-life conditions with greater variability and distractions, and the larger size of DB4, which supports learning richer KD patterns and enhances transferability to DB2. Within each transfer scenario, architectures that combine convolutional kernels with temporal recurrence (e.g., LSTM-FCN, GRU-FCN) consistently outperform pure RNNs or pure CNNs, suggesting that hybrid feature extractors best capture both local keystroke dynamics and longer-range dependencies. Finally, the optimal window and stride settings differ by source

Table 3. AUC-ROC scores comparison across DB3 and DB4 datasets for three balancing methods: Unbalanced (Unbal.), Undersample (Under.), and IMBALMED (IMB.) [9]. The highest score for each model is highlighted in bold.

Model	DB3			DB4		
	Unbal.	Under.	IMB.	Unbal.	Under.	IMB.
GRU	49.24%	65.93%	60.09%	64.51%	71.98%	**73.27%**
LSTM	46.06%	69.06%	58.49%	62.77%	59.75%	**73.86%**
GRU-FCN	58.79%	65.01%	63.80%	67.63%	67.73%	**75.47%**
LSTM-FCN	57.42%	**71.28%**	62.60%	56.07%	64.71%	68.88%
TCN	51.21%	57.82%	60.57%	63.42%	55.95%	**70.49%**
XCM	46.52%	64.33%	63.03%	58.41%	68.61%	**71.55%**
TSiT	48.12%	**61.20%**	57.96%	50.00%	51.97%	55.51%
TSTPlus	46.41%	63.90%	59.94%	57.94%	53.73%	**67.32%**

Table 4. Fine-tuning performance comparison (AUC-ROC and F1-Score) on DB3 and DB4 using the IMBALMED [9] method. The highest AUC-ROC score for each model is highlighted in bold.

Model	DB3 on DB2		DB4 on DB2	
	AUC-ROC	F1-Score	AUC-ROC	F1-Score
GRU	46.01%	63.87%	**75.20%**	34.44%
LSTM	55.87%	62.81%	**81.50%**	54.56%
GRU-FCN	37.71%	14.29%	**84.52%**	88.87%
LSTM-FCN	39.15%	36.11%	**88.94%**	78.07%
TCN	43.80%	51.02%	**88.04%**	64.67%
XCM	41.92%	41.98%	**82.64%**	61.81%
TSiT	66.61%	56.41%	**85.29%**	64.44%
TSTPlus	46.01%	18.33%	**79.15%**	63.92%

dataset: for DB3 (*free-text*), shorter and non-overlapping windows performed best, likely because uncontrolled typing benefits from clean, independent segments. For DB4 (*fixed-text*), mid-sized windows with small strides worked better, reflecting the structured and repetitive nature of the task.

The results of the external validation on DB1 are reported in Table 5, where we compare the performance of models using weights obtained after pre-training on DB4 (column *Pre-training on DB4*) and after subsequent fine-tuning on DB2 (*Fine-tuning on DB2*). We only report the results employing the pre-training and fine-tuning weights that yielded the best performance on the validation set during the 10-fold cross—validation. We show only DB4 as the pre-training source, as it outperformed DB3 across all eight models when fine-tuned on DB2 (see Table 4). From the reported results, it can be seen that, even before fine-tuning,

Table 5. External validation results on DB1 after fine-tuning on DB2 and pre-training on DB4. In bold is the highest AUC-ROC for each model. The columns *Best Fold* indicate the index of the fold from the fine-tuning cross-validation on DB2, whose checkpoint was used for external testing.

Model	Pre-training on DB4			Fine-tuning on DB2		
	AUC-ROC	F1-Score	Best Fold	AUC-ROC	F1-Score	Best Fold
GRU	**88.15%**	45.45%	5	75.29%	56.13%	1
LSTM	**86.67%**	57.82%	1	84.31%	65.12%	9
GRU-FCN	89.26%	78.26%	1	**89.41%**	79.39%	1
LSTM-FCN	82.96%	61.97%	2	**90.32%**	80.42%	1
TCN	81.85%	62.68%	2	**91.14%**	79.39%	9
XCM	70.37%	58.72%	10	**73.33%**	66.67%	9
TSiT	74.17%	57.91%	9	**85.77%**	72.14%	1
TSTPlus	62.75%	50.72%	1	**90.59%**	73.91%	9

models pre-trained on DB4 already perform strongly on DB1; this is an expected outcome given that both datasets use the same *fixed-text* protocol, which preserves similar keystroke patterns across domains. Fine-tuning on DB2 (a *free-text* dataset) further improves performance by adapting these representations to more variable typing behavior without compromising the knowledge gained from *fixed-text* pre-training. Among the architectures, TCN and TSTPlus emerged as the top performers, achieving AUC-ROC scores of 91.14% and 90.59%, respectively, after fine-tuning. Notably, TSTPlus, which initially underperformed compared to most models (see Table 3), benefits substantially from fine-tuning, underscoring the value of cross-protocol adaptation. Hybrid recurrent-convolutional models also demonstrate strong performance by combining convolutional feature extraction with recurrent dynamics. In contrast, pure RNNs exhibit a performance drop on free-text data, whilst TSiT and XCM register more modest gains. Overall, these findings confirm that leveraging a large *fixed-text* corpus for pre-training, followed by targeted adaptation on *free-text* data, yields the most generalizable keystroke-based biomarkers for PD detection.

5 Conclusion

In this work, we have demonstrated the effectiveness of a four-stage pipeline: preprocessing, deep-learning pre-training, targeted fine-tuning, and external validation for PD detection using KD. By leveraging large fixed-text datasets (DB4) for pre-training and adapting the learned representations on a free-text dataset (DB2), our framework achieves robust, generalizable performance. Hybrid recurrent and convolutional models (e.g., GRU-FCN, LSTM-FCN) achieve strong results, confirming the value of combining local and temporal features [11]. However, the TCN outperforms all, showing the effectiveness of deep temporal convolutions.

Our experiments further highlight the importance of tailored class-imbalance handling: although simple undersampling yields strong gains on smaller free-text corpora (DB3), the IMBALMED [9] strategy enables superior generalization on the larger fixed-text datasets by creating diverse, overlapping sub-distributions that better represent intra-class variability [20, 23]. Fine-tuning on DB2 delivers a clear uplift over zero-shot transfer from DB4, particularly rescuing transformer-based models (TSiT, TSTPlus) that initially underperform in the fixed-text pre-training phase.

External validation on the smallest independent dataset (DB1) confirms the real-world applicability of our approach: LSTM-FCN, TCN, and TSTPlus models achieve AUC-ROC scores above 90% and F1-Score exceeding 70%. These results, superior to the current state of the art, which relies solely on external validation, underscore the potential of smartphone-based keystroke monitoring as a noninvasive, scalable biomarker for telemonitoring, supporting both remote PD screening and progression tracking. Future work will explore the integration of multimodal sensor inputs (e.g., accelerometry, voice) [7] and the incorporation of explainability techniques to enhance both diagnostic accuracy and model transparency [4, 13].

Acknowledgments. Arianna Francesconi is a Ph.D. student enrolled in the National Ph.D. in Artificial Intelligence, XXXIX cycle, course on Health and Life Sciences, organized by Università Campus Bio-Medico di Roma. This work was partially funded by: (i) PNRR – DM 117/2023; (ii) Eustema S.p.A.; (iii) PNRR MUR, Italy project PE0000013 - FAIR. Resources are provided by the National Academic Infrastructure for Supercomputing in Sweden (NAISS) and the Swedish National Infrastructure for Computing (SNIC) at Alvis @ C3SE.

References

1. Alfalahi, H., et al.: Diagnostic accuracy of keystroke dynamics as digital biomarkers for fine motor decline in neuropsychiatric disorders: a systematic review and meta-analysis. Sci. Rep. **12**(1), 7690 (2022)
2. Bai, S., et al.: An empirical evaluation of generic convolutional and recurrent networks for sequence modeling. arXiv preprint arXiv:1803.01271 (2018)
3. Bernardo, L.S., et al.: Modified squeezenet architecture for Parkinson's disease detection based on keypress data. Biomedicines **10**(11), 2746 (2022)
4. Caragliano, A.N., et al.: Doctor-in-the-loop: an explainable, multi-view deep learning framework for predicting pathological response in non-small cell lung cancer. arXiv preprint arXiv:2502.17503 (2025)
5. Cho, K., et al.: Learning phrase representations using RNN encoder-decoder for statistical machine translation. arXiv preprint arXiv:1406.1078 (2014)
6. Dhir, N., et al.: Identifying robust markers of Parkinson's disease in typing behaviour using a CNN-LSTM network (2020)

7. Di Teodoro, G., et al.: A graph neural network-based model with out-of-distribution robustness for enhancing antiretroviral therapy outcome prediction for HIV-1. Comput. Med. Imaging Graph. **120**, 102484 (2025)

8. Fauvel, K., et al.: XCM: an explainable convolutional neural network for multivariate time series classification. Mathematics **9**(23), 3137 (2021)

9. Francesconi, A., et al.: Class balancing diversity multimodal ensemble for Alzheimer's disease diagnosis and early detection. Comput. Med. Imaging Graph. **123**, 102529 (2025)

10. Furia, L., et al.: Exploring early stress detection from multimodal time series with deep reinforcement learning. In: 2023 IEEE International Conference on Bioinformatics and Biomedicine (BIBM), pp. 1917–1920. IEEE (2023)

11. Giancardo, L., et al.: Computer keyboard interaction as an indicator of early Parkinson's disease. Sci. Rep. **6**(1), 34468 (2016)

12. Goldberger, A.L., et al.: Physiobank, physiotoolkit, and physionet: components of a new research resource for complex physiologic signals. Circulation **101**(23), e215–e220 (2000)

13. Guarrasi, V., et al.: Multimodal explainability via latent shift applied to covid-19 stratification. Pattern Recogn. **156**, 110825 (2024)

14. Hochreiter, S., Schmidhuber, J.: Long short-term memory. Neural Comput. **9**(8), 1735–1780 (1997)

15. Iakovakis, D., et al.: Touchscreen typing-pattern analysis for detecting fine motor skills decline in early-stage Parkinson's disease. Sci. Rep. **8**(1), 1–13 (2018)

16. Iakovakis, D., et al.: Early Parkinson's disease detection via touchscreen typing analysis using convolutional neural networks. In: 2019 41st Annual International Conference of the IEEE Engineering in Medicine and Biology Society (EMBC), pp. 3535–3538. IEEE (2019)

17. Iwana, B.K., Uchida, S.: An empirical survey of data augmentation for time series classification with neural networks. PLoS ONE **16**(7), e0254841 (2021)

18. Karim, F., et al.: LSTM fully convolutional networks for time series classification. IEEE Access **6**, 1662–1669 (2017)

19. Milne, A., Farrahi, K., Nicolaou, M.A.: Less is more: univariate modelling to detect early Parkinson's disease from keystroke dynamics. In: Soldatova, L., Vanschoren, J., Papadopoulos, G., Ceci, M. (eds.) DS 2018. LNCS (LNAI), vol. 11198, pp. 435–446. Springer, Cham (2018). https://doi.org/10.1007/978-3-030-01771-2_28

20. Mogensen, K., et al.: An optimized ensemble search approach for classification of higher-level gait disorder using brain magnetic resonance images. Comput. Biol. Med. **184**, 109457 (2025)

21. Oguiza, I.: tsai - a state-of-the-art deep learning library for time series and sequential data. Github (2023). https://github.com/timeseriesAI/tsai

22. Roy, S., et al.: Imbalanced ensemble learning in determining Parkinson's disease using keystroke dynamics. Expert Syst. Appl. **217**, 119522 (2023)

23. Ruffini, F., et al.: Multi-dataset multi-task learning for covid-19 prognosis. In: International Conference on Medical Image Computing and Computer-Assisted Intervention, pp. 251–261. Springer (2024)

24. Su, D., et al.: Projections for prevalence of Parkinson's disease and its driving factors in 195 countries and territories to 2050: modelling study of global burden of disease study 2021. BMJ **388** (2025)

25. Zerveas, G., et al.: A transformer-based framework for multivariate time series representation learning. In: Proceedings of the 27th ACM SIGKDD Conference on Knowledge Discovery & Data Mining, pp. 2114–2124 (2021)

Assessment and Compliance of Personalized Machine-Learning Pharmacokinetic Models in the European Regulatory Environment

Silvia Corte Metto[1], Federico Magnani[1]([✉]) [iD], and Gastone Castellani[1,2] [iD]

[1] Department of Medical and Surgical Sciences, University of Bologna, Bologna, Italy
{silvia.cortemetto2,federico.magnani9,
gastone.castellani}@unibo.it
[2] IRCCS, Azienda Ospedaliero-Universitaria di Bologna, Bologna, Italy

Abstract. The transformative potential of Deep Learning for the field of pharmacometrics is being extensively investigated by the scientific community. Latest models provide the innovative capability of differentiating the predictions at the level of individual patients, greatly fostering the personalization of the therapy. Still, due to the high-risk context of their application, there's the possibility that such technologies will not be employed soon in clinical settings at large scale. The European Union, through regulations such as the *Artificial Intelligence Act* and *Medical Device Regulation*, subjects the adoption of AI-based systems to careful risk assessment procedures, quality management, post market monitoring and, possibly, explicit safety thresholds. The safety of the individual patient cannot be exclusively derived from suitable and performant models; instead, it emerges from the interaction between the developer, the deployer and the user of the application. Accordingly, we present a harmonized methodology that explicitly links technical design decisions to sound legal reasoning. Developed through the interdisciplinary collaboration advocated in the literature and built on the tradition of jurimetrics, our proposed standard combines empirical performance metrics and theoretical engineering frameworks with formally verifiable compliance criteria. By basing technical requirements on measurable legal approximations, jurimetrics represents an epistemic bridge between pharmacometrics and regulatory oversight, guiding developers towards *legal-by-design* strategies that allow the seamless transition of technology from the research lab to routine care, and provides auditable evidence that protects stakeholders from liability, creating a common benchmark for the safe, compliant and equitable adoption of AI-driven pharmacometrics systems in healthcare.

Keywords: Jurimetrics · Pharmacometrics · Artificial Intelligence Act · Deep Learning · Model Assessment · Liability · Safety · Trustworthy AI · Inductive Bias

C. Tommasino et al. (Eds.): AIBIO 2025, CCIS 2696, pp. 75–87, 2026.
https://doi.org/10.1007/978-3-032-17216-7_7

1   Introduction

The integration of Machine Learning (ML) into classical pharmacological workflows is gaining increasing popularity among healthcare researchers, due to its potential towards precision medicine [20, 22, 32, 46]. Pharmacology could greatly benefit from advances in the individualized modeling of drug dynamics, which leads to better dose optimization and to enhanced prediction of pharmacological activity, of adverse effects and of drug interactions. Direct, off-the-shelf ML approaches to pharmacological tasks require large models, involving minimal domain knowledge. These black-box input-output relations, being not backed by pharmacological experts, can only live in research settings. On the other hand, the synergies between Deep Learning and dynamical systems are wide, robust and continuously expanding. A variety of modeling frameworks have been formalized for seamlessly merging mechanistic equations and neural modules into a unified mathematical system, such as physics-informed ML [25] (largely overlapped with hybrid models [45]) and Universal Differential Equations [42]. In pharmacokinetic settings, Neural ODEs [9, 29] are particularly promising, as testified by multiple successful applications [7, 15, 30, 41]. So called Deep Compartmental Models [21, 23] focus on a dedicated neural covariate model, while Compartment Model Informed Neural Networks (CMINNs [12]) extend the potential of Physics-Informed Neural Networks (PINNs, [43]) to the pharmacokinetic/pharmacodynamic (PK/PD) domain. The maturity of the field comprises a wide array of techniques for performing uncertainty quantification, allowing probabilistic predictions. Bayesian approaches have been formalized for the predictions of neural networks in general [6, 24] and for Neural ODEs in particular [10, 16, 39]. These techniques complement other possibilities for dealing with uncertainty, such as stochastic neural dynamics [37, 38].

Therefore, pharmacokinetics is among the most promising candidates for hosting the application of the latest ML techniques in a clinical setting. However, when embedded in decision-support devices, these models fall under the high-risk AI category of the 2024 EU Artificial Intelligence Act (AI Act). Consequently, developers must demonstrate – not merely claim – that, amongst others, their systems satisfy strict obligations on risk management, accuracy, robustness, cybersecurity, human oversight and post-market monitoring. Beyond the horizontal AI Act, AI-enabled pharmacokinetic systems that qualify as medical devices are simultaneously subject to the Medical Devices Regulation (MDR, Reg. (EU) 2017/745) [13] or, where applicable, the In Vitro Diagnostic Medical Devices Regulation (IVDR, Reg. (EU) 2017/746). Because they invariably process patient-level data, they must also comply with the General Data Protection Regulation (GDPR, Reg. (EU) 2016/679) for lawful-basis, purpose-limitation and data-subject-rights safeguard. From September 2025 the horizontal Data Act (Reg. (EU) 2023/2854), and since September 2023 the Data Governance Act (Reg. (EU) 2022/868), add rules on B2B/B2G data access, interoperability and data-intermediation, while the newly adopted European Health Data Space Regulation (Reg. (EU) 2025/327) establishes sector-specific conditions for both the primary and secondary use of electronic health data. These legislative layers impose high-level obligations – quality-and-safety management, data governance, transparency, cybersecurity and accountability – that must be demonstrated through recognized harmonized standards. In practice, conformity is evidenced via the medical-device standards suite (e.g., EN ISO 13485, EN ISO

14971, IEC 62304, ISO/IEC 81001-5-1) and the forthcoming AI-specific norms under CEN-CENELEC JTC 21, which will confer a presumption of conformity under the AI Act.

How does this legal framework interact with the cutting-edge technologies currently employed in pharmacokinetics, and how should the current regulation be applied to their deployment in clinical settings?

This question is especially important in view of the many different modeling techniques which characterize this field, pledging the identification of principles abstract enough to accommodate such variety, but targeted and clear. We believe such a need to be shared among the developers, the deployers and the hypothetical users of these systems, greatly preventing the adoption of potentially relevant innovations in healthcare. Some expert commentary even warns that AI tools used in pharmacology will only scale if explainability and auditability are embedded at design time [4].

This research paper embraces the emerging doctrine of *Secure- & Legal-by-Design* [2, 8, 47], in which every architectural choice – such as the inductive biases employed for driving the model to learn the intended relation – becomes an explicit legal argument that demonstrably reduces residual risk and clarifies liability allocation; combining it with jurimetrics, the application of quantitative and statistical methods to legal reasoning first formulated by Lee Loevinger in 1949 [27]. We identify grounded principles for developing quantitative arguments in the case of predictive pharmacometrics systems with ML components, providing developers with design strategies and guidelines for compliant products, and helping the clinicians in better understanding their source of safety, hence their limitations. We contribute to closing the gap between computer scientists, regulators and clinicians, and to creating a common ground for the discussion of complex, multidisciplinary issues.

The paper is organized as follows: Sect. 2 introduces the concept of Inductive Bias, which is the rationale guiding the scientific community in developing ML models; while Sect. 3 distills the core legal obligations contained in the EU AI Act and MDR into design imperatives that govern pharmacokinetic systems with ML components, indicating how software developers and informatic engineers could address each regulatory requirement.

2 Inductive Biases

Inductive biases are at the foundation of the generalization capability of ML systems since their earliest stages, as shown by classic books like Mitchell's Machine Learning ([34], p. 42), published almost 30 years ago. Inductive biases constrain the behavior of a given ML model in predictable ways, setting the boundaries of its operations and aiding the interpretation of its role in a larger system. Therefore, they carry huge relevance in compliance contexts. Inductive biases can be divided into three classes, adapting Karniadakis [25]:

- Observational biases, that correspond to the data employed for supervised learning, to which the predictions are asked to adhere. These can either be real measurements or synthetic datasets, produced by careful data augmentation procedures.

- Scientific biases, which are directly derived from the physical laws which govern the system, either high level as the energy or momentum conservation laws, or very specific like sets of equations finely describing the evolution of the quantitative variables which define the state of the system. This approach leads, depending on the context, to Physics-Informed NNs [43], Biology-Informed NNs [11], Compartment-Model Informed NNs [12], etc. Hybrid models [45], in general, can be regarded as the biasing of neural networks through mechanistic equations. Other strategies comprehend constraining some variables to predetermined ranges, using multibranch networks or dividing the parameters into different classes, one of which is personalized (see [21] on these possibilities).
- Learning biases consist in the appropriate choice of loss functions and learning algorithms guiding the training phase of a ML model: these can induce the model to favor the learning of behaviors that adhere to the underlying physics or to other constraints.

Scientific biases are spread in the world of pharmacometrics, due to their importance for data economy (which is key in a field characterized by sparse data) and to their flexibility in dealing with partially known physical systems. All these preliminary actions on the design of the model, while preserving its flexibility and its black-box nature, rule out vast classes of inadequate behaviors. Moreover, scientific biases can directly accommodate the intervention of experts in the field, for example by the specification or crafting of the most suitable compartment model to be employed, and they can be readily inspected by working clinicians, enhancing the transparency of the system. Actionable explanations foster confidence, awareness and responsibility in the final user, contributing to clarifying liability allocation.

3 Regulatory Obligations

Traditional regulatory dossiers have historically treated legal compliance and engineering evidence as two parallel tracks compiled ex-post, once a prototype is frozen [40]. Yet this approach is no longer tenable for medical technologies governed by MDR and for high-risk AI systems under the AI Act, both of which impose continuous, life-cycle risk-management obligations. As predicted by some academics [36], EU AI Act formalized these requirements, making compliance-by-design non-negotiable for high-risk healthcare applications: from design and development (MDR Annex I §3; AI Act Art. 9) through verification and validation (ISO 14971:2019) to post-market surveillance and performance monitoring (MDR Arts. 83–86; AI Act Art. 61), compliance must be embedded in every version iteration, design decision and dataset update, rather than bolted on the product retrospectively. A shift is required from retrospective compliance checks to a genuinely proactive *legal-by-design* mindset [5, 17, 18, 28].[1]

In practical terms, high-risk AI systems (AI Act, Art. 6; Annex III §5) embedded in medical applications must operate under a documented risk-management framework covering the entire life-cycle (Art. 9) of the product, in harmony with the MDR workflow for clinical evaluation and post-market surveillance (MDR Arts. 61 & 83–86). Five complementary duties arise:

---

[1] The principle *"legal by design"* in connection with AI was first introduced by Lippe et al. in [28]. A fuller doctrinal elaboration appears with Mireille Hildebrandt, in [17] and [18].

1. First, Article 10 obliges developers to maintain robust data governance, hence representative, complete, and biased-audited datasets.
2. Second, Article 12 mandates meticulous record-keeping so that every parameter, performance metric, and configuration change is hashed into an immutable log.
3. Third, Articles 13 and Recital 47 impose transparency and explainability obligations, requiring both the disclosure of the system's limitations and an output intelligible to professional users.
4. Fourth, Article 14 demands human oversight, translated here into predefined override and escalation mechanisms that preserve clinical autonomy.
5. Fifth, Article 15 couples accuracy, robustness, and cybersecurity into an integrated engineering target that must be demonstrated quantitatively through systematic stress-testing.

All the previous articles refer to the final product being introduced in the clinical context, comprising specific choices about the informatic system, the data storage or the versioning strategy, all aspects totally unrelated to the architecture of the model. For example, the regulation doesn't explicitly differentiate between systems implementing continuous learning and products undergoing periodical updates, through the usual process of version release. The two cases are subject to the same obligations, but in the former case the logging and the supervision would likely be automatic, while in the latter context they may be redacted manually, and a document could be associated with each release of the software. This choice has also a great impact on cybersecurity and on data governance. Similarly, differential privacy should be applied previously to data-ingestion to meet both GDPR and AI-Act confidentiality mandates [1, 49].

The focus of this work, instead, is on how the modeling procedure – comprising the choice of specific mathematical structures rather than others, the training strategy, and so on – affects these points. The obligations cover different aspects, transversally to the design, the development and the deployment phases of the model (in the ML community, the development and the deployment of the model are largely overlapped respectively with the training and inference phases), therefore, each modeling choice potentially contributes to the compliance with one or more of these principles. In the following subsections, we are going to see in deeper detail how to link model design choices to regulatory obligations. In Table 1, we report which articles of the AI Act can be addressed by each design aspect.

3.1 Article 10 - Robust Data Governance

Pharmacokinetics is characterized by sparse data settings, related to the impracticality of taking frequent blood samples from the patients, and due also to the high variability of the kinetics, which depends both on the drug and on the subject under consideration. This leads to fragmented datasets and to models tailored to specific drugs and patient cohorts. SOTA approaches, not leveraging ML techniques, employ a population-based approach (PopPK) based on Non-Linear Mixed Effects Models (NONMEM) [35]. These models have the capability of estimating subject-specific parameters, potentially allowing personalized predictions, but only after the collection of some data about the subject. Modern ML techniques promise preliminary subject-specific predictions. This scenario

Table 1. Regulatory obligations and the modeling choices which affect each of them. The table can be read as, for example: "Learning biases can be leveraged for demonstrating compliance with Articles 10, 12 and 13 of the AI Act".

		Obligations				
		Art 10	Art 12	Art 13	Art 14	Art 15
Design	Observational Bias	✓				✓
	Scientific Bias	✓		✓	✓	✓
Training	Learning Bias	✓	✓	✓		✓
Inference	Diagnostics Plots		✓	✓	✓	
	Uncertainty Quantification	✓	✓	✓	✓	✓

steered pharmacometrics towards trends such as data augmentation strategies and the strong use of scientific biases, both of which address the problem of data sparsity; hence, these measures can be used for demonstrating compliance.

Data augmentation has been leveraged by Giacometti et al. [15] for supervising the training of a Neural ODE tailored to the Dalbavancin antibiotic, while the devising of data-economic approaches is the main driver behind the introduction of the CMINN architectures [12]. Lu et al. [30] create a completely data-driven model, based only on observational biases, but they also provide a thoroughly analysis of the dataset for showing its representativeness, richness and adequacy with respect to the task. The quality of the datasets can be backed by domain experts, either via their assessment and validation or because the data are expert-curated.

Also, good training diagnostics can be leveraged to demonstrate retrospectively that the dataset employed was indeed sufficient to meet the intended performance expectations. Finally, a rigorous quantification of the epistemic component of uncertainty can be leveraged to show that the uncertainty in the predictions arises from the intrinsic variability of the system (aleatoric uncertainty) and is not derived from insufficient observational biases.

3.2 Article 12 – Record Keeping & Logging

From a legal perspective the record-keeping serves two functions.

First, evidentiary defense: although the Commission withdrew the draft AI Liability Directive in February 2025, the revised Product Liability Directive will still allow courts to shift the burden of proof onto providers that cannot supply complete, tamper-proof evidence of system behavior; hashed, time-stamped logs are therefore a pre-emptive shield against liability exposure. The software shall store the input and the corresponding output and diagnostics, any human action in semi-automatic frameworks, and in general all what's needed for the retrospective investigation of the system's behavior in producing specific predictions. If stochasticity is embedded in the system, the minimal information needed for reconstructing which statistical realization was produced, and not merely a statistical equivalent of the output, should be stored. In some cases, expliciting and storing the random seed could be enough. In the case continuous learning is implemented, weight updates and dataset revisions should be tracked, enabling conformity re-assessment whenever a *substantial modification* in the sense of the AI Act or MDR Annex IX occurs.

Second, regulatory reconciliation: the GDPR's data-minimization and storage-limitation principles (Art. 5(1)(c)–(e)) restrict what may be retained, whereas the MDR obliges manufacturers to keep post-market-surveillance data for at least ten years (Art. 10(8)) after the device is placed on the market (Art. 83). Purpose-bound retention schedules, pseudonymization, and selective-disclosure tooling are thus required to satisfy both regimes simultaneously.

3.3 Article 13 – Interpretability and Explainability

For high-risk AI systems in healthcare, interpretability is not merely desirable but mandated. Article 13 AI Act requires that professional users receive clear information on the system's logic, performance limits and appropriate use, while Article 14 links such transparency to effective human-oversight. Parallel obligations arise under the MDR: Annex I SPR 17.3 demands that software influencing clinical decisions be "understandable to the intended user", and MDCG 2020-1 stresses explainability as part of the clinical-evaluation evidence. Documented scientific biases and model-lineage artefacts (e.g., model cards [33], lineage graphs) therefore serve a dual role—technical insight and legal proof of compliance with these transparency and oversight duties.

Clearly, the model's architecture is a major component of this portion of compliance. Interpretability is not only linked to mechanistic interpretability or to post-hoc explainability techniques such as SHAP [31] or LIME [44], which furnish local attributions even for deep neural networks: scientific biases, as previously mentioned, can greatly enhance transparency, the safety and the interpretability of the model by design. Being backed by domain experts, scientific biases represent strong, clear and trustworthy communications both to the regulators and to the clinicians, together with laboratory staff and any other intended user of the application.

To convey the idea of the importance of scientific biases in these regards, let's consider some scenarios, depicted in the schematics of Fig. 1.

- With the Deep Compartment Model architecture (Fig. 1, a), Janssen et al. [23] employ a black-box module for determining the parameters of a classical compartment model. The output of the neural network is perfectly interpretable by the clinicians, that also specify the mechanistic model to employ, leaving to the black-box only the determination of patient-specific parameters. In such a way, the role of the black-box is to *assist* the creation of a personalized white-box model, which can be inspected autonomously by the clinicians.
- Universal Differential Equations [42] (Fig. 1, b) implement the parallel hybridization of black-box and white-box components, meaning that the preliminary prediction determined by the compartment model (again, chosen by the clinician) is then adjusted by a black-box module, which can leverage a wider array of patient-specific data with respect to the mechanistic model. In this case, the black-box module *adjusts* the predictions of a white-box module, for a specific subject.

- Giacometti et al. [15] (Fig. 1, c) pre-train a black-box model with a white-box, then they fine-tune it to a real dataset to introduce personalization. At the end, the whole system is made by a single black-box module, meaning that the intervention by the expert has been crucial in training phase, but it's not apparent at inference time.
- PINNs [43] (Fig. 1, d) are based on training a black-box module with observation data, under the close supervision of a white-box module. More specifically, the black-box module is continuously compared to a white-box model, and it's asked to be similar to it: such similarity can be controlled and quantified. Then, the prediction is made by the black-box only. In the last two cases, the role of the black-box modules is to *predict* end-to-end the target relation.

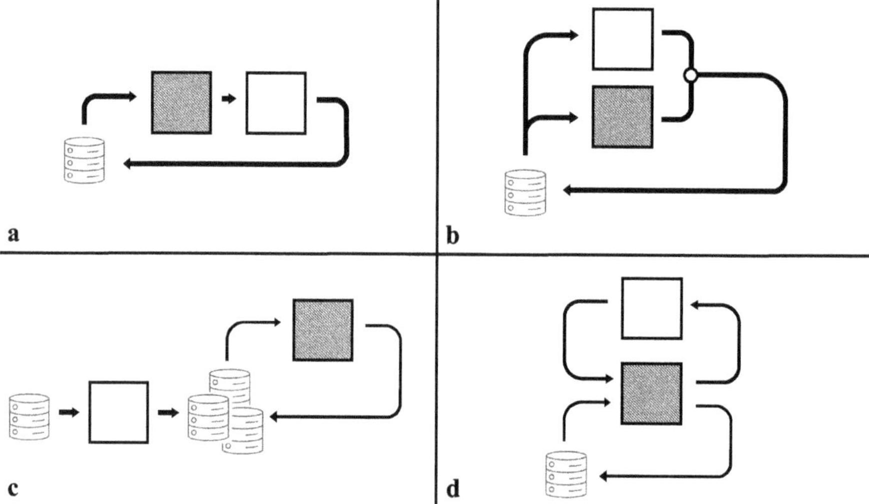

Fig. 1. Simplified schematics of the training procedure for different hybrid architectures. The white-boxes denote full interpretability, and their creation implies the intervention of a domain expert. Hence, their presence in the system guarantees, to varying extents, that the behavior of the black-boxes is bound to some restricted tasks, which depends on the specific case. The arrows denote the comparison cycle onto which the learning is based: comparisons can be made between predictions and observations (cycles between model and the datasets), or between the black-box model and a reference white-box model. a) The black-box module *assists* in the creation of a personalized white-box model. b) The black-box *adjusts* the predictions of a white-box model. c) Schematics of data augmentation: the black-box is trained by examples produced by a white-box. d) The black-box model is trained by data, but it's also bound to be similar to a reference white-box model.

These architectures are differentiated by their underlying mathematical framework (for example, in some cases the solution of the ODE system is approximated by the neural network, while in others it's the ODE system itself to be represented by the neural network, which is then integrated with classical numerical methods) but all these systems, as a net effect, provide personalized pharmacometrics predictions. Still, the roles taken by the black-boxes are very different, affecting the way the model should be communicated to the regulators and the way the user interprets the system. However, in all these cases, the clear and transparent communication of the system's logic is pivoted on the inductive biases characterizing their architecture. A clear user interface completes the chain of explanation, by aiding the correct interpretation of the results.

3.4 Article 14 – Human Oversight

Liability pivots on the availability and reasonable use of safeguards such as Out Of Distribution (OOD) detection [19, 26], abstention [14], and manual override, all measures expressly required by AI Act Art. 14(1)(a)–(c) to preserve human clinical autonomy and to mitigate burden-of-proof reversals in the event of harm. A core component towards this obligation lies in the quantification of the reliability of the predictions, usually based on Bayesian techniques. Apart for epistemic uncertainty, which is ubiquitous, in population pharmacokinetics the sources of variability are usually classified as Inter-Subject Variability, Intra-Subject Variability and Inter-Occasion Variability; while the variability due to different drugs is tackled by producing mathematical models specific to each drug [35]. ML approaches not aligned to this paradigm should carefully inform the user about their specificity, so to prevent misuse, ideally providing the decomposition of the uncertainty into separated components, that guides the clinicians into more responsible usage of the software.

Finally, standard diagnostics such as goodness-of-fit, individual plots, visual predictive checks and others, eventually adapted to the ML nature of the model, can further contribute to a compliant environment.

3.5 Article 15 – Accuracy, Robustness and Cybersecurity

Inductive biases aid in the training of performant and interpretable models in sparse data settings, but the most accurate model cannot be determined beforehand, by looking at the schematics regarding its architecture. Such diagrams can be leveraged to assess if the model is fatally flawed at its core, to enhance transparency and responsible usage in the users, to communicate the measures taken for addressing risk management. Statutory performance evidence must be generated on representative test sets and presented through harmonized metrics capable of supporting a conformity assessment under AI Act Art. 18 and MDR Annex VII. The robustness of the performance metrics is demonstrated by stressing the model with cross-validation and varying the random seeds of the stochastic optimizations and for the data splits. Robustness can also be attributed to the model itself, which should be tested under the whole range of inputs that the users could employ, while their usage away from tested conditions must be blocked or accompanied by explicit warnings and enlarged uncertainty, satisfying AI Act Art. Some frameworks are being developed for assisting the formal verification of the inference model so that all downstream safety metrics remain within legally defined bounds [3].

4 Conclusions

Collectively, the EU regulatory obligations show how privacy-by-design, explainability-by-design and risk-management-by-design converge into a coherent *legal-by-design* framework. Together, these trends underscore the urgency of proactive, engineering-informed measures. Only by embedding regulatory constraints directly into system architecture and governance processes can we ensure that frontier AI technology advances safely and equitably, protecting public interest while preserving the pace of innovation. The missing hinge between these high-level duties and day-to-day engineering practice is jurimetrics, the quantitative analysis of legal requirements, which translates statutory concepts into measurable technical targets and audit metrics. By embedding jurimetric indicators directly into system architecture, logging schemes and governance workflows, developers can demonstrate real-time conformity while regulators obtain verifiable evidence, shifting compliance from a retrospective paperwork exercise to a continuous, data-driven process. This makes regulatory requirements both implementable and enforceable, even as models grow more capable, and implements the shift from reactive fixes to proactive risk management [48].

This approach demands true interdisciplinarity. Engineers encode regulatory constraints as concrete controls; clinicians and ethicists validate clinical relevance; and legal scholars calibrate jurimetric thresholds. Inductive biases then act as built-in risk-control levers and interpretability "windows," allowing domain experts to inspect, challenge and refine the model's behavior throughout the lifecycle. Applied to pharmacometrics, these strategies show that state-of-the-art models can already meet EU high-risk obligations – provided that forthcoming standards embed jurimetric logic – ensuring consistent, harmonized evidence across jurisdictions.

5   Future Directions

Looking beyond the present analysis, three converging trajectories merit priority attention.

First, jurimetrics should be operationalized through publicly available scorecards that translate each statutory obligation – such as the robustness mandate in Article 15 AI Act or the post-market-surveillance duties in Article 83 MDR – into auditable technical key-performance indicators. These quantitatively anchored benchmarks would permit automated conformity checks and facilitate cross-study comparability, transforming compliance from an essentially documentary endeavor into a continuous, data-driven discipline.

Second, the on-going standardization work within CEN-CENELEC JTC 21 and the ISO technical committees offers an immediate channel for embedding pharmacometrics use-cases, uncertainty decomposition templates and cybersecurity profiles (e.g., IEC 81001-5-1) into the forthcoming horizontal AI standards. Aligning these documents with the proposed jurimetric indicators would create a harmonized evidentiary pipeline, capable of conferring a presumption of conformity under both the AI Act and the MDR/IVDR.

Third, governance mechanisms for continuous-learning systems must be prototyped in real-world settings. "Model passports" that record on-device weight updates trigger remote re-certification when jurimetric thresholds drift, and leverage EHDS-enabled data spaces for privacy-preserving applications represent a promising architecture. Evaluating such mechanisms in coordinated EMA–national sandboxes, with rigorous human-factors assessment of clinician trust and liability perceptions, will provide the empirical foundation required to fine-tune future product-liability reforms.

Together, these avenues aim to translate the legal-by-design blueprint into reproducible, scalable practice, ensuring that next-generation AI-driven pharmacometric systems remain scientifically rigorous, regulator-ready and clinically trustworthy.

Disclosure of Interests. The authors have no competing interests to declare that are relevant to the content of this article.

References

1. Abadi, M., et al.: Deep learning with differential privacy. In: Proceedings of the 2016 ACM SIGSAC Conference on Computer and Communications Security, pp. 308–318. Association for Computing Machinery, New York (2016). https://doi.org/10.1145/2976749.2978318
2. Abbate, E., et al.: Safe and sustainable by design chemicals and materials - methodological guidance (2024). https://doi.org/10.2760/28450, JRC138035
3. Athavale, A., Bartocci, E., Christakis, M., Maffei, M., Nickovic, D., Weissenbacher, G.: Verifying global two-safety properties in neural networks with confidence. In: Computer Aided Verification. CAV 2024. Springer, Cham (2024). https://doi.org/10.1007/978-3-031-65630-9_17
4. Ball, R., Dal Pan, G.: "artificial intelligence" for pharmacovigilance: ready for prime time? Drug Saf. **5** (2022). https://doi.org/10.1007/s40264-022-01157-4
5. Bate, A., Hobbiger, S.: Artificial intelligence, real-world automation and the safety of medicines. Drug Saf. **44** (2021). https://doi.org/10.1007/s40264-020-01001-7
6. Blundell, C., Cornebise, J., Kavukcuoglu, K., Wierstra, D.: Weight uncertainty in neural networks (2015). https://arxiv.org/abs/1505.05424
7. Bräm, D.S., Nahum, U., Schropp, J., Pfister, M., Koch, G.: Low-dimensional neural odes and their application in pharmacokinetics. J. Pharmacokinet. Pharmacodyn. **51** (2024)
8. Brodersen, J.B., et al.: Getting ready for the eu aiact in healthcare. A call for sustainable AI development and deployment (2025). https://arxiv.org/abs/2505.07875
9. Chen, R.T.Q., Rubanova, Y., Bettencourt, J., Duvenaud, D.: Neural ordinary differential equations. In: Proceedings of the 32nd International Conference on Neural Information Processing Systems, NIPS 2018, pp. 6572–6583. Curran Associates Inc., Red Hook (2018)
10. Dandekar, R., et al.: Bayesian neural ordinary differential equations (2022). https://arxiv.org/abs/2012.07244
11. Daneker, M., Zhang, Z., Karniadakis, G.E., Lu, L.: Systems Biology: Identifiability Analysis and Parameter Identification via Systems-Biology-Informed Neural Networks, pp. 87–105. Springer US (2023). https://doi.org/10.1007/978-1-0716-3008-2_4
12. Daryakenari, N.A., Wang, S., Karniadakis, G.: Cminns: compartment model informed neural networks—unlocking drug dynamics. Comput. Biol. Med. **184**, 109392 (2025)
13. European Parliament and Commission: Regulation (eu) 2017/745 of the European parliament and of the council of 5 April 2017 on medical devices, amending directive 2001/83/EC, regulation (EC) no 178/2002 and regulation (EC) no 1223/2009 and repealing council directives 90/385/eec and 93/42/eec (2017). http://data.europa.eu/eli/reg/2017/745/oj
14. Gandouz, M., Holzmann, H., Heider, D.: Machine learning with asymmetric abstention for biomedical decision-making. BMC Med. Inform. Decis. Mak. **294** (2021). https://doi.org/10.1186/s12911-021-01655-y
15. Giacometti, T., et al.: Leveraging neural odes for population pharmacokinetics of dalbavancin in sparse clinical data. Entropy **27** (2025)
16. Graf, O., Flores, P., Protopapas, P., Pichara, K.: Uncertainty quantification in neural differential equations (2021). https://arxiv.org/abs/2111.04207

17. Hildebrandt, M.: Smart technologies and the end (s) of law: novel entanglements of law and technology. Edward Elgar Publishing (2015)
18. Hildebrandt, M.: Law as computation in the era of artificial legal intelligence. Speaking law to the power of statistics. Univ. Toronto Law J. **68** (2017). https://doi.org/10.2139/ssrn.298 3045
19. Hong, Z., et al.: Out-of-distribution detection in medical image analysis: a survey (2024). https://arxiv.org/abs/2404.18279
20. Huang, Z., Denti, P., Mistry, H., Kloprogge, F.: Machine learning and artificial intelligence in PK-PD modeling: fad, friend, or foe? Clin. Pharmacol. Ther. **115** (2024)
21. Janssen, A., Bennis, F.C., Cnossen, M.H., Mathôt, R.A.A.: On inductive biases for the robust and interpretable prediction of drug concentrations using deep compartment models. J. Pharmacokinet. Pharmacodyn. **51** (2024)
22. Janssen, A., Bennis, F.C., Mathôt, R.A.A.: Adoption of machine learning in pharmacometrics: an overview of recent implementations and their considerations. Pharmaceutics **14** (2022)
23. Janssen, A., Leebeek, F.W.G., Cnossen, M.H., Mathôt, R.A.A.: Deep compartment models: a deep learning approach for the reliable prediction of time-series data in pharmacokinetic modeling. CPT Pharmacometrics Syst. Pharmacol. **11** (2022)
24. Jospin, L.V., Laga, H., Boussaid, F., Buntine, W., Bennamoun, M.: Hands-on Bayesian neural networks—a tutorial for deep learning users. IEEE Comput. Intell. Mag. **17**(2), 29–48 (2022). https://doi.org/10.1109/mci.2022.3155327
25. Karniadakis, G.E., Kevrekidis, I.G., Lu, L., Perdikaris, P., Wang, S., Yang, L.: Physics-informed machine learning. Nat. Rev. Phys. **3** (2021)
26. Kirchheim, K., Filax, M., Ortmeier, F.: Pytorch-ood: a library for out-of-distribution detection based on pytorch. In: Proceedings of the IEEE/CVF Conference on Computer Vision and Pattern Recognition (CVPR) Workshops, pp. 4351–4360 (2022)
27. Loevinger, L.: Jurimetrics - the next step forward. Minnesota Law Rev. **455** (1949)
28. Lippe, P., Katz, D.M., Jackson, D.: Legal by design: a new paradigm for handling complexity in banking regulation and elsewhere in law. Northeast. Univ. School Law Res. **93** (2014). https://doi.org/10.2139/ssrn.2539315
29. Losada, I.B., Terranova, N.: Bridging pharmacology and neural networks: a deep dive into neural ordinary differential equations. CPT Pharmacometrics Syst. Pharmacol. (2024)
30. Lu, J., Deng, K., Zhang, X., Liu, G., Guan, Y.: Neural-ode for pharmacokinetics modeling and its advantage to alternative machine learning models in predicting new dosing regimens. iScience (2021)
31. Lundberg, S.M., Lee, S.I.: A unified approach to interpreting model predictions. In: Guyon, I., et al. (eds.) Advances in Neural Information Processing Systems 30, pp. 4765–4774. Curran Associates, Inc. (2017). http://papers.nips.cc/paper/7062-a-unified-approach-to-interpreting-model-predictions.pdf
32. McComb, M., Bies, R., Ramanathan, M.: Machine learning in pharmacometrics: opportunities and challenges. Br. J. Clin. Pharmacol. (2022)
33. Mitchell, M., et al.: Model cards for model reporting. In: Proceedings of the Conference on Fairness, Accountability, and Transparency, FAT* 2019, pp. 220–229. Association for Computing Machinery, New York (2019). https://doi.org/10.1145/3287560.3287596
34. Mitchell, T.: Machine Learning. McGraw Hill Education (1997)
35. Mould, D.R., Upton, R.N.: Basic concepts in population modeling, simulation, and model-based drug development. CPT Pharmacometrics Syst. Pharmacol. (2012)
36. Nong, P., Hamasha, R., Singh, K., Adler-Milstein, J., Platt, J.: How academic medical centers govern AI prediction tools in the context of uncertainty and evolving regulation. NEJM AI **1**(3), AIp2300048 (2024). https://doi.org/10.1056/AIp2300048
37. Norcliffe, A., Bodnar, C., Day, B., Moss, J., Liò, P.: Neural ode processes (2021). https://arxiv.org/abs/2103.12413

38. O'Leary, J., Paulson, J.A., Mesbah, A.: Stochastic physics-informed neural ordinary differential equations. J. Comput. Phys. **468**, 111466 (2022). https://doi.org/10.1016/j.jcp.2022.111466
39. Ott, K., Tiemann, M., Hennig, P.: Uncertainty and structure in neural ordinary differential equations (2023). https://arxiv.org/abs/2305.13290
40. Petersen, C., et al.: Recommendations for the safe, effective use of adaptive CDS in the us healthcare system: an AMIA position paper. J. Am. Med. Inform. Assoc. JAMIA **28** (2021). https://doi.org/10.1093/jamia/ocaa319
41. Qian, Z., Zame, W.R., Fleuren, L.M., Elbers, P., van der Schaar, M.: Integrating expert odes into neural odes: pharmacology and disease progression (2021). https://arxiv.org/abs/2106.02875
42. Rackauckas, C., et al.: Universal differential equations for scientific machine learning (2021). https://arxiv.org/abs/2001.04385
43. Raissi, M., Perdikaris, P., Karniadakis, G.: Physics-informed neural networks: a deep learning framework for solving forward and inverse problems involving non-linear partial differential equations. J. Comput. Phys. **378** (2019)
44. Ribeiro, M.T., Singh, S., Guestrin, C.: "Why should I trust you?": explaining the predictions of any classifier. In: Proceedings of the 22nd ACM SIGKDD International Conference on Knowledge Discovery and Data Mining, San Francisco, CA, USA, 13–17 August 2016, pp. 1135–1144 (2016)
45. Schweidtmann, A.M., Zhang, D., von Stosch, M.: A review and perspective on hybrid modeling methodologies. Digit. Chem. Eng. (2024)
46. Stankevičiut'e, K., Woillard, J.B., Peck, R.W., Marquet, P., van der Schaar, M.: Bridging the worlds of pharmacometrics and machine learning. Clin. Pharmacokinet. (2023)
47. Tallam, K.: Engineering risk-aware, security-by-design frameworks for assurance of large-scale autonomous AI models (2025). https://arxiv.org/abs/2505.06409
48. The IEEE Global Initiative on Ethics of Autonomous and Intelligent Systems: Ethically aligned design. A Vision for Prioritizing Human Well-being with Autonomous and Intelligent Systems. IEEE (2019). https://standards.ieee.org/industry-connections/activities/ieeeglobal-initiative/
49. Veale, M., Borgesius, F.: Demystifying the draft EU artificial intelligence act. Comput. Law Rev. Int. **22**(4) (2021). https://ssrn.com/abstract=3896852

Data Generation and Augmentation

Knowledge Graph-Enhanced Retrieval-Augmented Generation for Nutrigenetics

Giovanni Maria De Filippis[1] , Domenico Benfenati[1(✉)] ,
Gianluca De Carlo[2] , and Antonio Maria Rinaldi[1]

[1] Department of Electrical Engineering and Information Technology,
University of Naples Federico II, Via Claudio 21, Naples, Italy
{giovannimaria.defilippis,domenico.benfenati,
antoniomaria.rinaldi}@unina.it
[2] Department of Computer, Control and Management Engineering "Antonio
Ruberti", Sapienza University of Rome, Rome, Italy
decarlo@diag.uniroma1.it

Abstract. This paper presents a domain-specific adaptation of GraphRAG framework for nutrigenetics, focusing on the extraction of genetic variant information relevant to personalized nutrition. By integrating Knowledge Graphs with Retrieval-Augmented Generation (RAG), we enhance biomedical knowledge discovery. A model selection study identifies optimal combinations of Large Language Models (LLMs) and embeddings, with Gemma2:9B paired with BERT achieving the highest quality score in graph construction. Evaluation against the naive RAG baseline shows significant improvements in response comprehensiveness, directness, and empowerment across diverse user profiles, including researchers, healthcare professionals, and consumers. These advancements highlight the potential of GraphRAG to accelerate hypothesis generation, support clinical decision-making, and empower individuals to make informed dietary choices based on genetic insights. These preliminary findings underscore the importance of structured knowledge representation in addressing biomedical challenges, with promising implications for advancing personalized nutrition and multi-domain biomedical applications.

Keywords: Knowledge Graphs · Retrieval Augmented Generation · Large Language Models · Nutrigenetics · Biomedical Knowledge Discovery · Personalized Nutrition

1 Introduction

The integration of Large Language Models (LLMs) and advanced embedding techniques has recently catalyzed significant advancements in the field of knowledge extraction and representation [20]. In particular, retrieval-augmented generation (RAG) [22] demonstrated remarkable capabilities to leverage unstructured

C. Tommasino et al. (Eds.): AIBIO 2025, CCIS 2696, pp. 91–104, 2026.
https://doi.org/10.1007/978-3-032-17216-7_8

text to enhance question answering [5,30], summarization [24], and complex information retrieval systems [10]. However, there remains a critical need for methods that structure and contextualize this retrieved knowledge in machine-interpretable formats, such as Knowledge Graphs (KG), which allows better reasoning, traceability, and domain-specific insights [34].

Personalized nutrition, situated at the intersection of genomics, biomedical research, and nutritional science, has emerged as a multidisciplinary domain [8]. The integration of individual-level data, particularly genetic variants, has been instrumental in understanding the mechanisms through which dietary interventions influence physiological responses and health outcomes [19]. The vast and continuously expanding biomedical corpus, such as that available in PubMed[1] and related repositories, presents both an unparalleled resource and a formidable challenge for automated knowledge discovery. Extracting domain-specific, actionable insights from this unstructured literature demands methodologies that efficiently blend robust language understanding with structured graph-based representations [2].

Recent developments at the intersection of LLMs and structured knowledge representation have led to novel methodologies that integrate KGs with LLM architectures [40]. Within this context, frameworks such as GraphRAG [12] are situated alongside a growing set of techniques that employ LLMs to distill and extract information encoded within KGs [4,29]. These methods build upon the intrinsic modular characteristics of graph structures [31], which allow for the division of graphs into nested, interconnected clusters. By employing established algorithms such as Louvain [6] and Leiden [38] for community detection, GraphRAG systematically organizes nodes into cohesive groups. Leveraging LLMs, the approach then generates progressively broader summaries that encompass these hierarchical groupings, resulting in summaries that reflect the layered relationships within the graph's community structure. In this work, we present an adaptation of GraphRAG framework [18]: a retrieval-augmented generation pipeline that constructs KGs from biomedical literature utilizing combinations of state-of-the-art LLMs and embedding models. Our approach systematically investigates the impact of different LLM and embedder pairs on KG structure and quality, with a focus on extracting genetic variant information relevant to personalized nutrition. Our findings contribute to the understanding of how retrieval-augmented methods and graph-based representations can be synergistically employed for complex, information-rich domains such as personalized nutrition, ultimately facilitating scalable, interpretable, and automated biomedical knowledge discovery.

2   Related Work

KGs have emerged as indispensable tools in the biomedical [32] and genomics [13] domains, offering effective strategies to organize and integrate heterogeneous biological data [9,25,27]. The construction of curated biomedical KGs

---

[1] https://pubmed.ncbi.nlm.nih.gov/.

enables comprehensive interlinking among heterogeneous data types, including genetic, proteomic, and phenotypic information, thus supporting sophisticated data exploration and hypothesis generation [26].

Specifically within genomics, KGs underpin many state-of-the-art analytical frameworks, facilitating the systematic discovery of gene-disease associations, pathway analysis, and identification of biomolecular interactions [14]. Large-scale resources such as PharmKG [42], PheKnowLator [9], and CKG [33] exemplify this trend, leveraging rich ontological and relational annotations to connect vast and diverse biomedical data silos.

Recent literature also reflects an increasing emphasis on the integration of multi-omics data—such as genomics, transcriptomics, and proteomics—within KG-driven systems [36], as researchers seek to address multifactorial biological questions through unified data frameworks [1]. This integrative approach enables enhanced pathway discovery and regulatory network inference, as demonstrated in several contemporary studies, and has led to meaningful advances in identifying disease-associated variants and critical therapeutic targets [14]. Within the context of RAG, recent works have begun to explore the combined use of KGs and LLMs to improve biomedical information extraction, semantic search, and evidence synthesis. For instance, Gao et al. developed the RAG framework [16], which utilizes a simple vector database with semantic retrieval capabilities for question answering. This approach was specifically applied to the nutrigenetics domain by Benfenati et al. [5], demonstrating its effectiveness in addressing complex question-answering tasks while significantly reducing computational demands for large language model (LLM) fine-tuning. Recent studies have demonstrated the potential of GraphRAG in the biomedical domain. For instance, the KG-RAG framework [28] leverages a massive biomedical KG (SPOKE) with LLMs such as Llama-2-13b, GPT-3.5-Turbo, and GPT-4 to generate meaningful biomedical text rooted in established knowledge. This framework optimizes context extraction, resulting in a significant reduction in token consumption without compromising accuracy. Another notable example is KRA-GEN [35], a KG-enhanced RAG framework that combines KGs, RAG, and advanced prompting techniques to solve complex biomedical problems. KRA-GEN converts KGs into a vector database and uses RAG to retrieve relevant facts, limiting hallucinations and improving the trustworthiness and accuracy of LLM-generated text. These studies highlight the versatility and potential of GraphRAG in addressing a range of biomedical challenges, including biomedical text generation and the resolution of complex problems.

3   Methods

In this paper, we present a domain-specific adaptation of the GraphRAG framework [12] for nutrigenetics applications. Rather than developing a new framework from scratch, we adapt and optimize the existing GraphRAG pipeline to address the unique challenges of extracting genetic variant information relevant to personalized nutrition. Our study investigates how different combinations of

LLMs and embedding models affect KG structure and quality in this specialized biomedical domain. Our adopted framework is shown in Fig. 1.

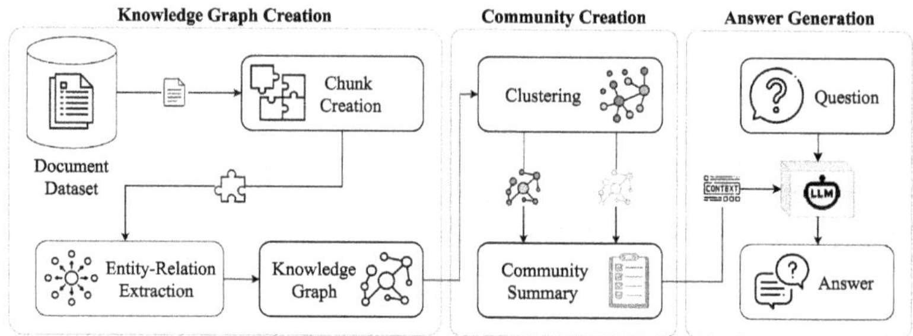

Fig. 1. Structure of the proposed GraphRAG pipeline.

3.1 Framework Architecture

The adapted GraphRAG pipeline operates through several interconnected stages:

- **Knowledge Graph Creation**: first, we segment the input document into chunks, preventing contextual bias relevant to biomedical literature. Subsequently, we modify the entity-relation extraction pipeline of GraphRAG [12] to identify target biomedical entities (genes, proteins, genetic variants (SNPs) and their interaction). These entities and relationships are aggregated in a comprehensive KG, with an hierarchical organization of genetic variant information and phenotypic associations. Using an embedding model, entity and chunks are indexed in a vector database.
- **Community Creation**: using community detection algorithm like Leiden [39] and Louvain [7], KG entities are clusterized into community that exhibit the same information. For each community, a summary and other information are created to describe the content of the entities and relationship included in the community.
- **Answer generation**: questions submitted to the system are propagated through communities, and partial responses are systematically aggregated across the graph structure. For complex queries, the framework generates thematic summaries of graph communities, which are then utilized to extend context and produce comprehensive global responses through a final query-focused summarization phase (map-reduce approach).

In our study, we adapted the original workflow to focus on extracting biomedical entities and relationships [12]. We have adapted the prompt design with domain-specific exemplars, including molecular entities (e.g., proteins, genes), physiological processes (e.g., nutrient uptake, lipid metabolsim), and genetic variants (e.g., SNPs). Few-shot learning with biomedical examples guided the model to extract contextually relevant entities and relationships. This approach improved the capture of genetic (e.g., gene-disease) and physical (e.g., protein-protein) interactions, enhancing the accuracy and relevance of the extracted information. Our domain-specific adaptations include:

- **Biomedical Prompt Engineering**: Designed prompts with nutrigenetics-specific terminology to enhance entity recognition of genetic variants, metabolic pathways, and nutrition-related phenotypes.
- **Domain-Specific Embeddings**: Employed BioBERT model to improve the modeling of biomedical semantic relationships.
- **Genetic Variant Focus**: Applied targeted preprocessing to prioritize segments containing genetic variant information, optimizing SNP-phenotype association extraction.
- **Evaluation Framework**: Established domain-specific evaluation metrics and question-generation protocols tailored to nutrigenetics.

The GraphRAG implementation of '*nano-graphrag*'[2] was used as baseline for our work.

3.2 Dataset Preprocessing

Our application is built upon the GRPM dataset [15]. We selected PubMed IDs corresponding to five research topics in personalized nutrition, as described in [15], resulting in 38,000 articles. Full-text retrieval via the PubMed Central (PMC) API yielded a final corpus of 24,000 articles. For the construction of our GraphRAG, we focused specifically on the *Results* sections of each full text, under the assumption that these segments contain the most salient data-driven findings. Articles were subsequently filtered based on the presence and sufficient length of the *Results* section, reducing the dataset to 18,000 articles.

We then applied Natural Language Processing (NLP) techniques to identify and retain only those *Results* sections containing explicit patterns related to genetic variants, which are key elements in nutrigenomics research. This final filtering step yielded a refined working dataset of 7,000 articles. For benchmarking purposes, we constructed a balanced evaluation set by randomly sampling 200 articles from the final collection, ensuring stratified representation across the five topics (i.e., 40 *Results* sections per topic) (Fig. 2).

3.3 Model Selection Study

To systematically evaluate the impact of different combinations of LLMs and embedding models on KG construction within our GraphRAG framework, we performed an extensive model assessment. We considered six LLMs (Gemma2:9b, Gemma2:27b [37], Llama3.1 [17], DeepSeek-v2 [23], Qwen2 and

---

[2] https://pypi.org/project/nano-graphrag.

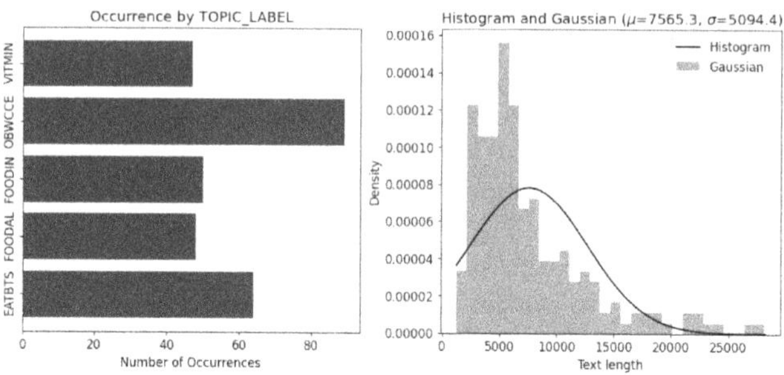

Fig. 2. Working dataset composition and length distribution. Legend: Obesity, Weight Control and Compulsive Eating (OBWCCE), Vitamin and Micronutrients Metabolism (VITMIN), Eating Behavior and Taste Sensation (EATBTS), Food Intolerances (FOODIN), Food Allergies (FOODAL). *Note: entries may contain multiple topics.*

Qwen2.5 [3]) and two embedding models (BERT [11] and BioBERT [21]), resulting in a total of 12 experimental configurations on a sample of 100 documents (20 per topic). KGs were constructed using each LLM-embedder pair and assessed on structural and semantic metrics, including the Largest Connected Component (LCC) and other graph-theoretic measures. The evaluation process included constructing the KG, conducting quantitative analysis (node degree distribution, LCC, clustering coefficient, graph density), and performing a qualitative assessment of extracted entities and relationships.

The composite score (S) for each configuration was calculated using a weighted combination of connectivity (C), structure quality (Q), and entity coherence (E):

$$S = 0.4 \cdot C + 0.3 \cdot Q + 0.3 \cdot E \tag{1}$$

where:

$$C = \frac{|\text{LCC}|}{N} \qquad Q = \max\left(0, 1 - \frac{I}{N}\right) \qquad E = \frac{V}{T} \tag{2}$$

- $|\text{LCC}|$ is the size of the largest connected component,
- N is the total number of nodes,
- I is the number of isolated nodes,
- V is the number of valid entities[3]
- T is the total number of extracted entities.

The composite score (S) comprehensively evaluates KG quality by integrating three critical dimensions. High *connectivity* ensures the KG's LCC encompasses most nodes, enabling robust reasoning and traversal across interconnected

---

[3] Valid entities: *"Gene", "Genetic Variant", "Transcript", "Protein", "Nutrient", "Food", "Dietary Pattern", "Physiological Process", "Metabolic Pathway", "Molecular Interaction", "Environmental Factor", "Disease".*

entities—essential for applications like biomedical discovery where relationships between genetic variants, nutrients, and metabolic pathways must be navigable. *Structure quality* penalizes isolated nodes, as fragmented components hinder holistic analysis and reduce the KG's utility for inference; minimizing isolation promotes cohesiveness. *Entity coherence* guarantees extracted entities align with domain-specific requirements, preventing irrelevant or erroneous entries that compromise semantic accuracy. Together, these metrics ensure the KG is topologically sound, analytically viable, and semantically precise for domain tasks.

3.4   Evaluation

In this section, we present the strategy employed for the performance evaluation of our framework. We designed a methodology to generate domain-specific questions for testing the generation pipeline using both the NaiveRAG baseline and our proposed approach. Subsequently, we developed an answer quality assessment pipeline, in which an LLM is used as a judge. Within this pipeline, we defined a set of metrics to evaluate the quality of the answers produced by both the NaiveRAG and GraphRAG.

Question Generation. To evaluate our system, we employed a LLM to generate domain-specific questions grounded in the information covered by the corpora within the dataset utilized. Starting from a high-level description of each domain and the intended purpose of the documents associated with it, we defined three user profiles designed to interact with the system:

- **User 1:** A researcher in nutrigenetics, interested in understanding how genetic variants influence dietary responses.
- **User 2:** A healthcare professional looking to apply nutrigenetic insights in clinical practice.
- **User 3:** A customer interested in personalized nutrition based on genetic information.

For each of the users, the LLM was prompted to generate T tasks that could be completed using GraphRAG system. Subsequently, for each of the T tasks, the LLM was prompted to generate Q questions that the user would need to ask in order to understand and accomplish the task. The complete methodology is outlined in Algorithm 1. In our evaluation phase, we set $N = 3$, $T = 5$ and $Q = 2$, resulting in a total of 30 questions for each of the 5 categories in the dataset. Consequently, the final dataset comprises 150 questions.

Answer Generation. We generated the answers using the Llama3.3:70b model, for its wide context window, querying both the Naive and GraphRAG systems.

Answer Evaluation Strategy. In the absence of an established benchmark for this task, we opted to employ an LLM as an evaluative judge, assessing performance according to a predefined set of criteria [41]. We defined three standard

---

Algorithm 1. Question Generation approach

Require: Corpus description D_c, N (#users), T (#tasks), Q (#questions)
Ensure: Set of $N * T * Q$ high-quality questions
  for all user $n \in [0, N]$ **do**
    User Description $d_u \leftarrow \text{LLM}(D_c)$
    for all task $t \in [0, T]$ **do**
      Task Description $d_t \leftarrow \text{LLM}(D_c, d_u)$
      for all question $q \in [0, Q]$ **do**
        Question generation $q \leftarrow \text{LLM}(D_c, d_u, d_t)$
      end for
    end for
  end for

Algorithm 2. Answer evaluation strategy

Require: Questions Q, Base Answers A_{BASE}, RAG Answers A_{RAG}, Evaluation criteria C
Ensure: Winners Codes W_C, Winning reasons W_R
  for all $q \in Q$ **and** $a_b \in A_{BASE}$ **and** $a_r \in A_{RAG}$ **and** $c \in C$ **do**
    prompt $\leftarrow \text{PROMPTGENERATION}(q, a_b, a_r, c)$
    $w_c, w_r \leftarrow \text{LLM(prompt)}$
    $W_C \leftarrow W_C \cup \{w_c\}$
    $W_R \leftarrow W_R \cup \{w_r\}$
  end for

---

criteria designed to cover different evaluative dimensions, enabling us to measure the quality of the responses from multiple perspectives. The evaluation strategy using the LLM as a judge is detailed in Algorithm 2.

We included the following evaluation criteria for the evaluation strategy design:

- **Comprehensiveness:** Evaluates how fully and accurately the answer addresses all relevant aspects of the question. A comprehensive answer is complete, well-organized, and avoids redundancy or irrelevant details.
- **Directness:** Measures how clearly and specifically the answer responds to the question. A direct answer should be concise and on-topic, avoiding vague or unrelated content.
- **Empowerment:** Reflects how well the answer helps the reader understand the topic and make informed decisions. An empowering answer explains its reasoning clearly, avoids misleading claims, and supports its statements with evidence when appropriate.

As described in Algorithm 2, during the evaluation phase, the LLM (*Llama4:scout*) is provided with the question, the responses generated by both the baseline framework and our proposed approach, as well as the specific evaluation criterion to be applied at that stage. For each evaluation quadruple $\{q, a_b, a_r, c\}$ the LLM is required to assign a score within the range $[0, 2]$. A score of "1" indicates that the baseline response is superior for criterion c, while a score of "2" signifies that the response produced by our framework is preferred. A score of "0" denotes that both responses are equivalent under the specified criterion. In addition to the numerical score, the LLM must provide a justification explaining its assessment. To mitigate biases introduced by the stochastic nature of generative models and to enhance the robustness of the evaluation, the algorithm was executed multiple times, and the results were averaged across different questions.

4   Results

The evaluation of our GraphRAG framework involved 12 configurations, combining six LLMs with two embedding models. For each setup, a KG was generated from 100 curated documents focusing on the Results sections of nutrigenetics literature. The results of the model assessment are summarized in Table 1, allowing the identification of optimal configurations and insights into the contributions of LLM and embedders.

Table 1. KG metrics for each LLM-Embedder configuration. LCC = Largest Connected Component; bert-base-v2 = all_mpnet-base-v2

Rank	LLM	Embedder	Score	Whole Graph			LCC			
				Nodes	Entities	Valid%	LCC%	Nodes	Entities	Valid%
8	gemma2:9b	biobert-v1.1	0.308	2909	258	15.89	19.8	577	68	20.59
1	gemma2:9b	bert-base-v2	**0.480**	2876	255	61.57	**26.6**	**765**	**82**	63.41
11	gemma2:27b	biobert-v1.1	0.263	2746	265	13.21	19.4	533	69	21.74
4	gemma2:27b	bert-base-v2	0.349	2576	231	41.56	16.0	411	49	69.39
5	llama3.1:8b	biobert-v1.1	0.343	3293	335	57.61	10.1	331	50	48.00
9	llama3.1:8b	bert-base-v2	0.285	3373	310	42.90	9.3	315	47	42.55
10	deepseek-v2:16b	biobert-v1.1	0.263	1645	298	64.43	2.9	47	14	**92.86**
12	deepseek-v2:16b	bert-base-v2	0.217	1772	325	48.00	4.5	79	20	65.00
6	qwen2:7b	biobert-v1.1	0.343	3945	721	56.73	5.1	200	35	60.00
7	qwen2:7b	bert-base-v2	0.340	**4008**	**812**	54.19	5.5	219	43	65.12
3	qwen2.5:14b	biobert-v1.1	0.416	3115	222	59.46	5.0	156	26	73.08
2	qwen2.5:14b	bert-base-v2	0.424	3040	174	59.77	6.1	186	19	78.95

The configurations using **gemma2:9b** with **bert-base-v2** embeddings consistently produced the highest-quality graphs, as indicated by the highest composite score of 0.48. These graphs were characterized by an LCC of 765 nodes, with 63.41% of valid entities, reflecting robust entity extraction and semantic coherence. The **bert-base-v2** embeddings, contrary to expectations, demonstrated superior performance compared to **biobert-v1.1**, with higher LCC coverage (26.6%) and fewer invalid entities (30 compared to 54 for biobert-v1.1). This suggests that bert-base-v2 embeddings contribute more effectively to graph quality and entity linking compared to biobert-v1.1. The top-performing configuration exhibited the most balanced node degree distribution, indicating improved entity linking and reduced sparsity. This configuration also demonstrated the highest number of valid entities (52) within the LCC, highlighting its effectiveness in extracting biomedical entities and their relationships.

Given these considerations, we selected the optimal configuration (**gemma2:9b** paired with **bert-base-v2**) for the KG construction based on our working set of 200 PMC nutrigenetics article results. This approach generated a high-quality KG comprising 5,896 nodes and 3,389 edges, with the LCC representing 30% of nodes, indicating a robust and well-connected graph structure. Notably, the entity coherence was 0.617, reflecting a high degree of semantic accuracy in extracted entities. To assess the effectiveness of our approach, we evaluated the retrieval and summarization performance of the resulting GraphRAG in comparison to both a NaiveRAG baseline (vector-based semantic retrieval without graph structure). GraphRAG consistently outperformed NaiveRAG baselines for every criteria we have defined. The results are summarized in Table 2, and plotted in Fig. 3.

Table 2. Winners number and percentage for the criteria established

	Comprehensiveness	Directness	Empowerment
NaiveRAG	5	57	17
NaiveRAG (%)	3.6 %	38 %	11.4 %
GraphRAG	145	92	128
GraphRAG (%)	**96.7 %**	**61.3 %**	**85.3 %**
Neutral	0	1	5
Neutral (%)	0 %	0.7 %	3.3 %

The LLM-as-a-judge evaluation reveals GraphRAG superior performance across all three criteria. For Comprehensiveness, GraphRAG significantly outperform the NaiveRAG in almost all the questions provided (145 out of 150). GraphRAG demonstrated also clear advantages in Directness, where it was rated superior in approximately 92 out of 150 evaluations compared to only 57 for NaiveRAG, with 1 case showing equivalent performance. An high difference was observed also in the Empowerment criterion, where GraphRAG outperformed NaiveRAG in 128 out of 150 evaluations, with 5 showing equivalent performance and 17 favoring NaiveRAG. These results indicate that while both approaches can provide specific answers, GraphRAG excels in delivering more direct, actionable responses that better empower users to understand complex nutrigenetics concepts and make informed decisions.

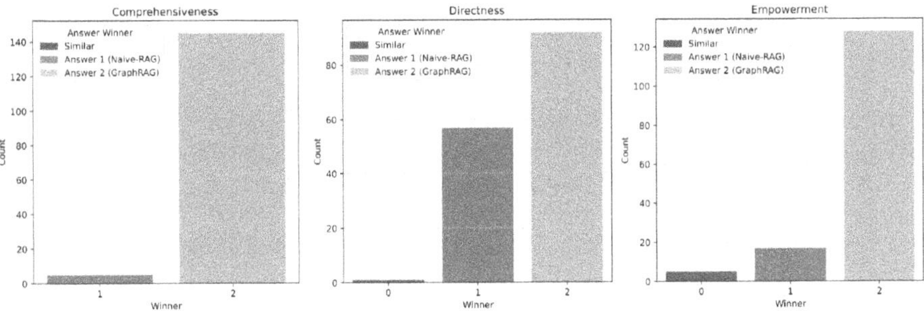

Fig. 3. Comparative evaluation of NaiveRAG vs. GraphRAG across three evaluation criteria. Distribution of LLM judge scores where 0: tie, 1: NaiveRAG and 2: GraphRAG.

5   Discussion and Conclusions

The results of our study demonstrate the effectiveness of the GraphRAG framework in enhancing retrieval and generation capabilities for biomedical applications, particularly in the domain of nutrigenetics. The framework's ability to construct and leverage structured KGs significantly outperformed traditional RAG approaches, as evidenced by its superior performance across all evaluation criteria. This improvement is particularly notable in the system's ability to provide comprehensive and empowering responses, which are critical for supporting informed decision-making in personalized nutrition. A key insight from our model selection study is the importance of selecting appropriate LLM and embedding model combinations. While the specific choice of models influenced the quality of the resulting KGs, the overall architecture of GraphRAG proved robust across different configurations. This suggests that the framework's design principles—combining hierarchical summarization with community detection—are more critical to its success than the specific models employed. The practical implications of this work are particularly significant for biomedical healthcare applications. For researchers, GraphRAG enables efficient exploration of large biomedical corpora, facilitating the discovery of genetic variant associations with dietary responses. This can accelerate hypothesis generation and experimental design, ultimately contributing to the advancement of personalized nutrition. For healthcare professionals, the system provides a valuable tool for translating complex genetic information into actionable insights, supporting the integration of nutrigenetic principles into clinical practice. Finally, for consumers, GraphRAG has the potential to empower individuals to make informed dietary choices based on their genetic profiles, fostering greater personalization and engagement in health management. The modular architecture of our GraphRAG framework makes it naturally extensible with minimal additional development effort. The system can readily accommodate the integration of additional biomedical ontologies to enhance KG interpretability, expand to multi-domain biomedical literature for broader clinical applicability, and incorporate user-specific interfaces and visualization tools for improved accessibility across diverse stakeholder groups in personalized healthcare.

Acknowledgments. We acknowledge financial support from the PNRR MUR project PE0000013-FAIR.

Author Contributions. Giovanni Maria De Filippis: Conceptualization, Methodology, Validation, Investigation, Data Curation, Writing - Original Draft, Writing - Review & Editing, Visualization. **Domenico Benfenati**: Methodology, Validation, Data Curation, Writing - Review & Editing. **Gianluca De Carlo**: Methodology, Validation, Data Curation, Writing - Review & Editing. **Antonio Maria Rinaldi**: Writing - Review & Editing, Supervision.

Data Availability. All datasets used in this study are publicly available. All code and datasets are available at https://github.com/johndef64/nutrig-graphrag.

Competing Interests. The authors declare that they have no competing interests.

References

1. Argelaguet, R., et al.: Multi-omics factor analysis–a framework for unsupervised integration of multi-omics data sets. Mol. Syst. Biol. **14**(6), e8124 (2018)
2. Ayams, J.N., et al.: Domain specific semantic categories in biomedical applications. Mining Biomedical Text, Images and Visual Features for Information Retrieval, pp. 607–634 (2025)
3. Bai, S., et al.: Qwen2. 5-vl technical report. arXiv preprint arXiv:2502.13923 (2025)
4. Ban, T., Chen, L., Wang, X., Chen, H.: From Query Tools to Causal Architects: Harnessing Large Language Models for Advanced Causal Discovery from Data (2023). https://doi.org/10.48550/arXiv.2306.16902
5. Benfenati, D., Filippis, G.M.D., Rinaldi, A.M., Russo, C., Tommasino, C.: A retrieval-augmented generation application for question-answering in nutrigenetics domain. Procedia Comput. Sci. **246**, 586–595 (2024). https://doi.org/10.1016/j.procs.2024.09.467
6. Blondel, V.D., Guillaume, J.L., Lambiotte, R., Lefebvre, E.: Fast unfolding of communities in large networks. J. Stat. Mech: Theory Exp. **2008**(10), P10008 (2008). https://doi.org/10.1088/1742-5468/2008/10/P10008
7. Blondel, V.D., Guillaume, J.L., Lambiotte, R., Lefebvre, E.: Fast unfolding of communities in large networks. J. Stat. Mech: Theory Exp. **2008**(10), P10008 (2008)
8. Bush, C.L., Blumberg, J.B., El-Sohemy, A., Minich, D.M., Ordovás, J.M., Reed, D.G., Behm, V.A.Y.: Toward the definition of personalized nutrition: a proposal by the american nutrition association. J. Am. Coll. Nutr. **39**(1), 5–15 (2020)
9. Callahan, T., Tripodi, I., Stefanski, A., et al.: An open source knowledge graph ecosystem for the life sciences. Sci. Data **11**(363) (2024). https://doi.org/10.1038/s41597-024-03171-w
10. Cuconasu, F., et al.: The power of noise: redefining retrieval for rag systems. In: Proceedings of the 47th International ACM SIGIR Conference on Research and Development in Information Retrieval, pp. 719–729 (2024)
11. Devlin, J., Chang, M.W., Lee, K., Toutanova, K.: Bert: pre-training of deep bidirectional transformers for language understanding. arXiv preprint (2018). https://doi.org/arXiv:1810.04805

12. Edge, D., et al.: From local to global: a graph rag approach to query-focused summarization (2025). https://arxiv.org/abs/2404.16130
13. Feng, F., et al.: Genomickb: a knowledge graph for the human genome. Nucleic Acids Res. **51**(D1), D950–D956 (2023)
14. Filippis, G.M.D., Amalfitano, D., Russo, C., Tommasino, C., Rinaldi, A.M.: A systematic mapping study of semantic technologies in multi-omics data integration. J. Biomed. Inform. **165**, 104809 (2025). https://doi.org/10.1016/j.jbi.2025.104809
15. Filippis, G.M.D., Monticelli, M., Pollice, A., Angrisano, T., Mele, B.H., Calabrò, V.: Computational strategies in nutrigenetics: constructing a reference dataset of nutrition-associated genetic polymorphisms. J. Biomed. Inform. **167**, 104845 (2025). https://doi.org/10.1016/j.jbi.2025.104845
16. Gao, Y., et al.: Retrieval-augmented generation for large language models: a survey (2023)
17. Grattafiori, A., et al.: The llama 3 herd of models. arXiv preprint arXiv:2407.21783 (2024)
18. Han, H., et al.: Retrieval-Augmented Generation with Graphs (GraphRAG) (2025). https://doi.org/10.48550/arXiv.2501.00309
19. Kiani, A.K., et al.: Polymorphisms, diet and nutrigenomics. J. Prev. Med. Hyg. **63**(2) (2022)
20. Kumar, P.: Large language models (LLMs): survey, technical frameworks, and future challenges. Artif. Intell. Rev. **57**(10), 260 (2024)
21. Lee, J., et al.: Biobert: a pre-trained biomedical language representation model for biomedical text mining. Bioinformatics **36**(4), 1234–1240 (2020)
22. Lewis, P., et al.: Retrieval-augmented generation for knowledge-intensive NLP tasks. Adv. Neural. Inf. Process. Syst. **33**, 9459–9474 (2020)
23. Liu, A., et al.: Deepseek-v2: a strong, economical, and efficient mixture-of-experts language model. arXiv preprint arXiv:2405.04434 (2024)
24. Liu, S., Wu, J., Bao, J., Wang, W., Hovakimyan, N., Healey, C.G.: Towards a robust retrieval-based summarization system. arXiv preprint arXiv:2403.19889 (2024)
25. Lobentanzer, S., Aloy, P., Baumbach, J., et al.: Democratizing knowledge representation with biocypher. Nat. Biotechnol. **41**, 1056–1059 (2023). https://doi.org/10.1038/s41587-023-01848-y
26. Lu, Y., Goi, S.Y., Zhao, X., Wang, J.: Biomedical knowledge graph: a survey of domains, tasks, and real-world applications. arXiv preprint arXiv:2501.11632 (2025)
27. Madeddu, F., et al.: VitaGraph: Building a Knowledge Graph for Biologically Relevant Learning Tasks (2025). https://doi.org/10.48550/arXiv.2505.11185
28. Matsumoto, N., et al.: KRAGEN: a knowledge graph-enhanced RAG framework for biomedical problem solving using large language models. Bioinformatics **40**(6), btae353 (2024). https://doi.org/10.1093/bioinformatics/btae353
29. Melnyk, I., Dognin, P., Das, P.: Knowledge Graph Generation From Text (2022). https://doi.org/10.48550/arXiv.2211.10511
30. Muludi, K., Fitria, K.M., Triloka, J., et al.: Retrieval-augmented generation approach: document question answering using large language model. Int. J. Adv. Comput. Sci. Appl. **15**(3) (2024)
31. Newman, M.E.J.: Modularity and community structure in networks. Proc. Natl. Acad. Sci. **103**(23) (2006)
32. Nicholson, D.N., Greene, C.S.: Constructing knowledge graphs and their biomedical applications. Comput. Struct. Biotechnol. J. **18**, 1414–1428 (2020)
33. Santos, A., et al.: A knowledge graph to interpret clinical proteomics data. Nat. Biotechnol. **40**(5), 692–702 (2022)

34. Sikos, L.F., Philp, D.: Provenance-aware knowledge representation: a survey of data models and contextualized knowledge graphs. Data Sci. Eng. **5**, 293–316 (2020)
35. Soman, K., et al.: Biomedical knowledge graph-optimized prompt generation for large language models. Bioinformatics **40**(9), btae560 (2024). https://doi.org/10.1093/bioinformatics/btae560
36. Su, C., Hou, Y., Wang, F.: GNN-based biomedical knowledge graph mining in drug development. Graph Neural Networks: Foundations, Frontiers, and Applications, pp. 517–540 (2022)
37. Riviere, M., et al.: Gemma 2: improving open language models at a practical size. arXiv preprint arXiv:2408.00118 (2024)
38. Traag, V.A., Waltman, L., van Eck, N.J.: From Louvain to Leiden: guaranteeing well-connected communities. Sci. Rep. **9**(1), 5233 (2019). https://doi.org/10.1038/s41598-019-41695-z
39. Traag, V.A., Waltman, L., Van Eck, N.J.: From louvain to leiden: guaranteeing well-connected communities. Sci. Rep. **9**(1) (2019)
40. Zhang, Q., Dong, J., Chen, H., Zha, D., Yu, Z., Huang, X.: Knowgpt: knowledge graph based prompting for large language models. Adv. Neural. Inf. Process. Syst. **37**, 6052–6080 (2024)
41. Zheng, L., et al.: Judging LLM-as-a-judge with mt-bench and chatbot arena. In: Oh, A., Naumann, T., Globerson, A., Saenko, K., Hardt, M., Levine, S. (eds.) Advances in Neural Information Processing Systems, vol. 36, pp. 46595–46623. Curran Associates, Inc. (2023)
42. Zheng, S., et al.: Pharmkg: a dedicated knowledge graph benchmark for bomedical data mining. Briefings Bioinform. **22**(4), bbaa344 (2021)

Generative Data Augmentation
by Dataset Distillation

Yuri Gordienko[1]([✉])(iD), Grzegorz Nowakowski[2](iD), Yuriy Kochura[1](iD),
Vladyslav Taran[1](iD), and Sergii Stirenko[1](iD)

[1] National Technical University of Ukraine "Igor Sikorsky Kyiv Polytechnic
Institute", Kyiv, Ukraine
`{gord,kochura,taran,stirenko}@comsys.kpi.ua`
[2] Cracow University of Technology, Krakow, Poland
`grzegorz.nowakowski@pk.edu.pl`

Abstract. Dataset distillation aims to create compact synthetic datasets that retain the generalization properties of real datasets. This study employs dataset distillation by matching training trajectories (DDMTT), a novel approach that utilizes expert trajectories (precomputed sequences of network parameters trained on the full dataset) to guide the distillation process. Experiments with the extremely increased number of images per class (IPC) were conducted using standard datasets such as CIFAR-10 and CIFAR-100, as well as medical benchmarking datasets from MedMNIST. The proposed method of generative data augmentation by dataset distillation (GDADD) demonstrated that, for CIFAR datasets, their smaller distilled versions containing 40,000 images achieved higher validation accuracy than the full datasets with 50,000 images, surpassing the original dataset's performance by 3.1% for CIFAR-10 and 2.9% for CIFAR-100. For the considered MedMNIST datasets (PathMNIST, DermaMNIST, RetinaMNIST), some distilled datasets (PathMNIST) exceeded the performance of models trained on full datasets, confirming the method's robustness across different domains and demonstrating the better results for the well balanced datasets.

Keywords: dataset distillation · classification · data augmentation · CIFAR-10 · CIFAR-100 · MedMNIST · ConvNet · health care

1 Introduction

Dataset distillation (DD) has emerged as a critical technique to address the increasing computational and storage demands of deep learning (DL) approaches [13]. Unlike traditional deep neural networks (DNN) that require vast amounts of data and computing power [5, 7–9, 12, 16, 19, 20, 25], DD synthesizes a small set of highly informative data points that retain the knowledge of large datasets [22]. Models trained on these distilled datasets can achieve performance comparable to those trained on full datasets, making DD a promising approach for efficient learning and storage. Overall, dataset distillation presents an efficient alternative to traditional data reduction, offering improved model training efficiency, storage savings, and generalization through synthetic data generation. DD's ability to compress and abstract key information makes it an essential tool in optimizing DL across explainability, design, and healthcare while improving efficiency and security. In this context, the challenges of scalability, multimodality, labeling complexity for the real datasets used in the practical setups are not resolved yet fully. That is why the further research of DD approaches should be performed for the DD better understanding. In this work, several experiments were performed to investigate the limits of DD with regard to its application to the standard and specific datasets to bring to the light the new ways for data augmentation and their effect of the dataset quality on the performance of classification tasks.

2 Background and Related Work

Due to the high-dimensional nature of DL data, distilling knowledge into a few points is challenging. DD methods can be broadly divided in several categories [13]. In meta-learning approaches, distilled data are treated as hyperparameters optimized in a nested loop to improve generalization [22]. Data-matching methods, on the other hand, update synthetic data by imitating the influence of real data on model training, either in parameter space or feature space [2,30,31].

Factorized dataset distillation (DD) leverages the idea that high-dimensional image data lie on a low-dimensional manifold and can be reconstructed using specific decoders [1,13,28]. Instead of directly storing synthetic images, factorized DD optimizes compact feature representations (codes) along with corresponding decoders, reducing storage needs and redundancy. This approach improves compression while preserving essential information. The factorized DD is categorized into three types: code-based DD, decoder-based DD, and code-decoder DD, each offering different trade-offs in efficiency and reconstruction quality, making it a powerful strategy for dataset distillation.

DD is used across various domains that demand efficient training and storage. It has been particularly useful in continual learning [18,24] and neural architecture search [15,23], where handling large datasets is computationally expensive. Additionally, since dataset distillation preserves gradient information, it plays a role in privacy preservation, federated learning, and adversarial robustness by reducing the exposure of raw data during training [6,21]. One notable application of DD is in explainable AI (XAI) algorithms [17]. Due to their small size, synthetic datasets allow precise measurement of how training examples influence test predictions. If both test and training images rely on the same synthetic images, it becomes easier to trace model decision-making, making dataset distillation a valuable tool for XAI. DD has also been employed in visual design where DD used to generate representative textures by cropping synthetic images and to model outfit compatibility, leveraging synthetic images to capture essential visual patterns [3,4]. In the health care, DD facilitates medical image sharing where DD can enhance data anonymization and secure data exchange between hospitals [14]. It allows healthcare institutions to collaboratively train AI models for computer-aided diagnosis with reduced privacy risks and lower costs.

3   Methodology

3.1   Datasets

The following benchmarking datasets were used in the work: 32×32 pixel CIFAR-10 and CIFAR-100 datasets that widely used for dataset distillation research [10,11], and 28×28 pixel specific MedMNIST datasets, actually PathM-NIST, DermaMNIST, and RetinaMNIST [26,27].

3.2   Dataset Distillation by Matching Training Trajectories

Here the dataset distillation by matching training trajectories (DDMTT) is used which introduces a novel approach to dataset distillation by leveraging expert trajectories to guide the learning process [2]. Expert trajectories are sequences of network parameters obtained by training a neural network on the full, real dataset. These trajectories represent an upper bound on performance for the distilled dataset, as they reflect the ideal learning process of a model trained on real data. To implement DDMTT, a large number of networks are trained on the real dataset, and their parameter snapshots are recorded at each epoch. These precomputed expert trajectories serve as references for guiding the learning process of a student model, which is trained on synthetic images. The student parameters) evolve during training, and the goal is to distill a synthetic dataset that induces a trajectory matching the real dataset's trajectory, ensuring that models trained on the distilled data perform similarly to those trained on the full dataset. A key advantage of DDMTT is that expert trajectories are computed before distillation, enabling faster and more efficient training. This precomputation allows for rapid experimentation, as the same expert trajectories can be used across multiple distillation attempts. By explicitly aligning the synthetic dataset with long-range network parameter evolution, DDMTT produces high-quality distilled datasets, ensuring that models trained on them generalize similarly to models trained on real data.

3.3   Network Architecture

The network architecture used for dataset distillation is based on ConvNet architectures [26] and primarily follows the intentionally simple design to enable direct analysis of the effectiveness of the distillation method while ensuring comparability with previous studies [2]. The network consists of several convolutional blocks, where the number of convolutional blocks is adapted based on the dataset resolution, with specific configurations defined for each dataset used in experiments. Each convolutional block contains 3×3 convolutional layer with 128 filters, ReLU activation functions, 2×2 average pooling and stride 2 and the more implementation details are given elsewhere [2]. By using this lightweight yet effective architecture, this work isolates the impact of the distillation method rather than introducing confounding effects from complex architectures. This design choice ensures that the results remain directly comparable to the previous works [2] and similar results [26,27], facilitating fair evaluation and benchmarking of the dataset distillation process.

3.4   Workflow

The dataset distillation workflow follows a standard evaluation protocol, where a randomly initialized neural network is trained from scratch on the distilled dataset and then evaluated on a validation set. This ensures a fair comparison of different distillation methods by assessing how well models generalize when trained on synthetic rather than real data. To generate distilled images, the workflow implements the distillation process and follows established techniques described in [2]. This includes applying a suite of differentiable augmentations, similar to those used in prior studies [29,30]. These augmentations help improve the generalization of the distilled dataset by introducing variations that mimic real-world transformations. The key hyperparameters for the distillation process, such as the number of real epochs per iteration, synthetic updates per iteration, and image learning rate, are documented elsewhere [2]. These hyperparameters are crucial in determining the efficacy of distillation, balancing training efficiency and synthetic data quality.

4   Results

4.1   Synthesized and Reconstructed Images

CIFAR Datasets. The dataset distillation results for CIFAR-10 (Fig. 1) and CIFAR-100 reveal that the synthetic images effectively capture class-specific information, even when highly compressed. The synthesized and reconstructed visualizations for 1 image per class (IPC) (Fig. 1, a and b) demonstrate vague, but recognizable representations, for example from the left to right: bird (1st), car (2nd), bird (3rd), cat (4th), deer (5th), dog (6th), ... for CIFAR-10 (Fig. 1). It indicates that the optimization process efficiently extracts key distinguishing features. Since the task is constrained to a single synthetic IPC, the model is forced to compress essential information into just one representation. When the constraint is relaxed to allow multiple synthetic IPC (e.g., 10 IPC), the optimization distributes the class's distinguishing features across multiple samples. This results in a more diverse and structured set of synthetic images (Fig. 1, c and d). For example, instead of a single compressed representation, the dataset contains varied examples of objects within a class, such as different versions of birds, cars, deers, etc. This outcome highlights that dataset distillation benefits from increased synthetic samples per class, as it enables the model to better approximate real-world diversity while maintaining a compact dataset size. The results support the effectiveness of dataset distillation in generating highly informative and expressive synthetic datasets with minimal storage requirements.

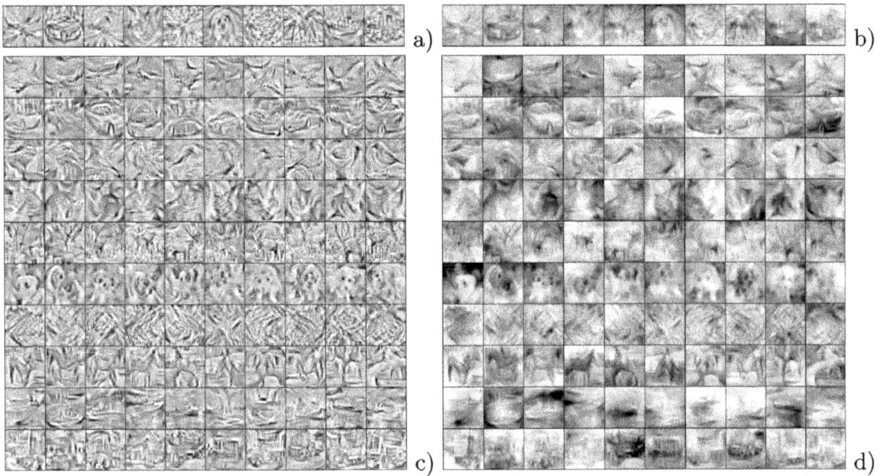

Fig. 1. Examples of synthesized (left) and reconstructed (right) images from CIFAR-10 dataset for various images per class: 1 (a,b) and 10 (c,d).

MedMNIST Datasets. But for the specific datasets like MedMNIST the synthesized and reconstructed images, for instance for PathMNIST (Fig. 2), are not so easily recognizable even for the higher values of IPCs due to the quite specific and complex patterns of some diseases.

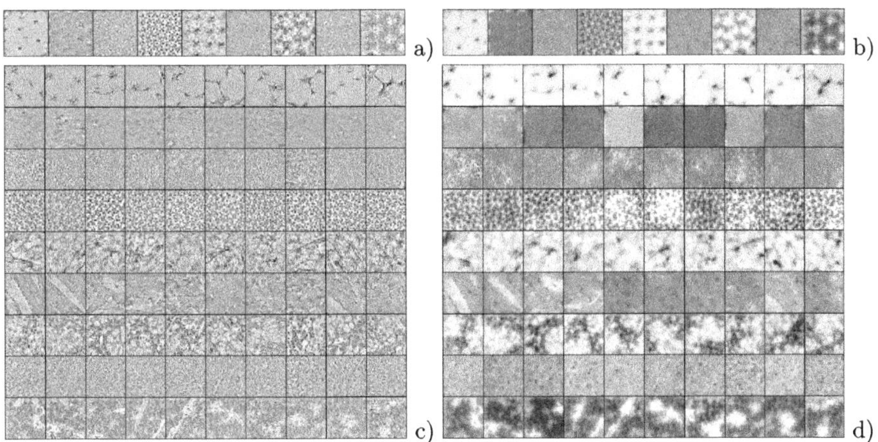

Fig. 2. Examples of synthesized (left) and reconstructed (right) images from PathM-NIST dataset for various images per class: 1 (a,b) and 10 (c,d).

4.2   Impact of Distilled IPC on Model Performance: CIFAR

In this part of research 5 trials of training on the distilled IPC were performed for the different IPC numbers from 1 up to 10000 to estimate the impact of IPC number on the actual performance of the model. The saturation (i.e. no decrease of the validation accuracy) was observed for various numbers of epochs, for example, for CIFAR-10 (Fig. 3): for IPC from 1 to 100 - up to 5000 epochs, for IPC from 1000 to 2000 - up to 1000 epochs, for IPC from 4000 to 5000 - up to 500 epochs, and for IPC 10000 - up to 120 epochs.

CIFAR-10. For each IPC (from 1 up to 10000 for CIFAR-10) the maximal validation accuracy values were plotted versus the IPC values in Fig. 3 (right). It should be noted that training on the IPC numbers from 1 to 50 (that were used in [2]) give the same results with regard to the maximal validation accuracy value obtained by averaging over 5 trials after the number of epochs when accuracy saturation was observed. Moreover, after some IPC value (4000 here) the maximal accuracy (0.879 ± 0.001) becomes higher than the accuracy obtained after training on the full original dataset (0.848 ± 0.001) (denoted by "+" symbol in Fig. 3, right). Here, "+" symbol corresponds the IPC number (5000) for the full dataset but the improvement beyond the standard deviation (0.001) was observed for the lower IPC equal to 4000. It means that distilled version of CIFAR-100 dataset with 40000 training images can provide the better performance than the original version of CIFAR-100 dataset with 50000 training images. For CIFAR-10 the overall improvement of the validation accuracy by DD is better than $3.1 \pm 0.1\%$ (Table 1).

CIFAR-100. Similarly, for CIFAR-100, after some IPC value (400 here) the maximal accuracy (0.591 ± 0.003) becomes higher than the accuracy obtained after training on the full original dataset (0.562 ± 0.003) (denoted by "+" symbol in Fig. 4, right). Here, "+" symbol corresponds the IPC number (500) for the full dataset but the improvement beyond the standard deviation (0.003) was observed for the lower IPC equal to 400. Again, it means that distilled version of CIFAR-100 dataset with 40000 training images can provide the better performance than the original version of CIFAR-100 dataset with 50000 training images. For CIFAR-100 the overall improvement of the validation accuracy by DD is better than $2.9 \pm 0.3\%$ (Table 1).

In general, DD used for CIFAR-10 and CIFAR-100 as a generative data augmentation by dataset distillation (GDADD) technique allows to use smaller synthetic (40000 images) datasets in comparison to the larger original (50000 images) datasets and get the accuracy which is higher by $\sim 3 \pm 0.3\%$.

4.3   Impact of Distilled IPC on Model Performance: MedMNIST

It worth to note that the results reported above relate to the standard datasets and their potential practical value should be checked for the more specific dataset

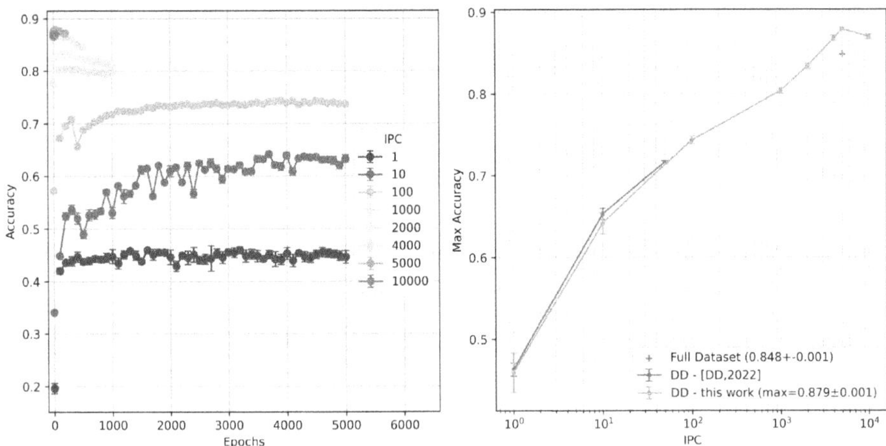

Fig. 3. CIFAR-10 dataset. Validation accuracy vs. epochs where the legend contains the distilled "images per class" (IPC) values (left) and maximal validation accuracy (observed for the stated IPC) vs. IPC (right) where the legend contains the reference values from [2]. The error bars denote the standard deviations of accuracy after 5 trials.

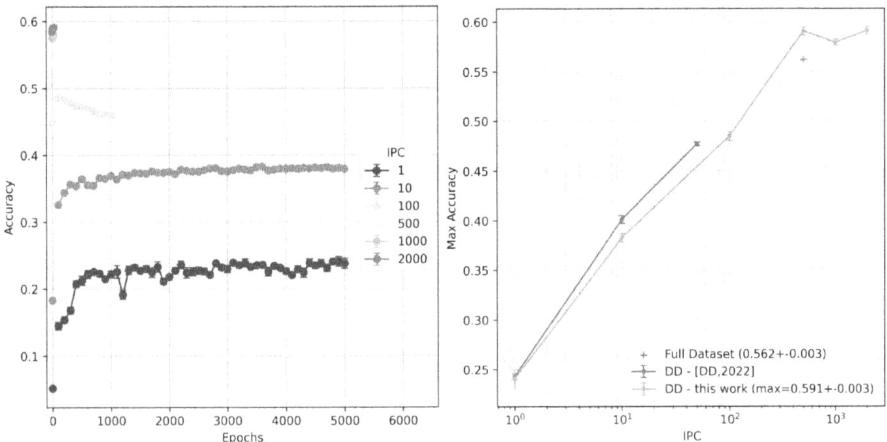

Fig. 4. CIFAR-100 dataset. Validation accuracy vs. epochs where the legend contains the distilled "images per class" (IPC) values (left) and maximal validation accuracy (observed for the stated IPC) vs. IPC (right) where the legend contains the reference values from [2]. The error bars denote the standard deviations of accuracy after 5 trials.

which are more closely reflect the real-world setups. For this purpose, the medical benchmarking datasets from MedMNIST collection were used [26,27].

PathMNIST. In this work, the performance improvement was obtained for ConvNet architecture and it is compared with the previously published results

Table 1. The maximal validation accuracy values for the balanced CIFAR datasets.

Experiment	CIFAR-10	CIFAR-100
DD, full original dataset [2]	0.848 ± 0.001	0.562 ± 0.003
Ours, distilled smaller dataset (Fig. 3, 4)	$\mathbf{0.879} \pm 0.001$	$\mathbf{0.591} \pm 0.003$

[26,27] obtained for various other methods including ResNet-18, ResNet-50, auto-sklearn, AutoKeras, and Google AutoML Vision (Fig. 5).

After some IPC value (100 here) the maximal accuracy values obtained by GDADD on the smaller synthetic version of PathMNIST dataset gradually become the better than accuracy values obtained by the aforementioned methods on the full original PathMNIST dataset. After some IPC value (10000 here) the maximal accuracy (0.917 ± 0.003) becomes higher than the best accuracy obtained after ResNet-50 training on the full original dataset (0.911) (denoted by the "·" symbol in Fig. 5, right). Here, "·" symbol corresponds the IPC number (10000) for the full dataset but the improvement at the brim of the standard deviation (0.003) was observed for the same IPC equal to 10000. Again, it means that distilled version of PathMNIST dataset with 900000 training images can provide the slightly better performance than the original version of PathMNIST dataset with same 90000 training images. For PathMNIST the overall improvement of the validation accuracy by DD is better than $0.6 \pm 0.3\%$ (Table 2). In comparison to the well balanced CIFAR-10/CIFAR-100 datasets this improvement is smaller and it can be explained by the slightly imbalanced distribution of images among classes in PathMNIST (see the details below).

DermaMNIST. Here the slight performance improvement was obtained with IPC growth and it was smaller in comparison with the previously published results [26, 27] obtained for various other methods including ResNet-18, ResNet-50, auto-sklearn, AutoKeras, and Google AutoML Vision (Fig. 6). In comparison to the well balanced CIFAR-10/CIFAR-100 datasets and the slightly imbalanced PathMNIST even this improvement is much smaller and, again, it can be explained by the imbalanced images distribution among classes.

RetinaMNIST. This dataset is similar to DermaMNIST by its imbalanced distribution of images among classes and the slight performance improvement with IPC growth that also is smaller in comparison with the previously published results [26, 27] obtained for various other methods including ResNet-18, ResNet-50, auto-sklearn, AutoKeras, and Google AutoML Vision (Fig. 7).

For the slightly (PathMNIST) and highly (DermaMNIST, RetinaMNIST) imbalanced datasets the impact of GDADD on the maximal validation accuracy values is summarized in Table 2.

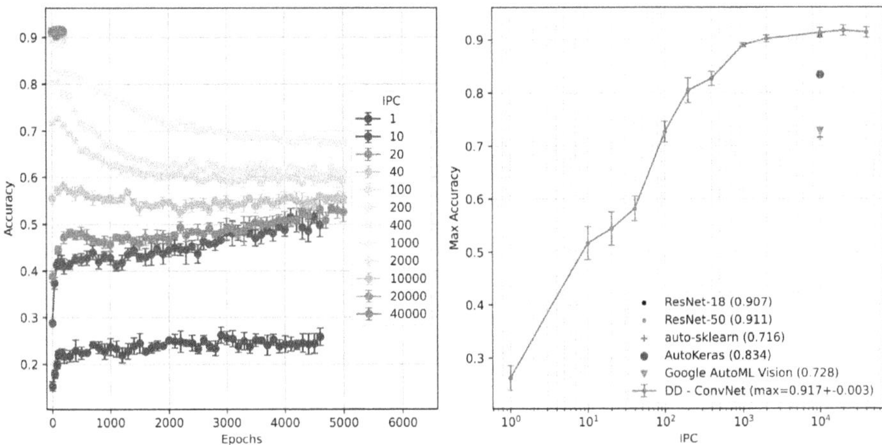

Fig. 5. PathMNIST dataset. Validation accuracy vs. epochs where the legend contains the distilled "images per class" (IPC) values (left) and maximal validation accuracy (observed for the stated IPC) vs. IPC (right) where the legend contains the reference values from [26, 27]. The error bars denote the standard deviations of accuracy after 5 trials.

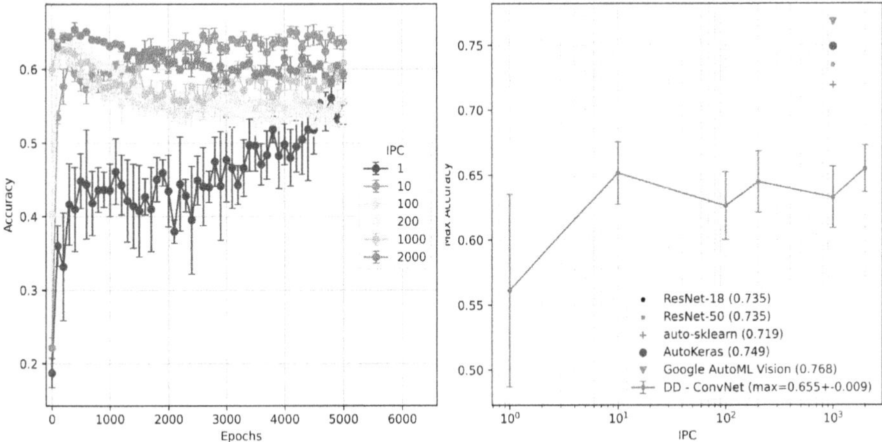

Fig. 6. DermaMNIST dataset. Validation accuracy vs. epochs where the legend contains the distilled "images per class" (IPC) values (left) and maximal validation accuracy (observed for the stated IPC) vs. IPC (right) where the legend contains the reference values from [26, 27]. The error bars denote the standard deviations of accuracy after 5 trials.

5 Discussion

The analysis was performed to calculate the overall maximal validation accuracy values determined over all IPC values for all datasets (synthetic and original)

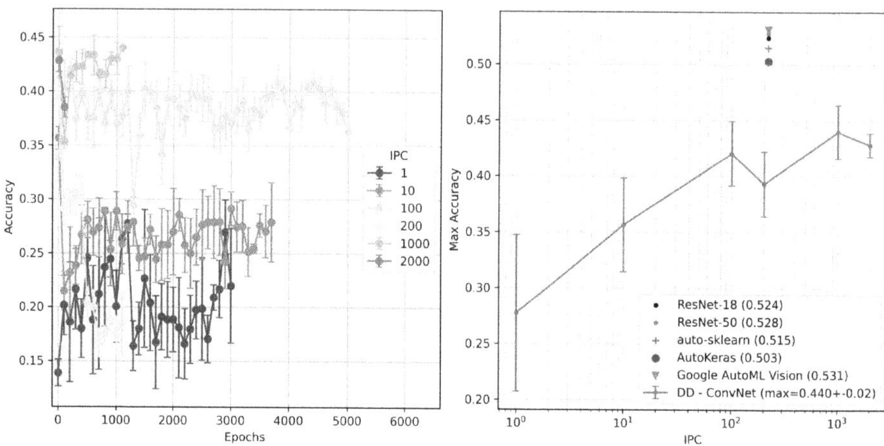

Fig. 7. RetinaMNIST dataset. Validation accuracy vs. epochs where the legend contains the distilled "images per class" (IPC) values (left) and maximal validation accuracy (observed for the stated IPC) vs. IPC (right) where the legend contains the reference values from [26,27]. The error bars denote the standard deviations of accuracy after 5 trials.

Table 2. The maximal validation accuracy values for the slightly (PathMNIST) and highly (DermaMNIST, RetinaMNIST) imbalanced datasets.

Model	Balanced	Imbalanced	
	PathMNIST	DermaMNIST	RetinaMNIST
ResNet-18 (28)	0.907	0.735	0.524
ResNet-50 (28)	0.911	0.735	0.528
auto-sklearn	0.716	0.719	0.515
AutoKeras	0.834	0.749	0.503
Google AutoML Vision	0.728	**0.768**	**0.531**
Ours (GDADD) (Fig. 5, 6 and 7)	**0.917** ± 0.003	0.655 ± 0.009	0.440 ± 0.020

and plot them versus the IPC values for which this overall maximal validation accuracy values were observed (Fig. 8).

It should be noted that the overall maximal validation accuracy values for synthetic versions of the datasets (the open symbols in Fig. 8) are aligned along a line (the dotted line in Fig. 8). But the overall maximal validation accuracy values for original versions of the datasets (the filled symbols in Fig. 8) are not aligned along a line and follow the broken line (the dashed line in Fig. 8). The error bars (red - for DermaMNIST and green - for RetinaMNIST) denote the standard deviations of IPC distribution for the original datasets after 5 trials. They characterize the imbalance of IPC distribution, the point's belonging to the trend line within the limits of standard deviation, and inability of the current GDADD setup to take it into account to improve the accuracy.

Actually, by this plot GDADD allow to obtain visual comprehension about advantages of the current GDADD setup to improve the accuracy for the well balanced datasets and disadvantages when the imbalance of IPC distribution is not considered (in the current setup).

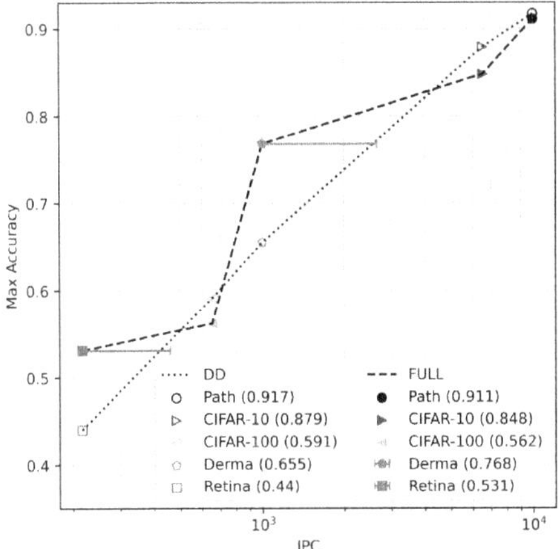

Fig. 8. Comparison of the overall maximal validation accuracy (determined over all IPC values) vs. the IPC for which this overall maximal validation accuracy was observed (right plot) where the legend contains the reference values from [2] and [26,27]. The error bars denote the standard deviations of IPC distribution for the original datasets after 5 trials. (Color figure online)

In general, GDADD presents an innovative method for augmenting datasets by leveraging expert trajectories obtained from training on real data. This approach allows for trajectory-guided augmentation where the expert trajectory guides the synthetic dataset's evolution, ensuring it captures key data characteristics. Even with a smaller number of distilled IPC, GDADD successfully encodes essential features, making it an efficient data augmentation method with the better performance. While effective for standard datasets like CIFAR-10 and CIFAR-100, performance on medical datasets like MedMNIST suggests the need for domain-specific enhancements. The potential of GDADD in healthcare applications, particularly in federated learning, is significant because synthetic datasets can replace real patient data, mitigating privacy concerns while enabling collaborative learning across institutions. Moreover, while medical imaging datasets often suffer from class imbalances and scarcity, GDADD can generate diverse synthetic samples, improving model robustness. By aligning the distilled datasets with training trajectories from multiple institutions, models can generalize better without direct access to real patient data.

GDADD offers several benefits over traditional dataset distillation and data augmentation techniques including reduce of computational overhead by utilizing previously trained models to guide distillation, enabling rapid experimentation; strong generalization with fewer samples, significantly reducing storage and computational requirements; preserved model performance by consequence that models trained on synthetic data closely follow performance trends of those trained on real data. The improved diversity with increased IPC values lead to more detailed synthetic datasets that better approximate real-world variability.

Despite its advantages, GDADD has some limitations related with dependency on initial expert trajectories, high computational cost of initial expert training, potential for bias propagation. The matter is the quality of distilled datasets is highly dependent on the effectiveness of the expert trajectory. Poorly trained expert models could lead to suboptimal synthetic data. Although distillation is efficient, generating expert trajectories requires significant computational resources upfront. Any biases present in the original dataset or training trajectory can be transferred to the distilled dataset, impacting generalization.

Beyond the stated limitations, our findings suggest that the DDMTT dependency on expert trajectories makes it inherently susceptible to the quality and bias of the initial training process. The poorer performance on imbalanced datasets indicates that the trajectory matching objective can prioritize majority classes. Furthermore, the significant computational cost of generating expert models presents a practical barrier to cheap entry for various applications. Future work will need to explore more efficient trajectory sampling methods and investigate regularization techniques to prevent bias amplification during distillation, moving beyond the current identification of limitations to their active mitigation.

To bridge the gap toward clinical applicability, future work must involve close collaboration with medical experts to validate the diagnostic relevance of synthesized images and to integrate domain-specific constraints directly into the distillation loss function. Furthermore, the varied performance on imbalanced medical datasets underscores the need for the specific domain adaptation. A key next step will be to tailor the GDADD framework specifically for healthcare, perhaps by incorporating class-balanced weighting or leveraging trajectories from models trained on rare classes to ensure the synthetic data effectively addresses clinical scarcity and imbalance.

6   Conclusions

The study investigates the impact of generative data augmentation by dataset distillation (GDADD) using the dataset distillation by matching training trajectories (DDMTT) technique. This method leverages expert trajectories to guide the learning process, improving the efficiency and quality of synthetic datasets for training neural networks. Results on the well balanced CIFAR-10 and CIFAR-100 datasets demonstrate that distilled images successfully capture class-specific information, even at a low image-per-class (IPC) setting. When IPC is increased, synthetic images better approximate real-world diversity, enhancing model performance. Specifically, for CIFAR-10, increasing IPC to 4000 improves validation accuracy significantly by $3.1 \pm 0.1\%$, for CIFAR-10, increasing IPC to 400 improves validation accuracy by $2.9 \pm 0.3\%$, and for PathMNIST the overall improvement of the validation accuracy by DD is better than $0.6 \pm 0.3\%$. For MedMNIST datasets, slightly imbalanced PathMNIST and strongly imbalanced DermaMNIST and RetinaMNIST, the synthesized images are less distinguishable compared to CIFAR datasets due to the IPC imbalances. However, increasing IPC still enhances performance, albeit with diminishing returns beyond a certain IPC threshold. Overall, GDADD enables models trained on synthetic datasets to achieve accuracy levels close and higher to those trained on the real data with a potetnial to generate compact yet informative datasets, reducing data storage needs while maintaining model generalization.

Acknowledgments. This research was supported by the National Research Fund of Ukraine under grant 2025.06/0100 in the part of the development of exploratory research on the new robust machine learning approaches for object detection and classification and by the Ministry of Education and Sciences of Ukraine (MESU), grant 2715r, as part of the search for advanced deep learning methods based on the requirements posed by devices on Edge Computing and Edge Intelligence layers.

References

1. Bengio, Y., Courville, A., Vincent, P.: Representation learning: a review and new perspectives. IEEE Trans. Pattern Anal. Mach. Intell. **35**(8), 1798–1828 (2013)
2. Cazenavette, G., Wang, T., Torralba, A., Efros, A.A., Zhu, J.Y.: Dataset distillation by matching training trajectories. In: Proceedings of the IEEE/CVF Conference on Computer Vision and Pattern Recognition, pp. 4750–4759 (2022)
3. Cazenavette, G., Wang, T., Torralba, A., Efros, A.A., Zhu, J.Y.: Wearable imagenet: synthesizing tileable textures via dataset distillation. In: Proceedings of the IEEE/CVF Conference on Computer Vision and Pattern Recognition, pp. 2278–2282 (2022)
4. Chen, Y., Wu, Z., Shen, Z., Jia, J.: Learning from designers: fashion compatibility analysis via dataset distillation. In: 2022 IEEE International Conference on Image Processing (ICIP), pp. 856–860. IEEE (2022)
5. Fukushima, K.: Neural network model for a mechanism of pattern recognition unaffected by shift in position-neocognitron. IEICE Tech. Rep. A **62**(10), 658–665 (1979)
6. Goetz, J., Tewari, A.: Federated learning via synthetic data. arXiv preprint arXiv:2008.04489 (2020)
7. Hochreiter, S., Schmidhuber, J.: Long short-term memory. Neural Comput. **9**(8), 1735–1780 (1997)
8. Ivakhnenko, A., Lapa, V.: Cybernetic predicting devices (1966). https://apps.dtic.mil/sti/citations/AD0654237. Accessed 24 Oct 2022
9. Kelley, H.J.: Gradient theory of optimal flight paths. ARS J. **30**(10), 947–954 (1960)
10. Krizhevsky, A., Hinton, G., et al.: Learning multiple layers of features from tiny images (2009)
11. Krizhevsky, A., Nair, V., Hinton, G.: The CIFAR datasets (2009). https://www.cs.toronto.edu/~kriz/cifar.html. Accessed 10 Oct 2024
12. LeCun, Y., Bengio, Y., Hinton, G.: Deep learning. Nature **521**(7553), 436–444 (2015)

13. Lei, S., Tao, D.: A comprehensive survey of dataset distillation. IEEE Trans. Pattern Anal. Mach. Intell. **46**(1), 17–32 (2023)
14. Li, G., Togo, R., Ogawa, T., Haseyama, M.: Dataset distillation for medical dataset sharing. arXiv preprint arXiv:2209.14603 (2022)
15. Li, G., Qian, G., Delgadillo, I.C., Muller, M., Thabet, A., Ghanem, B.: SGAS: sequential greedy architecture search. In: Proceedings of the IEEE/CVF Conference on Computer Vision and Pattern Recognition, pp. 1620–1630 (2020)
16. Linnainmaa, S.: Taylor expansion of the accumulated rounding error. BIT Numer. Math. **16**(2), 146–160 (1976)
17. Loo, N., Hasani, R., Amini, A., Rus, D.: Efficient dataset distillation using random feature approximation. Adv. Neural. Inf. Process. Syst. **35**, 13877–13891 (2022)
18. Rosasco, A., Carta, A., Cossu, A., Lomonaco, V., Bacciu, D.: Distilled replay: overcoming forgetting through synthetic samples. In: International Workshop on Continual Semi-Supervised Learning, pp. 104–117. Springer (2021)
19. Schmidhuber, J.: Deep learning in neural networks: an overview. Neural Netw. **61**, 85–117 (2015)
20. Schmidhuber, J., Blog, A.: The 2010s: our decade of deep learning/outlook on the 2020s. The recent decade's most important developments and industrial applications based on our AI, with an outlook on the 2020s, also addressing privacy and data markets (2020)
21. Wang, H.P., Chen, D., Kerkouche, R., Fritz, M.: Fed-GLOSS-DP: federated, global learning using synthetic sets with record level differential privacy. CoRR (2023)
22. Wang, T., Zhu, J.Y., Torralba, A., Efros, A.A.: Dataset distillation. arXiv preprint arXiv:1811.10959 (2018)
23. White, C., Jain, P., Nayak, S., Ramakrishnan, G., et al.: Speeding up nas with adaptive subset selection. arXiv preprint arXiv:2211.01454 (2022)
24. Wiewel, F., Yang, B.: Condensed composite memory continual learning. In: 2021 International Joint Conference on Neural Networks (IJCNN), pp. 1–8. IEEE (2021)
25. Williams, R.: Complexity of exact gradient computation algorithms for recurrent neural networks (technical report nu-ccs-89-27). Northeastern University, College of Computer Science, Boston (1989)
26. Yang, J., Shi, R., Ni, B.: Medmnist classification decathlon: a lightweight automl benchmark for medical image analysis. In: IEEE 18th International Symposium on Biomedical Imaging (ISBI), pp. 191–195 (2021)
27. Yang, J., et al.: Medmnist v2: a large-scale lightweight benchmark for 2D and 3D biomedical image classification. arXiv preprint arXiv:2110.14795 (2021)
28. Zhang, D., Yin, J., Zhu, X., Zhang, C.: Network representation learning: a survey. IEEE Trans. Big Data **6**(1), 3–28 (2018)
29. Zhao, B., Bilen, H.: Dataset condensation with differentiable siamese augmentation. In: International Conference on Machine Learning, pp. 12674–12685. PMLR (2021)
30. Zhao, B., Bilen, H.: Dataset condensation with distribution matching. In: Proceedings of the IEEE/CVF Winter Conference on Applications of Computer Vision, pp. 6514–6523 (2023)
31. Zhao, B., Mopuri, K.R., Bilen, H.: Dataset condensation with gradient matching. arXiv preprint arXiv:2006.05929 (2020)

Semantic Similarity in Radiology Reports via LLMs and NER

Beth Pearson[1(✉)], Ahmed Adnan[2], and Zahraa S. Abdallah[1]

[1] University of Bristol, Bristol, UK
{beth.pearson,zahraa.abdallah}@bristol.ac.uk
[2] Rosenfield Health Tech Ltd., Cardiff, UK
ahmed.adnan@rosenfieldhealth.com

Abstract. Radiology report evaluation is a crucial part of radiologists' training and plays a key role in ensuring diagnostic accuracy. As part of the standard reporting workflow, a junior radiologist typically prepares a preliminary report, which is then reviewed and edited by a senior radiologist to produce the final report. Identifying semantic differences between preliminary and final reports is essential for junior doctors, both as a training tool and to help uncover gaps in clinical knowledge. While AI in radiology is a rapidly growing field, the application of large language models (LLMs) remains challenging due to the need for specialised domain knowledge. In this paper, we explore the ability of LLMs to provide explainable and accurate comparisons of reports in the radiology domain. We begin by comparing the performance of several LLMs in comparing radiology reports. We then assess a more traditional approach based on Named-Entity-Recognition (NER). However, both approaches exhibit limitations in delivering accurate feedback on semantic similarity. To address this, we propose Llama-EntScore, a semantic similarity scoring method using a combination of Llama 3.1 and NER with tunable weights to emphasise or de-emphasise specific types of differences. Our approach generates a quantitative similarity score for tracking progress and also gives an interpretation of the score that aims to offer valuable guidance in reviewing and refining their reporting. We find our method achieves 67% exact-match accuracy and 93% accuracy within ± 1 when compared to radiologist-provided ground truth scores—outperforming both LLMs and NER used independently. Code is available at: github.com/otmive/llama_reports.

Keywords: LLM · Radiology · NER

1 Introduction

Radiology reports are important medical documents that capture the key findings from imaging modalities such as magnetic resonance imaging (MRI) scans, computed tomography (CT) scans and ultrasounds. In clinical practice, a preliminary report is drafted by a junior radiologist and subsequently reviewed by a senior radiologist who makes edits and produces the final report. Identifying

C. Tommasino et al. (Eds.): AIBIO 2025, CCIS 2696, pp. 119–131, 2026.
https://doi.org/10.1007/978-3-032-17216-7_10

semantic differences between preliminary and final radiology reports is essential for supporting the training of junior radiologists and improving the overall reporting process. These differences often reflect important corrections, clarifications, or additions made by senior radiologists and can reveal specific areas where clinical understanding can be strengthened. However, manually reviewing large numbers of reports to extract such insights is time-consuming and difficult to scale. Automating this process enables systematic feedback, supports targeted learning, and offers the potential for AI tools to assist in evaluating report quality and consistency across the workflow. [1–4]. While radiologists find these automated systems beneficial, particularly those with a visualisation of differences [1,3], the comparisons often fall short of expectations. Most rely on basic text comparisons, which fail to capture the clinical relevance or semantic nature of the differences, and do little to highlight broader trends or educational value. Radiology reports contain dense medical jargon and highly specialised terminology, making them particularly challenging to interpret, especially for methods not specifically designed to handle such complexity. More nuanced NLP techniques, such as NER using models trained on biomedical corpora have been explored in previous work [3,5,6]. However, these approaches often struggle to match the depth and nuance of feedback typically provided by experienced radiologists.

This paper investigates the potential of large language models (LLMs) to automate the semantic comparison of radiologist reports. We then propose a hybrid approach that combines LLMs with Named-Entity-Recognition (NER) to generate both a numerical similarity score and a qualitative interpretation. This dual output is designed to support feedback for junior radiologists and help identify common trends in report reviews. The inclusion of NER helps to ground the score in clinically relevant content by enabling a direct comparison between technical entities contained in both reports. Our use case focuses on providing structured, scalable feedback to junior doctors, allowing them to identify recurring gaps in their preliminary reports and track improvements over time. Due to the sensitive nature of radiology report data, we focus on open-source models which can be deployed on local servers to maintain patient confidentiality. We evaluate four LLMs on their ability to assess the semantic similarity of radiology reports and review the quality of their outputs. Building on these insights, we introduce Llama-EntScore - a novel method for comparing preliminary and final radiology reports using Llama 3.1 and NER to give a numerical score and interpretative feedback. While we use a base model LLM, the NER model has been pre-trained on biomedical data, enhancing the method's domain-specific relevance. The remainder of this paper is organised as follows: Sect. 2 reviews related work, Sect. 3 presents the proposed methods, Sect. 4 explains the results, and the paper concludes in Sect. 5.

2   Related Work

LLMs have been applied for a range of tasks in the radiology domain, including report generation [7], information extraction [8] and report summarisation [9,10].

Several studies have explored the use of LLMs to compare AI-generated reports with an expert-written ground truth [11–13], though comparing two human-written reports remains relatively unexplored. Zhu et al. [13] propose a method for comparing AI-generated reports with a ground truth using GPT-3.5 and GPT-4 with in-context learning. Bala et al. [14] use prompt-tuning with GPT-4 to identify missed diagnoses in preliminary radiology reports. Voinea et al. use Llama 3 to summarise MRI and CT radiology reports [15]. Doshi et al. use LLMs to simplify the impressions section of radiology reports, aiming to reduce medical jargon and improve readability for patients [16].

Several specialised models have also been developed for specific radiology tasks. CheXbert [17] is a model for labelling chest X-ray reports using a biomedically pre-trained version of BERT [18]. Tasks include marking specific diagnoses as positive, negative, or uncertain. However, this method is limited by its focus on chest X-rays only. RadCLiQ is a metric for evaluating cross-over entities between AI-generated and radiologist reports [19]. RadCLiQ combines four existing metrics, including RadGraph [6] - a language model trained on chest X-ray reports.

Recent work has explored the combination of LLMs and NER to handle tasks in the biomedical domain. Hu et al. [20] use GPT models to extract clinical entities from texts and develop task-specific prompts to refine their results. Ghali et al. [21] use in-context learning to leverage open-source LLMs for medical data extraction. Picha et al. [5] create a specific cosine similarity metric for chest X-ray reports using NER to extract key entities for calculating similarity. Zhang et al. [22] fine-tune an LLM for generating radiology report impressions from a given list of findings.

While prior work has largely focused on comparison involving AI-generated content or limited modalities such as chest X-rays, there is limited exploration of how LLMs can be used to compare two human-written radiology reports across broader imaging modalities. This paper addresses that gap by combining LLMs with NER to assess semantic similarities between preliminary and final radiology reports, offering feedback for junior radiologists during training.

3   Methodology

We propose a hybrid approach that combines NER and LLMs to compute both a semantic similarity score and an interpretable explanation of the differences between preliminary and final radiology reports. The goal is to produce feedback that aligns more closely with the nuanced understanding of a radiology expert. We begin by describing the NER component of the method.

3.1   Entity-Based Scoring via NER

NER is a widespread natural language processing (NLP) technique that is used to extract key information or clinical entities from text. In our approach, we extract entities from both the preliminary and final radiology reports and compute a cosine similarity score to assess semantic overlap based on the MCSE score from Picha et al. [5].

We begin by identifying entities that exactly match between the two reports. These are classified as matched entities. For each unmatched entity in the final report, we compute similarity scores with all unmatched entities in the preliminary report and assign the highest similarity score to the corresponding entity. The overall similarity score is then computed as:

$$Score_{NER} = \frac{C + \sum_{i=1}^{N} \max(S_j)}{T}, \quad j = 1, ..., M \tag{1}$$

where C is the number of matched entities, N and M are the number of unmatched entities in the final and preliminary reports, respectively, and T is the total number of entities in the final report.

While the NER-based similarity score offers a structured way to quantify differences between reports, it is inherently limited to surface-level comparisons. It cannot account for how an entity is used—whether a finding is negated, modified in severity, or described differently. These subtleties are often critical in clinical interpretation. To address this, we extend our method by incorporating an LLM that evaluates the contextual meaning of each shared entity, allowing us to distinguish not just presence but semantic intent.

3.2 Context-Aware Scoring with NER and LLMs

To address these limitations, we extend the method by introducing a context-sensitive scoring mechanism that incorporates the semantic use of entities, as judged by an LLM. We refer to this enhanced metric as the **Entity-Based Semantic Agreement Score (ESAS)**.

After extracting named entities from both reports, we first identify entities that are shared between the two. For each shared entity, we assess whether it is used in the same clinical context by prompting **LLaMA 3.1** with the following query:

> *Can you say whether the entity: '{entity}' is used in the same context or different context in these two texts?*
> *Text1: '{report1}'*
> *Text2: '{report2}'*
> *Please reply with a single-word answer: either 'same' or 'different'.*

Entities are then categorised based on both their presence and LLM response:

- **Matched**: Shared entities judged by the LLM to be used in the same context.
- **Mismatched**: Shared entities judged by the LLM to be used differently (e.g., differing severity or negation).
- **Missing**: Entities present only in the final report.
- **Surplus**: Entities present only in the preliminary report.

We compute the ESAS as follows:

$$\text{ESAS} = \frac{N_{\text{match}}}{N_{\text{match}} + \sum_{c \in \{\text{mismatch},\text{missing},\text{surplus}\}} W_c \cdot N_c} \tag{2}$$

Where N_{match} is the number of contextually matched entities, N_c is the number of entities in category c, where $c \in \{\text{mismatch}, \text{missing}, \text{surplus}\}$, and W_c is the penalty weight assigned to category c to reflect its clinical or educational impact.

The four categories were selected as they provide a robust framework for comparing differences that remain relevant across all scan types, and they align with the criteria radiologists typically consider when manually reviewing reports. The weighting values are designed to reflect the relative clinical and educational significance of each type of discrepancy. The weight W_{missing} corresponds to missing clinically important content in the preliminary report, which is penalised most heavily, as such omissions may indicate critical gaps in knowledge or pose risks to diagnostic accuracy. In contrast, W_{mismatch} accounts for contextual mismatches—such as incorrect severity, anatomical location, or negation—which are penalised slightly less but still reflect meaningful misunderstandings. Finally, W_{surplus} represents surplus entities, i.e., content present in the preliminary report but not retained in the final version. These are penalised the least, as they often reflect over-reporting or stylistic variation rather than substantive clinical error.

The weighting scheme is tunable and can be adapted for different training objectives—allowing for stricter evaluation in early training phases or more lenient interpretation when encouraging thorough documentation. In this way, ESAS provides a flexible, interpretable, and clinically grounded metric for assessing semantic similarity between radiology reports.

3.3   LLM-Based Interpretation of Similarity Scores

Following the calculation of the ESAS, we prompt the LLM to provide a qualitative explanation of the result. We observed that anchoring the prompt with a numerical score helps reduce hallucinations and guides the model toward more relevant, technical interpretations. The prompt used is:

> *These two reports have a similarity score of {score}. Report 1 is the final report, and Report 2 is the preliminary report.*
> *Can you give a reason for the similarity score? Focus on technical details rather than structure or style.*
> *Report 1: {report1}*
> *Report 2: {report2}*

This hybrid approach combines the structured, domain-specific strengths of NER with the interpretive capabilities of LLMs, resulting in both a quantitative similarity score and a human-readable explanation. To further support interpretability, we also provide a visualisation of the identified entities and their classification into *matched, mismatched, missing,* or *surplus.* An example of this visualisation is shown in Fig. 4.

4   Results

4.1   Dataset

Our dataset consists of 115 anonymised pairs of radiology reports, each comprising a preliminary report written by a junior radiologist and a corresponding final report reviewed by a senior radiologist. The dataset includes 56 MRI scans, 48 CT scans, 2 ultrasound scans, and 9 reports for which the imaging modality is unknown. Each report typically includes two sections: a *Findings* section, which details the observed anatomical and pathological features, and an *Impression* section, which summarises and prioritises the clinically significant findings. While our dataset is relatively small, it includes a variety of scan types from two different sources, one in the UK and one in Qatar, which supports the generalisability of our method to diverse clinical scenarios. We evaluate both the numerical similarity scores generated by our method and the quality of the corresponding LLM-generated interpretations. All data used in this study comes from a private, anonymised clinical dataset. Experiments are carried out in a Linux environment using an RTX 2080 GPU.

4.2   Evaluating LLMs

We evaluated four LLMs on their ability to compare radiology report pairs: **LLaMA-3.1-Instruct-8B** [23], **LLaMA-2-Chat-7B** [24], **Mistral-Instruct-7B** [25], and **BioMistral-7B** [26]. Our goal is to assess both the numerical similarity scores and the qualitative explanations generated by these models.

To test sensitivity to subtle semantic changes, we designed a small-scale experiment comparing (1) pairs of identical reports and (2) report pairs differing by a single negation. For example, a report stating "back muscle spasm" in the final version might have "no back muscle spasm" in the preliminary. These minimal negation changes are clinically significant but lexically similar, making them useful for evaluating contextual understanding.

To generate these modified reports, we used LLaMA-3.1 to create near-identical variations of existing reports with only one negation difference. The prompt used is:

> *Generate a report identical to this one but with one negation change, e.g.,* *"broken arm" becomes "no broken arm". Please only make one change from* *the original report.*
> `Report: {report_1}`
> *Please only output the report, no other text.*

Examples of generated pairs are shown in Fig. 1.

Each LLM was prompted to compare the two reports using the following format:

Original	Generated
Opinion:-	Opinion:-
Back muscle Spasm.	No back muscle spasm.
Degenerative changes as aforementioned with no corresponding level neural compromise.	Degenerative changes as aforementioned with corresponding level neural compromise
Opinion:-	Opinion:-
Secondary changes of back muscle spasm.	Secondary changes of back muscle spasm.
Degenerative changes with disc lesion as aforementioned more on the left side exerting mild neural compromise	Degenerative changes with no disc lesion as aforementioned more on the left side exerting mild neural compromise.
Impression:	Impression:
back muscle spasm spondylodegenerative changes with disc lesions as described above	no back muscle spasm, spondylodegenerative changes without disc lesions as described above

Fig. 1. Examples of small negation changes in report impression sections.

Please provide a similarity score out of 10 for these two reports. Focus on technical content rather than style or phrasing.

```
Score: <score>, Reasoning: <reasoning>
Report 1: {report_1}, Report 2: {report_2}
```

Table 1 shows the average similarity scores across the identical pairs and the small negation pairs.

Table 1. Average similarity scores produced by each LLM for identical and small-negation report pairs.

Model	Identical Report Score	Small Negation Score
Mistral	9.3	8.9
BioMistral	8.1	7.9
LLaMA 2	8.0	7.8
LLaMA 3.1	**9.7**	8.7

In addition to numerical scores, we analysed the textual explanations generated by each model which provide a justification for the similarity score based on the content in each report. We observed that **LLaMA 2** and **BioMistral** were more prone to hallucinations—describing differences that were not present in the input reports. While **Mistral** and **LLaMA 3.1** also occasionally produced hallucinations, their reasoning was generally more accurate and aligned with the report content.

Overall, we found that **LLaMA 3.1** generated the most detailed and contextually faithful outputs, both in terms of reasoning and numerical score reliability. As such, we selected LLaMA 3.1 as the base LLM for our hybrid Llama-EntScore method.

Despite its superior performance, LLaMA 3.1 still tended to assign overly high similarity scores to report pairs with clinically important differences—particularly in the small-negation cases. For instance, a change from "back muscle spasm" to "no back muscle spasm" would still receive a score of 8 or higher, even though the implication for diagnosis is substantial. This motivated the development of a more structured, entity-based similarity method to provide more granular and clinically grounded scoring.

4.3 Llama-EntScore Evaluation

We evaluate four similarity scoring methods for radiology report comparison: (1) a word-for-word overlap metric, (2) *LLaMA 3.1* alone, (3) cosine similarity based on NER, and (4) our proposed hybrid method, *Llama-EntScore*. The word-for-word metric computes the proportion of words in the final report that also appear in the preliminary report. NER is performed using SciSpacy [27] to extract clinically relevant terms from both reports. We choose the large core model as we found it to retrieve the highest number of entities for our report data. The implementation details of the LLaMA-based and cosine similarity approaches are described in Sects. 4.2 and 3.1, respectively. Our hybrid method, described in Sect. 3.2, combines the structured output of NER with the contextual understanding of a language model to produce a more interpretable and clinically aligned similarity score. For our experiments, the default weights in the Entity-Based Semantic Agreement Score (ESAS) are set as follows: $W_{\text{missing}} = 2$, $W_{\text{mismatch}} = 1.5$, and $W_{\text{surplus}} = 1$, reflecting their relative clinical significance. We made small adjustments to these weights and chose the values based on heuristic reasoning and alignment to ground-truth scores.

Figure 2 shows the score distributions produced by each method, and the ground truth score distributions. We compare these distributions, providing insight into how closely each method aligns with the ground truth scores assigned by radiology experts. Among the four approaches, Llama-EntScore demonstrates the closest match to expert annotations, with a wider spread of scores and better differentiation in mid-range values. Other methods tend to over-predict high similarity: the word-for-word and cosine methods cluster around perfect matches, while Llama 3.1 alone centres around 9 regardless of subtle changes.

Quantitative results are summarised in Table 2. Accuracy and related metrics are calculated by rounding predictions and comparing them to the integer-rounded ground truth scores. Therefore, a ground truth score of, for example, 9.3 and 9.2 are treated as a match. Llama-EntScore outperforms all other methods across every metric, with a 10% gain in strict accuracy over the next-best method. Its precision and recall also indicate more reliable alignment with expert judgment.

Confusion matrices in Fig. 3 illustrate the distribution of errors. While word-for-word and cosine scores skew rightward—suggesting consistent overestimation—Llama 3.1 exhibits vertical clustering near score 9. In contrast, Llama-EntScore forms a clean diagonal pattern, indicating more accurate predictions centred on true values.

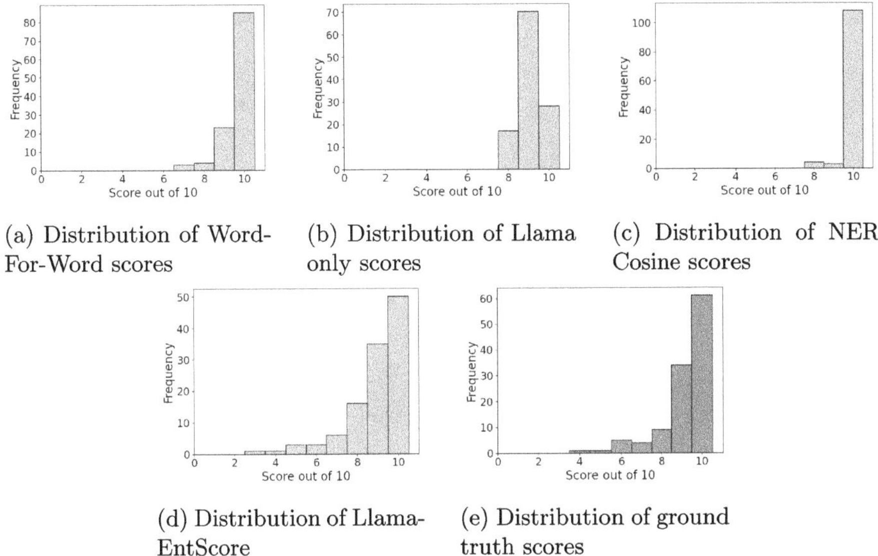

(a) Distribution of Word-For-Word scores

(b) Distribution of Llama only scores

(c) Distribution of NER Cosine scores

(d) Distribution of Llama-EntScore

(e) Distribution of ground truth scores

Fig. 2. Distribution of similarity scores for all methods. Llama-EntScore most closely follows the shape and spread of expert-annotated ground truth scores.

Table 2. Evaluation metrics for all methods. Scores are considered correct if they round to the same integer as the ground truth. ± 1 accuracy measures predictions within one point.

Method	Accuracy	Accuracy (± 1)	Precision	Recall	F1-Score
Word-For-Word	0.57	0.88	0.16	0.17	0.16
Llama 3.1	0.43	0.90	0.19	0.19	0.16
Cosine (NER Only)	0.55	0.83	0.18	0.15	0.12
Llama-EntScore	**0.67**	**0.94**	**0.38**	**0.46**	**0.40**

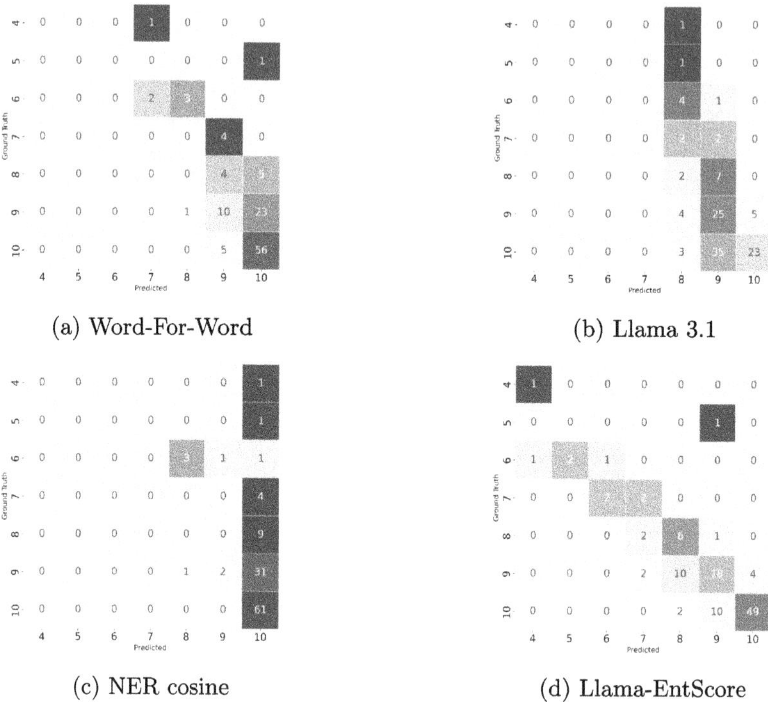

(a) Word-For-Word

(b) Llama 3.1

(c) NER cosine

(d) Llama-EntScore

Fig. 3. Confusion matrices for predicted vs. ground truth scores. Llama-EntScore produces a tighter diagonal pattern, indicating more precise estimates.

To enhance interpretability, we visualise the named entities found in each report, along with their classification as matched, mismatched, missing, or surplus (Fig. 4). This provides a concrete view of the differences driving the similarity score.

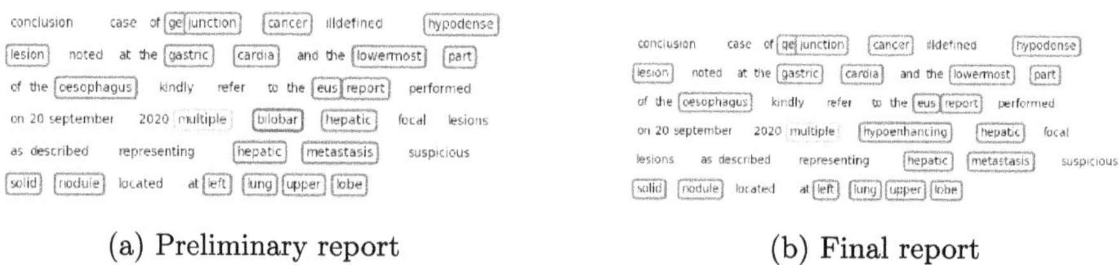

(a) Preliminary report

(b) Final report

Fig. 4. Entity comparison visualisation. Colour codes: green = matched, yellow = mismatched, red = missing, blue = surplus. (Color figure online)

Finally, Fig. 5 includes an example explanation generated by the Llama-EntScore, grounded in the content of both reports and the similarity score. This narrative feedback highlights which findings were consistent, which differed, and why the assigned score is appropriate. These explanations serve as valuable educational feedback for junior radiologists reviewing their preliminary reports.

The similarity score of 0.63 between the two reports suggests that they share a significant amount of technical content, but there are also some differences in the language and wording used. Here are some technical details that may contribute to the similarity score:

1. **Identical findings**: Both reports mention the same imaging findings, including:

* Left parietal craniotomy with 2 burr holes

* No evidence of acute intracranial hemorrhage

* Multiple ill-defined hypodensities in the basal ganglia and medial occipital lobes, likely representing chronic gliotic changes due to old infarction

* Bilateral periventricular chronic microangiopathic changes

* No focal areas showing oedematous changes to suggest acute infarction

* No extra-axial collections

* Aged-related atrophic changes in the form of prominent ventricles, cerebral sulci, and cerebellar folia

* Minimal mucosal thickening of the left maxillary antrum

* Clear rest of the paranasal sinuses and mastoid air cells

2. **Similar conclusions**: Both reports conclude that there is no evidence of acute intra- or extra-axial hemorrhage and no acute insult.

3. **Minor differences**: The main differences between the two reports

are minor and likely due to differences in wording or language usage:

* In Report 1, it is mentioned that ""no midline shift"" was observed, while in Report 2, this phrase is missing. However, this is not a significant difference.

* In Report 2, the phrase ""mass effect to suggest acute infarction"" is replaced with ""no focal areas showing oedematous changes to suggest acute infarction"". This change is minor and likely due to a difference in wording.

Fig. 5. Example LLM-generated explanation for a similarity score of 0.63 between a preliminary and final radiology report. The output highlights matched findings, similar conclusions, and minor wording differences.

5   Conclusion

We present Llama-EntScore - a semantic similarity method for comparing final and preliminary radiology reports, combining NER with Llama 3.1. Our approach generates a quantitative similarity score for tracking progress and also gives an interpretation of the score that aims to offer radiologists valuable guidance in reviewing and refining their reporting. We find that Llama 3.1 delivers the most insightful output among the LLMs tested; however, its numerical scoring lacks the precision required to meet radiologists' needs. Llama-EntScore achieves the best alignment with radiologist similarity scores across all metrics. Additionally, our numerical score can be adjusted to weigh different types of discrepancies more or less heavily, enabling customisation to align with the preferences of different radiologist groups or different report data distributions. Despite its promising performance, Llama-EntScore has some limitations. It currently handles only four categories of differences, and its effectiveness depends on the accuracy of the NER component. Unrecognised medical terms may be overlooked, affecting comparison outcomes. Additionally, on average, the hybrid method takes 90 s to process a single report pair running on an NVIDIA GeForce RTX 2080 Ti, limiting its scalability for large-scale datasets.

Future work will focus on several directions: (1) Exploring how the choice of NER model affects overall performance for example by comparing different models on their accuracy with ground truth scores. Additionally, fine-tuning the NER model on domain-specific radiology corpora to improve performance on specialised terminology, (2) Expanding the categories of entity differences in reports to include distinctions such as severity, anatomical location errors, or omitted findings. Categories could also be merged with domain knowledge, enabling identification of differences specific to the type of scan. (3) Reducing computational overhead to enable near real-time processing for clinical integration. Additionally, we plan to explore interactive feedback mechanisms, allowing radiologists to refine the system's outputs, and investigate its generalisability to other medical report types or specialties.

Acknowledgments. This work was supported by the Engineering and Physical Sciences Research Council (EPSRC) Impact Acceleration Account [grant number A100419], under the project AI Approach for Enhancing Radiology Reports.

References

1. Sharpe, R.E., Surrey, D., Gorniak, R.J., Nazarian, L., Rao, V.M., Flanders, A.E.: Radiology report comparator: a novel method to augment resident education. J. Digit. Imaging **25**, 330–336 (2012)
2. Harari, A.A., Conti, M.B., Bokhari, S.J., Staib, L.H., Taylor, C.R.: The role of report comparison, analysis, and discrepancy categorization in resident education. Am. J. Roentgenol. **207**(6), 1223–1231 (2016)
3. Kalaria, A.D., Filice, R.W.: Comparison-bot: an automated preliminary-final report comparison system. J. Digit. Imaging **29**, 325–330 (2016)
4. Alam, F., Afzal, M., Malik, K.M.: Comparative analysis of semantic similarity techniques for medical text. In: 2020 International Conference on Information Networking (ICOIN), pp. 106–109. IEEE (2020)
5. Picha, S.G., Chanti, D.A., Caplier, A.: Semantic textual similarity assessment in chest X-ray reports using a domain-specific cosine-based metric, arXiv preprint arXiv:2402.11908 (2024)
6. Jain, S., et al.: Radgraph: extracting clinical entities and relations from radiology reports, arXiv preprint arXiv:2106.14463 (2021)
7. Wang, Z., Liu, L., Wang, L., Zhou, L.: R2gengpt: radiology report generation with frozen LLMs. Meta-Radiol. **1**(3), 100033 (2023)
8. Le Guellec, B., et al.: Performance of an open-source large language model in extracting information from free-text radiology reports. Radiol. Artif. Intell. e230364 (2024)
9. Hu, D., Zhang, S., Liu, Q., Zhu, X., Liu, B.: The current status of large language models in summarizing radiology report impressions, arXiv preprint arXiv:2406.02134 (2024)
10. Liu, Z., et al.: Radiology-llama2: best-in-class large language model for radiology, arXiv preprint arXiv:2309.06419 (2023)

11. Wang, Z., Luo, X., Jiang, X., Li, D., Qiu, L.: LLM-RadJudge: achieving radiologist-level evaluation for X-ray report generation, arXiv preprint arXiv:2404.00998 (2024)
12. Xu, S., et al.: Reasoning before comparison: LLM-enhanced semantic similarity metrics for domain specialized text analysis, arXiv preprint arXiv:2402.11398 (2024)
13. Zhu, Q., et al.: Leveraging professional radiologists' expertise to enhance LLMs' evaluation for radiology reports, arXiv preprint arXiv:2401.16578 (2024)
14. Bala, W., Li, H., Moon, J., Trivedi, H., Gichoya, J., Balthazar, P.: Enhancing radiology training with GPT-4: pilot analysis of automated feedback in trainee preliminary reports. Curr. Probl. Diagnostic Radiol. (2024)
15. Voinea, V., et al.: GPT-driven radiology report generation with fine-tuned llama 3. Bioengineering **11**(10), 1043 (2024)
16. Doshi, R., Amin, K.S., Khosla, P., Bajaj, S.S., Chheang, S., Forman, H.P.: Quantitative evaluation of large language models to streamline radiology report impressions: a multimodal retrospective analysis. Radiology **310**(3), e231593 (2024)
17. Smit, A., Jain, S., Rajpurkar, P., Pareek, A., Ng, A.Y., Lungren, M.P.: Chexbert: combining automatic labelers and expert annotations for accurate radiology report labeling using bert, arXiv preprint arXiv:2004.09167 (2020)
18. Devlin, J., Chang, M.-W., Lee, K., Toutanova, K.: Bert: pre-training of deep bidirectional transformers for language understanding. In: Proceedings of the 2019 Conference of the North American Chapter of the Association for Computational Linguistics: Human Language Technologies, Volume 1 (Long and Short Papers), pp. 4171–4186 (2019)
19. Yu, F., et al.: Evaluating progress in automatic chest X-ray radiology report generation. Patterns **4**(9) (2023)
20. Hu, Y., et al.: Improving large language models for clinical named entity recognition via prompt engineering. J. Am. Med. Inform. Assoc. ocad259 (2024)
21. Ghali, M.-K., Farrag, A., Sakai, H., Baz, H.E., Jin, Y., Lam, S.: Gamedx: generative AI-based medical entity data extractor using large language models, arXiv preprint arXiv:2405.20585 (2024)
22. Zhang, L., et al.: Constructing a large language model to generate impressions from findings in radiology reports. Radiology **312**(3), e240885 (2024)
23. Dubey, A., et al.: The llama 3 herd of models, arXiv preprint arXiv:2407.21783 (2024)
24. Touvron, H., et al.: Llama 2: open foundation and fine-tuned chat models, arXiv preprint arXiv:2307.09288 (2023)
25. Jiang, A.Q., et al.: Mistral 7b, arXiv preprint arXiv:2310.06825 (2023)
26. Labrak, Y., Bazoge, A., Morin, E., Gourraud, P.A., Rouvier, M., Dufour, R.: Biomistral: a collection of open-source pretrained large language models for medical domains, arXiv preprint arXiv:2402.10373 (2024)
27. Neumann, M., King, D., Beltagy, I., Ammar, W.: Scispacy: fast and robust models for biomedical natural language processing, arXiv preprint arXiv:1902.07669 (2019)

From Scarce to Sufficient: Imaginary Image-Like Features via Diffusion Models for Imbalanced Medical Data

Halan Villarroel[1], Christian Pieringer[2] , and Billy Peralta[1]

[1] Facultad de Ingeniería, Universidad Andres Bello, Santiago, Chile
`h.villarroeldueas@uandresbello.edu`, `billy.peralta@unab.cl`
[2] Facultad de Ingeniería y Negocios, Universidad de Las Américas, Santiago, Chile
`cpieringer@udla.cl`

Abstract. The growing use of artificial intelligence in modern medicine poses significant challenges due to the lack and imbalance of high-quality clinical data, which arises from ethical, logistical, and technical limitations. We propose a framework that addresses this challenge by utilizing diffusion models, a state-of-the-art generative technique, to provide high-fidelity and diverse synthetic features rather than images. The framework implements a complete pipeline that combines feature extraction with pre-trained convolutional networks and a U-Net-based diffusion model to generate new clinical representations in scenarios with strong imbalance, such as melanoma diagnosis. Through rigorous experiments on two real datasets, we demonstrated that this technique consistently improves critical standard performance metrics compared to classical augmentation methods such as replication or Gaussian noise, positioning it as an effective and reproducible solution for data augmentation. The document describes the method and empirical results that validate this approach, presenting a practical and replicable method to enhance the robustness of models used in medical applications. Our results suggest that synthetic feature generation with diffusion not only enhances classification in limited clinical contexts but also paves the way for future research in domains where data access remains a persistent bottleneck.

Keywords: Data augmentation · Diffusion models · Melanoma diagnosis

1 Introduction

Artificial intelligence has become a transformative tool in the healthcare industry., with applications ranging from diagnostic assistance to treatment planning [1]. However, the development of robust predictive systems faces a critical bottleneck: the scarcity of high-quality clinical data constrained by ethical, logistical, and economic factors that make large-scale clinical data collection difficult. Moreover, the inherent variability in medical images, resulting from differences

C. Tommasino et al. (Eds.): AIBIO 2025, CCIS 2696, pp. 132–148, 2026.
https://doi.org/10.1007/978-3-032-17216-7_11

in acquisition protocols, equipment specifications, and patient characteristics, exacerbates the challenge of training machine learning models with effective generalization capabilities [2]. In this context, diffusion models have emerged as promising tools for synthetic data generation, offering unprecedented capabilities in maintaining clinical fidelity while addressing data scarcity [3].

Current data generation techniques, particularly GANs and traditional augmentation methods, show significant limitations in preserving clinical semantics while generating diverse samples [4,5]. These limitations become especially critical in scenarios with severe class imbalance, such as rare disease diagnosis, where traditional methods fail to capture the underlying distribution of minority classes [4]. Crucially, augmentation models typically aim to recreate realistic instances, which can be complex to synthesize [6] and also require more computational resources [7]. An alternative possibility is to augment the data by considering the features of the images directly, where it becomes feasible to explore diffusion models applied to this task.

We propose an approach for synthetic data generation that operates directly on latent feature representations extracted from pre-trained convolutional networks, explicitly targeting the generation of clinically relevant features rather than complete images [8]. Our implementation utilizes a U-Net-based diffusion model architecture, trained on compressed representations from a ResNet-18 pre-trained model, to generate synthetic features that preserve the semantic structure of medical data [3]. We validate our approach through extensive experiments on two real-world skin cancer datasets, employing a comprehensive evaluation protocol that includes standard metrics such as accuracy, precision, recall, and F1-score. The proposed methodology demonstrates significant improvements over traditional augmentation techniques, particularly in scenarios of severe class imbalance, while maintaining computational efficiency and clinical relevance.

This work makes three key contributions to the application of machine learning in the medical domain: *i*) a feature-level diffusion approach that reduces computational complexity compared to full-image generation while preserving clinical relevance; *ii*) a detailed methodology for generating features using efficient diffusion model libraries; and *iii*) a comprehensive evaluation framework for synthetic data generation in imbalanced medical scenarios, benchmarking against state-of-the-art methods. Results demonstrate that our proposed approach significantly improves classification performance in data-limited settings, offering a practical solution for real-world medical applications [1]. The findings suggest promising avenues for further research in domains where data access remains a persistent challenge, particularly in rare disease diagnosis and personalized medicine [9]. Through this work, we aim to contribute to the development of more robust and accessible AI systems for medical applications, while addressing the critical challenge of data scarcity in healthcare.

The remainder of the document is organized as follows: Sect. 2 reviews related work in medical data augmentation and diffusion models. Section 3 presents our proposed methodology, detailing the feature extraction and diffusion-based generation pipeline. Section 4 describes the experimental setup, including datasets, evaluation metrics, and implementation details. Section 5 presents and analyzes the results, comparing our approach with traditional augmentation methods. Section 6 the implications of our findings and their potential impact on medical AI applications. Finally, Sect. 7 concludes the paper and outlines future research directions.

2   Related Work

The scarcity and imbalance of medical data represent fundamental challenges in developing robust AI systems for healthcare. Recent advances in deep learning have primarily focused on two complementary approaches: few-shot learning strategies to minimize dependency on large labeled datasets and synthetic data generation through advanced generative models. This section critically examines six seminal works that have shaped these methodological directions, highlighting their contributions and limitations in addressing the scarcity of medical data.

Few-shot learning approaches have emerged as promising solutions for medical image analysis with limited data. Wang et al. [10] pioneered a novel meta-learning framework that emulates human-like image variation imagination capabilities. Their approach introduces a "hallucinator" network that generates synthetic examples through meta-learning, achieving significant improvements in classification accuracy for underrepresented classes. While their method shows promising results, it faces challenges in maintaining anatomical consistency and clinical relevance in generated variations, particularly for complex medical conditions.

Medical image segmentation presents unique challenges in few-shot scenarios due to the need for precise anatomical boundaries. Ye and Zhang [9] address this challenge through an innovative, dynamic self-training framework that generates pseudo-labels for continuous medical data streams. Their method shows significant effectiveness in the applications of CT and MRI., maintaining temporal consistency while avoiding model collapse. However, the method's performance heavily depends on the quality of initial annotations and may struggle with highly variable anatomical structures.

Early disease detection in ophthalmology requires precise analysis of subtle features in fundus images. Kim, Zuallaert, and Neve [11] contribute to this field by developing a hybrid architecture that combines deep convolutional networks with matching network techniques. Their idea enables the successful preservation of high-resolution details, which are crucial for glaucoma diagnosis and achieving a competitive performance with limited training data. However, the method's effectiveness depends on the high-quality image acquisition and the need for expert validation in clinical settings.

The evolution of generative models has significantly impacted medical image synthesis, with diffusion models emerging as a breakthrough technology in this field. Ho, Jain, and Abbeel [3] introduce Denoising Diffusion Probabilistic Models (DDPM), establishing a new paradigm in generative modeling through a progressive Gaussian noise process and learned denoising phase. The diffusion model architecture achieves unprecedented levels of sample quality and diversity in high-dimensional spaces, offering a stable alternative to adversarial training. However, the computational complexity of the noise process and the need for extensive training data remain significant challenges for medical applications.

The control and precision of generated medical images are crucial for clinical applications. Dhariwal and Nichol [12] address this challenge by introducing classifier guidance in diffusion models, achieving superior performance in both diversity and precision compared to GANs. The explicit control over generated classes is a critical requirement for diagnostic applications. However, the method's effectiveness in preserving subtle pathological features and maintaining anatomical consistency requires further validation in clinical settings.

Computational efficiency and clinical relevance are paramount in the generation of medical images. Rombach et al. [8] address these requirements through Latent Diffusion Models (LDMs), which operate in compressed feature spaces while maintaining high visual quality. In addition, they include a multi-resolution pyramidal strategy, which is particularly effective for high-resolution medical images and offers a practical solution for clinical deployment. However, the performance in preserving fine-grained pathological features and its adaptability to different medical imaging modalities require further investigation.

Recent advances in medical image synthesis have demonstrated the potential of diffusion models in dermatology applications. Akrout et al. [13] presents a comprehensive study on diffusion-based data augmentation for skin disease classification, showing that these models can maintain classification accuracy even when trained on fully synthetic datasets. In addition, Sagers et al. [14] demonstrate that diffusion models can effectively generate high-quality skin images without compromising classifier performance.

Furthermore, Abbasai [15] extend these findings to other medical imaging domains, highlighting the versatility of diffusion-based approaches in generating clinically relevant synthetic data. These studies collectively validate the effectiveness of diffusion models in generating medical images and maintaining clinical relevance and diagnostic accuracy in synthetic samples.

We summarize existing approaches that have made a significant progress in addressing medical data scarcity. However, they primarily focus on generating complete images or synthesizing labels in highly supervised environments. Our work introduces a different perspective by generating intermediate features directly applicable to classifier training, offering several advantages: reduced computational complexity maintained clinical relevance, and effective class imbalance mitigation without complete image reconstruction. Through comparative evaluation with classical augmentation techniques, we demonstrate that our diffusion-based approach achieves better performance in key metrics, particularly in severely imbalanced scenarios.

3   Proposed Method

The core of our proposal utilizes a UNet-based diffusion model, chosen for its proven effectiveness in capturing hierarchical features and preserving spatial relationships, which are essential for maintaining the clinical relevance of medical data representations. This architecture is specifically adapted to operate on fixed-dimension vector representations instead of raw images, ensuring a balance between computational efficiency and the preservation of meaningful clinical features. The choice of a UNet architecture is motivated by its characteristic encoder-decoder structure, which effectively extracts and reconstructs complex features at multiple scales, making it particularly well-suited for modeling the intricate variations present in medical data.

To exploit the inductive biases inherent in image-based diffusion architectures and enhance visual interpretability, we reshape the extracted feature vectors into two-dimensional formats, effectively treating them as synthetic images. *Can these image-like representations enable more effective learning by allowing direct reuse of well-established visual diffusion architectures?* This formulation allows the adoption of diffusion models originally designed for image generation, such as DDPMs, which are well-suited for learning spatially coherent representations. Furthermore, this approach facilitates future integration with image-level generative tasks, potentially enabling a unified framework for both feature and image synthesis.

In summary, our proposed method synthesizes features directly in latent space using diffusion models, enabling effective data augmentation under severe class imbalance. First, we describe the general architecture of the diffusion model used. Finally, we outline the full generation pipeline—from feature extraction and preprocessing to training and evaluation.

3.1   Diffusion Model Architecture

Following the framework of Denoising Diffusion Probabilistic Models (DDPM) [3], our approach implements a forward process in which Gaussian noise is progressively added to the input data over a fixed number of T time steps. This process transforms clean inputs into a sequence of increasingly noisy versions, defined as a Markov chain:

$$q(x_t|x_{t-1}) = \mathcal{N}(x_t; \sqrt{1 - \beta_t}x_{t-1}, \beta_t\mathbf{I}), \tag{1}$$

where $\beta_t \in (0, 1)$ denotes a variance schedule controlling the noise magnitude at each step t. By choosing a well-designed schedule, we ensure that x_T approaches an isotropic Gaussian distribution, effectively decoupling semantic structure from noise.

Using the law of total probability, the marginal distribution $q(x_t|x_0)$ can be computed in closed form:

$$q(x_t|x_0) = \mathcal{N}(x_t; \sqrt{\bar{\alpha}_t}x_0, (1 - \bar{\alpha}_t)\mathbf{I}), \tag{2}$$

where $\bar{\alpha}_t = \prod_{s=1}^{t}(1 - \beta_s)$ represents the cumulative product of retained signal. This expression enables efficient sampling of noisy training pairs (x_t, x_0) without computing the full chain.

The reverse process is learned by estimating $p_\theta(x_{t-1}|x_t)$, a denoising step parameterized by a neural network (here, a UNet) trained to predict the added noise. This is commonly rephrased as minimizing the expected error in estimating the noise ϵ:

$$\mathcal{L}_{\text{simple}} = \mathbb{E}_{x_0,\epsilon,t}\left[\|\epsilon - \epsilon_\theta(x_t, t)\|^2\right], \tag{3}$$

where $x_t = \sqrt{\bar{\alpha}_t}x_0 + \sqrt{1 - \bar{\alpha}_t}\epsilon$ and $\epsilon \sim \mathcal{N}(0, \mathbf{I})$.

Finally, the model approximates the full data likelihood by minimizing a variational upper bound:

$$\min_\theta \mathbb{E}_{q(x_{0:T})}\left[-\log p_\theta(x_0|x_{1:T})\right]. \tag{4}$$

This formulation ensures that the learned reverse process progressively refines x_t toward a high-fidelity sample x_0, enabling the generation of realistic and semantically meaningful synthetic features.

3.2   Feature Generation Pipeline

Our framework includes a comprehensive feature generation pipeline that systematically transforms raw medical images into balanced, clinically relevant feature sets. This pipeline is visually represented in Fig. 1, illustrating the flow of data from preprocessing to final evaluations. The process consists of four interconnected stages, each carefully designed to maintain data integrity, enhance feature representation, and address the challenge of class imbalance in medical datasets:

1. **Preprocessing and Initial Feature Extraction:** In this stage, we begin by selecting the appropriate dataset and performing crucial preprocessing steps, including resizing, tensor conversion, and normalization. These steps ensure consistent dimensionality and intensity distributions across the dataset, reducing computational overhead while maintaining clinical feature integrity. We then employ a pre-trained ResNet18 network (with the final layer removed) to extract 512-dimensional feature vectors from the standardized images, creating a robust and informative feature representation that balances information preservation and efficiency.

2. **Dataset Refinement and Feature Preparation:** After extracting features, the pipeline proceeds with dataset filtering and the construction of data loaders that organize the features into coherent subsets. Features are separated by class and re-normalized to ensure consistency in the learning process. Additionally, repetitive sampling and normalization of the features are performed to increase dataset richness and further balance class distributions. This step also includes the conversion of features into an image-like representation, leveraging the flexibility of deep learning frameworks.

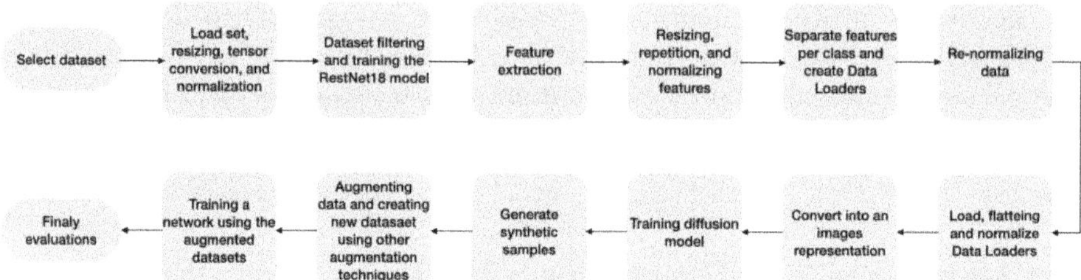

Fig. 1. Our proposed pipeline architecture illustrates the transformation from original medical images to the generation of synthetic features. We demonstrate how our class-trained diffusion model processes and enhances the data flow, highlighting the key stages of feature extraction and augmentation.

3. **Diffusion Model Training:** The core of the pipeline involves training a UNet-based diffusion model on the prepared feature representations. This model undergoes class-specific training, with 400 iterations per class, to learn the reconstruction of clean features from progressively noisier inputs. This learning process approximates the reverse denoising diffusion process, enabling the model to generate new, high-quality feature samples that preserve the underlying clinical semantics.

4. **Synthetic Generation, Augmentation, and Evaluation:** In the final stage, the trained diffusion model generates synthetic feature samples specifically for the minority classes, which are then seamlessly integrated with the original features to create a balanced dataset. Additional augmentation techniques are optionally applied to further enhance data diversity. A new network is subsequently trained using this enriched dataset, and its performance is rigorously evaluated against state-of-the-art benchmarks to confirm the effectiveness of our approach.

This four-stage pipeline ensures that the generated synthetic data not only addresses the inherent class imbalance problem but also maintains the clinical relevance and diversity essential for robust predictive modeling. The modularity and adaptability of this framework make it particularly suitable for real-world medical applications where data scarcity and class imbalance remain persistent challenges.

4   Experimental Design

4.1   Datasets and Imbalance Problem

Our experiments leverage three distinct subsets derived from the same publicly available dermatological image dataset [15] to thoroughly evaluate the effectiveness of the proposed model. This section describes the analysis, preprocessing, training, and validation procedures implemented to ensure a rigorous assessment.

The first subset contains 204 images categorized as either *Cancer* or *Non-Cancer*, with a pronounced class imbalance—162 images in the majority class and only 42 in the minority class, highlighting the need for advanced augmentation techniques.

The second subset expands the evaluation to 4,094 images, offering a more balanced distribution of *benign* and *malignant* cases and providing a broader context for validating the model's generalization capabilities.

Finally, the third subset encompasses 10,605 images, representing a large-scale scenario to assess the robustness and scalability of the proposed methodology in a more comprehensive setting.

By systematically analyzing these three related yet distinct subsets, we ensure that our conclusions are robust, generalizable, and relevant to real-world medical data challenges.

4.2 Statistical Analysis of Data

Descriptive statistics were calculated to understand the nature of the images. The mean pixel intensity was 103.60, with a median of 100.0, indicating a prevalence of dark tones. The standard deviation reached 49.79, suggesting moderate variability in intensities. Additionally, 6,325 outliers were identified, distributed as expected in complex medical images. Finally, a slight right skewness and negative kurtosis were observed, confirming a skewed and dispersed distribution. Figure 2 shows a set of representative images, where the first row illustrates benign instances and the second row contains malignant examples.

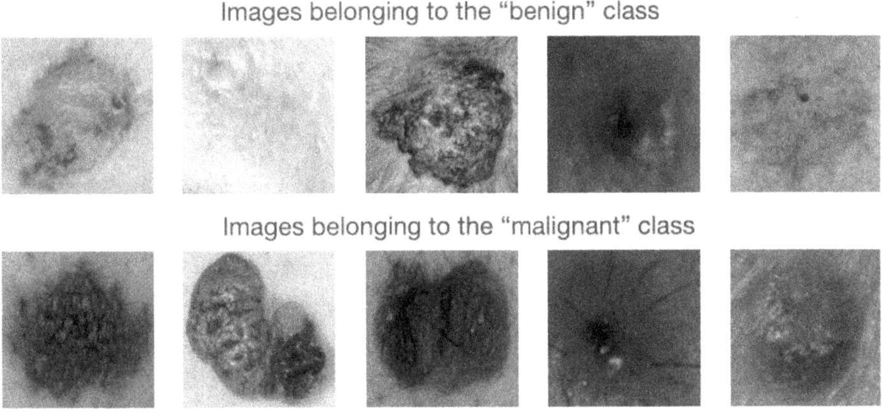

Fig. 2. Representative examples from our dataset show both positive (Cancer) and negative (Non-Cancer) cases. We selected these images to demonstrate the visual complexity and variability that our model must be able to handle.

4.3 Preprocessing and Feature Extraction

All images were resized to a fixed resolution and normalized to maintain consistency between samples. Subsequently, a pre-trained ResNet18 network was used as a feature extractor, omitting its final layer to obtain 512-dimensional vector representations. This approach ensures significant semantic reduction of information, allowing the diffusion model to operate on a more compact but clinically representative space.

4.4   Diffusion Model Training

We trained a separate diffusion model for each class in order to better capture class-specific feature distributions and structural variability. Each model was trained for 400 iterations using a U-Net backbone with increasing resolution multipliers $(1, 2, 4, 8)$ and a base dimensionality of 64. To enhance efficiency and representation power, we enabled *flash attention* modules [16] within the UNet, improving both training stability and memory usage. This architectural choice allows the network to operate over multiple feature scales and capture both local and global patterns essential for synthetic feature reconstruction.

During training, we employed a continuous validation scheme using a hold-out partition comprising 20% of the training set. We monitored loss dynamics and qualitative outputs across iterations to ensure convergence and prevent over-fitting. All models were implemented using the `denoising-diffusion-pytorch` library by Lucidrains [17], which provides modular and optimized components for efficient diffusion-based generation.

4.5   Generation and Evaluation

After training, the model generated synthetic samples for the minority class, converting them back into vectors and combining them with the original features to balance the dataset. Meanwhile, we compared the model's performance with other traditional augmentation techniques, such as replication and Gaussian noise [18]. We used metrics such as precision, recall, F1-score, and a confusion matrix to evaluate our model on a completely independent test set.

4.6   Partition and Validation

We applied a `hold-out` strategy with an $80/20$ division to separate the validation data from our training set. We kept the test set independent to evaluate generalization effectively. This configuration allowed us to achieve reliable and consistent performance evaluations under realistic conditions of limited data.

5   Results

This section presents the results of our experiments, providing a comprehensive assessment of the proposed diffusion-based synthetic feature generation approach across three dermatological image datasets. We systematically evaluate the performance improvements of our method compared to traditional augmentation techniques, using standard classification metrics such as accuracy, precision, recall, and F1-score. Furthermore, we analyze how these improvements manifest across different dataset scales and class imbalance scenarios, offering a better understanding of the practical implications of our approach in real-world medical applications. In order to obtain the replicability of experiments, a demo source code of experiments is available in https://drive.google.com/file/d/1EOOPvDcAhcG4TJzSSeGzEXIS24lTXoPw/view?usp=sharing.

5.1   Evaluation Protocol

Our evaluation framework systematically assesses the effectiveness of the proposed diffusion-based augmentation approach across multiple dimensions. We conducted comprehensive experiments on three dermatological datasets of varying scale and class balance, comparing our method against three established augmentation techniques: replication, Gaussian noise [18], and scaled noise. We carefully select evaluation metrics to capture different aspects of the model's performance: accuracy for overall correctness, precision for controlling false positives, recall for sensitivity to minority classes, and F1-score for balanced performance assessment.

5.2   Results on Skin-Data-Cancer

In the first dataset, which includes 204 images (162 Non-Cancerous and 42 Cancerous), we observed a significant class imbalance that poses a clear challenge for classifier performance. This imbalance amplifies the tendency of models to favor the majority class, often at the expense of correctly identifying minority class samples. As shown in Table 1, our approach, which leverages diffusion-augmented data, demonstrates a substantial improvement over the baseline model trained on unbalanced data, with the *F1 score* improving by 20.8%. This significant gain highlights the efficacy of synthetic feature generation in mitigating the class imbalance problem.

Furthermore, our method consistently outperforms other straightforward strategies, such as simple replication of minority samples and the addition of Gaussian noise, in terms of both precision and recall. This suggests that the synthetic features generated by our diffusion-based pipeline contribute meaningfully to the classifier's ability to generalize beyond the limited real data available. Such improvements are especially relevant in medical applications, where the correct identification of minority class instances (e.g., cancerous cases) can be critical for clinical decision-making. This dataset thus serves as a compelling example of how diffusion-augmented data can effectively address the dual challenges of data scarcity and class imbalance in real-world medical contexts.

5.3   Results on Skin Cancer Dataset

In our second dataset, which contains 4,094 images divided into benign and malignant classes, we observed that the introduction of synthetic features generated by the diffusion model led to consistent improvements across all key metrics.

Table 1. Summary of the performance metrics for the Skin-data-Cancer dataset. This results allow us to demonstrate the effectiveness of our diffusion-based approach in improving classification outcomes by 20.8%.

Technique	Accuracy	Precision	Recall	F1 Score
Original - Original Model	0.599	0.728	0.599	0.532
Original - Diffusion Data	0.747	0.766	0.747	0.740
Original - Replication	0.643	0.746	0.643	0.586
Original - Scaled Noise	0.677	0.748	0.677	0.642
Original - Gaussian Noise	0.728	0.766	0.728	0.712

As shown in Table 2, the approach achieved an *F1 score* of 0.809 while maintaining a high precision of 0.867. This demonstrates the method's ability to enhance minority class detection and overall model robustness in a more balanced yet challenging dataset. The consistent performance gains indicate that the proposed diffusion-based feature generation method generalizes well beyond the initial dataset, offering practical value for diverse real-world medical applications.

Table 2. Report of the classification performance on the expanded Skin Cancer dataset. We highlight the consistent improvements achieved across all evaluation metrics.

Technique	Accuracy	Precision	Recall	F1 Score
Original - Original Model	0.744	0.863	0.744	0.768
Original - Diffusion Data	0.791	0.867	0.791	0.809
Original - Replication	0.749	0.864	0.749	0.773
Original - Scaled Noise	0.735	0.863	0.735	0.761
Original - Gaussian Noise	0.754	0.864	0.754	0.777

5.4   Results on Skin Cancer Test (Expanded)

We further evaluated our approach on an expanded dataset comprising 10,605 images to test its scalability and robustness in a large-scale scenario. As summarized in Table 3, while the observed performance differences were more modest compared to the smaller datasets, our diffusion-based method still achieved the best balance between precision and recall. These subtle yet consistent improvements underscore the ability of the approach to maintain competitive performance even when faced with more complex and better-balanced data distributions, reinforcing its practicality for real-world medical applications.

Table 3. Summary of the performance metrics for the large-scale Skin Cancer Test dataset. Results show the robustness of our method in handling extensive medical data.

Technique	Accuracy	Precision	Recall	F1 Score
Original - Original Model	0.853	0.856	0.853	0.852
Original - Diffusion Data	0.854	0.856	0.854	0.854
Original - Replication	0.852	0.855	0.852	0.851
Original - Scaled Noise	0.852	0.855	0.852	0.851
Original - Gaussian Noise	0.853	0.855	0.853	0.852

5.5 Feature Images

We conducted a detailed visual analysis of the feature representations generated by each model, comparing them to the original feature distributions. These visualizations reveal consistent and discernible differences between the classes, with our diffusion-based approach producing a broader and more evenly distributed feature space. Importantly, these differences are maintained across all models, with only minimal variations observed. This suggests that the synthetic features generated by our diffusion model enhance class separability and preserve the underlying semantic structure of the data. Figures 3, 4, 5, 6 and 7 illustrate these feature spaces, providing further evidence of the improvements achieved through our proposed methodology.

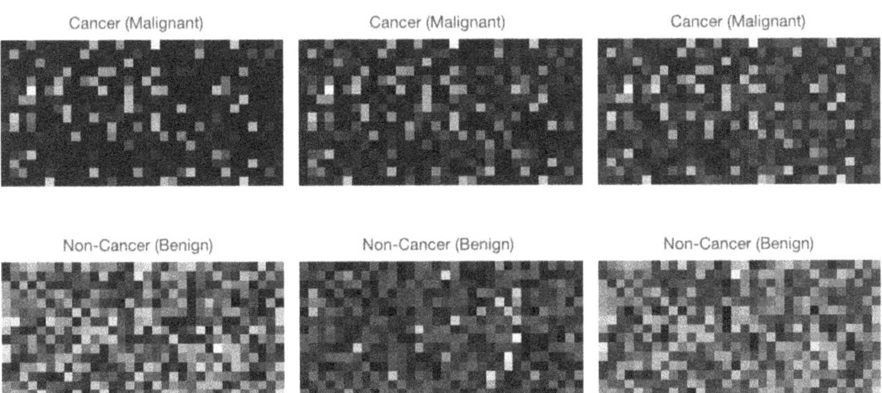

Fig. 3. We visualize the feature representations obtained from the original embedding neural network (ResNet-18), showing the natural distribution of features before augmentation.

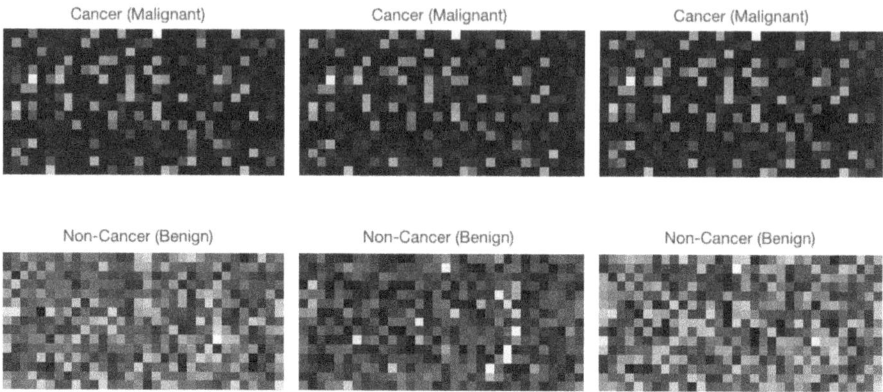

Fig. 4. Our diffusion-based method's feature visualization demonstrates enhanced feature diversity while maintaining clinical relevance, as evidenced by the improved classification metrics.

5.6 Highlights and Significance

Our comprehensive evaluation across three datasets of varying scales and balances shows that our diffusion-based approach consistently proves effective. We observed significant improvements in F1-score, with the most remarkable enhancement of 39.1% (from 0.532 to 0.740) in the severely imbalanced Skindata-Cancer dataset. Additionally, we achieved a balanced enhancement of precision and recall across all datasets. Our method demonstrated stable performance across different dataset sizes, maintaining consistent improvements even in the larger dataset of 10,605 images. Importantly, we preserved clinical relevance in the generated features. These results validate our approach as an effective and

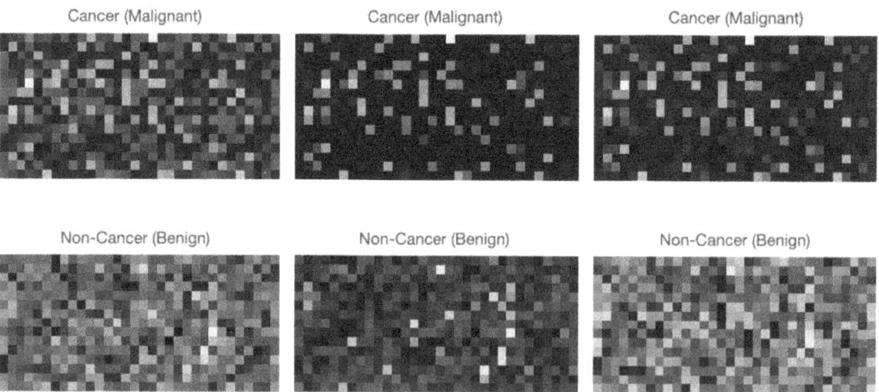

Fig. 5. Feature visualization from the replication method reveals limited diversity in the augmented features, explaining its lower performance in our experiments.

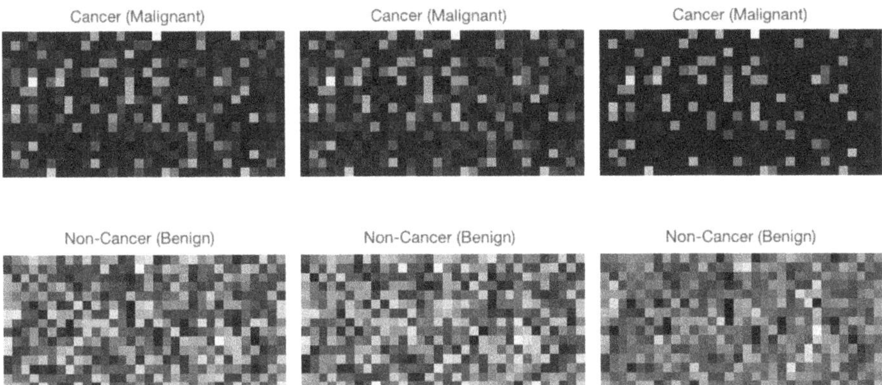

Fig. 6. The Gaussian noise method's feature visualization illustrates how random perturbations impact the feature space, resulting in suboptimal augmentation outcomes.

robust solution for medical data augmentation, particularly in challenging situations such as class imbalance and data scarcity. We highlight that our method maintains strong performance across different scales, underlining its potential for real-world clinical applications.

6   Discussion

Our study provides solid empirical evidence that diffusion models serve as a highly effective alternative for generating synthetic data in medical contexts facing data scarcity. We specifically differentiate our approach from previous works by operating directly in the feature space. This strategy helps us avoid the computational complexity associated with complete image generation and facilitates seamless integration into supervised classification workflows.

One of our main contributions is validating that the synthetic vectors generated by diffusion preserve the semantic structure of clinical data while introducing sufficient diversity. This diversity enhances the generalization capacity of classifiers trained with these vectors. We observed consistent improvements in key metrics such as F1-score and recall, which are especially critical in imbalanced scenarios.

Additionally, we conducted a systematic comparison with traditional augmentation techniques, such as sample replication and Gaussian noise addition. While these methods offer quick benefits, they often generate redundancy or introduce non-informative noise. In contrast, our diffusion approach enables more controlled and adaptive generation, making it particularly suitable for domains where clinical precision is crucial.

However, we acknowledge certain limitations of our study. First, we validated our model on only two datasets related to dermatological images. Although our results are promising, we recognize the need to explore its applicability to

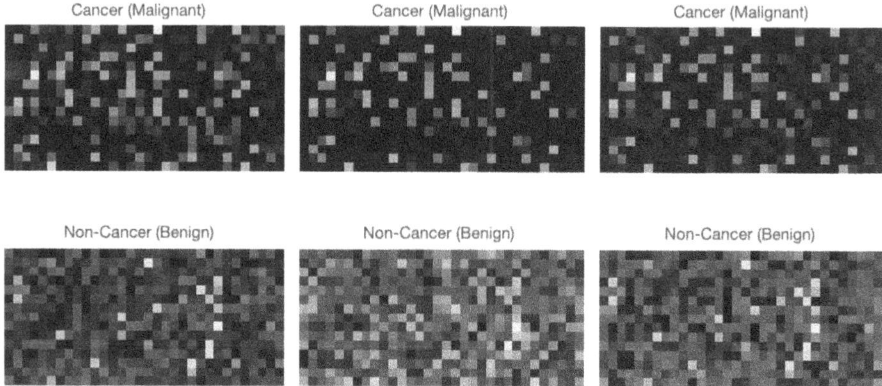

Fig. 7. The feature visualization of our scaled Gaussian noise approach illustrates the impact of controlled noise addition on feature distribution, showing moderate improvements over basic noise addition.

other clinical modalities, such as X-ray images, magnetic resonance imaging, and histopathology. Second, the conversion process between image and feature spaces introduces some dependence on the extractor—in our case, ResNet18. Future research should focus on exploring more specific or domain-adaptive variants to address this dependency.

7   Conclusions

We present a data augmentation approach that leverages diffusion models operating directly in the feature space, specifically designed to tackle class imbalance in medical data. The method proposed a rigorous pipeline of extraction, generation, and evaluation that allows us to demonstrate that synthetic features not only increase the volume of data but also enhance the semantic representativeness and diversity of the training set. Our results reveal significant improvements across all evaluated datasets, with the most notable being a 39.1% increase in F1-score (from 0.532 to 0.740) in the severely imbalanced Skin-data-Cancer dataset.

Our empirical results on three dermatological datasets demonstrate that our proposed model consistently outperforms traditional augmentation methods, achieving notable improvements in key metrics, including precision (up to 0.867), recall, and F1-score. These findings validated our central hypothesis and open new opportunities for integrating this model into critical medical tasks where data access is limited. The model's ability to maintain performance across different scales (from 204 to 10,605 images) suggests potential for real-world clinical applications.

Nevertheless, our study also reveals important limitations that should inform our future research. Our current implementation relies on ResNet18 as a feature extractor, highlighting the need for more domain-specific architectures. Furthermore, our validation is confined to dermatological images, indicating a necessity to explore applicability across various medical modalities.

As we look ahead, we should focus on three main directions: (1) developing domain-adaptive feature extractors specifically designed for medical imaging, (2) extending our validation to other clinical domains such as X-ray imaging and histopathology, and (3) investigating how we can integrate diffusion models with self-supervised learning techniques to reduce our dependence on labeled data further. By combining these improvements, we can create even more robust and efficient solutions for medical data augmentation.

Together, our work contributes to the state of the art in deep learning for medicine by proposing an effective, efficient, and clinically plausible tool to address the persistent challenge of limited and imbalanced data while providing clear directions for future research and development.

Acknowledgments. B. Peralta appreciates the support of the National Center for Artificial Intelligence CENIA FB210017, Basal ANID and Chilean National Agency for Research and Development (ANID), Fondecyt grant ID 1241882.

References

1. Topol, E.J.: High-performance medicine: the convergence of human and artificial intelligence. Nat. Med. **25**(1), 44–56 (2019)
2. Litjens, G., et al.: A survey on deep learning in medical image analysis. Med. Image Anal. **42**, 60–88 (2017)
3. Ho, J., Jain, A., Abbeel, P.: Denoising diffusion probabilistic models. arXiv preprint arXiv:2006.11239 (2020)
4. Frid-Adar, M., et al.: GAN-based synthetic medical image augmentation for increased CNN performance in liver lesion classification. Neurocomputing **321**, 321–331 (2018)
5. Chen, Y., et al.: Generative adversarial networks in medical image augmentation: a review. Comput. Biol. Med. **144**, 105382 (2022)
6. Woodland, M., et al.: Evaluating the performance of StyleGAN2-ADA on medical images. In: International Workshop on Simulation and Synthesis in Medical Imaging, pp. 142–153. Springer, Heidelberg (2022)
7. Huang, T., Lee, I., Ahn, E., et al.: Computationally efficient diffusion models in medical imaging: a comprehensive review. arXiv preprint arXiv:2505.07866 (2025)
8. Rombach, R., et al.: High-resolution image synthesis with latent diffusion models. In: Proceedings of the IEEE/CVF Conference on Computer Vision and Pattern Recognition, pp. 10684–10695 (2022)
9. Ye, Z., Zhang, W.: A dynamic few-shot learning framework for medical image stream mining based on self-training. EURASIP J. Adv. Signal Process. 2023(1), 1–16 (2023). https://asp-eurasipjournals.springeropen.com/articles/10.1186/s13634-023-00999-z
10. Wang, Y.X., et al.: Low-shot learning from imaginary data. In: Proceedings of the IEEE Conference on Computer Vision and Pattern Recognition (CVPR), pp. 7278–7286 (2018). https://openaccess.thecvf.com/content_cvpr_2018/html/Wang_Low-Shot_Learning_From_CVPR_2018_paper.html

11. Kim, M., Zuallaert, J., De Neve, W.: Few-shot learning using a smallsized dataset of high-resolution fundus images for glaucoma diagnosis. In: Proceedings of the 2nd International Workshop on Multimedia for Personal Health and Health Care, pp. 89–92 (2017). https://dl.acm.org/doi/10.1145/3132635.3132650
12. Dhariwal, P., Nichol, A.: Diffusion models beat GANs on image synthesis. Adv. Neural. Inf. Process. Syst. **34**, 8780–8794 (2021). https://papers.nips.cc/paper/2021/hash/49ad23d1ec9fa4bd8d77d02681df5cfa-Abstract.html
13. Akrout, M., et al.: Diffusion-based data augmentation for skin disease classification: Impact across original medical datasets to fully synthetic images. In: International Conference on Medical Image Computing and Computer-Assisted Intervention, pp. 99–109. Springer, Heidelberg (2023). https://doi.org/10.1007/978-3-031-53767-7_10
14. Sagers, L.W., et al.: Augmenting medical image classifiers with synthetic data from latent diffusion models. arXiv preprint arXiv:2308.12453 (2023)
15. Abbasai, F.: Skin Data Cancer (2022). https://www.kaggle.com/datasets/faresabbasai/skin-cancer. Accessed 29 Nov 2024
16. Dao, T., et al.: Flashattention: fast and memory-efficient exact attention with io-awareness. Adv. Neural. Inf. Process. Syst. **35**, 16344–16359 (2022)
17. Wang, P.: Denoising Diffusion Pytorch (2021). https://github.com/lucidrains/denoisingdiffusion-pytorch. Accessed 04 June 2025
18. Taniguchi, T., Furuta, R.: Learning gaussian data augmentation in feature space for one-shot object detection in manga. In: Proceedings of the 6th ACM International Conference on Multimedia in Asia, pp. 1–8 (2024)

Flow-Based Synthetic Data Generation: A Unified Approach for Biomedical Tasks

Tommaso Giacometti[1,2], Nico Curti[1,2(✉)], Adriano Zaghi[3], Daniel Remondini[1,2], and Gastone Castellani[3,4]

[1] Department of Physics and Astronomy, University of Bologna, Bologna, Italy
`nico.curti2@unibo.it`
[2] INFN Istituto Nazionale di Fisica Nucleare, Bologna, Italy
[3] Department of Medical and Surgical Sciences, University of Bologna, Bologna, Italy
[4] IRCCS Azienda Ospedaliero-Universitaria di Bologna, Bologna, Italy

Abstract. Synthetic data is becoming an essential tool for overcoming data scarcity, class imbalance, and privacy concerns in all research fields, including the biomedical one. We propose Conditional Flow Matching (CFM) as a unified and efficient generative framework applicable across diverse biomedical modalities. CFM leverages conditional optimal transport to model complex data distributions, while maintaining architectural simplicity and computational efficiency. We evaluate CFM on three representative tasks of increasing complexity in data structure. We show applications to the following case studies: (i) mixed type tabular data from Acute Myeloid Leukemia patient cohort, including genomic landscape and survival data; (ii) standard 2D RGB biomedical images belonging to discrete classes, given by slit lamp eye images stratified according to conjunctival hyperemia; (iii) 3D Computed Tomography chest volumes for lung segmentation. Across these use cases, CFM generates high-fidelity, anatomically and semantically consistent samples, validated according to *ad hoc* metrics and pipelines. Despite some modality-specific limitations, our results highlight CFM's versatility and potential as a general-purpose synthetic data generation framework for healthcare and biomedical domains.

Keywords: Biomedical data · Synthetic data · Conditional Flow Matching · Synthetic Validation · Image Synthesis

1 Introduction

Synthetic data generation offers a promising solution to key challenges in data-driven biomedical research, particularly in settings where data is scarce, sensitive, or difficult to collect. In healthcare, legal, ethical, and budget constraints often limit data availability and small or biased datasets can effect model generalization, especially for rare pathologies. Synthetic data can augment limited datasets, correct class imbalances, and enhance model training.

C. Tommasino et al. (Eds.): AIBIO 2025, CCIS 2696, pp. 149–156, 2026.
https://doi.org/10.1007/978-3-032-17216-7_12

To be acceptable and useful, synthetic data must satisfy four core criteria: fidelity (indistinguishable from real samples), diversity (coverage of real-world variability), utility (usefulness for downstream tasks), and privacy (ensuring patient anonymity). Recent generative modeling approaches, such as Generative Adversarial Networks, Variational Autoencoders, and diffusion models, have shown promise in biomedical applications; however, limitations in stability, interpretability, or diversity have so far prevented widespread adoption [2,6,8]. Diffusion models, as also shown by Kazerouni et al. [6], combine the advantages of VAEs and GANs by producing high-quality synthetic samples while preserving stable and reliable convergence during training. Their main limitation, however, lies in their inherently slow generation process.

A more recent flow-based approach to generative tasks is Conditional Flow Matching (CFM), introduced by Lipman et al. [7], which uses optimal transport to generate high-fidelity synthetic data and provides better performance and significantly faster sampling than diffusion models. Yazdani et al. [12] applied CFM to generate 2D and 3D synthetic grayscale medical images (echocardiograms and MRIs) using 2D and 3D Convolutional Neural Network (CNN) architectures, respectively. Similarly, Fuchi et al. [3] demonstrated the effectiveness of rectified flows for tabular data across multiple benchmarks.

In this work, we adopt CFM [7,10] as a unifying framework for synthetic data generation and investigate its capabilities across three diverse biomedical use cases of increasing complexity:

- generation of tabular patient data with mixed binary and continuous features;
- class-conditional synthesis of 2D RGB conjunctival hyperemia images;
- generation of 3D lung computed tomography (CT) volumes employing a 2D CNN approach to maintain computational efficiency.

To assess the quality of the generated samples for each use case, we employed dedicated pipelines and evaluation metrics.

Through these applications, we demonstrate CFM's potential to produce high-quality synthetic data that satisfies key evaluation criteria and supports ongoing research in data augmentation, model development, and controlled simulation of pathological conditions.

2   Materials and Methods

For all the three different applications, the CFM models are implemented through suitably designed neural networks, customized to the specific data type and task requirements. In each case, the network is trained to approximate the vector field governing the CFM process [7,10], enabling the generation of synthetic samples that follow the learned data dynamics. The models are trained using optimal transport (OT) flows to map the source Gaussian distributions to the target data distributions, with the flow being class-conditioned for the 2D Conjunctival Hyperemia Images and 3D Lung CT tasks.

2.1   Tabular Data

The Acute Myeloid Leukemia (AML) dataset includes 2017 subjects described by 175 variables. Each subject's mutational profile is captured by 155 binary features, indicating the presence or absence of specific genetic or cytogenetic mutations. In addition, there are six pairs of variables (one continuous and one binary per pair) describing the patient's clinical trajectory. The continuous variables record the follow-up time until the patient either left the study (censored) or experienced a specific event (e.g., remission, relapse, or death). The corresponding binary variables indicate whether the event occurred. For instance, the binary variable for relapse is set to 1 if the patient relapsed, and 0 if the patient was censored. The dataset further contains 8 clinical and demographic features, including platelet count, sex, and age. This database, taken from [9], has been used to define AML subtypes and to assign patients to different risk categories.

To model the vector field underlying the data generation process, we use a Feedforward Neural Network (FNN) comprising three hidden layers, totaling approximately $2.7 \cdot 10^5$ parameters. Each layer employs LeakyReLU activation function, with dropout ($p = 0.1$) applied for regularization (Fig. 1a). Temporal information is integrated via an auxiliary FNN with a single hidden layer of 20 neurons and a Sigmoid activation function, which modulates the output of the main network multiplicatively, as shown in Fig. 1a.

A synthetic dataset comprising the same number of patients as the real tabular dataset is generated to evaluate the model's ability to approximate the underlying probability distribution.

2.2   2D Conjunctival Hyperemia Images

The eye dataset consists of 1299 RGB slit lamp images collected at varying resolutions from 350 subjects at the IRCCS Azienda Ospaliero-Universitaria di Bologna [1]. Each image was manually cropped to focus on the scleral region, resized to $224 \times 224 \times 3$, and globally labeled by an expert clinician using a standard hyperemia grading scale from 1, minimal redness (low inflammation), to 5, severe redness (severe inflammation). Pixel intensities are rescaled to the $[-1, 1]$ range to facilitate model training.

The dataset is affected by a strong class imbalance, with clinically significant redness levels 4 and 5 representing only 29% of samples. This motivates the need for synthetic data generation to balance class representation, particularly in underrepresented but clinically important categories.

To model the data, a U-Net architecture is employed with four downsampling layers and residual blocks, augmented with a multi-head cross-attention mechanism inserted between the residuals blocks and the downsampling/upsampling layers, to capture both local and global features while preserving morphological structure. Redness class conditioning is introduced through embedding layers integrated into the network.

To assess the quality of the synthetic data, 600 images are generated per class, creating a balanced dataset. Two classifiers are trained, one on synthetic data and the other on real data, and evaluated on a real test set for comparative performance.

Additionally, image sequences are generated by fixing the initial noise vector of the CFM process across redness levels, enabling visual inspection of morphological consistency as redness increased.

2.3   3D Lung CT

The lung dataset used in this study is sourced from The Cancer Imaging Archive (TCIA) [4], consisting of 61 chest CT scans in 3D. These scans vary in slice thickness, spatial resolution, and the number of axial slices, totaling 4682 axial images with a resolution of 512×512 pixels. On average, each scan comprises approximately 77 slices, equating to roughly $20 \cdot 10^6$ voxels per volume. This dataset was selected for its anatomical clarity and manageable size, providing a suitable starting point for early-stage experimentation on complex thoracic structures.

To address inconsistencies in slice count and resolution, a standard preprocessing pipeline is implemented. Lung regions are segmented using the lungmask tool [5], and only slices containing lung portions were retained. Each volume is resampled to a fixed shape of $30 \times 256 \times 256$, ensuring spatial consistency while adjusting the average axial spacing to approximately 8.6 mm. Voxel intensities, originally in Hounsfield Units (HU), are, finally, clipped between -1024 and 1024 and rescaled to the range $[-1, 1]$.

Due to the high computational demands of 3D processing, training is performed on individual 2D axial slices instead of full 3D volumes. Each axial index is treated as a class label, resulting in 30 distinct classes. This allowed the model to remain lightweight and computationally tractable, effectively reducing the task requirements to a conditional 2D generation problem.

The used model architecture was adapted from that applied in the above 2D image synthesis, with an expanded embedding layer to accommodate the larger number of class labels.

During generation, axial slices are sequentially synthesized by varying the class index, while keeping fixing the initial noise vector of the CFM process. This strategy, similar to that used in conjunctival redness synthesis, promotes spatial continuity across the axial dimension.

To evaluate the quality of the synthetic lung data, the Fréchet inception distance (FID) between real and generated slices is computed. Anatomical coherence is further validated through segmentation using TotalSegmentator [11] and lungmask [5], confirming the presence of realistic and continuous 3D structures.

3   Results

3.1   Tabular Data

To qualitatively assess the distributional similarity between real and synthetic samples, a Principal Component Analysis (PCA) is performed on the real dataset and subsequently used to project both real and synthetic data into a shared latent space (Fig. 1b).

In addition, Shannon entropy is employed as a quantitative measure of data variability. The real dataset exhibited an entropy of $H = 11.0$, while the synthetic dataset show reduced variability with an entropy of $H = 7.6$.

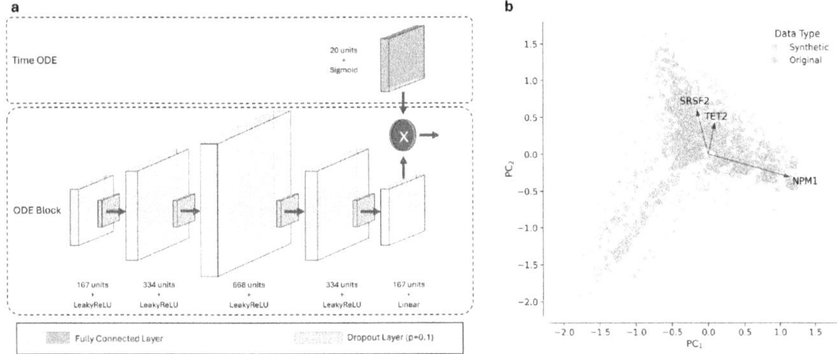

Fig. 1. (**a**) FNN model structure used to learn the vector field to generate tabular data. (**b**) PCA projection of real and synthetic datapoints and directions of the three most important features.

3.2   2D Conjunctival Hyperemia Images

Figure 2a and 2b presents the confusion matrices for the two classifiers trained respectively on real and synthetic data. The reported performances are quantified considering a test set composed only by real images.

Figure 2c illustrates a sequence of synthesized eye images that maintain morphological consistency while varying in redness level, demonstrating the model's ability to control class-conditional features while preserving anatomical structure.

3.3   3D Lung CT

The FID computed for a set of 50 3D synthetic generated patients results to be $\text{FID} = 15.2$.

Most generated lung volumes exhibit coherent 3D anatomical structure, with clear differentiation between lobes and plausible spatial continuity. An example of a complete lung volume, reconstructed from slice-wise segmentations, is shown in Fig. 3.

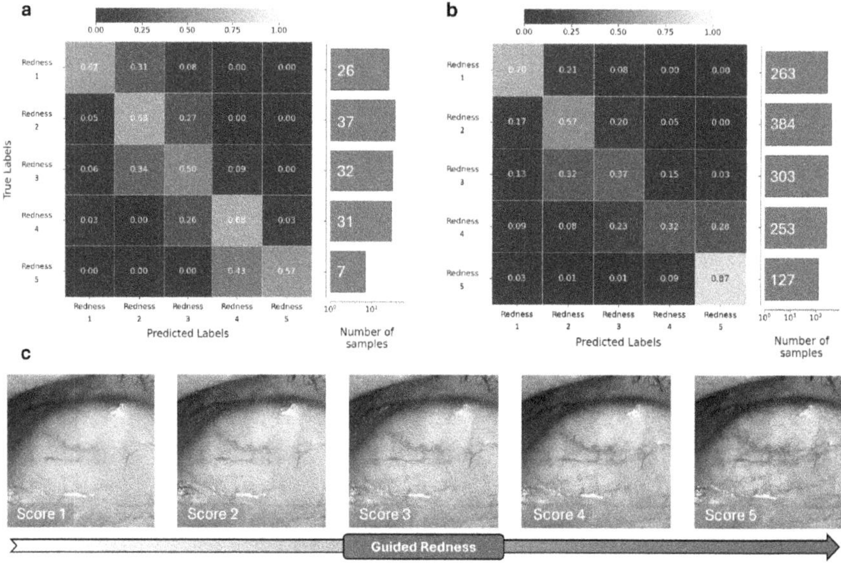

Fig. 2. (**a**) Confusion matrix of the classifier trained and tested on real data (sample counts per redness class shown). (**b**) Confusion matrix of a classifier trained on synthetic data and tested on real images. (**c**) Representative synthetic eye images across redness levels, preserving morphology.

4   Discussion

This study highlights the flexibility of CFM as a generative framework for biomedical data across diverse modalities and levels of complexity. Our results demonstrate that CFM can model conditional distributions with high fidelity while preserving both structural and semantic integrity.

In the tabular domain, the overlap between real and synthetic samples in the PCA space (Fig. 1b) indicates that our simple FNN-based CFM effectively captures the main modes of variation in the original data. However, the reduced entropy observed in the synthetic dataset suggests a loss of variability, likely due to the mismatch between the Gaussian prior and the binary nature of most features. Ongoing works are exploring more expressive priors, as proposed in [3], to better accommodate mixed data types and close the entropy gap.

For 2D conjunctival hyperemia images, the model successfully generates morphologically consistent samples across redness levels, demonstrating precise class conditional control. Notably, classifiers trained solely on synthetic data generalized compatibly to real images, even in the underrepresented redness classes, confirming the utility of CFM for class-aware data augmentation. Moreover, the generation of redness progression sequences with fixed initial noise showcases the model's ability to isolate and modulate specific visual attributes while preserving identity (Fig. 2c).

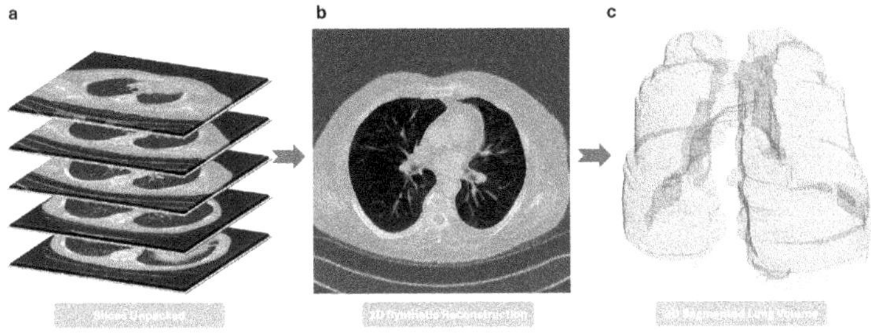

Fig. 3. (a) Generated 2D slices. (b) Central slice contoured with segmentation predicted by lungmask. (c) 3D reconstruction of the segmented lung's lobes.

Similarly, in the case of 3D lung CT scans, although individual slices are generated independently, sometimes resulting in discontinuities along the sagittal and coronal planes, the use of axial position as a conditioning variable helps maintain spatial coherence across the axial dimension. Most generated volumes exhibit anatomically realistic structures, including accurate lobe boundaries, as confirmed by automated segmentation tools (Fig. 3c). These findings demonstrate the potential of CFM for medical image synthesis, with ongoing work aimed at improving inter-slice continuity and incorporating pathological features. Moreover, the FID achieved is consistent with that reported in [12] for 3D structures, despite our dataset being one order of magnitude smaller. In general, an FID of 15.2 suggests the synthetic images are reasonably close to real ones and suitable for exploratory tasks (e.g., augmentation or benchmarking), though clinical use would require lower FID and further task-specific validation (e.g., SSIM, PSNR, etc.).

Across all modalities, CFM enables efficient, class-conditional sampling, making it a strong candidate for standardized biomedical data synthesis.

5   Conclusion

We presented CFM as a unified and efficient framework for synthetic biomedical data generation, demonstrating its applicability across tabular, 2D, and 3D modalities. CFM produces high-fidelity, class-controllable samples that preserve structural and semantic integrity, despite its architectural simplicity.

While some limitations remain, such as reduced variability in binary tabular data and slice, wise discontinuity in volumetric synthesis, our results underscore CFM's potential for tasks like class balancing and data augmentation. Future work will focus on richer priors, enhanced 3D consistency, and pathology-aware generation. CFM thus offers a scalable and interpretable approach to synthetic data generation in biomedical research.

Acknowledgments. GC acknowledged for the support by European Union—Horizon 2020/23 program GenoMed4All project n° 101017549, Synthema project n° 1101095530, Innovative Health initiative (IHI), Synthia project n° 101172872, AIRC Foundation (Associazione Italiana per la Ricerca contro il Cancro, Milan Italy-Project n° 26216) and PRIN (Ministry of University & Research, Italy-Project 20229B28PE).

Disclosure of Interests. The authors have no competing interests to declare that are relevant to the content of this article.

References

1. Curti, N., et al.: A fully automated pipeline for a robust conjunctival hyperemia estimation. Appl. Sci. **11**(7) (2021). https://doi.org/10.3390/app11072978
2. Ehrhardt, J., Wilms, M.: Chapter 8 - autoencoders and variational autoencoders in medical image analysis. In: Burgos, N., Svoboda, D. (eds.) Biomedical Image Synthesis and Simulation. The MICCAI Society book Series, Academic Press (2022). https://doi.org/10.1016/B978-0-12-824349-7.00015-3
3. Fuchi, M., Takagi, T.: Rectable: fast modeling tabular data with rectified flow (2025). https://arxiv.org/abs/2503.20731
4. Grove, O., Berglund, A.E., Schabath, M.B., Aerts, H.J.W.L., Dekker, A., Wang, H., et al.: Data from: quantitative computed tomographic descriptors associate tumor shape complexity and intratumor heterogeneity with prognosis in lung adenocarcinoma (2015). https://doi.org/10.7937/K9/TCIA.2015.A6V7JIWX
5. Hofmanninger, J., Prayer, F., Pan, J., Röhrich, S., Prosch, H., Langs, G.: Automatic lung segmentation in routine imaging is primarily a data diversity problem, not a methodology problem. Eur. Radiol. Exp. **4**(1), 50 (2020). https://doi.org/10.1186/s41747-020-00173-2
6. Kazerouni, A., et al.: Diffusion models in medical imaging: a comprehensive survey. Med. Image Anal. **88**, 102846 (2023). https://doi.org/10.1016/j.media.2023.102846
7. Lipman, Y., Chen, R.T.Q., Ben-Hamu, H., Nickel, M., Le, M.: Flow matching for generative modeling (2023). https://arxiv.org/abs/2210.02747
8. Saad, M.M., O'Reilly, R., Rehmani, M.H.: A survey on training challenges in generative adversarial networks for biomedical image analysis (2023). https://arxiv.org/abs/2201.07646
9. Tazi, Y., Ossa, J.A., Zhou, Y.Y., Bernard, E., Thomas, I., Gilkes, A., et al.: Unified classification and risk-stratification in acute myeloid leukemia. Nat. Commun. (2022). https://doi.org/10.1038/s41467-022-32103-8. http://hdl.handle.net/10541/625598
10. Tong, A., Fatras, K., Malkin, N., Huguet, G., Zhang, Y., Rector-Brooks, J., et al.: Improving and generalizing flow-based generative models with minibatch optimal transport (2024). https://arxiv.org/abs/2302.00482
11. Wasserthal, J., Breit, H.C., Meyer, M.T., Pradella, M., Hinck, D., Sauter, A.W., et al.: Totalsegmentator: robust segmentation of 104 anatomic structures in ct images. Radiol. Artif. Intell. **5**(5) (2023). https://doi.org/10.1148/ryai.230024
12. Yazdani, M., Medghalchi, Y., Ashrafian, P., Hacihaliloglu, I., Shahriari, D.: Flow matching for medical image synthesis: bridging the gap between speed and quality (2025). https://arxiv.org/abs/2503.00266

Multimodal Techniques

Multimodal Machine Learning Architecture for Predictive Diagnosis and Treatment of Ophthalmic Diseases

Asmaa Abdelmawgoud[1,2] and Andrea M. Tonello[1(✉)]

[1] University of Klagenfurt, 9020 Klagenfurt am Wörthersee, Austria
`andrea.tonello@aau.at`
[2] Arab Academy for Science and Technology, 21919 Alexandria, Egypt

Abstract. Artificial intelligence (AI) and deep learning (DL)-based systems have gained significant attention in the diagnosis of ophthalmic diseases, including cataracts, glaucoma, diabetic retinopathy (DR), and age-related macular degeneration (AMD). This work proposes a multimodal system that integrates fundus images, patient demographics, and clinical pathology data, achieving a diagnostic accuracy of 98.78% and a treatment recommendation accuracy of 93.19%. The model employs EfficientNet-B0 for image feature extraction and dense layers for processing tabular clinical data. Comprehensive evaluations using confusion matrices and ROC analysis demonstrate robust performance. The proposed system provides clinicians with an objective, data-driven decision-support tool that enhances diagnostic precision and improves patient outcomes.

Keywords: artificial intelligence · deep learning · ophthalmic diseases · fundus images · treatment recommendation · image processing · multimodal system · patient demographics · clinical pathology

1 Introduction

Ophthalmic diseases such as cataracts, diabetic retinopathy (DR), age-related macular degeneration (AMD), and glaucoma are among the leading causes of blindness worldwide. In Europe, individuals aged 40 to 75 are particularly affected, bearing a significant burden of vision-threatening conditions [25]. According to 2024 estimates [26], approximately 39 million cases of cataracts, glaucoma, DR, AMD, and retinal detachment were reported within this age group. Although cataracts account for nearly 60% of these cases, the majority of preventable blindness—estimated at 82%—is attributed to AMD (8.6 million cases), DR (3.4 million cases), and glaucoma (3.9 million cases). These conditions also impose a substantial financial burden, accounting for 71% of the European Union's total expenditure on eye diseases, which amounts to approximately €14.3 billion annually in healthcare costs and lost productivity.

© The Author(s), under exclusive license to Springer Nature Switzerland AG 2026
C. Tommasino et al. (Eds.): AIBIO 2025, CCIS 2696, pp. 159–176, 2026.
https://doi.org/10.1007/978-3-032-17216-7_13

Recent advancements in AI-powered screening tools (e.g., Retina AI's optimized algorithms) [1] offer a promising avenue for early detection and intervention. Tailored specifically for individuals aged 40–75, these tools have demonstrated high accuracy in identifying early-stage AMD and proliferative DR. When integrated into workplace and primary care screening initiatives, they could potentially prevent up to 58% of severe vision loss cases (EURETINA Age-Stratified Analysis, 2024) [26]. Early detection is essential for preventing blindness; however, traditional diagnostic methods often rely on subjective interpretation of medical images, which can lead to inconsistencies and diagnostic delays [27].

Optical Coherence Tomography (OCT), a widely adopted non-invasive imaging technique, provides high-resolution cross-sectional views of the retina and is instrumental in diagnosing eye diseases. However, its interpretation requires specialized clinical expertise, which is not always readily accessible. Another key diagnostic method is fundus photography—a painless procedure that captures detailed images of the eye's interior structures, critical for assessing eye health. With the advent of artificial intelligence (AI) and deep learning techniques [1], automated image analysis has become increasingly accurate and efficient, significantly enhancing diagnostic capabilities.

While most existing approaches in the literature focus primarily on image-based analysis, this paper proposes an AI-driven algorithm that integrates multiple data modalities—including images (particularly, fundus ones), and patient medical records, e.g., blood test results and demographic data, to predict eye diseases, as illustrated in Fig. 1. Furthermore, the algorithm also serves as a recommender system, providing personalized treatment plans based on patient-specific data. The objective of this study is to bridge the gap between AI research and clinical application by equipping ophthalmologists with a robust decision-support tool that enhances diagnostic accuracy and supports improved patient outcomes.

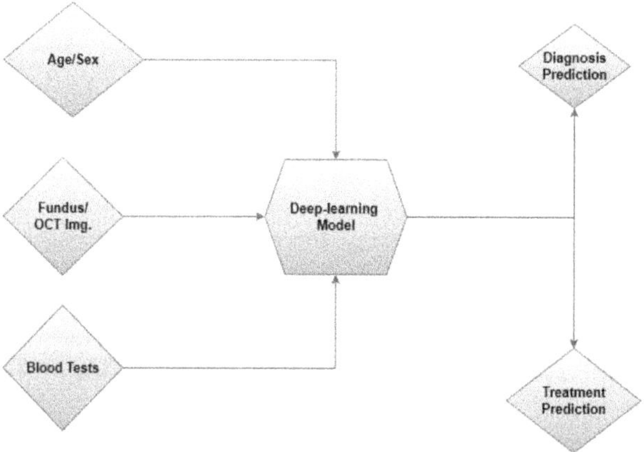

Fig. 1. Proposed AI model for diagnosis and treatment of ophthalmic diseases.

The remainder of the paper is structured as follows. Section 2 reviews related work. Section 3 highlights the key contributions of our study. Section 4 details the proposed methodology and deep learning framework. Section 5 presents and analyzes the results. Finally, Sect. 6 concludes the paper and outlines directions for future research.

2 Related Work

In this section, we present an overview of relevant literature organized by specific ophthalmic diseases. While comprehensive surveys exist [1–3], we provide an updated summary of recent contributions in Tables 1–4.

2.1 Diabetic Retinopathy (DR)

Diabetic retinopathy (DR) remains one of the leading causes of visual impairment worldwide. Numerous studies have applied deep learning (DL) techniques for DR detection using fundus photography, OCT, or hybrid modalities. For instance, Liu et al. [1] employed EfficientNet-B5 on a dataset of more than 1.17 million fundus images, achieving an AUC between 0.88 and 0.96. Similarly, Dai et al. [1] combined ResNet with Mask R-CNN, improving early-stage DR detection with an AUC range of 0.92–0.97 across 666,383 images. Table 1 summarizes key contributions in this domain.

Table 1. Summary of AI-based methods for diabetic retinopathy (DR) detection. Abbreviations: AUC – area under curve; Sens – sensitivity; Spc – specificity; DME – diabetic macular edema; TFI – traditional fundus images; SFI – smartphone fundus images; VT – vision-threatening; Ref. – referable; Acc – accuracy.

Contribution	Year	Data	AI Model	Task	Avg. AUC/Sens/Spc
Refat et al. [2]	2025	Hybrid (5 sources)	VR-FuseNet (VGG19 + ResNet50V2)	DR grading	−/−/Acc: 91.8
Dalahma et al. [3]	2025	4.1K FI	CNN + Gaussian preprocessing	DR detection	−/−/Acc: 95.5
Zhu et al. [4]	2023	EyePACS FI	MobileNet CNN	DR detection	−/−/Acc: >90%
Bora et al. [5]	2023	575.3K FI	Inception-V3	DR detection	0.79/−/−
Li et al. [6]	2023	717K FI	ResNet-50 + self-attention	DR progression	−/−/−
Liu et al. [1]	2022	1M TFI	EfficientNet-B5	DME detection	0.92/85.5/77
Dai et al. [1]	2021	660K TFI	ResNet + R-CNN	DR grading	0.94/90.6/82.2
Lee et al. [1]	2021	300K TFI	7 AI models (5 vendors)	Referable DR detection	−/68.5/72.1
Araujo et al. [1]	2020	100K TFI	Gaussian MI framework	Referable DR detection	−
Heydon et al. [1]	2020	120K TFI	EyeArt v2.1	Referable DR detection	−/95.7/54.0
Natarajan et al. [1]	2019	57K SFI	Medios AI (DL system)	Referable DR detection	−/97.9/83.6
Li et al. [1]	2018	177K TFI	Inception-V3	Vision-threatening DR	0.97/94.7/95.0
Ting et al. [1]	2017	189K TFI	VGGNet	DR detection	0.94/95.2/82.7 (Ref.); 0.96/100/91 (VT)
Gulshan et al. [7]	2016	140K TFI	Inception-V3	Referable DR detection	0.99/92.2/96.2
Takahashi et al. [8]	2015	9.9K TFI	GoogleNet	DR detection	−/−/Acc: 81.0

2.2 Glaucoma

Glaucoma is a progressive optic neuropathy that leads to irreversible vision loss and often remains asymptomatic in its early stages. Early detection is therefore essential, as timely intervention can prevent further damage. OCT and fundus imaging are the most widely used modalities for glaucoma screening. Recent advances in AI have enhanced diagnostic performance. For instance, Xiong et al. [1] developed FusionNet, a multimodal algorithm trained on 2,463 OCT–fundus image pairs, achieving AUCs between 0.87 and 0.92 for glaucomatous optic neuropathy (GON) detection. Zhang et al. [10] employed ResNet-34 with more than 7,000 fundus images, reporting an AUC of 0.94. Table 2 summarizes notable contributions in this area.

Table 2. Summary of AI-based methods for glaucoma detection. Abbreviations: GON – glaucomatous optic neuropathy; POAG – primary open-angle glaucoma; PACG – primary angle-closure glaucoma; NIA – narrow iridocorneal angles; PAS – peripheral anterior synechiae; VF – visual field; OCT – optical coherence tomography; TFI – traditional fundus images; UWFI – ultra-widefield fundus images; Acc – accuracy; F1 – F1-score.

Contribution	Year	Data	AI Model	Task	AUC/Sens/Spc
Roy et al. [9]	2025	EyePACS-AIROGS-light V2	DeepEyeNet	Glaucoma detection	−/−/Acc: 95%
Zhang et al. [10]	2024	7K FI	ResNet-34 + U-Net	GON detection	0.94/−/−
Islam et al. [11]	2023	ORIGA, STARE, REFUGE	ResNet-50 + InceptionV3	Early detection	−/−/F1: 0.98
Wang et al. [12]	2023	Not specified	ResNet-50 + U-Net	Glaucoma classification	−/−/Acc: 98% (Train); 96% (Test)
Xiong et al. [1]	2022	5K VF/OCT	FusionNet	GON detection	0.89/79.3/87.7
Al Mahrooqi et al. [13]	2022	EyePACS-AIROGS	Multi-view CNN	Glaucoma classification	0.92/−/−
Fan et al. [1]	2022	66K TFI/VF	ResNet-50	POAG detection	0.83/81.0/82.5
Li et al. [1]	2021	1M ANT-SEG	ResNet-34/50	PACG (NIA, PAS) detection	0.94/86.7/87.8 (NIA); 0.90/90.0/89.0 (PAS)
Dixit et al. [1]	2021	600K VF + 300K Clinical	CMNN	Glaucoma progression	0.91/−/−
Medeiros et al. [1]	2021	180K OCT/TFI	ResNet-50	GON progression	0.91/−/−
Li et al. [1]	2020	23K UWFI	InceptionResNet-V2	GON detection	0.99/97.8/96.3
Yousefi et al. [1]	2020	31.5K VF	PCA + Manifold Learning	Glaucoma monitoring	−/77.0/94.0
Ran et al. [1]	2019	7K OCT	ResNet	GON detection	0.93/84.0/87.5
Martin et al. [1]	2018	435 Clinical (IOP, SUB)	Random Forest	POAG detection	0.76/−/−
Li et al. [1]	2018	48K TFI	Inception-V3	GON detection	0.99/95.6/92.0
Asaoka et al. [1]	2016	279 VF	DFFNN	Pre-glaucoma detection	0.93/77.8/90.0

2.3 Age-Related Macular Degeneration (AMD)

Age-related macular degeneration (AMD) is a degenerative retinal disease that primarily affects the macula, leading to central vision loss in individuals over the age of 50. It is broadly classified into two forms: dry (atrophic) and wet (neovascular). OCT imaging plays a central role in identifying structural abnormalities such as drusen accumulation and subretinal fluid.

Several AI-based approaches have been proposed for AMD detection and progression monitoring. For example, Potapenko et al. [1] trained a deep learning model on 106,840 OCT images, achieving an AUC between 0.90 and 0.98. Similarly, Hwang et al. [1] employed ResNet-50 with OCT images, reporting AUC values between 0.98 and 0.99 for different AMD subtypes. Table 3 summarizes notable contributions in this field.

Table 3. Summary of AI-based methods for AMD detection and classification. Abbreviations: CNV – choroidal neovascularization; SSNPID – self-supervised non-parametric instance discrimination; Acc – accuracy.

Contribution	Year	Data	AI Model	Task	AUC/Sens/Spc
Ngoc Thien Le et al. [14]	2024	Unspecified FI	Vision Transformer (ViT)	AMD classification	-/-/Acc: 97%
Potapenko et al. [1]	2022	106K OCT	Temporal DL model	CNV detection in AMD	0.94/88.1/90.2
Yellapragada et al. [1]	2022	101K TFI	SSNPID	AMD severity classification	-/-/Acc: 87%
Rakocz et al. [1]	2021	2K OCT	SLIVER-net	AMD progression detection	0.91/-/-
Yim et al. [1]	2020	130K OCT	U-Net + PredNet	Predict conversion to wet AMD	0.82/-/-
Hwang et al. [1]	2019	35.9K OCT	VGG16, Inception-V3, ResNet-50	AMD subtype classification	0.98/-/Acc: 92%
Keel et al. [1]	2019	143K TFI	Inception-V3	AMD detection	0.98/98.4/95.0
Peng et al. [1]	2019	59K TFI	Inception-V3	AMD classification	0.95/-/-
Grassmann et al. [1]	2018	125K TFI	Ensemble of 6 NNs	AMD classification	-/-/Acc: 63%
Kermany et al. [1]	2018	208K OCT	Inception-V3	AMD detection	0.99/97.2/95.7
Burlina et al. [1]	2017	133K TFI	AlexNet	AMD detection	0.95/80.6/92.8
Schlegl et al. [15]	2017	354 OCT volumes	CNN + anomaly detection	AMD detection	0.94/-/-

2.4   Cataract

Cataract refers to the clouding of the eye's natural lens, leading to impaired vision or blindness. It is the most common cause of blindness worldwide, particularly in elderly populations. Although surgical treatment is effective, early detection is especially critical in resource-constrained settings.

Several deep learning methods have been developed for cataract detection and grading. For instance, Tham et al. [1] applied ResNet-50 on 25.7K fundus images and achieved an AUC between 0.92 and 0.97 for visually significant cataract detection. Lu et al. [1] reported AUC values ranging from 0.80 to 0.98 for cataract grading using slit-lamp images. Table 4 provides a summary of representative studies.

Table 4. Summary of AI-based methods for cataract detection and grading. Abbreviations: FI – fundus images; TFI – traditional fundus images; SLI – slit-lamp images; GLN – global-local attention network; GLR – global-local representation; Acc – accuracy.

Contribution	Year	Data	AI Model	Task	AUC/Sens/Spc
Walaa N. Ismail et al. [16]	2024	ODIR-5K (FI)	Multi-label CNN	Cataract classification	0.98/–/–
Amr ElSawy et al. [17]	2023	AREDS2	Deep CNN	Cataract detection	–/–/Acc: 95%
Keenan et al. [1]	2022	19K SLI	DeepLensNet	Age-related cataract classification	–/–/Mean Acc: 16.6%
Tham et al. [19]	2022	25.7K TFI	ResNet-50 + XGBoost	Visually significant cataract detection	0.94/92.4/85.7
Xu et al. [1]	2021	9.9K TFI	GLN	Cataract detection and grading	–/–/Acc: 85–90%
Lu et al. [1]	2021	847 SLI	R-CNN + ResNet-50	Cataract grading	0.89/90.2/78.4
Lin et al. [1]	2020	1.7K patient history	Random Forest	Congenital cataract detection	0.89/69.0/88.0
Xu et al. [1]	2020	8K TFI	Hybrid GLR	Cataract grading	–/87.4/85.9 (Acc: 86.2%)
Wu et al. [1]	2019	37.6K SLI	ResNet-50	Refractive cataract detection	0.92–0.95/–/–
Zhang et al. [1]	2019	1.3K TFI	ResNet-18 + SVM + FCNN	Cataract grading	–/90.9/89.9
Ran et al. [1]	2018	TFI	CNN + Random Forest	Cataract detection and grading	–/–/Acc: 96%
Qiao et al. [21]	2017	FI	SVM + Genetic Algorithm	Cataract classification	–/–/Acc: 92%
Yang et al. [22]	2016	1.2K FI	Ensemble learning	Cataract detection and grading	–/–/Acc: 93%
Gao et al. [23]	2015	5K SLI	CNN	Cataract grading	–/–/–

2.5   Commercial Platforms

Several AI-driven commercial platforms have been developed for ophthalmic disease detection. Representative examples include:

- **IDx-DR**: The first FDA-approved AI system for detecting diabetic retinopathy [29].
- **DeepMind Health**: Employs deep learning for analyzing OCT scans, enabling the detection of conditions such as age-related macular degeneration [30].
- **Eyenuk**: An AI-powered screening platform for diabetic retinopathy [31].
- **RetinaNet**: An AI-based system for retinal disease classification [32].

While these platforms demonstrate strong performance, their scope is limited. Most focus exclusively on disease identification without offering personalized treatment recommendations. Furthermore, many address only a single disease category and typically do not exploit multimodal clinical data sources. To the best of our knowledge, no prior multimodal architectures have been developed that jointly integrate fundus images with structured clinical variables for both disease diagnosis and treatment recommendation. This research gap motivates our proposed framework, which aims to bridge visual and clinical data to deliver both diagnostic classification and therapeutic guidance within a single unified system.

3   Contribution

This work introduces several innovations that distinguish it from existing approaches:

1. **Comprehensive training data:** The model was trained on the publicly available **ODIR-5K** dataset [28] as a baseline. To enhance clinical utility, the dataset was augmented with *physician-developed annotations* formulated in collaboration with ophthalmologists. These annotations include:
   - Detailed clinical pathology descriptions
   - Treatment recommendations tailored to each diagnosis.

   This integration of fundus images with expert-driven decision elements enables the model to capture nuanced associations between image features, disease manifestations, and therapeutic interventions.
2. **Dual functionality:** In contrast to many prior methods that focus solely on disease detection, the proposed model additionally provides personalized treatment recommendations.
3. **Multimodal data integration:** The framework leverages diverse data sources—including fundus images, demographic attributes, and clinical pathology results—thereby improving prediction robustness.
4. **Unified architecture:** A single deep learning framework is employed, combining EfficientNet-B0 for image processing with fully connected layers for tabular clinical data. This design eliminates the need for disease-specific models.
5. **High performance:** The model achieves an AUC of 0.99, sensitivity of 92.1%, specificity of 78.3%, and an overall diagnostic accuracy of 98.7%. For treatment recommendation tasks, an accuracy of 93.19% is reported.

4   Methods

This section outlines the methodology adopted for the design and implementation of the proposed deep learning framework. The pipeline begins with multimodal data preprocessing, followed by model architecture design, training, and evaluation. The workflow is optimized to handle heterogeneous clinical inputs and to deliver both diagnostic and treatment outputs within a unified framework.

4.1   Problem Statement and Objective

Clinical Challenge. The diagnosis of ophthalmic diseases is clinically complex due to the need to distinguish among eight categories that often exhibit overlapping visual features in retinal fundus images. For example, diabetic retinopathy and hypertensive retinopathy may present similar abnormalities, complicating differentiation. Furthermore, systemic comorbidities frequently influence ocular manifestations, adding another layer of diagnostic difficulty.

Limitations of Existing Works. Most existing AI models target a single disease category (e.g., diabetic retinopathy), thereby limiting generalizability in broader clinical contexts. Co-existing ocular conditions—such as glaucoma co-occurring with cataracts—are seldom addressed jointly, reducing practical clinical applicability. Moreover, many approaches rely exclusively on a single modality (e.g., fundus images or OCT), overlooking the complementary value of integrating multimodal clinical data.

Objective. To overcome these limitations, our objective is to develop a unified AI framework capable of diagnosing multiple ophthalmic diseases by leveraging a combined dataset of retinal images (fundus, OCT) and structured clinical data (demographics, pathology reports). The model is designed to provide side-specific diagnosis by distinguishing between conditions affecting the left and right eyes, while also delivering personalized treatment recommendations through a decision-support module that integrates disease classification with clinical context.

4.2   Multimodal Data

The proposed machine learning model is built on multimodal data derived from the publicly available Ocular Disease Intelligent Recognition (ODIR-5K) dataset [28]. This dataset comprises records from 3,500 patients and includes demographic information, color fundus photographs of both eyes, and clinician-provided diagnostic annotations. It reflects a realistic clinical distribution, as it was collected by Shanggong Medical Technology Co., Ltd. from multiple hospitals and medical centers across China.

The fundus images were captured using a variety of commercially available cameras (e.g., Canon, Zeiss, Kowa), resulting in diverse image resolutions. This variability mirrors real-world acquisition conditions and enhances the generalization ability of trained models.

We primarily focus on fundus images due to their wide availability and utility in mass screening, especially in resource-limited settings where OCT may not be accessible. Fundus images provide a 2D projection of retinal structures, enabling the visualization of blood vessels, hemorrhages, and microaneurysms—critical features for early detection of several ophthalmic diseases (Table 5).

Table 5. Example of multimodal entries showing structured variables and fundus images. Disease codes: N – Normal, D – Diabetic Retinopathy, G – Glaucoma, C – Cataract, A – AMD, H – Hypertension, M – Myopia, O – Others. Blood tests: Cholesterol (Ch), Hemoglobin (HbG), HbA1c, Glucose (Gl).

Patient Age Sex (M / F)	LT–RT Diagnosis (N, D, G, C, A, H, M, O)	Blood Tests (Ch / HbG / HbA1c / Gl)	Fundus Images (LT–RT)
69 F	C–N	210 / 11.5 / 6.8 / 130	
57 M	N–N	190 / 12.5 / 5.3 / 85	

Table 6. Preprocessing strategies applied to structured clinical data. Numerical variables are imputed and standardized, whereas categorical variables are transformed into numerical format using one-hot encoding.

Feature Type	Example	Preprocessing Steps	Tools Used
Numerical	Age,Cholesterol,Hbg, HbA1c,Glucose	1. Handle missing values via mean imputation 2. Standardize values $(\mu = 0, \sigma = 1)$	`SimpleImputer`, `StandardScaler`
Categorical	Sex (Male/Female)	Convert to numerical format using one-hot encoding	`OneHotEncoder`

As shown in Table 6, numerical features (e.g., age, cholesterol, hemoglobin, HbA1c, and glucose) were standardized after handling missing values through mean imputation. Categorical features, such as patient sex, were converted into machine-readable format using one-hot encoding. This preprocessing ensured uniformity across heterogeneous clinical data and facilitated integration with image-based features.

4.3   Data Pre-processing

The overall model architecture is shown in Fig. 2. This subsection describes the data pre-processing stage.

Image Pre-processing. Fundus images were uniformly resized to a resolution of 224×224 pixels to ensure compatibility with the model's input layer. Pixel intensity values were normalized to the range $[0, 1]$, standardizing the input distribution and facilitating model convergence. For patients without available image data, the missing input was replaced with a zero-filled array of the same dimensions. **Tabular Data Pre-processing.** The tabular data consisted of numerical features (e.g., age, cholesterol, hemoglobin, HbA1c, glucose) and categorical features (e.g., patient sex). As summarized in Table 6, missing values in numerical features were imputed using the mean, followed by standardization (zero mean, unit variance). Categorical variables were transformed into numerical format using one-hot encoding.

Feature Integration. After preprocessing, all features—standardized numerical values and one-hot encoded categorical variables—were concatenated along the feature dimension to form a unified feature matrix. This matrix was later fused with image-derived feature vectors during the multimodal integration stage.

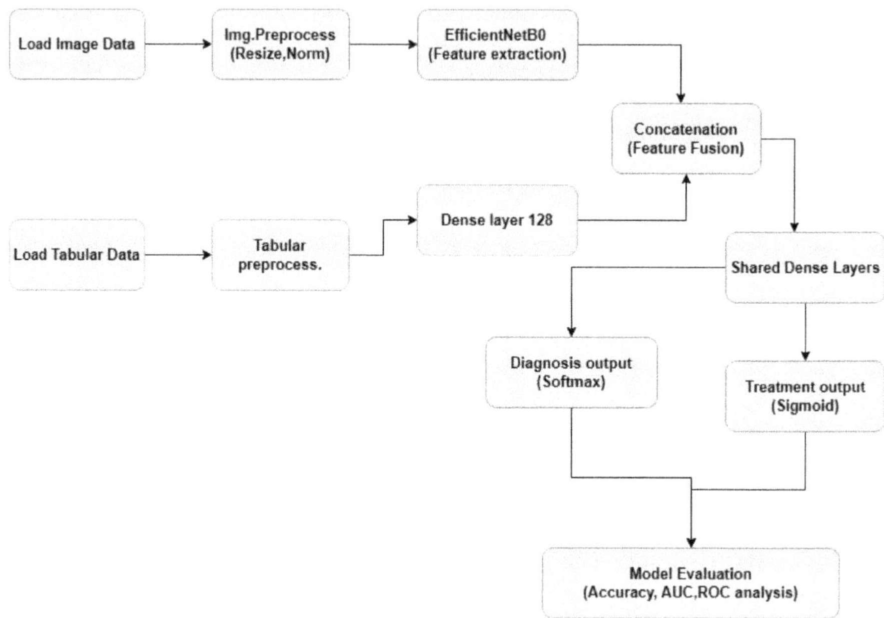

Fig. 2. Overview of the proposed model architecture.

4.4 Model Design

The proposed architecture is a multi-input deep learning framework designed to jointly exploit retinal fundus images and structured clinical data for both diagnosis and treatment recommendation. The model consists of two main components: an image feature extractor and a clinical data processor, which are integrated through a feature fusion mechanism, as illustrated in Fig. 2.

1. **Image Processing Block.** This branch employs the EfficientNet-B0 architecture, a computationally efficient convolutional neural network pre-trained on ImageNet. It processes RGB fundus images resized to $224 \times 224 \times 3$. Convolutional layers extract spatial features relevant to ophthalmic pathology, which are then flattened and passed through fully connected layers to encode high-level semantic information such as retinal lesions and atrophic regions.
2. **Clinical Data Block.** The second branch processes structured tabular data consisting of five numerical features (age, glucose, HbA1c, cholesterol, hemoglobin) and one categorical feature (sex). Numerical values were standardized, while categorical variables were one-hot encoded. This branch comprises fully connected layers with ReLU activation, batch normalization, and dropout regularization, enabling the network to capture patterns among demographics and biomarkers.
3. **Feature Fusion and Classification.** Outputs from the two branches are concatenated to form a joint feature representation, enabling the model to

learn associations between visual and clinical modalities. For example, the presence of microaneurysms in fundus images can be linked with elevated glucose levels, which is critical for detecting diabetic retinopathy.

The fused representation is processed through a fully connected layer with 64 neurons and ReLU activation, followed by a dropout layer (rate = 0.5) to mitigate overfitting. The model then produces two parallel predictions:

- *Diagnosis Prediction:* A softmax-activated output layer classifies cases into Normal (N), Cataract (C), Diabetic Retinopathy (D), Glaucoma (G), Age-related Macular Degeneration (A), or Other (O). The "Other" category encompasses conditions such as drusen, retinitis pigmentosa, epiretinal membrane, myopia, post-laser coagulation, myelinated nerve fibers, and chorioretinal atrophy. These were grouped into a single class due to limited representation in the dataset and inconsistent treatment recommendations, ensuring training stability and preserving clinical coherence.
- *Treatment Recommendation:* A second softmax layer predicts the recommended treatment modality, selecting from: Observation, Surgery, Laser, Medication, or Injection.

This dual-headed architecture emulates real-world clinical workflows by providing both diagnostic classification and evidence-based therapeutic guidance within a single unified framework.

4.5   Model Training

The proposed deep learning model was trained using both fundus images and corresponding tabular clinical data. The target outputs consisted of two components: (1) diagnostic classes indicating ophthalmic pathologies and (2) treatment recommendation labels.

Treatment supervision was based on rule-based mappings derived from standard ophthalmology guidelines. For each disease category (e.g., DR, Cataract, Glaucoma, AMD), one or more expected treatment options were defined from the set Observation, Surgery, Laser, Medication, Injection. These mappings were later summarized in the Results section.

The neural network was optimized using the Adam optimizer with a weighted combination of two task-specific loss functions:

- A multi-class diagnostic branch with softmax activation and categorical cross-entropy loss, used to predict mutually exclusive conditions (Normal, DR, Glaucoma, Cataract, AMD, Other).
- A multi-label treatment branch with sigmoid activation and binary cross-entropy loss, used to predict concurrent therapies, where each treatment option was treated as an independent binary prediction task.

4.6 Model Evaluation

The model was evaluated on an independent test set to assess predictive performance. Metrics included overall accuracy for both diagnosis and treatment outputs. Performance was calculated per diagnostic instance (eye cases) rather than per patient, as patients may present multiple ocular pathologies across both eyes. This design reflects real-world scenarios where coexisting diseases are common.

Detailed evaluation included:

- **Confusion matrices**, showing the distribution of true versus predicted classes for diagnosis.
- **Classification reports**, including precision, recall, and F1-score for each diagnostic class.
- **AUC-ROC curves**, used to evaluate discriminative ability for both diagnostic and treatment tasks.

These complementary metrics provided a comprehensive understanding of the model's effectiveness and reliability. Further quantitative results are presented below.

5 Results

5.1 Dataset Composition

The study utilized an enhanced version of the ODIR-5K dataset [28], comprising 7,000 fundus images (left/right eyes) from 3,500 patients. Of these, 1,500 patients were clinically enriched with expert-estimated blood test values (glucose, HbA1c, cholesterol) and treatment recommendations. A total of 4,130 ocular pathology cases among 3,000 fundus images were identified, indicating that patients may exhibit more than one coexisting eye condition. The distribution of pathologies is reported in the last column (support) of Table 8.

To ensure a fair evaluation and prevent potential data leakage, dataset partitioning was performed strictly at the *patient level*. All fundus images and associated clinical information from the same patient (both left and right eyes) were assigned exclusively to one subset—training or testing—without overlap. Specifically, 80% of the patients were allocated to the training set and 20% to the test set. During model development, the test set was also used to monitor validation performance and prevent overfitting. The final reported performance metrics are therefore based on this same patient-level test partition, ensuring that the model was evaluated only on patients it had not seen during training.

Since the original ODIR-5K dataset does not contain explicit treatment annotations, *disease-to-treatment mappings* were introduced to supervise the therapeutic recommendation task. These mappings were derived from established ophthalmology guidelines (e.g., Euretina, ICO) and represent the most likely interventions for each disease category, independent of individual variability. This ensures that treatment predictions remain clinically meaningful and reproducible (Table 7).

Table 7. Rule-based mappings between ophthalmic disease categories and treatment options.

Disease Category	Expected Treatment Options
Normal (N)	Observation
Cataract (C)	Surgery, Observation
Diabetic Retinopathy (DR)	Laser, Medication, Injection, Observation
Glaucoma (G)	Medication, Surgery, Observation
AMD (A)	Injection, Laser, Observation
Other (O)	Observation

To illustrate the end-user perspective of the AI clinical tool, Fig. 3 shows medical report summaries for three randomly selected patients. The AI-generated predictions for both diagnosis and treatment align closely with clinical ground truth decisions.

MEDICAL REPORT SUMMARY	MEDICAL REPORT SUMMARY	MEDICAL REPORT SUMMARY
Patient ID: 772 **Age/Sex:** 63 Years- old Female **Clinical findings:** Left eye: wet age-related macular degeneration. Right eye: Dry age-related macular degeneration **Model prediction:** Diagnosis: AMD (Confidence: 94%) Treatment: Injection (Confidence: 92%) **Clinical Validation:** -Model correctly identified AMD based on bilateral macular degeneration findings -Treatment recommendation aligns with AAO guidelines for wet AMD management	**Patient ID: 1463** **Age/Sex:** 42 Years- old Male **Clinical findings:** Left eye: laser spot, moderate NPDR Right eye: NPDR **Model prediction:** Diagnosis: DR (Confidence: 95%) Treatment: Laser (Confidence: 90%) **Clinical Validation:** -Model correctly identified Diabetic Retinopathy based on clinical findings of moderate NPDR in both eyes. -Treatment recommendation of Laser therapy aligns with standard care for moderate NPDR with laser spots.	**Patient ID: 198** **Age/Sex:** 57 Years- old Male **Clinical findings:** Left eye: Normal Right eye: Normal **Model prediction:** Diagnosis: Normal (Confidence: 95%) Treatment: Observation (Confidence: 90%) **Clinical Validation:** -Model correctly identified Normal based on clinical findings. -Treatment recommendation of No Treatment aligns with standard care.

Fig. 3. Example of three patient summary reports showing AI-predicted diagnosis and treatment aligned with clinical ground truth.

5.2 Overall Performance

The model achieved high performance across all metrics. Overall precision was 98.5%, recall 98.7%, F1-score 98.6%, AUC 0.99, and accuracy 98.78%. Table 8 provides class-wise performance results.

Table 8. Diagnostic performance metrics per class: precision, recall, F1-score, AUC, true positives (TP), and support.

Class	Precision	Recall	F1	AUC	TP	Support
Normal (N)	1.000	1.000	1.000	1.000	900	900
Diabetic Retinopathy (DR)	1.000	1.000	1.000	1.000	480	480
Glaucoma (G)	0.967	0.967	0.967	0.990	493	509
Cataract (C)	1.000	1.000	1.000	1.000	500	500
AMD (A)	0.940	0.940	0.940	0.995	884	939
Other (O)	1.000	1.000	1.000	1.000	700	700
Overall	0.985	0.987	0.986	0.998	3957	4028

From Table 8, the model achieved 98.78% overall accuracy. Perfect classification was obtained for Normal, DR, Cataract, and Other categories, with slight degradation for Glaucoma and AMD. Figure 4 shows strong alignment between predicted and actual pathology distributions, with minimal over/underprediction across categories.

To further analyze laterality effects, Table 9 reports eye-specific results, showing consistent performance between the two eyes.

Finally, Fig. 5 shows confusion matrices for both eyes, demonstrating strong diagonal dominance with minimal misclassification.

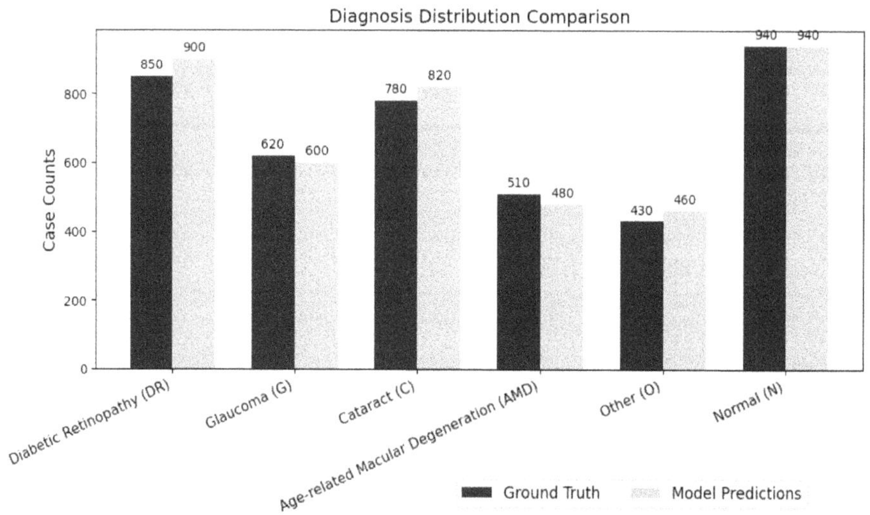

Fig. 4. Distribution of diagnostic classes: ground truth (dark blue) vs. model predictions (light blue). (Color figure online)

Table 9. Eye-specific performance for diabetic retinopathy detection.

Metric	Left Eye	Right Eye	Interpretation
Accuracy	89.4%	90.1%	Comparable performance
Precision	90.3%	92.1%	Higher confidence in right eye
Recall	88.4%	87.2%	Left eye detects more true DR
F1-Score	89.3%	89.6%	Balanced performance

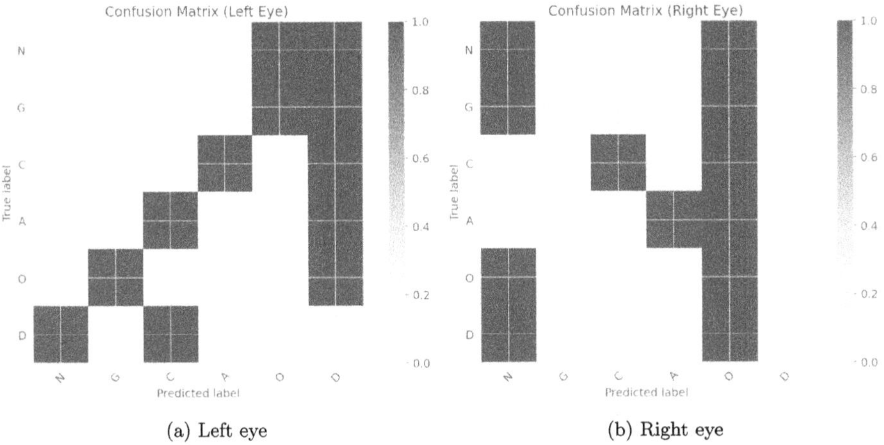

(a) Left eye   (b) Right eye

Fig. 5. Confusion matrices for left and right eyes, showing high accuracy and consistent performance across classes.

5.3 Treatment Recommendation Performance

The model's treatment recommendations were evaluated across five intervention categories: observation (no treatment), laser, surgery, injection, and medication. Comparative results are presented in Table 10 and Fig. 6.

Table 10. Percentage Distribution of Treatment Recommendations.

Treatment Class	Ground Truth (%)	Model (%)
Observation	24.5	29.7
Laser	58.95	58.95
Surgery	33.85	40.99
Medication	17.22	20.89
Injection	63.6	65.2

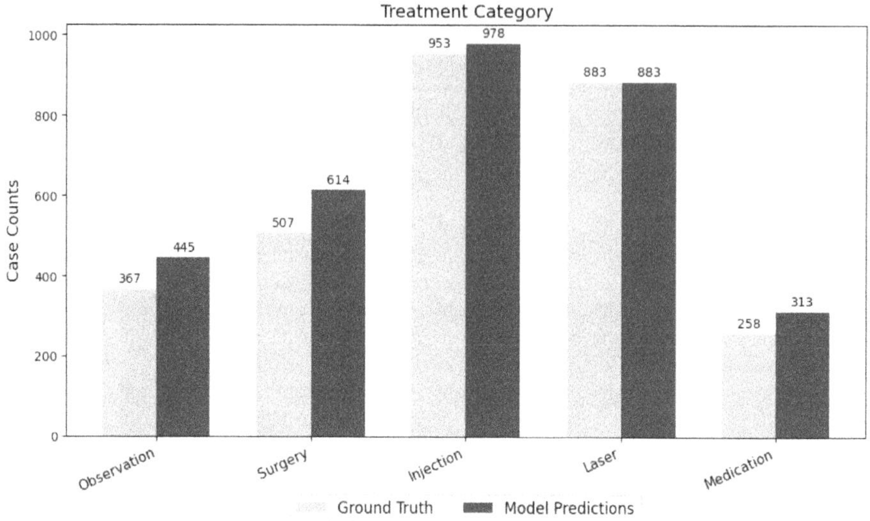

Fig. 6. Comparative frequencies of treatment recommendations.

As shown in Fig. 6, the model successfully captures important treatment decision patterns. Except for laser therapy, which matches clinical data precisely, the model tends to slightly overestimate the need for active interventions, with surgery showing the largest deviation. Nonetheless, the overall treatment ranking (injection, laser, surgery, medication, observation) is preserved.

6   Conclusion and Future Directions

This work presented a multimodal deep learning framework that integrates fundus images with structured clinical data to jointly predict ocular disease diagnosis and treatment recommendations. The system achieved strong performance (98.78% accuracy for diagnosis and 93.19% for treatment prediction), demonstrating the value of multimodal integration for comprehensive and individualized patient assessment. Importantly, the model addresses multiple diseases simultaneously, whereas many prior works remain restricted to single-pathology detection.

Nevertheless, several limitations should be acknowledged. Firstly, evaluation was conducted only on an enhanced version of the ODIR-5K dataset. Although a strict patient-level split was enforced to prevent data leakage, no additional dataset validation was performed, limiting the proof of being able to generalize across populations and imaging devices. Secondly, treatment recommendation labels were generated using guideline-based mappings rather than real-world therapeutic records, introducing a level of abstraction. Thirdly, no direct multimodal baselines exist for comparison in this scope, and ablation studies to isolate modality contributions were not performed.

Future work will address these limitations by enlarging the training dataset, validating performance on external cohorts and incorporating real-world treatment outcomes as they become available. In addition, longitudinal screening capability will be explored to enable monitoring of disease progression over time. Finally, expanding the diagnostic scope to include rare ophthalmic pathologies through targeted data augmentation and specialized training.

Acknowledgments. The authors received no external funding for this work. The work of Asmaa Abdelmawgoud was carried out during her research visit at the University of Klagenfurt.

Disclosure of Interests. The authors have no competing interests to declare that are relevant to the content of this article.

References

1. Li, Z., et al.: Artificial intelligence in ophthalmology: the path to the real-world clinic. Cell Rep. Med. (2023)
2. Refat, A., et al.: Artificial intelligence in ophthalmology: the path to the real-world clinic. arXiv:2504.21464 (2025)
3. Dalahma, M., et al.: Deep learning convolutional neural network diabetic retinopathy detection using Gaussian filter preprocessing. In: Proceedings of 3rd International Ophthalmology Conference (2025)
4. Zhu, X., et al.: nnMobileNet: rethinking CNN for retinopathy research. arXiv:2306.01289 (2023)
5. Bora, A., et al.: A hybrid approach for diagnosing diabetic retinopathy from fundus image exploiting deep features. Heliyon **9** (2023)
6. Li, X., et al.: Artificial intelligence in ophthalmology: the path to the real-world clinic. Cell Rep. Med. **4** (2023)
7. Gulshan, V., et al.: Development and validation of a deep learning algorithm for detection of diabetic retinopathy in retinal fundus photographs. JAMA Ophthalmol. (2016)
8. Takahashi, H., et al.: Applying artificial intelligence to diabetic retinopathy screening in Japan. Jpn. J. Ophthalmol. (2015)
9. Roy, S., et al.: DeepEyeNet: Adaptive genetic Bayesian algorithm based hybrid ConvNeXtTiny framework for multi-feature glaucoma eye diagnosis. arXiv:2501.11168 (2025)
10. Zhang, Y., et al.: External validation of a deep learning detection system for glaucomatous optic neuropathy: a real-world multicentre study. Br. J. Ophthalmol. (2024)
11. Islam, M., et al.: A framework for early detection of glaucoma in retinal fundus images using deep learning. Eng. Proc. (2023)
12. Wang, H., et al.: Segmentation and classification of glaucoma using U-Net with deep learning model. J. Healthc. Eng. (2022)
13. Al-Mahrooqi, H., et al.: GARDNet: robust multi-view network for glaucoma classification in color fundus images. arXiv:2205.12902 (2022)
14. Le, N.T., et al.: ViT-AMD: a new deep learning model for age-related macular degeneration diagnosis from fundus images. Int. J. Intell. Syst. (2024)

15. Schlegl, T., et al.: Unsupervised anomaly detection with generative adversarial networks to guide marker discovery. In: Proceedings of International Conference on Information Processing on Medical Imaging (IPMI) (2017)
16. Ismail, W.N., et al.: CataractNetDetect: a novel deep learning model for effective cataract classification through data fusion of fundus images. Disc. Artif. Intell. (2024)
17. Elsawy, A., et al.: DeepOpacityNet: a deep network for detection of cataracts from color fundus photographs. Commun. Med. (2023)
18. Tham, Y.C., et al.: Detecting visually significant cataract using retinal photograph-based deep learning. Nat. Aging (2022)
19. Xu, K., et al.: GLA-net: a global-local attention network for automatic cataract classification. J. Biomed. Inf. (2021)
20. Lu, W., et al.: Lens opacities classification system III–based artificial intelligence program for automatic cataract grading. J. Cataract Refract. Surg. (2021)
21. Qiao, Y., et al.: Application of SVM based on genetic algorithm in classification of cataract fundus images. In: IEEE International Conference on Imaging Systems and Technology (IST) (2017)
22. Yang, J., et al.: Exploiting ensemble learning for automatic cataract detection and grading. Comput. Methods Prog. Biomed. (2016)
23. Gao, X., et al.: Automatic feature learning to grade nuclear cataracts based on deep learning. IEEE Trans. Biomed. Eng. (2015)
24. Ting, D., et al.: Artificial intelligence and deep learning in ophthalmology. Br. J. Ophthalmol. (2019)
25. GBD 2019 Blindness and Vision Impairment Collaborators: Causes of blindness and vision impairment in 2020 and trends over 30 years. Lancet Glob. Health (2021)
26. European Society of Retina Specialists (Euretina): Guidelines for the management of retinal diseases in Europe. https://www.euretina.org. Accessed 15 Aug 2025
27. Wong, T.Y., et al.: Guidelines on diabetic eye care: the international Council of Ophthalmology recommendations for screening, follow-up, referral, and treatment based on resource settings. Ophthalmology (2016)
28. Andrew, M.D.: Ocular disease recognition dataset (ODIR-5K). https://odir2019.grand-challenge.org. Accessed 15 Aug 2025
29. Abràmoff, M.D., Lavin, P.T., Birch, M., Shah, N., Folk, J.C.: Pivotal trial of an autonomous AI-based diagnostic system for detection of diabetic retinopathy in primary care offices. NPJ Digit. Med. **1**, 39 (2018). https://doi.org/10.1038/s41746-018-0040-6
30. De Fauw, J., Ledsam, J.R., Romera-Paredes, B., et al.: Clinically applicable deep learning for diagnosis and referral in retinal disease. Nat. Med. **24**, 1342–1350 (2018). https://doi.org/10.1038/s41591-018-0107-6
31. Eyenuk Inc.: Eyenuk receives FDA clearance for EyeArt AI system for autonomous detection of diabetic retinopathy. https://eyenuk.com/eyeart-ai-system/. Accessed 15 Aug 2025
32. Lin, T.Y., Goyal, P., Girshick, R., He, K., Dollár, P.: Focal loss for dense object detection. In: Proceedings of IEEE International Conference on Computer Vision (ICCV), pp. 2980–2988 (2017). https://doi.org/10.1109/ICCV.2017.324

GNN-Based Multimodal Analysis of Brain Anatomical and Functional Features for Parkinson's Disease and Cognitive Decline Detection

Patrizia Ribino[1,3(✉)], Alessandro Pensabene[2,3], and Maria Mannone[1,3]

[1] ICAR, National Research Council (CNR), Palermo, Italy
`{patrizia.ribino,maria.mannone}@icar.cnr.it`
[2] Università degli Studi di Palermo, Palermo, Italy
`alessandro.pensabene02@community.unipa.it`
[3] Institute of Physics and Astronomy, University of Potsdam, Potsdam, Germany

Abstract. Parkinson's Disease (PD) is a progressive neurodegenerative disorder characterized by motor dysfunction and, in many cases, cognitive impairment. While substantial progress has been made in understanding PD's clinical manifestations, distinguishing PD patients from healthy controls and identifying cognitive impairment subtypes remains challenging. In this study, we present a Graph Neural Network (GNN) framework that leverages both structural anatomical data (SA) and functional connectivity (FC) to enhance the classification of PD patients and the stratification of cognitive impairment subtypes. Our approach includes an ablation study to evaluate the individual and combined contributions of SA and FC in distinguishing between PD patients and healthy controls (HC) and between PD patients with normal cognition (PD-NC) and those with mild cognitive impairment (PD-MCI). Experimental results show that the GNN-based approach reveals the distinct roles of anatomical and functional connectivity in disease phenotypes.

Keywords: Parkinson's Disease · Cognitive Decline · GNN

1 Introduction

Parkinson's Disease (PD) is a progressive neurodegenerative disorder primarily characterized by motor dysfunction, which arises from the degeneration of dopamine-producing neurons in the substantia nigra, a region in the midbrain essential for dopamine production and also responsible for movement [11]. First described by James Parkinson in 1817 as the "Shaking Palsy", PD is now recognized as the second most prevalent neurodegenerative disease worldwide, following Alzheimer's disease [12]. Over the past two decades, the global incidence of PD has increased substantially, a trend attributed not only to improvements

C. Tommasino et al. (Eds.): AIBIO 2025, CCIS 2696, pp. 177–185, 2026.
https://doi.org/10.1007/978-3-032-17216-7_14

in diagnostic precision but also to demographic shifts, particularly the ageing global population [2,4]. The risk of developing PD increases significantly with age, mostly after 60 years. Epidemiological studies reveal a marked gender disparity, with men being approximately 1.4 times more likely to develop PD than women, suggesting potential biological and hormonal influences in disease susceptibility [5,14]. Despite significant advances in research, the exact PD aetiology remains largely unknown. About 5–10% of cases are attributed to monogenic mutations [8,10], while the vast majority are sporadic, stemming from a complex interplay of genetic predispositions and environmental factors [1,6].

Beyond its well-known motor symptoms, cognitive impairment represents a significant non-motor manifestation of PD, profoundly affecting patients' quality of life [3]. Cognitive decline in PD ranges from mild cognitive impairment (PD-MCI) to PD dementia (PDD), with distinct patterns of cognitive deficits that include executive dysfunction, memory impairment, and difficulties with visuospatial processing. These deficits are linked to widespread structural and functional brain alterations, which are increasingly studied through Magnetic Resonance Imaging (MRI). MRI techniques have been crucial in detecting brain volume changes in PD, particularly in subcortical structures such as the caudate nucleus and putamen. These regions often show atrophy, while some paradoxically increase in volume, possibly reflecting compensatory responses to neurodegeneration [15]. Advanced imaging approaches, such as resting-state functional MRI (rs-fMRI), further enable the exploration of functional connectivity (FC) disruptions that correlate with cognitive impairment and disease progression.

Recently, Machine Learning (ML) has become increasingly prominent in the field of healthcare for enhancing diagnosis, predicting disease progression, and refining patient stratification. In PD research, ML models are used to identify biomarkers, track disease trajectories, and differentiate patient subtypes with greater precision [13]. Among these methods, Graph Neural Networks (GNNs) have currently shown particular promise in exploiting complex relationships within brain connectivity data [9,16]. When combined with rs-fMRI, GNNs enable the characterization of brain network disruptions in PD patients, facilitating the identification of cognitive impairments linked to disease progression.

In this study, we exploit the GNN power to classify Parkinson's Disease, incorporating both structural anatomical data (SA) and functional connectivity (FC) to enhance patient differentiation. Specifically, we perform an ablation study to evaluate the individual and combined contributions of the brain's anatomical structural view and functional connectivity in distinguishing PD patients from healthy controls and further categorizing PD patients with mild cognitive impairment (PD-MCI) from those with normal cognition (PD-NC).

To achieve this, we designed two targeted experiments in a cohort of 48 patients extracted from a publicly available dataset. *PD vs. Healthy Controls*, which encompasses the full cohort of 48 subjects and assesses the capacity of SA and FC to discriminate between PD patients and healthy individuals, and *PD-MCI vs. PD-NC*, which narrows the focus to the 30 PD patients, evaluating the role of SA and FC in distinguishing cognitive impairment subtypes.

2 Materials and Methods

2.1 Parkinson's Disease Dataset

The data used in this work are extracted from a dataset provided by the Open-Neuro platform, a free and open platform for validating and sharing BIDS-compliant MRI, PET, MEG, EEG, and iEEG data[1] The dataset originates from a longitudinal study focused on exploring Parkinson's Disease and its related cognitive impairments [7]. It includes resting-state fMRI data collected from participants classified into three groups: healthy controls (HC), PD patients with normal cognition (PD-NC), and those with mild cognitive impairment (PD-MCI). The dataset is structured into several main components. Participant information, including demographics and group classifications, is documented in a metadata file. For each individual in the study, there is a dedicated subdirectory named after their participant ID (e.g., sub-01, sub-02), which is further organized into two sections: *anat/* and *func/*. The *anat/* folder contains anatomical MRI scans, specifically T1-weighted images, while the *func/* folder stores resting-state fMRI data. The original dataset contains information about 55 individuals. However, only 48 have all the information necessary for our study. In this cohort, males and females are equally distributed, and their average age is 68.8 ± 7.5. Among them, 40% are HC, 26% are PD-MCI, and 34% are PD-NC.

2.2 GNN Model

Graph Neural Networks are a class of deep learning models specifically designed to work with data structured as graphs. Unlike traditional neural networks that operate on fixed-grid data such as images or sequences, GNNs excel at learning patterns and relationships in data represented as graphs. A graph $G = (V, E)$ consists of a set of nodes V and edges E that represent relationships or connections between these nodes. In the context of neuroscience, nodes represent brain regions (known as Regions of Interest, ROIs), and edges reflect functional or structural connectivity between them, derived from imaging techniques like resting-state fMRI (rs-fMRI). GNNs iteratively update each node's representation by aggregating information from neighbors. The message-passing process lets each node incorporate its own features and those from connected nodes, capturing local and global graph structure.

In this study, we employ a custom-designed GNN architecture that leverages the capabilities of Edge Convolution layers to effectively learn from graph-structured data. As shown in Fig. 1, the model is composed of three main Edge Convolution blocks, each followed by batch normalization. EdgeConv layer dynamically constructs local neighborhoods for each node, computing edge features based on the differences and similarities between connected nodes. Each EdgeConv layer is equipped with its own Multi-Layer Perceptron (MLP). These layers use max pooling as an aggregation mechanism, ensuring that only the

---

[1] Data are available at https://openneuro.org/.

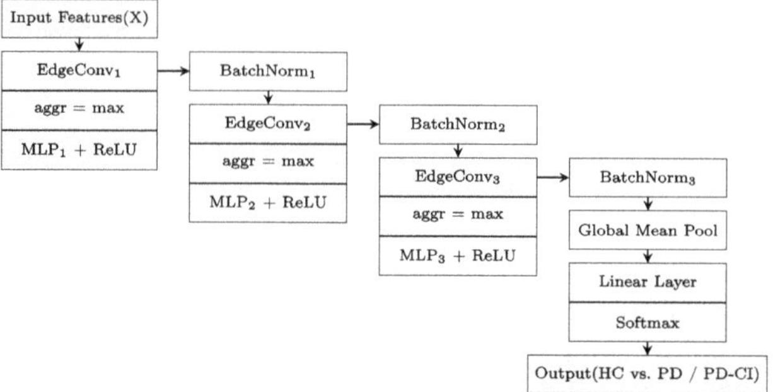

Fig. 1. Architecture of the GNN model.

most relevant features are retained from each neighborhood. After each Edge-Conv operation, batch normalization is applied to stabilize the learning process. This normalization helps the network generalize better by preventing overfitting and accelerating convergence. Finally, the processed node embeddings are passed through a linear layer that maps them to a two-dimensional output, representing the two classes under study (e.g., HC vs. PD or PD-NC vs. PD-MCI).

2.3   MRI Graph-Based Classification Pipeline

The following steps describe the whole classification process:

- *Feature extraction*: SA and FC matrices are constructed independently for each subject. Anatomical features are extracted from high-resolution T1-weighted MRI scans. This process involves resampling atlas labels to align with the resolution of the T1 image, followed by the computation of the mean intensity values for each predefined brain region. These features serve as node attributes in the graph representation. Functional connectivity matrices are generated from rs-fMRI data. This involves standardizing fMRI signals and calculating Pearson correlations between brain regions' time series. The resulting FC matrix reflects synchronized neural activity strength.
- *Graph Representation*: For graph-based learning, SA and FC matrices have to be represented as weighted, undirected graphs. Each node corresponds to a specific brain region, enriched with features that concatenate anatomical properties from SA and temporal synchronization metrics from FC. Edge attributes are populated with the corresponding connectivity strengths, providing weighted indicators of connection intensity.
- *Label Assignment and Data Storage*: Subjects are by diagnostic status from the dataset's TSV metadata. Graph objects, along with their labels, are stored locally for efficient retrieval during model training and evaluation.
- *Model Training and Evaluation*: The constructed graphs serve as input to the GNN model, optimized using a cross-entropy loss function with the Adam optimizer. The learning rate is set to 0.001, and the model is trained for 150 epochs. Early stopping is employed based on validation loss (Fig. 2).

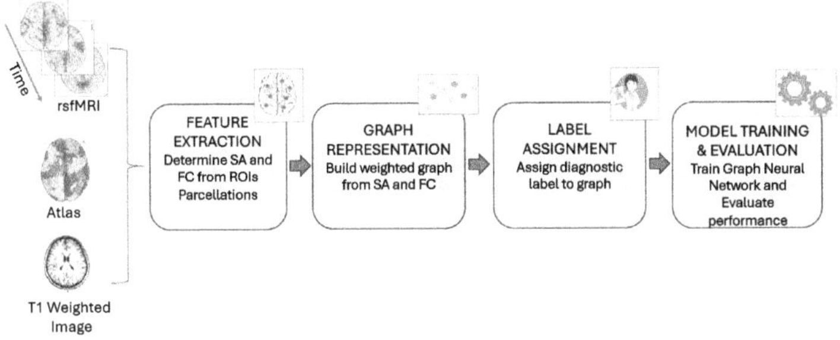

Fig. 2. Pipeline for detecting Parkinson's Disease and related cognitive decline.

3   Experimental Setup

We conducted an ablation study to assess the individual and combined contributions of anatomical features and functional connectivity in distinguishing Parkinson's patients from healthy subjects and separating PD patients with mild cognitive impairment from those with normal cognition. We performed two experiments. The first one concerned the classification of PD patients versus Healthy Controls (HC) by including all 48 subjects in the dataset. The second one focused on the classification of PD-MCI versus PD-NC by analyzing only the 30 PD patients. For each experiment, the model is trained under three different configurations: i) *Only SA features* where graph representation for each patient is derived solely from structural data; ii) *Only FC features* where graph representation is derived exclusively from functional connectivity; iii) *Combined features (SA + FC)* where graph representation is derived that integrates both SA and FC. Each experiment consisted of several runs to evaluate average performance.

3.1   Results and Discussions

The results of the classification tasks are reported in Table 1, showing the metrics for the PD vs. HC and PD-MCI vs. PD-NC classification.

PD vs. HC Classification - For distinguishing Parkinson's Disease (PD) patients from Healthy Controls (HC), the use of Functional Connectivity (FC) alone as input features in the proposed GNN model achieved a mean accuracy of 80.00% $\pm$ 0.00% with a maximum accuracy of 80.00% and a test loss of 0.6282 ± 0.0026. In contrast, Structural Anatomical features (SA) alone performed slightly worse with an accuracy of 72.00% $\pm$ 4.22% and a maximum accuracy of 80.00%. Interestingly, the combined use of SC and FA maintained the mean accuracy at 80.00%, but the maximum accuracy increased to 90.00%, suggesting that integrating both feature types may capture complementary information, enhancing the upper bounds of classification performance. However, it is notable that the loss value for SA+FC (0.6124 ± 0.0919) did not improve significantly compared to FC alone, hinting that, while the combination is beneficial for peak performance, it does not consistently optimize the learning process.

Table 1. Results of GNN Classification

Experiment	Features	Accuracy Mean ± STDV	Loss	Acccuracy Max
PD vs HC	SA	72.00% ± 4.22%	0.5071 ± 0.0337	80.00%
	FC	80.00% ± 0.00%	0.6282 ± 0.0026	80.00%
	SC+FA	80.00% ± 8.16%	0.6124 ± 0.0919	90.00%
PD-MCI vs PD-NC	SA	98.33% ± 3.51%	0.3318 ± 0.0384	100.00%
	FC	53.33% ± 7.03%	0.7892 ± 0.0716	67.00%
	SA+FC	78.33% ± 8.05%	0.5733 ± 0.0805	83.00%

PD-MCI vs. PD-NC Classification - The findings show more differences when differentiating PD patients with Mild Cognitive Impairment (PD-MCI) from those with Normal Cognition (PD-NC). The SA feature alone achieved an impressive 98.33% ± 3.51% mean accuracy with a perfect maximum accuracy of 100.00%. This result indicates that structural brain changes are highly predictive of cognitive status within PD patients. Conversely, the FC feature alone performed poorly with a mean accuracy of 53.33% ± 7.03%, just marginally above random chance, and a maximum accuracy of 67.00%. This implies that functional connectivity patterns are less distinguishable between PD-MCI and PD-NC groups when considered independently. When both SA and FC are combined, the mean accuracy drops to 78.33% ± 8.05% from the 98.33% seen with SA alone. This reduction suggests that including FC may add noise or redundant information that does not contribute meaningfully to this type of classification.

Analysis of Functional and Anatomical Brain Differences between HC vs PD and PD-NC vs PD-MCI - To support our earlier findings, we analysed three male subjects: a healthy control (HC, sub-MJF003), a PD patient with normal cognition (PD-NC, sub-MJF014), and a PD patient with mild cognitive impairment (PD-MCI, sub-MJF001). Our goal was to identify differences in both functional connectivity and anatomical structure between each pair of subjects based on their MRI scans. For functional connectivity, we extracted connectivity matrices for each subject, computed the absolute differences between pairs, and highlighted the most significant region-to-region discrepancies. In parallel, we conducted an anatomical analysis using structural T1-weighted MRI images. Using the same atlas, we measured the volumetric size of each brain region for each subject and compared these volumes to identify regions with notable structural differences. These anatomical differences were displayed in sorted bar charts for easy interpretation. As illustrated in Fig. 3 and Fig. 4[2], the observed functional and anatomical differences correspond well with the classifier's predictions. Functional connectivity differences are less pronounced between PD subjects (Fig. 3c) compared to the differences observed when comparing the HC

---

[2] Magnified images can be found here.

subject with PD patients (Fig. 3a and 3b). Conversely, the anatomical analysis reveals more prominent differences, particularly in the visual cortex, which distinguishes PD patients with normal cognition from those with MCI.

While this analysis is exploratory due to the limited sample size, it provides preliminary evidence that the classifier's predictions may reflect meaningful, measurable changes in brain structure and connectivity.

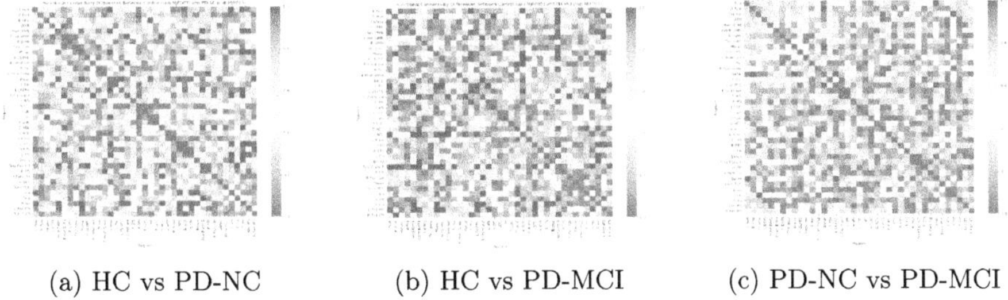

(a) HC vs PD-NC   (b) HC vs PD-MCI   (c) PD-NC vs PD-MCI

Fig. 3. Functional connectivity comparison with stronger difference in red. (Color figure online)

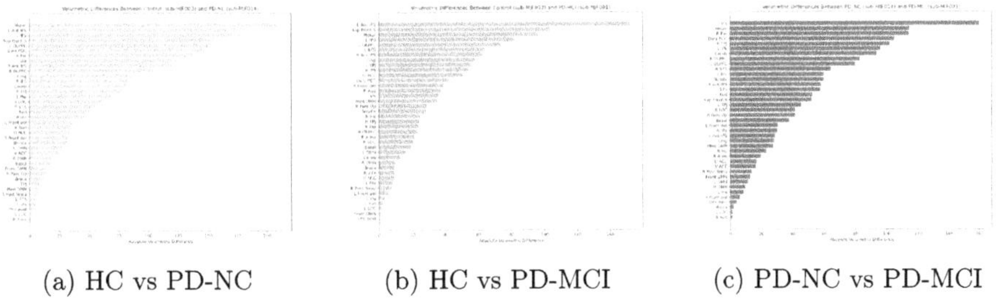

(a) HC vs PD-NC   (b) HC vs PD-MCI   (c) PD-NC vs PD-MCI

Fig. 4. Comparison of anatomical differences across subjects.

4   Conclusions

By leveraging graph-based learning, GNNs can effectively distinguish between Healthy Controls (HC) and PD patients, as well as detect subtle network changes associated with cognitive impairment in PD. The results indicate that the predictive power of SA and FC is task-dependent. For PD vs. HC, FC is strong on its own, but the combination of SA and FC marginally improves the best-case scenario. For PD-MCI vs. PD-NC, SA alone is significantly more powerful, and adding FC seems to dilute its predictive strength. This could reflect the fact that structural changes are more distinct and localized when cognitive impairment is present, while functional patterns are more variable and potentially less distinguishable in cognitive classifications. Further analysis might explore longitudinal studies to understand how SC and FC changes evolve with disease progression and cognitive decline, offering deeper insights into their roles as biomarkers for early detection and monitoring of PD-related cognitive changes.

Acknowledgments. This paper was developed within the project funded by Next Generation EU – "Age-It – Ageing well in an ageing society" project (PE0000015), National Recovery and Resilience Plan (NRRP) – PE8 – Mission 4, C2, Intervention 1.3, CUP B83C22004880006.

References

1. Ascherio, A., Schwarzschild, M.A.: The epidemiology of Parkinson's disease: risk factors and prevention. Lancet Neurol. **15**(12), 1257–1272 (2016)
2. Bloem, B.R., Okun, M.S., Klein, C.: Parkinson's disease. Lancet **397**(10291), 2284–2303 (2021)
3. Cao, D., et al.: Magnetic resonance imaging of brain structural and functional changes in cognitive impairment associated with Parkinson's disease. Front. Aging Neurosci. **16**, 1494385 (2024)
4. Dorsey, E.R., Bloem, B.R.: The Parkinson pandemic–a call to action. JAMA Neurol. **75**(1), 9–10 (2018)
5. Gillies, G.E., Pienaar, I.S., Vohra, S., Qamhawi, Z.: Sex differences in Parkinson's disease. Front. Neuroendocrinol. **35**(3), 370–384 (2014)
6. Goldman, S.M.: Environmental toxins and Parkinson's disease. Ann. Rev. Pharmacol. Toxicol. **54**(1), 141–164 (2014)
7. Kemp, A.S., Eubank, J., Younus, Y., Galvin, J.E., Prior, F.W., Larson-Prior, L.J.: Resting State MRI data from healthy control (HC), Parkinson's disease with normal cognition (PD-NC), and Parkinson's disease with mild cognitive impairment (PD-MCI) cohorts (2025). https://doi.org/10.18112/openneuro.ds005892.v1.0.0
8. Klein, C., Westenberger, A.: Genetics of Parkinson's disease. Cold Spring Harb. Perspect. Med. **2**(1), a008888 (2012)
9. Li, S., Yang, Y., Lv, Y., Xia, J., Wang, X.: ResGAT: embedding adjacent connectivity of brain regions from fMRI for accurate parkinson's disease recognition. In: International Conference on Advanced Data Mining and Applications, pp. 94–108. Springer, Heidelberg (2024). https://doi.org/10.1007/978-981-96-0840-9_7
10. Nalls, M.A., et al.: Identification of novel risk loci, causal insights, and heritable risk for Parkinson's disease: a meta-analysis of genome-wide association studies. Lancet Neurol. **18**(12), 1091–1102 (2019)
11. Poewe, W., et al.: Parkinson's disease. Nat. Rev. Dis. Primers **3**(1), 1–21 (2017)
12. Pringsheim, T., Jette, N., Frolkis, A., Steeves, T.D.: The prevalence of Parkinson's disease: a systematic review and meta-analysis. Mov. Disord. **29**(13), 1583–1590 (2014)
13. Tabashum, T., Snyder, R.C., O'Brien, M.K., Albert, M.V., et al.: Machine learning models for Parkinson disease: systematic review. JMIR Med. Inf. **12**(1), e50117 (2024)
14. Wooten, G., Currie, L., Bovbjerg, V., Lee, J., Patrie, J.: Are men at greater risk for Parkinson's disease than women? J. Neurol. Neurosurg. Psychiat. **75**(4), 637–639 (2004)

15. Yun, J.J., de Taurines, A.G., Tai, Y.F., Haar, S.: Anatomical abnormalities suggest a compensatory role of the cerebellum in early Parkinson's disease. Neuroimage **310**, 121121 (2025)
16. Zhang, X., Bai, P., Zhang, M., Yuan, M., Ren, Y.: Analysis of Parkinson's disease multi-connectivity brain functional networks based on graph convolutional neural networks. In: Proceedings of the 2024 7th International Conference on Signal Processing and Machine Learning, pp. 202–211 (2024)

Data Donation for Digital Twins in Healthcare: Potential and Challenges in the European Context

Martina Baltuzzi[(✉)] [ID]

University of Turin, Turin, Italy
`martina.baltuzzi@unito.it`

Abstract. Digital Twins, due to their ability to simulate and predict complex systems, are set to transform healthcare by improving personalised medicine, potentially tailoring diagnostics and reducing treatment costs. However, as their effectiveness depends on the availability of large, high-quality and inclusive datasets, current challenges pertain to fragmented health records, underrepresentation of minority groups, and the risk of algorithmic bias resulting from flawed information. To address these issues, the concept of data altruism, as set out in the EU Data Governance Act, has emerged as a promising strategy to diversify and improve the data pools needed to train DTs. Nevertheless, these practices carry significant ethical implications and normative challenges. This article explores the potential of the adoption of data donation mechanisms to better medical DTs within the European context, taking the first steps in analysing related ethical challenges while highlighting the importance of data quality and equity.

Keywords: Digital Twins · Healthcare · Ethics · Data donation

1 Digital Twins in Healthcare

Digital twins (DTs) are virtual replicas of tangible products or processes which, utilising data streams to generate digital representations of the physical counterpart, can simulate and mirror real-world alterations[1]. Since the early 2000s, when Michael Grieves first introduced them at the University of Michigan [9], they have experienced increasing popularity, capturing attention from both the industry and academia[2] [2]. In recent years, particularly during the COVID-19 pandemic, the life sciences industry began exploring

---

[1] The notion at the basis of digital twins can be traced back at least to the 1960s, when NASA pioneered the idea of using digital models to generate accurate simulations during the Apollo missions [19], then describing them as "an integrated multiphysics, multiscale, probabilistic simulation of an as-built vehicle or system that uses the best available physical models, sensor updates, fleet history, etc., to mirror the life of its corresponding flying twin" [8].

[2] DTs may soon be implemented in numerous sectors [1], ranging from the integration into smart cities settings [2], where they could achieve remarkable results in planning and maintenance, to the optimization of product design in the manufacturing field [1].

© The Author(s), under exclusive license to Springer Nature Switzerland AG 2026
C. Tommasino et al. (Eds.): AIBIO 2025, CCIS 2696, pp. 186–193, 2026.
https://doi.org/10.1007/978-3-032-17216-7_15

new ways to improve efficiency and reduce costs in the medical field, thereby accelerating digital transformation; within this shift, digital twins have emerged as a promising technology that could soon revolutionise traditional healthcare practices. Specifically, DTs could enhance the importance of the individual and thus accelerate the development of personalised medicine, as transforming patients into virtual entities may significantly improve treatment precision and shorten diagnostic timelines[3]. There are various health areas where DTs could be used: in cardiology they could serve to create virtual heart models to improve surgery; in pharmacy they could help determining the impact of medications on specific individuals by taking into account personal habits and diet [5]; furthermore, in orthopaedics, the advancements in wearable devices could drive DTs among the most promising technologies for real-time monitoring and analysis, connecting physical models to virtual reconstructions [20].

2 Data for Digital Twins

Digital twins have been defined as "data intense scenario[s]" [17], potentially impacting healthcare by empowering patients and promoting equitable treatment. To achieve these ambitious goals, it is essential to gather and have access to large amounts of both clinical and non-clinical data, enabling the DT model to define the most effective treatment strategies or to select tailored diagnoses. Meaningfully, data should be provided in an uninterrupted, consistent and high-quality stream that is representative of minorities and marginalised groups[4], as biased or incomplete information may undermine the algorithmic integrity of DTs and result in unreliable predictions[5]. The health sector may be particularly affected by erroneous algorithmic predictions: forecasting the future based on biased input could profoundly impact society, since relying on partial or prejudiced medical information may run the risk of perpetuating injustices and worsen their elimination, risking to reiterate the implementation of health practices as "designed around the white male" [17]. Therefore, acquiring quality data is one of the main challenges of using DTs in healthcare, given that electronic health records are often fragmented or difficult to interoperate. Taking into account the possible incompleteness of the datasets used to train the algorithms – and following the steps traced by the EU Data Governance Act – data donation could be a feasible tool capable of remedying the underrepresentation of uncommon patient traits, while also promoting individual participation in scientific progress, specifically within the European context.

---

[3] According to Sun et al. [20], to effectively customize medicine by adapting treatments to specific cases, it becomes highly useful to develop a "virtual physiological human body", with the aim of bridging the gap between computational physiology and clinical practice.

[4] A study conducted by Liu et al. [12] highlighted that IBM's Watson for Oncology showed reduced reliability when applied to non-Western populations, as the dataset used to train the program mainly contained information about Western populations.

[5] Indeed, to detect hidden correlations between many variables in an effective way, aiming at conducting predictive analysis with a high degree of accuracy, Digital Twins may need to be equipped with machine learning technologies based on algorithms; however, the dependability of such processes may be at risk if the datasets at disposal maintain certain prejudices [7].

3   The Promises of Data Donation

In response to the growing demand for diversity and completeness in datasets, the concept of data altruism emerged as a promising strategy to facilitate voluntary data sharing for the public good. The moral desirability of data donation can be traced back to specific arguments in favour of persons engaging in the practice: for example, individuals may choose to allow their data to support scientific research and to contribute to the advancement of the common good [14]. The March 2020 Eurobarometer report [23] examined the impact of digitalisation on everyday lives, including public attitudes towards personal data sharing. Among the questions posed, respondents were asked to indicate under what circumstances they would have been willing to share their personal data: the majority expressed a disposition to do so to support medical research and healthcare improvement. However, in seven EU member states, respondents showed aversion to sharing their data irrespective of the purpose. Given the critical role of data in the development of digital twins, such reluctance may eventually limit their inclusiveness and effectiveness. To enable informed consent on data donation and increase public awareness, it is therefore fundamental to demonstrate trustworthiness and transparency in the donation mechanism, as well as to carefully balance the complex ethical, technical, and social considerations involved in the functioning of medical DTs [11].

In September 2023, the Regulation (EU) 2022/868 on European Data Governance (Data Governance Act) [29] became applicable, seeking to "increase trust in data sharing, strengthen mechanisms to increase data availability and overcome technical obstacles to the reuse of data" [26]. In particular, the Regulation recognises the crucial role played by health data in advancing personalised treatments and in enhancing the quality of medical services[6]. Data altruism is defined under Article 2(16) DGA as follows:

> 'data altruism' means the voluntary sharing of data on the basis of the consent of data subjects to process personal data pertaining to them, or permissions of data holders to allow the use of their non-personal data without seeking or receiving a reward [...] for objectives of general interest as provided for in national law, where applicable, such as healthcare [29].

Integrating data donation to enrich DT training datasets could facilitate the creation of more representative and comprehensive resources through the inclusion of data from patient categories that are typically underrepresented in medical research. Data donation could enhance datasets by providing both clinical information and real-world data [18], the latter potentially generated through mobile applications and wearable devices[7]. The data altruism mechanism introduced by the DGA, a formalised framework aimed at

---

[6] The EU estimates around 120 billion in savings a year through the effective use of data in the medical sector. [26]

[7] To help with data collection, one solution could be represented by the integration of real-time information via smart health devices such as fitness trackers, wearable heart monitors, or connected mobile applications. While these technologies may promise improvements in monitoring costs and in the quality of personalization for the treatment, their employment also introduces complex ethical issues that need to be addressed, to allow responsible innovation in the medical sector [10].

enabling individuals and organisations to donate data for objectives of general interest voluntarily, rests on three specific pillars. First, the principle of public benefit, second, the institutionalisation of non-profit data altruism organisations under national supervision, and last, the operationalisation of data repositories and consent mechanisms. The model represents an important attempt to implement data altruism at scale, but it currently faces both technical and normative limitations that hinder its full realisation, including definitional ambiguity around the concept of general interest and legal uncertainties regarding data processing roles [15]. Currently, in Europe, only three entities are officially registered as data altruism organisations: the Spanish non-profit association DATALOG and the Belgian initiatives 101 Genomes and European Brain Data Hub (EBDH) [25]. Yet, despite the promising early results of the mechanism, so far this form of data donation, as regulated by the DGA, has not delivered the expected outcomes [15].

4 Ethical Implications and Normative Challenges

It has been suggested that donating personal data may, in some cases, be more psychologically or ethically challenging than donating blood or even organs [11], underlining the reluctance to adhere to this practice. Conducting an ethical assessment of data donation in this domain is therefore fundamental, as it highlights potential obstacles and enhances public trust and participation. One of the main factors that could reduce the public's trust in how their shared data will be used is the "black box" nature of machine learning algorithms embedded in the structure of Digital Twins. The opacity of ML systems' internal logic, which in some cases may remain hidden even from their developers, can hinder interpretation of the model's input and thus make accountability difficult [21]. Furthermore, data-related issues – such as acquisition and management, privacy and transparency – may pose serious concerns, in particular in contexts where various DTs are operating at different levels, exchanging information and influencing one another. Data donors may wonder where their data will eventually end up, making questions about data destination and control increasingly important. In this respect, at least two risk scenarios can be delineated. The first issue concerns the ownership and potential misuse of patient data by private entities. In this case, privacy may be at risk if personal data becomes accessible to, or even the property of, organisations that may not prioritise individual welfare[8]. This scenario, other than raising challenges about privacy, may also evolve into a broader concern about individual autonomy, as the ability of entities to use personal data to shape personal choices might eventually risk eroding personal freedom. A second scenario relates to data security and the risk of breaches. Accessing real-time data or sourcing information from genomic databases to train DTs might indeed amplify the risk of data being lost or stolen, as its sensitivity and volume may significantly exceed those found in traditional electronic health records. Given the distributed and often opaque nature of such digital infrastructures, responsibility for breaches may remain uncertain [17]. Thus, to ensure secure data donation in this context, it is fundamental to reach a fair balance between protecting individual privacy and

---

[8] A frequently cited example is the use of predictive analytics by insurance companies to make increasingly precise risk assessments on the basis of features tied to personal identity, such as age or medical history. [28]

advancing scientific research. Reliance on anonymisation techniques may not offer a fully satisfactory solution, as it could significantly diminish the quantity and quality of available data while also hindering the linking of specific datasets on critical dimensions, such as socioeconomic indicators [17] (Fig. 1).

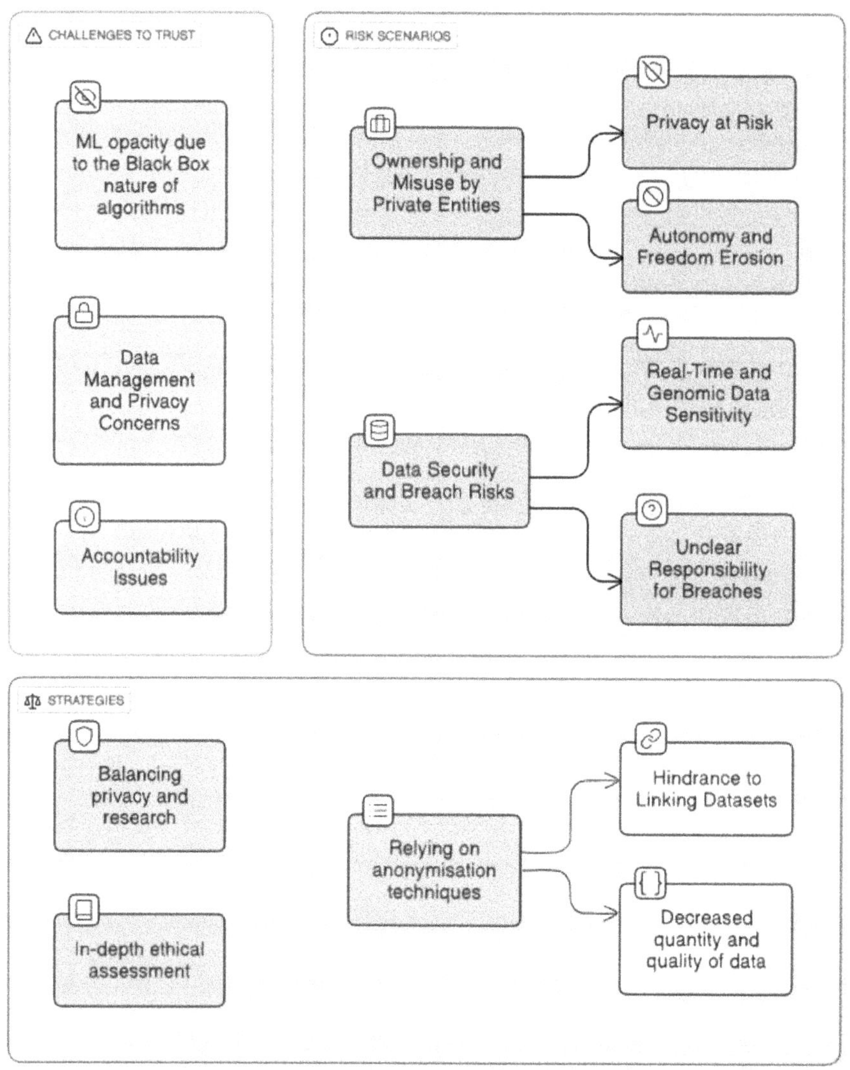

Fig. 1. Challenges of data donation for medical DTs

5 Future Research

To move towards the responsible integration of data donation in the training of medical DTs, several steps appear particularly urgent. First, clear governance frameworks must be consolidated under instruments such as the EU Data Governance Act, ensuring transparency and accountability. Second, building public trust remains central: targeted awareness initiatives and participatory design processes are needed to engage citizens and address concerns about privacy and data misuse. Third, technical infrastructures require further development, with emphasis on secure, interoperable platforms and the adoption of privacy-preserving techniques that balance data utility with individual rights. Then, data quality and representativeness must be strengthened by systematically addressing the underrepresentation of minority groups and by introducing continuous monitoring mechanisms. Finally, ethical assessment should be embedded into practice through the application of established bioethical principles, such as Childress and Beauchamp's principles of biomedical ethics – autonomy, beneficence, non-maleficence and justice –, often adopted in guiding decision-making processes and in evaluating clinical practices, [3], and the testing of frameworks such as AI4People by Floridi et al. [6]. Progress along these axes will depend on sustained collaboration between regulators, healthcare providers, technology developers, and civil society, thereby ensuring that data donation mechanisms can contribute to more equitable and trustworthy medical digital twins.

6 Conclusion

The integration of digital twins into healthcare presents promising potential for improving personalised care by enhancing diagnostic accuracy, enabling real-time monitoring, and introducing new dimensions of patient-centred values. The success of DTs, however, depends on access to large volumes of diverse high-quality data. The concept of data altruism, as set out in the EU Data Governance Act, proposes a way to expand and diversify datasets by encouraging people to donate their data voluntarily, potentially increasing inclusiveness and equity in the medical field. This model raises, however, significant challenges related to ethical governance, as building and maintaining public trust requires transparency and accountability, as well as a careful balance between individual privacy and collective benefits of scientific progress. This article has taken the first steps in the analysis of the normative and ethical implications of integrating data donation to better train medical DTs; future research will explore these challenges through established principles, such as Beauchamp and Childress' principles of biomedical ethics and the AI4People framework.

7 Disclosure of Interests

The author has no competing interests to declare that are relevant to the content of this article.

References

1. Attaran, M., Celik, B.G.: Digital twin: benefits, use cases, challenges, and opportunities. Decis. Anal. J. **6**, 100165 (2023)
2. Batty, M.: Digital twins. Environ. Plan. B: Urban Anal. City Sci. **45**(5), 817–820 (2018)
3. Beauchamp, T.L., Childress, J.F.: Principles of Biomedical Ethics, 4th edn. Oxford University Press, New York (1994)

4. Bruynseels, K., Santoni de Sio, F., van den Hoven, J.: Digital twins in health care: ethical implications of an emerging engineering paradigm. Front. Genet. **9**, 31 (2018)
5. Erol, T., Mendi, A.F., Doğan, D.: The digital twin revolution in healthcare. In: 4th International Symposium on Multidisciplinary Studies and Innovative Technologies (ISMSIT), pp. 1–7 (2020)
6. Floridi, L., et al.: AI4People—an ethical framework for a good ai society: opportunities, risks, principles, and recommendations. Minds Mach. **28** (2018)
7. Fuller, A., Fan, Z., Day, C., and Barlow, C., Digital Twin: Enabling Technologies, Challenges and Open Research, *IEEE Access*, vol. 8, (2020)
8. Glaessgen, E., Stargel, D.: The digital twin paradigm for future NASA and U.S. Air force vehicles. In/l Paper for the 53rd Structures, Structural Dynamics, and Materials Conference: Special Session on the Digital Twin (2012)
9. Grieves, M.: Origins of the digital twin concept. Florida Inst. Technol. **8**, 3–20 (2016)
10. Hassani, H., Huang, X., MacFeely, S.: Impactful digital twin in the healthcare revolution. Big Data Cogn. Comput. **6**, 83 (2022)
11. Kerina, H.: Jones Chapter 5 incongruities and dilemmas in data donation: juggling our 1s and 0s. In: Krutzinna, J., Floridi, L. (eds.) The Ethics of Medical Data Donation, vol. 137. Springer, Heidelberg (2019)
12. Liu, C., Liu, X., Wu, F., Xie, M., Feng, Y., Hu, C., Using artificial intelligence (Watson for oncology) for treatment recommendations amongst Chinese patients with lung cancer: feasibility study. J. Med. Internet Res. (2018)
13. Matsumi, H., Solove, D.J.: The Prediction Society: AI and the Problems of Forecasting the Future. GWU Legal Studies (2024)
14. Pagallo, U.: Il dovere alla salute: Sul rischio di sottoutilizzo dell'intelligenza artificiale in ambito sanitario. Mimesis, Milan (2022)
15. Paseri, L.: Il governo dei dati: interesse pubblico, altruismo e partecipazione, University of Turin (2025)
16. Paseri, L.: The ethical and legal challenges of data altruism for the scientific research sector. In: Arias-Oliva, M., Pelegrin-Borondo, J., Murata, K., Lara Palma A.M., Ollé Sensé M., (Eds), Smart Ethics in the Digital World Proceedings of the ETHICOMP 2024, pp. 137–141 (2024)
17. Popa, E.O., van Hilten, M., Oosterkamp, E., Bogaardt, M.-J.: The use of digital twins in healthcare: Socio-ethical benefits and socio-ethical risks. Life Sci. Soc. Policy **17**(1), 6 (2021)
18. Re Ferrè, G.: Data donation and data altruism to face algorithmic bias for an inclusive digital healthcare. BioLaw J. (2023)
19. Rosen, R., Von Wichert, G., Lo, G., Bettenhausen, K.D.: About the importance of autonomy and digital twins for the future of manufacturing. IFAC-PapersOnLine **48**(3) (2015)
20. Sun T., He X., Song X., Shu L., Li Z.: The digital twin in medicine: a key to the future of healthcare? Front. Med. (2022)
21. Sun, T., He, X., Li, Z.: Digital twin in healthcare: recent updates and challenges. Dig. Health (2023)
22. Vayena, E., Blasimme, A., Cohen, I.G.: Machine learning in medicine: addressing ethical challenges. PLoS Med. (2018)
23. Attitudes towards the impact of digitalisation on daily lives, https://europa.eu/eurobarometer/surveys/detail/2228, last accessed 2025/07/27
24. Data Governance Act Explained. https://digital-strategy.ec.europa.eu/en/policies/data-governance-act-explained. Accessed 23 Aug 2025
25. EU register of recognised data altruism organisations. https://digital-strategy.ec.europa.eu/en/policies/data-altruism-organisations. Accessed 23 Aug 2025
26. European Data Governance Act. https://digital-strategy.ec.europa.eu/en/policies/data-governance-act. Accessed 02 Aug 2025

27. Launch of European funding instrument to upscale Digital Twins towards the Citi-Verse through Living-in.EU. https://eurocities.eu/latest/launch-of-european-funding-instrument-to-upscale-digital-twins-towards-the-citiverse-through-living-in-eu/. Accessed 28 July 2025
28. OECD, Leveraging technology in insurance to enhance risk assessment and policyholder risk reduction. https://www.oecd.org/content/dam/oecd/en/publications/reports/2023/12/leveraging-technology-in-insurance-to-enhance-risk-assessment-and-policyholder-risk-reduction. Accessed 04 Aug 2025
29. Regulation (EU) 2022/868 of the European Parliament and of the Council of 30 May 2022 on European data governance

Image Segmentation

Quality-Guided Focal Loss: Enhancing Minority Class Detection in Haematological Imaging

Thabang Fenge Isaka[1]([✉])(iD), Claire Wynne[2](iD), and Jane Courtney[1](iD)

[1] School of Electrical and Electronic Engineering, Technological University Dublin, Dublin, Ireland
`D23125116@mytudublin.ie`
[2] School of Biological, Health and Sports Sciences, Technological University Dublin, Dublin, Ireland

Abstract. In the critical race against malaria, the most dangerous parasites often hide in plain sight. When parasitaemia falls below 1%, precisely when early detection matters most, conventional AI detection systems falter despite impressive aggregate metrics. This paradox of "seeing everything except what matters most" stems from a fundamental detection dilemma: infected cells comprise a vanishingly small minority that conventional approaches systematically overlook. We propose a methodical Quality-Guided Focal Loss (QGFL), a framework that reconceptualizes how detection systems learn from imbalanced data. By integrating class-specific focusing parameters, quality-guided weighting, and spatial awareness through UIoU, QGFL achieves a remarkable improvement in detecting infected cells in the clinically vital 1–3% parasitaemia range. Our cross-dataset validation confirms QGFL's generalizability across diverse imaging conditions without requiring dataset-specific tuning. This work advances the approach to minority class detection in medical imaging, demonstrating how prediction quality can guide model optimization, ensuring that what matters clinically also matters computationally.

Keywords: Medical Image Analysis · Object Detection · Class Imbalance · Adaptive Focal Loss · Malaria Detection

1 Introduction

In the fight against malaria, early detection can mean the difference between life and death. Yet in resource-constrained settings where malaria remains endemic, diagnostic capabilities are severely limited by the availability of trained microscopists. Automated detection systems offer transformative potential, but face a fundamental challenge: infected red blood cells often constitute merely 1–3% of all visible cells, creating extreme class imbalance that causes conventional AI systems to miss critical infections. Microscopy faces similar challenges, with

C. Tommasino et al. (Eds.): AIBIO 2025, CCIS 2696, pp. 197–211, 2026.
https://doi.org/10.1007/978-3-032-17216-7_16

average microscopists detecting only 50–100 parasites/μl versus expert limits of 5 parasites/μl [13], consistent with broader medical image imbalance issues [3]. This "needle-in-haystack" problem is particularly acute in low-density infections, precisely when early intervention is most critical. Mosquera et al. [7] demonstrated that imbalanced datasets can lead to 20% drops in F1-score for malaria detection systems, while Ramos-Briceño et al. [9] showed that state-of-the-art neural networks struggle with species-level Plasmodium identification in sparse distributions. As illustrated in Fig. 1, morphological similarity between infected and uninfected cells creates scenarios where subtle infections are easily missed, representing the most dangerous failure mode in automated diagnosis.

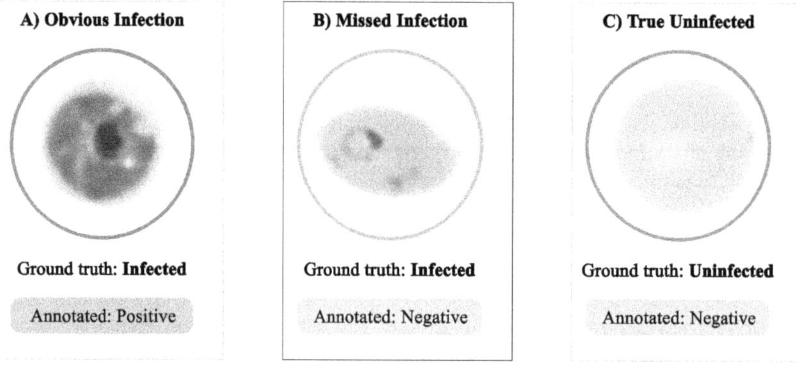

Fig. 1. Critical detection scenarios: (A) obvious infection correctly identified, (B) missed infection incorrectly classified as negative, (C) true uninfected cell correctly identified.

While focal loss approaches have shown promise for addressing class imbalance in object detection [6], their application to medical imaging with extreme intra-image imbalance remains underexplored. Current approaches lack systematic frameworks addressing minority class detection challenges where false negatives carry severe clinical consequences. Additionally, difficulty thresholding emerges as critical, requiring mechanisms to focus on challenging examples while avoiding noise from trivial cases [2]. This paper proposes a Quality-Guided Focal Loss (QGFL), a progressive adaptation framework for haematological imaging that addresses intra-image class imbalance through quality-guided components and difficulty thresholding. Building upon recent advances in quality-guided approaches [17], our framework demonstrates substantial improvements in detecting infected cells in low-density scenarios, showing promise for enhanced automated malaria detection applications.

The key contributions of this work are:

1. A progressive focal loss adaptation framework building from basic focal loss through quality-guided components to difficulty thresholding.

2. A quality-guided component that dynamically adjusts loss contribution based on detection quality, improving performance without sacrificing majority class accuracy.
3. Comprehensive validation across three datasets with varying imbalance characteristics, demonstrating consistent improvements in low-density scenarios.
4. A difficulty thresholding strategy that focuses training on genuinely challenging examples while avoiding noise from trivial cases.

2 Related Work

2.1 Object Detection Architectures for Haematological Imaging

Object detection in haematological imaging has evolved from traditional image processing to sophisticated deep learning architectures. Davidson et al. [1] implemented a two-stage approach achieving 92% accuracy on balanced test sets but showing significant performance degradation on images with natural parasite distributions. This limitation stems from treating detection as sequential segmentation and classification tasks, failing to leverage contextual information across the entire field of view. Hung and Carpenter [5] pioneered Faster R-CNN application to malaria microscopy, improving localization accuracy but relying heavily on mean Average Precision (mAP), which obscured performance disparities between infected and uninfected cell detection. Recent approaches focus on computational efficiency while maintaining accuracy. Guemas et al. [4] employed Real-Time Detection Transformer (RT-DETR) for species-level recognition, demonstrating improved species classification but continued struggles with intra-image class imbalance. Their evaluation showed detection recall for *P. falciparum* dropped from 87% to 63% when infection ratio fell below 3%, highlighting persistent minority class detection challenges. Current architectures face critical limitations: optimization for balanced datasets, evaluation methodologies masking performance disparities, and lack of specialized components for haematological imaging challenges such as morphological similarity and variable staining conditions.

2.2 Class Imbalance and Focal Loss Adaptations in Medical Imaging

Class imbalance in medical imaging manifests at both dataset and intra-image levels with distinct performance implications. Gao et al. [3] distinguished between these imbalance types, achieving AUC of 0.91 on LUNA16 and 0.87 on DDSM using deep autoencoder architectures, though primarily effective for dataset-level imbalance. Mosquera et al. [7] demonstrated F1-scores dropping up to 20% when minority classes constitute less than 5% of datasets, with melanoma detection showing 17.3% lower F1-score compared to majority classes. Focal Loss, introduced by Lin et al. [6], represented significant advancement in addressing class imbalance by dynamically adjusting loss contribution of well-classified examples, achieving 3.2% Average Precision improvement in RetinaNet.

Medical imaging adaptations include Yeung et al. [15] Unified Focal Loss framework, achieving 7.3% Dice score improvement for brain tumor segmentation, and Su et al. [11] Adaptive Focal Loss with dynamic focusing parameter adjustment, achieving 4.7% improvement in medical X-ray keypoint detection. Zhao et al. [17] proposed cross-domain Focal Loss adaptation for low-contrast medical image segmentation, demonstrating significant improvements through adversarial learning integration. Current approaches face limitations: few address extreme intra-image imbalance in haematological imaging, most focus on either classification or segmentation tasks, and quality-guided component integration with Focal Loss requires exploration.

2.3   Threshold Calibration and Quality-Guided Components

Threshold calibration represents a critical aspect of object detection in imbalanced scenarios, where minority classes require substantially lower confidence thresholds for optimal recall. Esposito et al. [2] demonstrated that class-specific calibration significantly improves minority class detection without compromising overall performance. Rajaraman et al. [8] revealed Expected Calibration Error (ECE) 2.3 times higher for minority classes, highlighting fundamental trade-offs between calibration and discrimination in imbalanced contexts. Quality assessment in object detection extends beyond simple IoU metrics to incorporate localization precision, classification confidence, and contextual relevance. Zhao et al. [17] demonstrated that quality-guided components improve performance by dynamically shifting attention between low-quality and high-quality prediction regions. Zhan et al. [16] showed detection performance drops by 27.3% when image quality falls below PSNR threshold of 25dB, particularly affecting small, low-contrast objects analogous to haematological imaging challenges. Current approaches inadequately address extreme threshold disparities in haematological imaging, focus primarily on post-hoc adjustment rather than integrated training considerations, and insufficiently explore quality assessment's relationship with detection reliability in low-density scenarios. This analysis of current approaches across object detection architectures, class imbalance methods, focal loss adaptations, threshold calibration, and quality-guided components identifies specific limitations that the Quality-Guided Focal Loss framework addresses, providing a comprehensive solution to minority class detection challenges in haematological imaging.

3   Materials and Methods

3.1   Dataset Characteristics and Preprocessing

This study utilized three publicly available malaria microscopy datasets: D1 [1], D2 [5], and D3 [4], all characterized by pronounced intra-image sparsity. Table 1 reveals that 87–98% of images contain ≤ 2 infected cells, creating a clinically realistic "needle-in-haystack" detection scenario.

Table 1. Intra-Image Class Imbalance Across Datasets

Dataset	Split	Img.	Inf.	Uninf.	Mean Inf.%	Std. Dev	≤ 2 Inf.
D1	Train	279	1,614	23,372	2.8%	±1.1%	243 (87%)
	Valid	79	599	6,799	3.2%	±1.4%	62 (78%)
	Test	40	164	3,516	1.9%	±1.0%	38 (95%)
D2	Train	930	1,791	57,912	0.7%	±0.6%	915 (98%)
	Valid	265	446	16,825	0.8%	±0.5%	259 (98%)
	Test	133	215	8,400	0.6%	±0.4%	131 (98%)
D3	Train	865	3,600	65,678	1.4%	±1.2%	812 (94%)
	Valid	247	997	18,221	1.7%	±1.3%	226 (91%)
	Test	123	467	9,565	1.3%	±1.0%	117 (95%)

D1 comprises 398 microscopy images from laboratory *P. falciparum* cultures with standardized Giemsa staining. D2 consists of 1,328 images from ex vivo *P. vivax* patient samples, presenting severe class imbalance with 97% uninfected cells. D3 represents the largest collection with 29,228 images from 475 patient samples across 6 French hospitals, spanning multiple *Plasmodium* species. All datasets were standardized to binary infected/uninfected COCO-annotated classifications and partitioned using 70/20/10% splits to prevent data leakage [14]. D3 required strategic subsampling: retaining 100% of images containing infected cells and 5% of uninfected-only images, preserving natural intra-image sparsity essential for clinical relevance. No synthetic augmentation or artificial class balancing was employed, aligning with findings that preserving natural distributions improves generalization in medical imaging [10].

3.2 Base Architecture

The Quality-Guided Focal Loss framework builds upon RetinaNet with ResNet50 backbone pre-trained on ImageNet, selected for established performance in detecting small objects under class imbalance [6]. The architecture integrates Feature Pyramid Network for multi-scale feature representation, critical for detecting parasites across developmental stages. Domain-specific adaptations included reconfiguring the classification head for binary classification and disabling in-place ReLU operations for stable gradient flow. Training employed SGD with momentum 0.9, learning rate 0.003, and weight decay 0.0005. For our experiments, the Baseline (B) model in Table 2 refers to the RetinaNet architecture that uses default library parameters for its standard focal loss. In contrast, our Standard Focal Loss (FL) model, which represents the first level of our progressive framework, utilizes the standard implementation from Lin et al. [6] with our own tuned hyperparameters:

$$FL(p_t) = -\alpha_t(1 - p_t)^\gamma \log(p_t) \tag{1}$$

where p_t represents predicted probability for the true class, α_t is class-balancing weight (0.9 for infected, 0.1 for uninfected), and γ is the focusing parameter (2.0) that down-weights easy examples.

3.3 Progressive Loss Adaptations

The Quality-Guided Focal Loss framework in Fig. 2 employs progressive adaptation, systematically building upon standard focal loss [6] to address minority class detection challenges. This methodical progression, inspired by adaptive focal loss methodologies [11] and calibration-aware approaches [17], enables precise identification of effective components while maintaining experimental control.

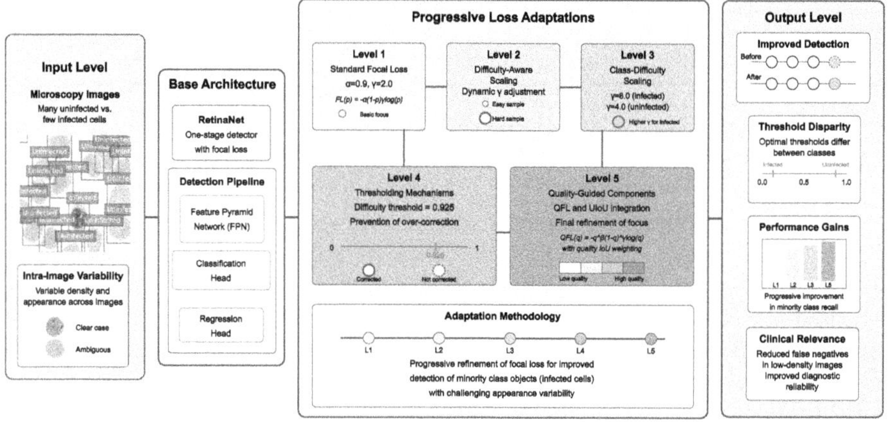

Fig. 2. The five-level progressive adaptation approach, from standard focal loss through difficulty-aware and class-specific modifications, to the complete quality-guided framework with UIoU integration.

Level 2: Difficulty-Aware Scaling. Dynamic adjustment of focusing parameter based on sample difficulty, building upon adaptive focal loss approaches [11]:

$$\mathrm{FL}_{\mathrm{diff}}(p_t) = -\alpha_t(1 - p_t)^{\gamma_{\mathrm{eff}}} \log(p_t) \tag{2}$$

where $\gamma_{\mathrm{eff}} = \gamma + (\max_\gamma - \gamma) \times \text{difficulty}$ with difficulty $= (1 - p_t)$ and optimal $\max_\gamma = 4.0$. This adaptation addresses the inherent challenge where difficult examples often receive insufficient attention under standard focusing mechanisms.

Level 3: Class-Difficulty Scaling. Class-specific maximum focusing parameters, extending class-aware focal loss methodologies [12]:

$$\text{FL}_{\text{class-diff}}(p_t) = -\alpha_t(1 - p_t)^{\gamma_{\text{eff}}} \log(p_t) \tag{3}$$

This is the case where γ_{eff} applies class-specific parameters: infected_max$_\gamma$ = 8.0 and uninfected_max$_\gamma$ = 4.0, recognizing the inherent asymmetry in detection tasks.

Level 4: Thresholding Mechanisms. Difficulty thresholding to focus on challenging examples, adapting threshold calibration principles [2]:

$$\text{FL}_{\text{thresh}}(p_t) = -\alpha_t(1 - p_t)^{\gamma_{\text{eff}}} \log(p_t) \tag{4}$$

where difficulty is calculated as:

$$\text{difficulty} = \frac{\max\left(\text{raw\_difficulty} - \text{threshold},\ 0\right)}{1 - \text{threshold}} \tag{5}$$

With raw_difficulty = $(1 - p_t)$ and optimal threshold = 0.925.

Level 5: Quality-Guided Components. Integration of quality measurement and Unified IoU components, following calibration error principles and synthesizing quality-guided approaches [17]:

$$\text{QGFL}(p_t) = -\alpha_t(1 - p_t)^{\gamma_{\text{eff}}}(1 + \text{quality\_weight}) \times \text{uiou\_ratio} \times \log(p_t) \tag{6}$$

where quality is measured as the absolute difference between prediction and target:

$$\text{quality} = |p - \text{target}| \tag{7}$$

Adjusted using:

$$\text{quality\_adjusted} = \max(\text{quality} - \text{quality\_margin},\ 0) \tag{8}$$

And transformed to:

$$\text{quality\_weight} = \min(\text{quality\_adjusted}^{\text{quality\_factor}},\ 10.0) \tag{9}$$

With quality_margin = 0.5 and quality_factor = 2.0. The UIoU component varies from 2.0 to 0.5 using linear decay during training.

3.4 Adaptation Methodology

The progressive refinement methodology systematically isolates challenges of minority class detection, as visualized in Fig. 2. Parameter calibration followed rigorous grid search on Dataset D1: alpha (0.25–0.9), gamma (1.0–4.0), max gamma (4.0–20.0), and thresholds (0.05–0.96). Error analysis employed TIDE methodology categorizing detection failures. Cross-dataset validation employed direct parameter transfer from D1 to D2 and D3 without dataset-specific tuning, providing stringent generalizability testing across varying class imbalance ratios, parasite species, and imaging protocols.

4 Results

4.1 Cross-Dataset Performance

Table 2 reports the performance of the Quality-Guided Focal Loss (QGFL) framework across three haematological imaging datasets. Relative to the baseline RetinaNet, QGFL improves mean average precision (mAP) by 5.7% on D1, 11.2% on D2, and 10.4% on D3. Infected-class F1 scores show substantial gains in D1 (from 0.562 to 0.655) and D2 (from 0.648 to 0.743), corresponding to 16.5 and 14.7 percent relative improvement, respectively. On D3, recall increases from 0.675 to 0.807, indicating improved coverage of sparse positives. The Class-Diff+Thresh adaptation yields mAP improvements of 10.3% on D1 and 12.6% on D2, suggesting that explicit modulation of class difficulty contributes significantly to overall performance.

Table 2. Performance comparison of QGFL variants and baseline RetinaNet across three haematological imaging datasets. See legend below for full adaptation level names.

Adapt.	D1				D2				D3			
	mAP	Prec.	Recall	F1	mAP	Prec.	Recall	F1	mAP	Prec.	Recall	F1
B	0.672	0.824	0.427	0.562	0.681	0.718	0.591	0.648	0.772	0.903	0.675	0.772
FL	0.741	0.683	**0.604**	0.641	0.763	0.682	0.767	**0.722**	0.815	0.700	**0.794**	0.744
DA	0.704	0.674	0.579	0.623	0.752	0.652	0.740	0.693	0.845	0.661	0.812	0.729
CD	0.690	0.674	0.543	0.601	0.720	0.667	0.698	0.682	0.808	0.746	0.717	0.731
CD+T	**0.741**	0.650	**0.634**	**0.642**	**0.767**	**0.731**	0.735	0.733	0.815	0.701	**0.797**	0.745
FL+Q	0.713	0.754	0.598	**0.667**	0.726	0.747	0.688	0.717	0.812	0.717	0.760	0.738
FL+Q+U	0.711	**0.797**	0.573	**0.667**	0.759	0.728	**0.758**	0.743	0.816	0.732	0.784	**0.757**
QGFL	0.710	0.786	0.561	0.655	0.757	0.728	**0.758**	0.743	**0.852**	**0.735**	**0.807**	**0.769**

Adaptation Legend:
B = Baseline RetinaNet, **FL** = Standard Focal Loss, **DA** = Difficulty-Aware, **CD** = Class-Difficulty, **CD+T** = Class-Difficulty + Threshold, **FL+Q** = Focal Loss + Quality, **FL+Q+U** = Focal Loss + Quality + UIoU, **QGFL** = Complete Quality-Guided Focal Loss Framework.

Figure 3 supports these findings. Average precision for the infected class increases across all datasets: from 0.557 to 0.627 in D1, from 0.554 to 0.666 in D2, and from 0.764 to 0.795 in D3. The QGFL curves consistently span a broader recall range, particularly in D1 and D2 where intra-image imbalance is more severe.

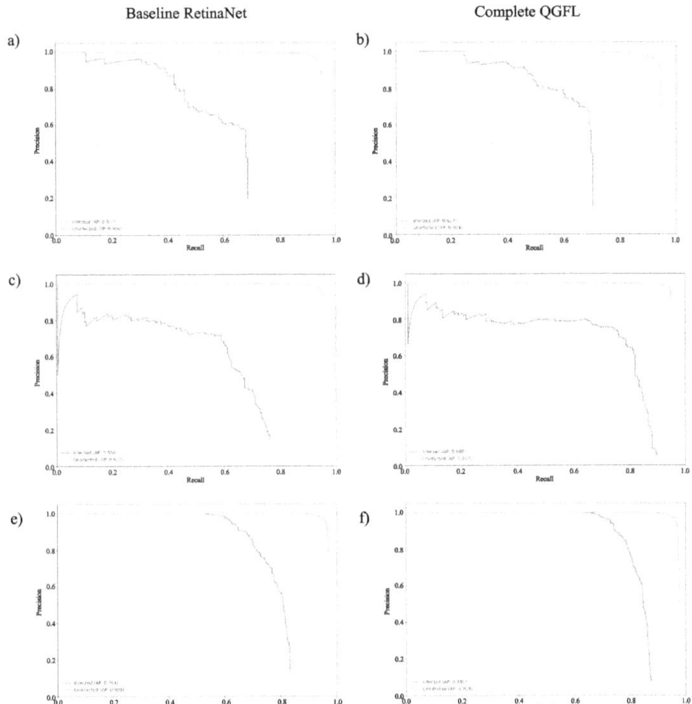

Fig. 3. Precision-recall curves comparing the baseline RetinaNet against the complete QGFL framework for infected-class detection across datasets D1, D2, and D3

4.2 Confidence Calibration and Error Analysis

Figure 4 presents optimal confidence thresholds across adaptation strategies and datasets. Infected-class thresholds consistently fall below the standard 0.5 detection threshold, ranging from 0.14–0.87, while uninfected cells achieve optimal performance at 0.56–0.93. This pattern persists across all three datasets regardless of adaptation complexity. Complete QGFL demonstrates more consistent infected-class thresholds across datasets while preserving uninfected performance above 0.8.

Figure 5 presents missed detection rates for infected cells across adaptation strategies. Complete QGFL achieves the lowest error rates across all datasets (38.1%, 18.8%, and 14.9% on D1, D2, and D3), with D1 showing the most substantial improvement from baseline (52.5% to 38.1%).

4.3 Low-Density Performance

Figure 6 examines recall performance across infection density bins, focusing on the clinically critical 1–3% range where Complete QGFL demonstrates substantial improvements: 46% enhancement on D1 (0.42 to 0.61 recall), 93% on D2

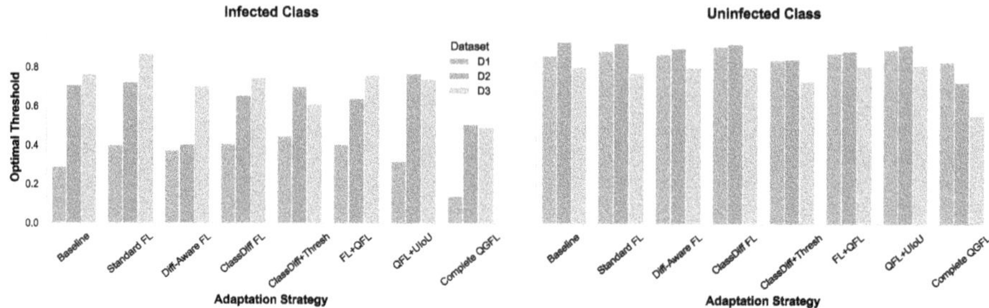

Fig. 4. Optimal confidence thresholds for infected and uninfected classes. A systematic disparity is observed, with infected cells consistently requiring lower thresholds across all datasets.

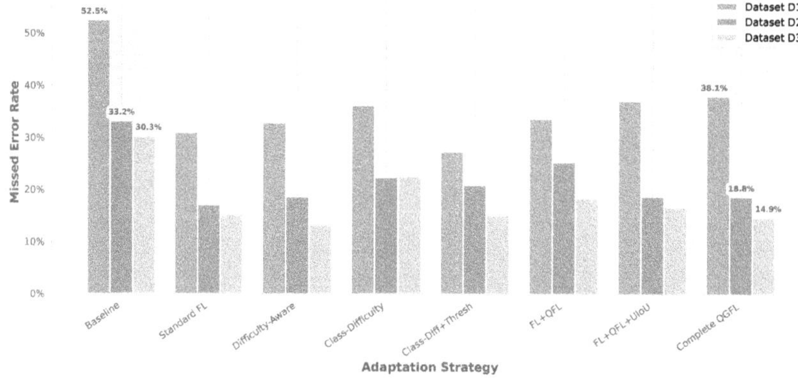

Fig. 5. Missed detection rates for infected cells across all datasets, where the complete QGFL model consistently achieves the lowest error rates.

(0.28 to 0.54), and 8% on D3 (0.71 to 0.76). These density-stratified results validate that QGFL's systematic approach addresses minority class detection precisely where clinical impact is greatest.

4.4   Qualitative Results

Figure 7 presents representative detection outputs across adaptation strategies, illustrating progressive improvement in minority class detection. Complete QGFL demonstrates the most comprehensive detection performance, consistently identifying infected cells across density scenarios while maintaining precision.

5   Discussion and Limitations

This study introduced Quality-Guided Focal Loss (QGFL), a progressive adaptation framework addressing minority class detection in haematological imag-

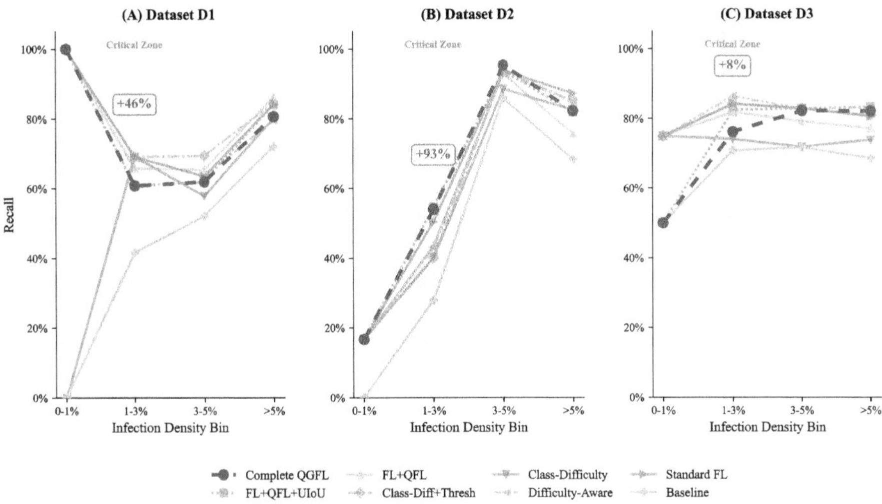

Fig. 6. Density-stratified recall performance, highlighting the substantial improvements by QGFL in the clinically critical 1–3% infection density range across all three datasets.

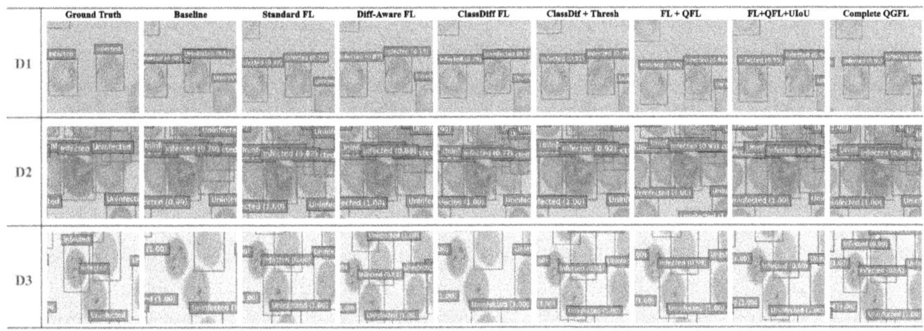

Fig. 7. Qualitative results for datasets D1-D3, where the complete QGFL framework demonstrates superior detection coverage of infected cells.

ing. QGFL substantially improves infected cell detection across three diverse datasets, with notable gains in clinically relevant low-density scenarios. The progressive adaptation methodology revealed critical insights about focal loss modifications for medical object detection. Class-specific threshold calibration yielded substantial performance improvements (10.3% mAP improvement on D1, 12.6% on D2), confirming that explicit modulation of class difficulty contributes significantly to overall performance. This aligns with Rajaraman et al. [8], who found that deep learning models are poorly calibrated for minority classes in medical imaging, with Expected Calibration Error 2.3 times higher for minority classes. QGFL addresses this calibration challenge through targeted adjustments to gradient weighting and loss formulation.

Density-stratified recall analysis in Fig. 6 provides compelling evidence for QGFL's clinical utility. In the critical 1–3% infection density range where early diagnosis is crucial, QGFL demonstrated substantial improvements: 46% enhancement on D1, 93% on D2, and 8% on D3. This pattern suggests that QGFL's effectiveness scales inversely with baseline performance, offering the most substantial improvements in the most challenging detection scenarios. The 93% improvement on D2, which features the most severe class imbalance (0.7% infected cells), demonstrates that QGFL effectively addresses the fundamental challenge of extreme intra-image sparsity. Confidence calibration properties (Fig. 4) reveal a systematic pattern with direct clinical implications. The consistent disparity between infected-class thresholds (0.14–0.87) and uninfected thresholds (0.56–0.93) across all datasets explains why conventional detection systems fail in low-prevalence scenarios. This threshold disparity creates a fundamental detection dilemma: using a single global threshold inevitably sacrifices either sensitivity or specificity for the minority class. QGFL resolves this dilemma by dynamically adjusting loss contributions based on class membership and prediction quality, enabling the model to maintain high sensitivity for infected cells without compromising overall precision. The stability of this threshold pattern across adaptation levels confirms it represents an intrinsic property of the detection task rather than an artifact of model design. It is important to note that this focus on improving recall involves a deliberate trade-off with precision. For instance, on dataset D1, QGFL improves recall from a baseline of 0.427 to 0.561, while precision moves from 0.824 to 0.786. Our framework is designed to manage this balance, prioritizing the reduction of clinically critical false negatives in alignment with the goals of early-stage screening. The integration of quality-guided components with focal loss represents a significant contribution that addresses a specific gap in medical object detection. While previous approaches like Zhao et al. [17] demonstrated quality-guided components for segmentation tasks, and Lin et al. [6] introduced focal loss for general object detection, neither approach adequately addressed the unique challenges of haematological imaging where objects of interest are morphologically similar but functionally distinct. QGFL bridges this gap by combining three critical elements: (1) class-specific focusing parameters that acknowledge the asymmetric detection challenges, (2) quality-guided weighting that dynamically adjusts loss contribution based on prediction quality, and (3) UIoU integration that addresses the spatial aspects of detection. This comprehensive framework specifically targets the needle-in-haystack detection scenario encountered in early-stage infection. Our evaluation is centered on the RetinaNet architecture, a choice made deliberately as it was the pioneering architecture for focal loss, thus providing the most direct and logical platform to isolate and rigorously evaluate the impact of our progressive loss adaptations.

While these results are promising, three primary limitations affect clinical applicability. First, while the QGFL framework is theoretically more complex, our empirical analysis found its practical computational overhead to be modest. For example, on a representative dataset (D3), it required only 5.1% more training time, demonstrating that its performance benefits are accessible without a prohibitive resource burden. Second, our analysis is constrained in two main ways: its focus on binary classification and its evaluation on a single architecture. The binary approach, while effective for proving the core concept, does not address the clinical need for species-level Plasmodium identification. Similarly, while our choice of RetinaNet was justified for isolating the effects of our loss function, the performance of QGFL on other modern architectures remains unevaluated. Third, while datasets preserved natural class distributions, they represent controlled laboratory conditions rather than the full variability encountered in clinical practice, including staining quality variations and microscope calibration differences.

Future work will address these limitations through optimized implementations that maintain performance while reducing computational requirements, extension to multi-class scenarios with hierarchical class relationships, and prospective validation in clinical environments. Additionally, systematic evaluation of established class balancing techniques alongside the progressive QGFL framework will identify synergistic combinations and optimize performance across diverse medical imaging applications. Crucially, future validation will involve implementing QGFL across state-of-the-art architectures, including YOLO variants and transformer-based models, to rigorously establish its generalizability.

6   Conclusion

This work demonstrates that by reconceptualizing loss functions through a quality-guided approach, we can achieve improved detection capabilities in minority class scenarios. The Quality-Guided Focal Loss framework achieves consistent improvements in detecting infected cells, with up to 93% improvement in recall for the clinically critical 1–3% parasitaemia range where early intervention matters most. Beyond the quantitative gains, QGFL represents a systematic approach that moves from treating all predictions equally to acknowledging their inherent quality differences. This principle extends beyond haematological imaging, offering a methodical pathway toward more reliable automated detection across medical domains where subtle abnormalities demand heightened sensitivity, ultimately contributing to earlier diagnosis and improved patient outcomes.

Acknowledgments. Funded by Taighde Éireann – Research Ireland through the Research Ireland Centre for Research Training in Machine Learning (18/CRT/6183).

Disclosure of Interests. The authors have no competing interests to declare that are relevant to the content of this article.

References

1. Davidson, M.S., et al.: Automated detection and staging of malaria parasites from cytological smears using convolutional neural networks. Biol. Imaging **1**, e2 (2021). https://doi.org/10.1017/s2633903x21000015
2. Esposito, C., Landrum, G.A., Schneider, N., Stiefl, N., Riniker, S.: GHOST: adjusting the decision threshold to handle imbalanced data in machine learning. J. Chem. Inf. Model. **61**(6), 2623–2640 (2021). https://doi.org/10.1021/acs.jcim.1c00160
3. Gao, L., Zhang, L., Liu, C., Wu, S.: Handling imbalanced medical image data: a deep-learning-based one-class classification approach. Artif. Intell. Med. **108**, 101935 (2020). https://doi.org/10.1016/j.artmed.2020.101935
4. Guemas, E., et al.: Automatic patient-level recognition of four plasmodium species on thin blood smear by a real-time detection transformer (RT-DETR) object detection algorithm: a proof-of-concept and evaluation. Microbiol. Spectrum **12**(2), e01440-23 (2024). https://doi.org/10.1128/spectrum.01440-23
5. Hung, J., et al.: Applying faster R-CNN for object detection on malaria images. In: 2017 IEEE Conference on Computer Vision and Pattern Recognition Workshops (CVPRW), pp. 808–813 (2017). https://doi.org/10.1109/cvprw.2017.112
6. Lin, T.Y., Goyal, P., Girshick, R., He, K., Dollár, P.: Focal loss for dense object detection. IEEE Trans. Pattern Anal. Mach. Intell. **42**(2), 318–327 (2018). https://doi.org/10.1109/tpami.2018.2858826
7. Mosquera, C., Ferrer, L., Milone, D.H., Luna, D., Ferrante, E.: Class imbalance on medical image classification: towards better evaluation practices for discrimination and calibration performance. Eur. Radiol. **34**(12), 7895–7903 (2024). https://doi.org/10.1007/s00330-024-10834-0
8. Rajaraman, S., Ganesan, P., Antani, S.: Deep learning model calibration for improving performance in class-imbalanced medical image classification tasks. PLoS ONE **17**(1), e0262838 (2022). https://doi.org/10.1371/journal.pone.0262838
9. Ramos-Briceño, D.A., et al.: Deep learning-based malaria parasite detection: convolutional neural networks model for accurate species identification of plasmodium falciparum and plasmodium vivax. Sci. Rep. **15**(1), 3746 (2025). https://doi.org/10.1038/s41598-025-87979-5
10. Shen, L., et al.: Deep learning to improve breast cancer detection on screening mammography. Sci. Rep. **9**(1), 12495 (2019). https://doi.org/10.1038/s41598-019-48995-4
11. Su, Z., Adam, A., Nasrudin, M.F.: Adaptive focal loss for keypoint-based deep learning detectors addressing class imbalance. IEEE Access **13**, 31842–31856 (2025). https://doi.org/10.1109/access.2025.3538917
12. Tan, J., et al.: Equalization loss for long-tailed object recognition. In: 2020 IEEE/CVF Conference on Computer Vision and Pattern Recognition (CVPR), pp. 11659–11668 (2020). https://doi.org/10.1109/cvpr42600.2020.01168
13. Tangpukdee, N., Duangdee, C., Wilairatana, P., Krudsood, S.: Malaria diagnosis: a brief review. Korean J. Parasitol. **47**(2), 93–102 (2009). https://doi.org/10.3347/kjp.2009.47.2.93
14. Willemink, M.J., et al.: Preparing medical imaging data for machine learning. Radiology **295**(1), 4–15 (2020). https://doi.org/10.1148/radiol.2020192224
15. Yeung, M., Sala, E., Schönlieb, C.B., Rundo, L.: Unified focal loss: generalising dice and cross entropy-based losses to handle class imbalanced medical image segmentation. Comput. Med. Imaging Graph. **95**, 102026 (2022). https://doi.org/10.1016/j.compmedimag.2021.102026

16. Zhan, B., Song, E., Liu, H.: FSA-net: rethinking the attention mechanisms in medical image segmentation from releasing global suppressed information. Comput. Biol. Med. **161**, 106932 (2023). https://doi.org/10.1016/j.compbiomed.2023.106932
17. Zhao, Y., Shen, X., Chen, J., Qian, W., Ma, H., Sang, L.: ARD loss for low-contrast medical image segmentation. Mach. Learn. Sci. Technol. **5**(1), 015013 (2024). https://doi.org/10.1088/2632-2153/ad1d06

Auto-prompting Foundation Models for Clinical Segmentation: The Case of Pathological Scapula

Michele Signori[1]([✉])(iD), Mattia Savardi[2](iD), Fabio Casiraghi[1](iD),
Maristella Francesca Saccomanno[2,3](iD), Giuseppe Milano[2,3](iD),
and Alberto Signoroni[2](iD)

[1] Department of Information Engineering, University of Brescia, Brescia, Italy
`{michele.signori,fabio.casiraghi}@unibs.it`
[2] Department of Medical and Surgical Specialties, Radiological Sciences, and Public Health, University of Brescia, Brescia, Italy
`{mattia.savardi,maristella.saccomanno,giuseppe.milano,`
`alberto.signoroni}@unibs.it`
[3] Department of Bone and Joint Surgery, Spedali Civili, Brescia, Italy

Abstract. Automatic segmentation of the scapula in CT volumes is critical for surgical planning and other clinically relevant morphometric tasks, but especially pathological cases pose significant challenges due to high anatomical variability, complex geometry, and proximity to adjacent structures. Standard deep learning methods, including large-scale segmentation models such as TotalSegmentator, often fail on this task due to the scarcity of high-quality, annotated pathological data. Conversely, general-purpose foundation models such as SAM2 require manual prompting, precluding full automation. In this work, we introduce a novel, fully automatic, and prompt-free segmentation framework. Our key idea is to cascade existing tools, repurposing the imperfect output of an automatic segmentation model (TotalSegmentator) not as a final result, but as a mechanism to generate robust 3D prompts for a SAM-based foundation model. This approach creates a fully automatic pipeline that requires no user interaction or task-specific fine-tuning. We evaluated our framework on a challenging dataset of about 40 expert-annotated pathological scapulae. Quantitative and qualitative results demonstrate that our method significantly outperforms both the baseline automatic segmentation model and prompted general-purpose medical foundation models (MedSAM2), reaching an average Dice Score of 92.40%, compared to 81.24% of TotalSegmentator and 82.41% of MedSAM2. Our auto-prompting strategy offers a powerful and data-efficient paradigm for tackling complex segmentation tasks in clinically realistic, low-data scenarios, bridging the gap between large-scale models and specialized clinical needs.

Keywords: Medical Image Segmentation · Vision Foundation Models · Scapula Segmentation · Automatic Prompting · Zero-shot Segmentation

© The Author(s), under exclusive license to Springer Nature Switzerland AG 2026
C. Tommasino et al. (Eds.): AIBIO 2025, CCIS 2696, pp. 212–225, 2026.
https://doi.org/10.1007/978-3-032-17216-7_17

1   Introduction

Accurate 3D segmentation of bone structures from Computed Tomography (CT) images is a fundamental prerequisite for a growing number of clinical procedures in orthopedics and computational anatomy [5]. In particular, the segmentation of the scapula is critical for the pre-operative assessment of glenoid morphology, the virtual planning of complex shoulder arthroplasty, and the design of patient-specific implants and surgical guides [7,15]. However, this task presents formidable challenges, especially in pathological cases where anatomy is significantly altered. The scapula's intrinsically complex, non-convex geometry, combined with its close proximity to the humerus and clavicle, often leads to indistinct or non-existent tissue boundaries, particularly in cases of pathological fusion [2]. These geometric complexities are exacerbated by a critical data scarcity problem. Publicly available, expert-annotated datasets of pathological scapulae are virtually non-existent, primarily because healthy scapulae are often partially cropped in standard thoracic CT acquisitions, while annotating pathological cases is an extremely time-consuming and expertise-intensive process.

The advent of deep learning, particularly architectures based on U-Net [14] and its volumetric variants such as V-Net [11], has revolutionized medical image segmentation, yielding remarkable successes across numerous applications [1,13]. This has led to the development of large-scale, general-purpose segmentation models such as TotalSegmentator [17], a powerful SOTA tool based on the robust nnU-Net framework [6] capable of identifying over 100 anatomical structures. The same authors also recently released another version of the model that is able to segment 59 anatomical structures from Magnetic Resonance (MR) Images [3]. Despite their general effectiveness, these models often falter when segmenting structures with significant anatomical variance. This failure stems from an inherent bias in their vast training sets, which lack the diversity to model atypical or pathological morphologies. The pathological scapula perfectly exemplifies this challenge. Consequently, its complex, out-of-distribution variations lead to unreliable and inaccurate segmentations, making these tools unsuitable for high-precision clinical applications in this context.

A different paradigm is offered by foundation models, such as the Segment Anything Model (SAM) and its successor, SAM2 [8,12]. Trained on billions of natural images, these models possess remarkable zero-shot generalization capabilities but are not fully automatic, as their design requires user-provided prompts (e.g., points, masks, or bounding boxes). To bridge this gap for medical use, fine-tuned versions such as MedSAM [9] and MedSAM2 [10] have been developed. MedSAM2 cleverly adapts the video segmentation capabilities of SAM2 to 3D volumes by treating sequential slices as video frames, enabling robust object tracking across the volume from a single initial prompt. However, as we demonstrate in this work, even this extensive medical fine-tuning is insufficient to guarantee accuracy on highly specialized tasks. The training data, although extensive, primarily consist of common anatomical structures such as organs and tumors, and do not capture the specific and complex shape variations of pathological bones. Similar efforts have also been reported [18], but they face the same fundamental limitation, leaving a clear gap for a solution that is both fully automatic and highly accurate for this specific clinical need.

In this work, we bridge this gap by introducing a novel, fully automatic framework that intelligently cascades existing SOTA tools to overcome their individual limitations. Our core contribution is an auto-prompting pipeline that establishes a powerful synergy: it uses the coarse anatomical awareness of TotalSegmentator to generate an initial, imperfect segmentation, which is then repurposed as a fully automatic 3D prompt for the SAM2 foundation model. This allows us to harness the fine-grained segmentation acuity and remarkable zero-shot power of SAM2 without requiring any manual interaction or resource-intensive, task-specific fine-tuning. Furthermore, using a small amount of expert-annotated images, we managed to further improve the segmentation performance, exploiting SAM2's few-shot capabilities. Our method effectively circumvents the two primary bottlenecks in modern medical segmentation: the need for manual labor and the dependence on large, curated datasets. The main contributions of this paper are:

- A novel auto-prompting framework that enables the fully automatic use of foundation models for complex 3D medical segmentation tasks.
- A comprehensive quantitative and qualitative evaluation on a challenging, expert-annotated dataset of pathological scapulae.
- A demonstration that our cascaded approach significantly outperforms both leading automatic segmentation models and fine-tuned foundation models, establishing a new SOTA for this specific clinical problem.
- A powerful and data-efficient paradigm for other challenging segmentation tasks where annotated data is scarce.

2   Methods

This paper evaluates and compares several models for the challenging task of pathological scapula segmentation. Our primary comparisons are against TotalSegmentator [17], various configurations of the SAM2 foundation model [12], and its medically fine-tuned version, MedSAM2 [10]. For SAM2, we also developed a fine-tuning procedure on a small set of annotated data to assess performance improvements.

The following sections first provide an analysis of the baseline models, with a focus on the limitations of TotalSegmentator that motivate our work. Subsequently, we present an in-depth description of our proposed automatic pipeline, detailing each stage from preprocessing to final mask generation, followed by a description of our fine-tuning process.

2.1   Analysis of Baseline Models

TotalSegmentator: Capabilities and Limitations. The TotalSegmentator model offers a state-of-the-art solution for multi-organ segmentation, but its performance on specific structures is highly dependent on its training data composition [17]. Through our analysis, we identified significant inconsistencies in the ground truth masks used to train TotalSegmentator for the scapula. This limitation is central to understanding its suboptimal performance on our task.

Figure 1 highlights this issue, comparing a complete anatomical scapula with two ground truth examples from the public TotalSegmentator training dataset. It is evident that the training masks are often incomplete. The middle mask in the figure shows a nearly complete segmentation, but omits part of the acromion. The mask on the right is far more deficient, entirely lacking the supraspinous fossa, the inferior angle, and the acromion. Our investigation of the training set revealed that very few CT scans contain the entire scapula, as scans are often focused on thoracic organs, thus partially cropping the bone. Even when the scapula is fully visible in the CT, the corresponding ground truth masks can be incomplete, as demonstrated by mask 2 in Fig. 1. These training data deficiencies directly lead to the model's systematic errors in segmenting the scapula, motivating its use in our pipeline as a generator of coarse anatomical priors rather than as a precise segmentation tool.

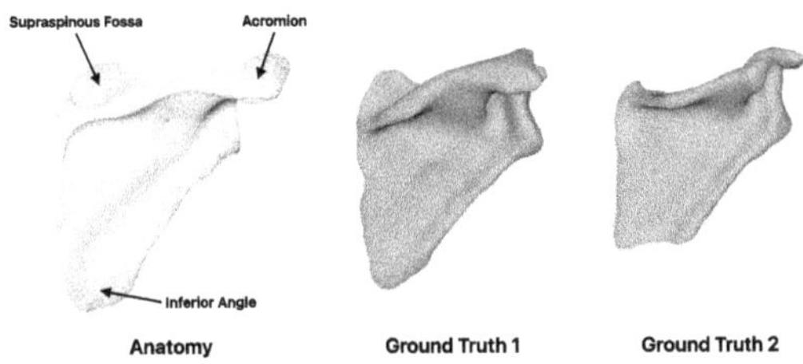

Fig. 1. Figure showing the anatomy of the scapula (image retrieved from Anatomy Standard website (www.anatomystandard.com/ossa-et-juncturae/extremitas-superior/scapula.html)) and two different quality TotalSegmentator ground truth masks.

Foundation Model Baselines: SAM2 and MedSAM2. To establish a clear performance benchmark, we evaluate the SAM2 [12] foundation model using the official checkpoints across its different sizes: Tiny, Small, Base Plus, and Large, to understand the impact of model size on segmentation quality. We also evaluate MedSAM2 [10], which is a version of SAM2 fine-tuned on a large, general-purpose medical dataset. All the listed baseline models receive the exact same automatically generated prompt for each case, according to the auto-prompting technique described below, ensuring a fair and direct comparison of their ability to refine a coarse input.

2.2 Proposed Method: The Auto-prompting SAM2 Pipeline

The core of our work is a fully automated pipeline that leverages SAM2 for high-fidelity segmentation without manual intervention. The overall scheme is illustrated in Fig. 2. The key innovation is to use the imperfect but automatic output of TotalSegmentator to generate a prompt for SAM2, creating a synergistic end-to-end process.

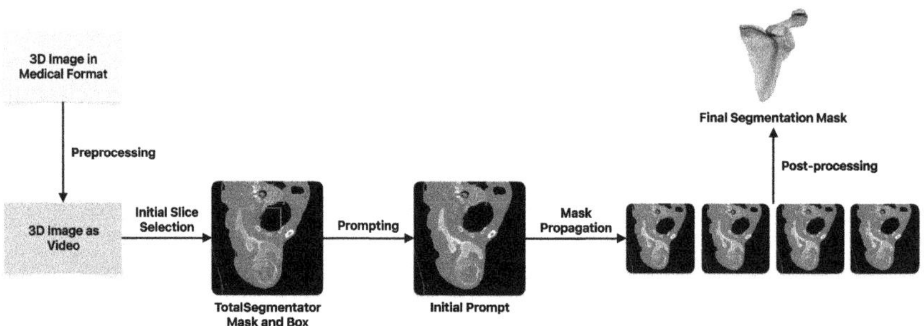

Fig. 2. A picture showing the entire SAM 2 pipeline with examples coming from one of the considered CT scans. These steps allow the model to generate a final segmentation mask starting from a 3D image in medical format.

Data Preprocessing. Since foundation models like SAM2 were originally developed for natural images, medical CT data requires a preprocessing phase. To adapt our 3D volumes for the SAM2 video predictor, each CT slice is individually converted into a normalized JPG image. As our objective is bone segmentation, we first apply an intensity windowing to the CT data, clipping Hounsfield Unit (HU) values to the range of [-100, +900] to highlight bone structures. These clipped values are then rescaled to the [0, 255] range and saved as unsigned integer images, creating a sequence of JPG images that the model can process as a video.

Automatic Prompt Initialization. While promptable models typically require manual input during inference [10], our pipeline fully automates this stage. We use the coarse segmentation mask produced by TotalSegmentator as the source for the initial prompt. The process is as follows: first, we identify the single slice that contains the largest scapula area as segmented by TotalSegmentator. Our tests show this slice is typically well-recognized and provides a robust starting point. On this selected slice, we provide a dual prompt to SAM2: both the binary segmentation mask and its tightest bounding box. This allows SAM2 to leverage both spatial location and a strong shape prior to refine the initial, often inaccurate, mask. This entire process, from selecting the optimal slice to generating the prompt, is performed automatically.

Mask Propagation. Starting from the single prompted slice, SAM2 propagates the segmentation mask across the entire 3D volume. The model is capable of propagating the mask in a single pass per direction. We therefore apply this process bidirectionally from the centrally-located initial slice once towards the final slice and once towards the first. This approach allows the model to leverage inter-slice context, enhancing segmentation consistency and accuracy, especially in low-quality slices, by drawing on information from neighboring slices.

Post-processing. Once the mask has been propagated to all slices, a final refinement is performed. To eliminate potential noise or minor, disconnected artifacts, we apply a 3D connected component analysis and retain only the single largest object corresponding to the scapula bone. Finally, the refined binary mask is converted back into the original medical image format of the input CT, ensuring it can be correctly stored and visualized in medical imaging software for qualitative assessment.

3   Experimental Evaluation

In this section, we present the comprehensive quantitative and qualitative evaluation of our proposed auto-prompting framework against a suite of baseline and state-of-the-art models.

3.1   Dataset and Experimental Design

Dataset. We assembled a clinical dataset of 39 pathological shoulder CT scans from internal archives. A high-quality ground truth for each case was generated using specialized medical imaging software (Mimics Medical 27.0, Materialise, Leuven, Belgium). The segmentation process was semi-automatic, initiated by an expert operator and subsequently reviewed by a second expert who individually verified and approved the quality of each case.

The creation process involved several steps to handle the complexity of the data. Initially, a curvature flow filter was applied to the CT scans to enhance image quality. Subsequently, an automatic segmentation was performed by adjusting a seed threshold based on Hounsfield Units (HU); possibly varying between different CT scans, this threshold was typically set between 150 and 250 HU to separate the scapula from the humerus while excluding the clavicle and other irrelevant structures. In the most difficult cases with bone fusion, manual corrections were performed slice-by-slice. Following this, two semi-automatic functions were used to refine thinner or missing regions of the scapula and to close any remaining holes in the bone structures. The first tool requires the expert to manually indicate areas where the scapula is not adequately covered by the mask. The software then automatically fills these regions by detecting bone tissue based on HU values. Similarly, the second tool closes remaining holes, requiring the user to provide a few points near the gaps to guide the algorithm effectively. Finally, an automatic smoothing tool was applied to regularize the segmentation contours, yielding a precise 3D mask. The time required for this process ranged from 5 to 30 min per case (average: 15–20 min). This parameter strictly depends on the quality of the CT scan and the closeness of the bones, both influencing the amount of manual intervention needed. This fact highlights how difficult and time-consuming the pathological scapula segmentation task is, even for an expert and with the presence of an advanced commercial tool (not always available in every setting), and therefore the need for a robust, fully automatic solution.

Experimental Setup. The dataset of 39 scans was randomly partitioned into a training set of 11 cases and a test set of 28 cases, simulating a common scenario with limited annotated data. The training set was used exclusively for our SAM2 Fine-Tuned model. All other models were evaluated on the 28 test cases. Performance was quantitatively measured primarily using the Dice Similarity Coefficient (DSC) [4], the standard metric for volumetric medical image segmentation. We additionally included the Average Symmetric Surface Distance (ASSD), a distance-based metric reported in millimeters, which provides an intuitive measure of boundary discrepancies and complements DSC by offering a spatial perspective [16].

To investigate the benefits of task-specific adaptation, we fine-tuned the SAM2.1-Base Plus model checkpoint. While retaining most of the original architecture as reported in [12], we adjusted parameters to fit our data and resources. The input image dimension was set to 512×512. We trained the model for 100 epochs with a batch size of 4. The training was performed on a 40GB A100 GPU and lasted about 1 h. Each training sample consisted of 8 consecutive slices randomly sampled from a CT volume, with resampling at each epoch to ensure the model inspected a large portion of each CT. A differential learning rate was used, set to 3.0×10^{-6} for the image encoder to preserve its learned features, and 5.0×10^{-6} for all other components to encourage adaptation to the specific domain.

3.2   Quantitative Results

The quantitative performance of all models on the test set in terms of DSC is summarized in Table 1. We present results with and without the final post-processing step to transparently assess the raw model output alongside the refined result.

The data in Table 1 reveal several key insights. Our ap-SAM2 Fine-Tuned model clearly provides the best performance, achieving a mean DSC of **92.40%**. This represents a significant improvement of over 11% points (p.p.) compared to the TotalSegmentator baseline.

Notably, in all configurations, post-processing yields only negligible gains for the foundation models. This finding underscores the effectiveness of the auto-prompting framework itself, which consistently generates segmentations that are already topologically clean and require minimal refinement.

A noteworthy comparison is between TotalSegmentator and the zero-shot ap-SAM2 models. The SAM2 Tiny variant achieves the best performance in this group (88.95% DSC), with a relatively low standard deviation, indicating

Table 1. Quantitative comparison between the considered and proposed automatic segmentation models in terms of Dice Similarity Coefficient (DSC). The **ap** prefix identifies models evaluated using our proposed auto-prompting framework.

	No Post Processing	With Post Processing
TotalSegmentator	81.24% ± 3.27%	81.24% ± 3.27%
ap-SAM2 Tiny	88.07% ± 4.20%	88.95% ± 3.45%
ap-SAM2 Small	85.95% ± 5.87%	86.49% ± 5.61%
ap-SAM2 Base Plus	86.97% ± 7.71%	86.97% ± 7.74%
ap-SAM2 Large	82.83% ± 8.83%	84.90% ± 7.74%
ap-MedSAM2	82.11% ± 16.00%	82.41% ± 15.79%
ap-SAM2 Fine-Tuned	**92.03% ± 6.49%**	**92.40% ± 6.45%**

consistent results. This demonstrates that even without any specific training, our auto-prompting framework boosts performance by over 7.5 p.p. compared to the initial segmentator. It also suggests that for this 3D task, increasing model size within the SAM2 family does not necessarily lead to better performance.

Conversely, ap-MedSAM2, despite its medical-specific fine-tuning, performs poorly. Its average DSC is lower than most base SAM2 models, and its standard deviation is exceptionally high (15.79%), indicating highly variable and quite unreliable results. This suggests that a general medical fine-tuning process can fail or even degrade performance on highly specific and complex pathological tasks.

Figure 3 displays box plots of the DSC and ASSD distributions across all evaluated cases, providing a comprehensive comparison of the models. ASSD, as an absolute distance-based measure, is presented on a logarithmic scale to effectively capture the wide variability in its values and to improve interpretability. Several pronounced outliers are evident in the ASSD plot, corresponding to cases with substantial surface discrepancies. In our specific context, these outliers are primarily associated with instances in which a considerable portion of the humerus is erroneously included in the scapula segmentation. The magnitude of these values largely depends on the extent of the missegmented bone. Consequently, the ASSD distribution exhibits a greater number of outliers compared to the overlap-focused DSC distribution. Our fine-tuned model demonstrates the best overall performance across both metrics, characterized by a high median DSC, a low median ASSD, a narrow interquartile range (IQR), and a limited number of outliers. Notably, 75% of the cases achieve a DSC above 90% and an ASSD below 0.2 mm, indicating highly accurate and consistent segmentation performance. In the ASSD box plot, two prominent outliers exceed 10 mm, likely reflecting cases in which a substantial portion of the humerus was mistakenly included in the scapula segmentation. However, the remaining four outliers lie below 2 mm, suggesting acceptable boundary accuracy even in those less consistent cases. In contrast, MedSAM2 exhibits a wide performance spread, with several severe outliers falling below 60% DSC and exceeding 6 mm ASSD, reflecting lower robustness.

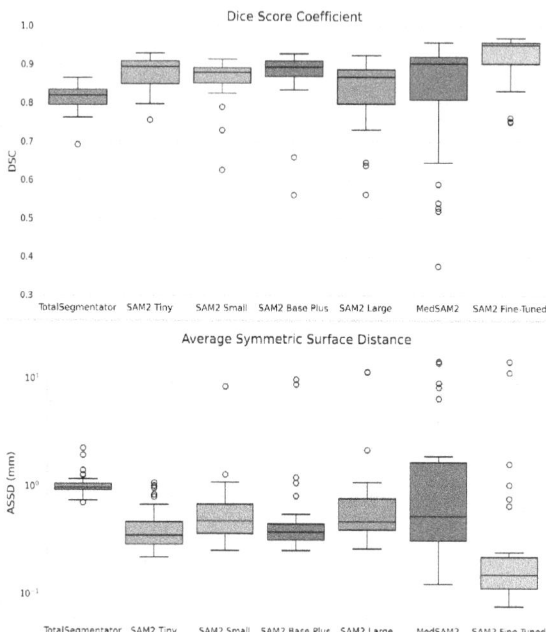

Fig. 3. Box plots showing the distribution of the DSC and ASSD values on the test set. The ASSD values are shown in log scale to better visualize outliers and distribution spread.

TotalSegmentator yields very consistent results with a tight IQR, yet with lower overall accuracy. Among the SAM2-based variants, the Base Plus model appears to provide a favorable balance between overlap and surface-based performance, although it still produces some low-scoring outliers indicative of segmentation failures in specific cases.

3.3 Qualitative Analysis

Qualitative analysis is fundamental to understanding the models' behavior in specific, challenging scenarios. Figure 4 presents three representative examples from the test set. In the first case, our SAM2 Fine-Tuned model produces a mask that closely matches the ground truth, whereas TotalSegmentator's result is coarse, and MedSAM2 fails to segment large portions of the scapula. The second example shows an anatomically simpler case where all models perform better; however, TotalSegmentator's mask remains less precise than the nearly equivalent outputs from MedSAM2 and the SAM2 variants. In the third case, MedSAM2 incorrectly includes the humerus in the segmentation, a critical error, while TotalSegmentator again fails to capture a large part of the supraspinous fossa, consistent with the training data issues shown in Fig. 1.

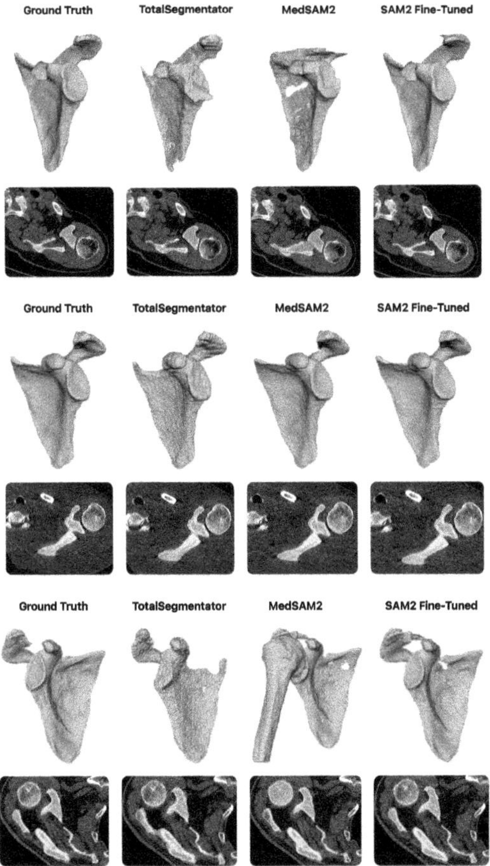

Fig. 4. Qualitative comparison of three different CT scans with good SAM2 performance. On the first line of each example, the 3D segmentation masks are displayed. On the second line, the 2D view of the overlapping between the CT and the segmentation mask of a significant slice is presented.

Figure 5 illustrates a particularly challenging case with severe glenoid pathology, corresponding to an outlier for our fine-tuned model (easily recognizable in Fig. 3). Here, both MedSAM2 and our SAM2 Fine-Tuned model failed to correctly separate the scapula from the humerus.

In this instance, the initial prompt generated by TotalSegmentator was itself flawed, including a portion of the humerus. Due to the extreme proximity and pathological fusion of the joint, neither the zero-shot nor the fine-tuned SAM2 models were able to fully correct this initial error, leading to a poorer segmentation. This highlights a limitation of our current pipeline, where the final quality is still partially dependent on receiving an anatomically coherent (as TotalSegmentator usually provides) and topologically reasonable, albeit coarse, initial prompt. Such extreme cases may require specialized refinement solutions beyond the purview of this work. Nevertheless, potential mitigation strategies exist; for instance, incorporating a coarse humerus mask generated by TotalSegmentator could effectively exclude this bone from the final segmentation without requiring substantial additional effort.

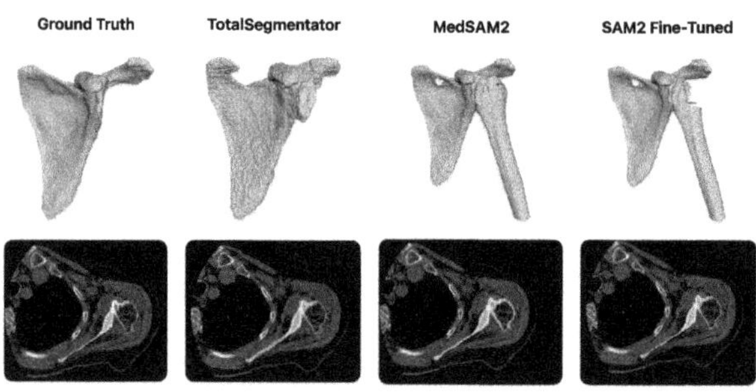

Fig. 5. Example of a CT scan in which the scapula is inaccurately segmented even by SAM 2 (outlier).

4   Discussion

Our experimental results offer several crucial insights into the application of foundation models for complex medical segmentation tasks.

Firstly, we demonstrate that a generalist foundation model, when guided by a coarse, automatically-generated prompt, can significantly outperform highly specialized, state-of-the-art tools. Our auto-prompting framework, even when driving a zero-shot SAM2 model, surpassed the performance of TotalSegmentator on the challenging task of pathological scapula segmentation. This suggests a paradigm shift: instead of relying on models trained on vast but potentially flawed specialized datasets, leveraging the powerful, fine-grained refinement capabilities of a generalist model can yield superior results, provided it is initialized effectively.

Secondly, our findings reveal a potential "paradox of fine-tuning" for large foundation models. The poor and highly variable performance of MedSAM2 is particularly revealing. Despite being fine-tuned on an extensive medical dataset, its generalization capabilities on our specific, out-of-distribution pathological cases were compromised. This suggests that large-scale, broad-domain fine-tuning may cause the model to over-specialize on the patterns within its training data, paradoxically reducing its zero-shot flexibility when faced with novel anatomical variations. This highlights a critical trade-off that must be carefully considered when adapting large models for niche clinical applications.

Thirdly, we show the remarkable efficiency of "smart" data over "big" data. In stark contrast to MedSAM2's performance, our SAM2 Fine-Tuned model, trained on just 11 relevant examples, achieved the highest accuracy by a significant margin. This strongly indicates that for complex, specific tasks, minimalist fine-tuning on a small, highly curated dataset is a more effective and data-efficient strategy than relying on models trained on massive but less specific data collections.

Finally, our auto-prompting pipeline itself represents a robust framework for the fair evaluation of different foundation models. By providing the exact same imperfect starting point to each model, we can directly compare their intrinsic error correction and segmentation refinement capabilities, removing the confounding variable of manual prompt quality.

4.1   Limitations and Future Work

While our approach is effective, we acknowledge its limitations. The primary challenge arises in cases of extreme pathological bone fusion where no discernible boundary exists in the CT data. As shown in our qualitative analysis, foundation models, being inherently agnostic to this specific anatomical context, struggle to resolve such ambiguities. This defines the current boundary of applicability for purely data-driven segmentation methods in these scenarios.

This observation opens several avenues for future research. A promising direction is the development of hybrid models that integrate our auto-prompting framework with anatomical atlases or statistical shape models. Such priors could provide the necessary constraints to resolve pathological fusions. Furthermore, the modularity of our pipeline allows for the exploration of alternative methods for generating the initial coarse prompt, potentially increasing its robustness.

The most immediate future work, however, is to validate the generalizability of our framework. Its success on the scapula suggests strong potential for other challenging segmentation tasks characterized by high anatomical variability and data scarcity, such as other complex joints, pediatric anatomies, or tumors with infiltrative boundaries. Owing to the modularity of our pipeline, this objective is expected to be readily attainable. Specifically, the SAM2 mask propagation phase employed in the baseline models is agnostic to the anatomical structure, implying that the primary variations involve the initial coarse mask provided by TotalSegmentator and, potentially, minor adjustments in the preprocessing steps, such as windowing parameters for anatomical structures other than bones. Furthermore, we demonstrated that fine-tuning with only a limited number of examples can yield substantial performance gains. Therefore, once ground truth masks are available, this process can be readily adapted to any anatomical structure of interest.

5   Conclusion

In this work, we introduced a fully automatic auto-prompting framework that effectively harnesses the power of generalist foundation models for a complex medical segmentation task. Our results demonstrate that this approach not only surpasses specialized segmentation tools but also reveals critical insights into the trade-offs of large-scale versus minimalist fine-tuning. By converting a coarse segmentation into a high-quality prompt, our method provides a data-efficient, accurate, and automated solution, paving the way for a broader and more effective application of foundation models to solve challenging problems in clinical imaging.

Acknowledgments. We would like to thank Medacta International S.A. (Castel San Pietro, Switzerland) for their valuable collaboration throughout the course of this research.

Disclosure of Interests. The authors have no competing interests to declare that are relevant to the content of this article.

References

1. Antonelli, M., et al.: The medical segmentation decathlon. Nat. Commun. **13**(1), 4128 (2022)
2. Chaoui, J., Hamitouche, C., Stindel, E., Roux, C.: Recognition-based segmentation and registration method for image guided shoulder surgery. In: 2011 Annual International Conference of the IEEE Engineering in Medicine and Biology Society, pp. 6212–6215. IEEE (2011)
3. D'Antonoli, T.A., et al.: Totalsegmentator MRI: sequence-independent segmentation of 59 anatomical structures in MR images. arXiv preprint arXiv:2405.19492 (2024)
4. Dice, L.R.: Measures of the amount of ecologic association between species. Ecology **26**(3), 297–302 (1945)
5. Fu, Y., Liu, S., Li, H.H., Yang, D.: Automatic and hierarchical segmentation of the human skeleton in CT images. Phys. Med. Biol. **62**(7), 2812 (2017)
6. Isensee, F., Jaeger, P.F., Kohl, S.A., Petersen, J., Maier-Hein, K.H.: nnu-net: a self-configuring method for deep learning-based biomedical image segmentation. Nat. Methods **18**(2), 203–211 (2021)
7. Jacquot, A., et al.: Proper benefit of a three dimensional pre-operative planning software for glenoid component positioning in total shoulder arthroplasty. Int. Orthop. **42**(12), 2897–2906 (2018). https://doi.org/10.1007/s00264-018-4037-1
8. Kirillov, A., et al.: Segment anything. arXiv:2304.02643 (2023)
9. Ma, J., He, Y., Li, F., Han, L., You, C., Wang, B.: Segment anything in medical images. Nat. Commun. **15**, 1–9 (2024)
10. Ma, J., et al.: Medsam2: segment anything in 3D medical images and videos. arXiv preprint arXiv:2504.03600 (2025)
11. Milletari, F., Navab, N., Ahmadi, S.A.: V-net: fully convolutional neural networks for volumetric medical image segmentation. In: 2016 Fourth International Conference on 3D Vision (3DV), pp. 565–571. IEEE (2016)
12. Ravi, N., et al.: Sam 2: segment anything in images and videos. arXiv preprint arXiv:2408.00714 (2024)
13. Rayed, M.E., Islam, S.S., Niha, S.I., Jim, J.R., Kabir, M.M., Mridha, M.: Deep learning for medical image segmentation: state-of-the-art advancements and challenges. Inform. Med. Unlocked 101504 (2024)

14. Ronneberger, O., Fischer, P., Brox, T.: U-net: convolutional networks for biomedical image segmentation. In: Navab, N., Hornegger, J., Wells, W.M., Frangi, A.F. (eds.) MICCAI 2015. LNCS, vol. 9351, pp. 234–241. Springer, Cham (2015). https://doi.org/10.1007/978-3-319-24574-4_28
15. Satir, O.B., et al.: Automatic quantification of scapular and glenoid morphology from CT scans using deep learning. Eur. J. Radiol. **177**, 111588 (2024)
16. Taha, A.A., Hanbury, A.: Metrics for evaluating 3D medical image segmentation: analysis, selection, and tool. BMC Med. Imaging **15**, 1–28 (2015)
17. Wasserthal, J., et al.: Totalsegmentator: robust segmentation of 104 anatomic structures in CT images. Radiol. Artif. Intell. **5**(5) (2023)
18. Zhu, J., Qi, Y., Wu, J.: Medical SAM 2: segment medical images as video via segment anything model 2. arXiv preprint arXiv:2408.00874 (2024)

Keynote Papers

Towards Segmenting the Invisible: An End-to-End Registration and Segmentation Framework for Weakly Supervised Tumour Analysis

Budhaditya Mukhopadhyay[1], Chirag Mandal[1], Pavan Tummala[1], Naghmeh Mahmoodian[3], Andreas Nürnberger[1,4], and Soumick Chatterjee[1,2(✉)]

[1] Institute of Technical and Business Information Systems, Faculty of Computer Science, Otto von Guericke University Magdeburg, Magdeburg, Germany
contact@soumick.com
[2] Human Technopole, Milan, Italy
[3] Institute of Medical Engineering, Faculty of Electrical Engineering and Information Technology, Otto von Guericke University Magdeburg, Magdeburg, Germany
[4] Centre for Behavioural Brain Sciences, Magdeburg, Germany

Abstract. Liver tumour ablation presents a significant clinical challenge: whilst tumours are clearly visible on pre-operative MRI, they are often effectively invisible on intra-operative CT due to minimal contrast between pathological and healthy tissue. This work investigates the feasibility of *cross-modality weak supervision* for scenarios where pathology is visible in one modality (MRI) but absent in another (CT). We present a hybrid registration-segmentation framework that combines MSCGUNet for inter-modal image registration with a UNet-based segmentation module, enabling registration-assisted pseudo-label generation for CT images. Our evaluation on the CHAOS dataset demonstrates that the pipeline can successfully register and segment healthy liver anatomy, achieving a Dice score of 0.72. However, when applied to clinical data containing tumours, performance degrades substantially (Dice score of 0.16), revealing the fundamental limitations of current registration methods when the target pathology lacks corresponding visual features in the target modality. We analyse this "domain gap" and "feature absence" problem, demonstrating that whilst spatial propagation of labels via registration is feasible for visible structures, segmenting truly invisible pathology remains an open challenge. Our findings highlight that registration-based label transfer cannot compensate for the absence of discriminative features in the target modality, providing important insights for future research in cross-modality medical image analysis.

Keywords: Inter-modal Image Registration · Image Segmentation · Liver Tumour Segmentation · Weakly-supervised Learning · Cross-modality Supervision

© The Author(s), under exclusive license to Springer Nature Switzerland AG 2026
C. Tommasino et al. (Eds.): AIBIO 2025, CCIS 2696, pp. 229–242, 2026.
https://doi.org/10.1007/978-3-032-17216-7_18

1   Introduction

The application of deep learning methods in medical image analysis has demonstrated substantial promise [7,8], with increasing efficiency and accuracy fostering trust among healthcare professionals and patients alike [10]. This research investigates the feasibility of cross-modality weak supervision for liver tumour segmentation, a clinically important yet technically challenging problem. We employ image registration and segmentation techniques within a multi-step framework that combines supervised and weakly-supervised learning approaches [3,12].

A fundamental challenge in liver tumour ablation surgery is the "invisibility paradox": tumours that are clearly visible on pre-operative MRI are often undetectable on intra-operative CT due to insufficient contrast between pathological and healthy tissue. This work addresses this challenge by proposing a deep learning framework that aims to transfer tumour localisation information from MRI to CT through registration-assisted pseudo-label generation [4,11]. It is essential to acknowledge that when discriminative features are absent from the pixel data in CT, a convolutional neural network cannot directly "see" the tumour—it can only propagate spatial information learned through registration with MRI.

In this approach, image registration [2] and segmentation [9] are combined in an end-to-end framework. The MRI and CT images are registered to obtain a warped output that spatially aligns the modalities, and the registered image is subsequently passed through a segmentation model to predict the tumour location. The contributions of this work are threefold: (1) a hybrid registration-segmentation framework for cross-modality label transfer; (2) an evaluation on a standard dataset (CHAOS) demonstrating that the method functions correctly on healthy anatomy; and (3) a failure analysis on real-world clinical data, highlighting the fundamental limitations of registration-based approaches when the target pathology lacks corresponding visual features in the target modality. These methods are intended as a supporting tool for medical professionals during surgery, complementing their experience rather than replacing clinical judgement.

1.1   Problem Statement

Hepatic abscess formation represents a significant clinical challenge for patients with liver pathology. A conventional approach for treating such conditions involves ablation, whereby the tumour or abscess is destroyed through thermal energy delivered via percutaneously inserted needles. Whilst this pathology is readily detectable on MRI, CT imaging typically fails to visualise such lesions, as illustrated in Fig. 1. Given the impracticality of accommodating MRI equipment within an operating theatre, medical professionals must perform pre-operative MRI and subsequently correlate these findings with intra-operative CT during the procedure.

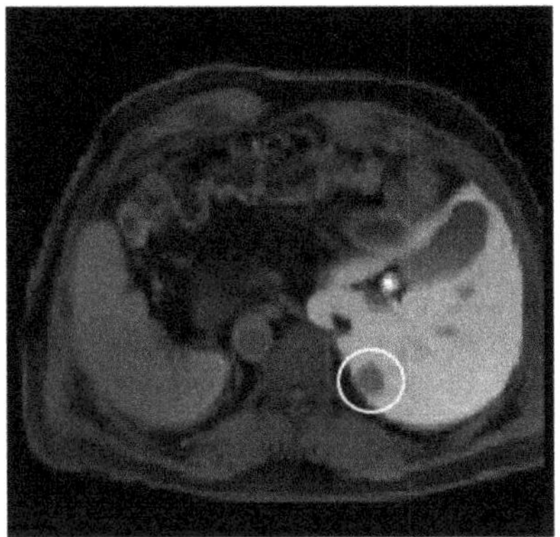 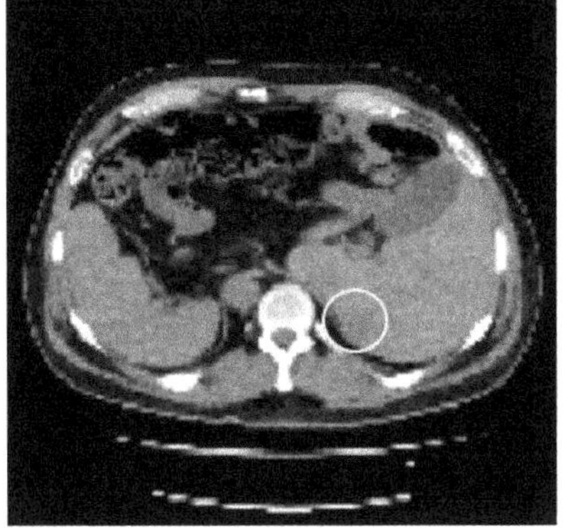

Fig. 1. Comparison between MRI (on the left, showing the tumour) and CT (on the right, for the same patient, the tumour is not distinguishable) depicting the problem statement.

During the operation, the clinician analyses the intra-operative CT scans to visualise the patient's anatomy and needle positioning, yet these images frequently provide insufficient information regarding the precise tumour location. The clinician must therefore continuously cross-reference the pre-operative MRI with current CT slices to estimate the lesion boundaries. This approach presents several inherent challenges: the procedure remains heavily dependent upon the clinician's experience and spatial reasoning abilities, and there is an attendant risk of inadvertent damage to healthy tissue during the ablation process.

From an information-theoretic perspective, the mutual information between the input CT voxel intensities ($\mathbf{z}$) and the tumour label is negligible ($I(\mathbf{z}; Y) \approx 0$). Consequently, the network cannot rely on discriminative features but must depend entirely on the spatial priors transferred via registration.

1.2   Related Work

A conventional approach in medical image analysis involves developing supervised learning methods, which typically achieve high accuracy when adequate labelled data are available. For combined CT-MRI abdominal segmentation, the CHAOS challenge [5] provides a comprehensive benchmark. This challenge addresses the performance of deep learning for multi-modal and cross-modality segmentation tasks. A principal finding was that deep learning models performing multi-organ segmentation generally achieved inferior performance compared to organ-specific segmentation models, with performance degrading substantially in cross-modality tasks, particularly for liver segmentation. Participants were assigned separate tasks for segmenting abdominal organs from CT, MRI, and combined CT-MRI datasets, implementing various network architectures to optimise challenge performance. One of the leading teams, OvGUMemorial, proposed a modified Attention 2D U-Net [1] employing soft attention gates and a multi-scaled input image pyramid for improved feature representation.

The team additionally proposed parametric ReLU activation instead of standard ReLU, incorporating a learnable leakage coefficient during training. The ISDUE team proposed a model comprising two encoder-decoder modules and one 2D UNet module, where the UNet module enhanced the second decoder and provided improved localisation capabilities. The Lachinov team employed a 3D UNet model with skip connections between contracting and expanding paths, utilising an exponentially growing number of channels across consecutive resolution levels [6]. A residual network constructed the encoding path for efficient training, with pixel shuffle serving as the up-sampling operator.

1.3 Hypothesis

Let $\mathcal{D}_{MR} = \{(\mathbf{x}_i, y_i)\}$ be the source domain of labelled MRI volumes, where $\mathbf{x} \in \mathbb{R}^{H \times W \times D}$ represents the volumetric intensity data and $y \in \{0,1\}^{H \times W \times D}$ represents the binary tumour mask. Let $\mathcal{D}_{CT} = \{\mathbf{z}_j\}$ be the target domain of unlabelled intra-operative CT volumes.

The "invisibility paradox" posits that the conditional probability of detecting a tumour y given CT input $\mathbf{z}$ is significantly lower than given MRI input $\mathbf{x}$ due to low contrast-to-noise ratio in pathological regions: $P(y|\mathbf{z}) \ll P(y|\mathbf{x})$. Crucially, this represents a regime of *aleatoric uncertainty* (data-inherent noise arising from the physical invisibility of the tumour in CT) rather than *epistemic uncertainty* (insufficient training data). This distinction is fundamental: acquiring additional CT training samples cannot resolve the underlying feature absence, as the discriminative information is physically absent from the modality.

Our hypothesis is that we can approximate the target mapping function $f : \mathcal{D}_{CT} \to y$ by learning a non-linear spatial transformation ϕ that aligns the domains. We define the pseudo-label generation for the target domain as:

$$\tilde{y}_{CT} = y_{MR} \circ \phi$$

where $\circ$ denotes the spatial resampling (warping) operation. The objective is to train a segmentation network S such that $S(\mathbf{x}_{reg}) \approx \tilde{y}_{CT}$, where $\mathbf{x}_{reg} = \mathbf{x} \circ \phi$.

It is important to clarify the nature of supervision in this framework. Whilst the term "weakly supervised" is employed, this differs from the conventional usage where weak supervision implies image-level tags (e.g., "contains tumour"). Here, strong supervision is available from the MRI, but it is *unpaired* with the CT initially. The framework therefore performs *registration-assisted pseudo-label generation*: the "ground truth" for CT segmentation is generated by warping the MRI mask through the learned spatial transformation. Both modules work collaboratively, with registration quality directly influencing segmentation accuracy.

2 Methods

2.1 Methodology

This section presents the overall methodology of the research. The architecture comprises two interconnected modules that function in an end-to-end manner, with the registration module providing spatial alignment that enables pseudo-

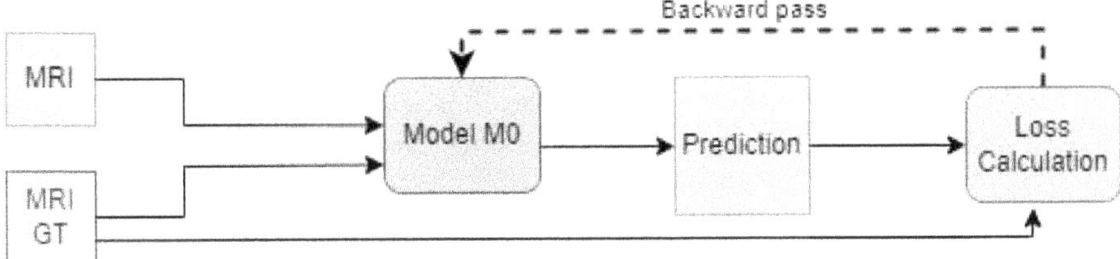

Fig. 2. Module M0.

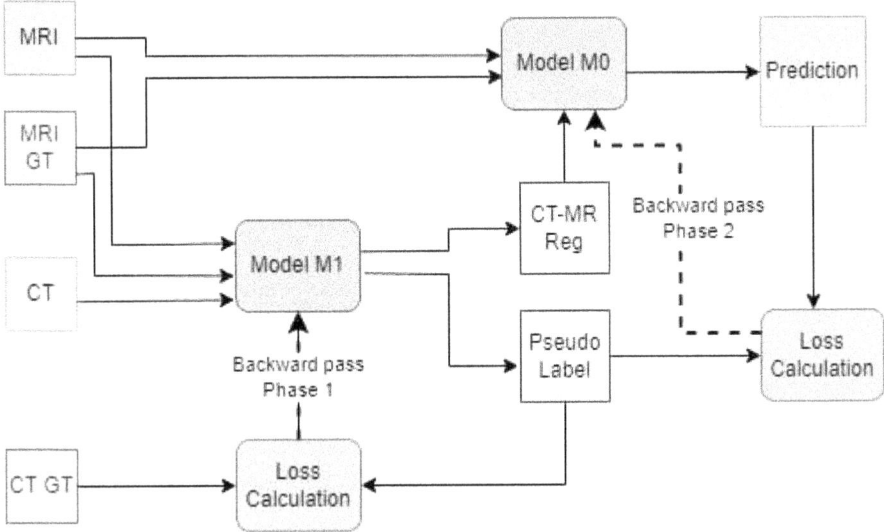

Fig. 3. Combined Modules.

label generation for the subsequent segmentation module. Code of this research (including the trained model weights) can be found on GitHub[1] (Figs. 2 and 3).

Several data pre-processing steps are employed. Firstly, the level and window values of the CT image are adjusted to enhance tissue visualisation, with the level set to 50 and the window to 350. Secondly, the MRI and CT images are resampled to equalise voxel spacing using zero padding and interpolation. Additional processing includes min-max normalisation of all images.

Image Registration (Module M0). We employ a Multi-Scale UNet with Self-Constructing Graph Latent (MSCGUNet) [2] to parameterise the deformation field. Let F be the fixed image (CT) and M be the moving image (MRI). The network learns a dense deformation field $\phi : \Omega \to \mathbb{R}^3$ over the spatial domain Ω, such that the warped moving image $M(\phi)$ aligns with F.

The registration is formulated as an energy minimisation problem:

$$\hat{\phi} = \arg \min_{\phi} \left[\mathcal{L}_{sim}(F, M \circ \phi) + \lambda \mathcal{L}_{reg}(\phi) \right]$$

---

[1] GitHub: https://github.com/BudhaTronix/Weakly-Supervised-Tumour-Detection.

where $\mathcal{L}_{sim}$ quantifies the dissimilarity between modalities, and $\mathcal{L}_{reg}$ imposes smoothness constraints on the deformation field to ensure topological preservation (i.e., ensuring the Jacobian determinant $\det(J_\phi) > 0$).

This network was selected for several reasons: its multi-scale supervision capability enables effective handling of both small and large deformations, which is critical for inter-modal registration where organs may undergo significant non-rigid transformations between acquisitions. The multi-scale architecture of MSC-GUNet is particularly pertinent here, as it captures both the global organ shift (due to respiration) and the local tissue compression caused by the tumour mass. Additionally, the self-constructing graph mechanism improves the model's generalisation by learning structural relationships within the image. Cycle consistency is another important feature, ensuring consistent deformations in both forward (moving to fixed) and backward (fixed to moving) directions, which regularises the learning process.

The combined loss equation for the MSCGUNet comprises different loss components. In Eq. 1, l_{sim} denotes the similarity loss for inter-modal registration, l_{sm} represents the smoothness loss penalising sharp deformations, and l_{scg} is the self-constructing graph loss that facilitates learning of similar features in input image pairs. The fixed image is denoted by f and the moving image by m, with subscript d indicating downsampled versions. The hyper-parameters α, α_d, β, β_d, and λ control the relative contribution of each loss component.

$$
\begin{aligned}
l_{\text{total}} &= \alpha \left(l_{sim_{f \to m}} + l_{sim_{m \to f}} \right) + \alpha_d \left(l_{sim_{f_d \to m_d}} + l_{sim_{m_d \to f_d}} \right) \\
&+ \beta \left(l_{sm_{f \to m}} + l_{sm_{m \to f}} \right) + \beta_d \left(l_{sm_{f_d \to m_d}} + l_{sm_{m_d \to f_d}} \right) \\
&+ \lambda \left(l_{scg_{f \to m}} + l_{scg_{m \to f}} \right)
\end{aligned} \tag{1}
$$

The final values of the hyper-parameters were set to -1.2, -0.6, 0.5, 0.25, and 5, respectively, following the experimental validation in the original paper.

Pseudo-label Propagation. Once the optimal deformation field $\hat{\phi}$ is computed, it serves as the bridge for weak supervision. Since the ground truth tumour labels y_{MR} exist only in the moving domain, we generate the pseudo-ground truth for the CT space, denoted as $\tilde{y}_{CT}$, by applying the learned transformation:

$$
\tilde{y}_{CT}(\mathbf{p}) = y_{MR}(\mathbf{p} + \hat{\phi}(\mathbf{p}))
$$

where $\mathbf{p}$ represents the voxel coordinates. This step assumes that the anatomical location of the pathology is invariant to the modality, despite the difference in voxel intensity representation.

Segmentation Network (Module M1). The segmentation module S is a 2D UNet [9] trained to map the registered MRI volume (now spatially aligned with the CT coordinate system) to the pseudo-labels.

$$
\hat{y} = S(M \circ \hat{\phi}; \theta_S)
$$

where θ_S are the learnable parameters of the segmentation network.

2.2   Dataset

CHAOS Dataset. For method development and validation with properly labelled data for both modalities, the CHAOS dataset [5] was employed. This dataset comprises T1-weighted and T2-weighted MRI alongside CT images, with corresponding liver labels. Importantly, all subjects are healthy, meaning the dataset contains no pathological tissue. This serves as a control dataset, enabling validation that the registration-segmentation pipeline functions correctly when consistent anatomical features are present in both modalities. The CHAOS dataset contains CT images, CT ground truth masks (CT_GT), MRI images, and MRI ground truth masks (MR_GT) for abdominal organs.

Clinical Dataset. The clinical dataset was obtained from Universitätsklinikum Magdeburg (IRB No: 66/22). This dataset comprises 11 volumes of paired MRI and CT scans from patients with liver pathology. Strict exclusion criteria were applied to ensure registration viability. Four volumes were excluded due to severe motion artefacts, metallic implant artefacts, or low signal-to-noise ratio that would render deformation field estimation unreliable. The remaining seven volumes constitute the high-quality cohort for validation. These volumes were employed for cross-modality image registration (MRI to CT). Notably, one patient had a severely damaged liver prior to ablation, precluding use of that volume for training purposes.

The CHAOS dataset was selected as the primary development dataset for several reasons: the superior image quality compared to the clinical dataset, which would otherwise impair deep learning model training; the larger number of available volumes; and the availability of consistent ground truth annotations. The clinical dataset, whilst smaller and more challenging, provides the critical test case for evaluating the framework on pathological tissue that is invisible on CT.

2.3   Loss Functions

The loss functions employed for the segmentation module are Focal Tversky Loss and Dice Loss. Focal Tversky Loss was selected specifically to address the class imbalance inherent in tumour segmentation, where the tumour region typically comprises a small fraction of the total image volume compared to the surrounding liver parenchyma and background. This loss function provides enhanced control over false negative and false positive penalties, which is particularly important when segmenting small structures.

The similarity loss $\mathcal{L}_{sim}$ in Eq. 1 is critical for multi-modal alignment. We utilise a metric robust to intensity non-uniformities (such as Local Cross-Correlation or MIND), defined generally as:

$$\mathcal{L}_{sim}(F, M') = -\sum_{\mathbf{p}\in\Omega} \mathrm{Sim}(F(\mathbf{p}), M'(\mathbf{p}))$$

For the segmentation module M1, we minimise a compound loss function combining the Dice score and Focal Tversky estimation to handle class imbalance. The Dice Loss $\mathcal{L}_{DSC}$ is defined as:

$$\mathcal{L}_{DSC} = 1 - \frac{2\sum_i p_i g_i + \epsilon}{\sum_i p_i + \sum_i g_i + \epsilon}$$

where $p_i \in [0, 1]$ is the predicted probability of the tumour class at voxel i, $g_i \in \{0, 1\}$ is the ground truth (pseudo-label), and ϵ is a smoothing term.

The Focal Tversky Loss ($\mathcal{L}_{FTL}$) introduces a focusing parameter γ to down-weight easy background examples:

$$\mathcal{L}_{FTL} = (1 - TI)^\gamma$$

where TI is the Tversky Index defined as:

$$TI = \frac{TP}{(TP + \alpha FN + \beta FP)} \tag{2}$$

Here, TP, FN, and FP denote true positives, false negatives, and false positives, respectively. The parameters α and β control the trade-off between precision and recall: when $\alpha = \beta = 0.5$, the Tversky index reduces to the Dice coefficient; when $\alpha = \beta = 1$, it becomes the Jaccard index. The parameter γ in the Focal Tversky Loss controls the nonlinearity, down-weighting easy examples and focusing training on difficult cases.

2.4   Evaluation Metrics

The evaluation metrics employed are the Jaccard Index and Dice Coefficient.

The Jaccard Index, also known as Intersection over Union (IoU), measures the ratio of the intersection to the union of the sample sets:

$$J(A, B) = \frac{|A \cap B|}{|A \cup B|} = \frac{|A \cap B|}{|A| + |B| - |A \cap B|} \tag{3}$$

The Dice Coefficient provides an alternative measure of similarity between two sample sets:

$$DSC = \frac{2|X \cap Y|}{|X| + |Y|} \tag{4}$$

Both metrics range from 0 (no overlap) to 1 (perfect overlap). Median values are reported to provide robustness against outliers.

3   Results and Analysis

This section presents the experimental results, structured to distinguish between the proof-of-concept evaluation on healthy anatomy (CHAOS dataset) and the challenging clinical application on pathological tissue.

Table 1. Training Paradigm Selection: Comparison of Sequential vs End-to-End Training

Training Paradigm	Loss Func	Model	Jaccard	Dice
Unified	FTL	DeepSup	0.61 ± 0.00	0.53 ± 0.00
	FTL	UNet	0.61 ± 0.01	0.56 ± 0.04
	Dice	DeepSup	0.64 ± 0.00	0.60 ± 0.01
	Dice	UNet	0.61 ± 0.01	0.57 ± 0.03
Sequential	FTL	DeepSup	$\mathbf{0.69 \pm 0.04}$	$\mathbf{0.67 \pm 0.07}$
	FTL	UNet	$\mathbf{0.69 \pm 0.04}$	$\mathbf{0.72 \pm 0.04}$
	Dice	DeepSup	$\mathbf{0.71 \pm 0.02}$	$\mathbf{0.72 \pm 0.04}$
	Dice	UNet	$\mathbf{0.69 \pm 0.07}$	$\mathbf{0.67 \pm 0.11}$

Table 2. Model and Loss Function Selection: Cross-validation Results

Training Paradigm	Combination	Jaccard	Dice
Sequential	Dice - DeepSup	0.71 ± 0.00	0.69 ± 0.01
	FTL - DeepSup	0.72 ± 0.00	0.70 ± 0.01
	FTL - UNet	0.71 ± 0.00	0.71 ± 0.00
	Dice - UNet	$\mathbf{0.72 \pm 0.00}$	$\mathbf{0.72 \pm 0.00}$

3.1 Training Paradigm Selection

The framework was evaluated using both Focal Tversky Loss and Dice Loss, with median values computed for Jaccard and Dice scores. Sequential training, where the registration and segmentation modules are trained separately, substantially outperforms end-to-end training. Sequential training achieved scores ranging from 0.67 to 0.72, whilst end-to-end training achieved only 0.53 to 0.60. Table 1 summarises these findings.

3.2 Model and Loss Function Selection

Table 2 presents the Jaccard and Dice scores for different combinations of loss functions and models following six-fold cross-validation with different subjects from the dataset. For the UNet DeepSup model, the Focal Tversky Loss performs better, whilst for the standard UNet model, Dice Loss yields superior results.

3.3 Proof of Concept: CHAOS Dataset

The CHAOS dataset provides a controlled environment with healthy subjects where anatomical features are consistent between CT and MRI. Table 3 compares the weakly supervised approach against fully supervised baselines. The supervised results for the Dice Loss and UNet combination achieve a median score of 0.92, whilst the corresponding weakly supervised results achieve 0.72. Similarly, the supervised FTL and UNet DeepSup combination achieves 0.93, with the weakly supervised counterpart achieving 0.70.

Table 3. Comparison with Supervised Baseline: CHAOS Dataset

Training Type	Combination	Jaccard	Dice
Supervised	Dice - UNet	0.92 ± 0.01	0.92 ± 0.02
Weakly Supervised	Dice - UNet	0.72 ± 0.00	0.72 ± 0.00
Supervised	FTL - DeepSup	0.93 ± 0.00	0.93 ± 0.01
Weakly Supervised	FTL - DeepSup	0.72 ± 0.00	0.70 ± 0.01

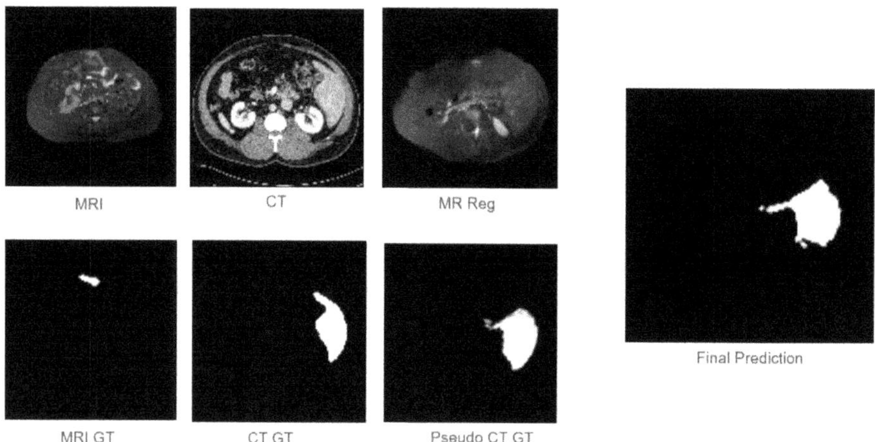

Fig. 4. CHAOS Results: Pipeline stages showing accurate registration and segmentation of healthy liver anatomy.

These results demonstrate that the registration-segmentation pipeline functions correctly: when anatomical features are visible and consistent in both modalities, the framework achieves acceptable performance despite never directly observing CT ground truth during training. The performance gap between supervised (0.92–0.93) and weakly supervised (0.70–0.72) approaches can be attributed to registration imperfections and the inherent challenge of cross-modality feature transfer.

Figure 4 illustrates the pipeline stages for CHAOS data. The close similarity between CT_GT and Pseudo CT_GT confirms that registration is performed accurately. The final liver segmentation prediction demonstrates the viability of the approach for visible anatomical structures.

3.4   The Clinical Challenge: Invisible Tumour Segmentation

Application to clinical data containing tumours reveals the fundamental limitations of the approach. Tables 4 and 5 present the results for the weakly supervised and baseline approaches, respectively.

The substantial performance degradation from CHAOS (Dice: 0.72) to clinical data (Dice: 0.16) represents a critical finding rather than merely "poor results". This degradation warrants careful analysis.

Table 4. Weakly Supervised Model on Clinical Data

Model	Loss Function	Jaccard	Dice
UNet	Dice Loss	0.35±0.09	0.16±0.14

Table 5. Clinical Data Baseline (Supervised)

Model	Loss Function	Jaccard	Dice
UNet	Dice Loss	0.46±0.01	0.19±0.06

3.5 Failure Analysis: Understanding the Performance Gap

The poor performance on clinical tumour segmentation stems from several interconnected factors that illuminate the fundamental challenges of cross-modality weak supervision.

The Feature Absence Problem. The core issue is that tumours visible on MRI are effectively invisible on CT due to minimal contrast between pathological and healthy tissue. Unlike the CHAOS dataset where the liver boundary is visible in both modalities, tumour boundaries exist only in MRI pixel data. A convolutional neural network cannot segment structures that lack discriminative features in the input image; it can only propagate spatial information learned through registration.

The Spatial Prior Adherence. In the absence of discriminative CT features, the network correctly learned to prioritise the spatial prior (ϕ) over the visual evidence. The network acts as a faithful "registration warp", propagating the label based solely on the deformation field. This confirms the model's adherence to the weak supervision signal. However, any registration error, even minor misalignment, causes the segmentation to miss the target completely because there is no visual cue in the CT to refine the boundaries. The network effectively transfers the tumour location based solely on spatial correspondence, without any confirmatory signal from the CT image content.

Registration Limitations. Determining tumour boundaries in a deformed liver presents substantially greater challenges than segmenting the whole organ. The liver may undergo respiratory motion, patient positioning differences, and tissue deformation between MRI and CT acquisition. Whilst registration can accommodate global organ displacement, precise local alignment at tumour boundaries is considerably more difficult, particularly when the tumour has altered the local tissue characteristics.

Dataset Constraints. Additional factors include the limited dataset size (four training, two test, and one validation subject), contrast variations between subjects, the presence of multiple tumours in some subjects, and data acquisition from different MRI devices affecting image quality consistency.

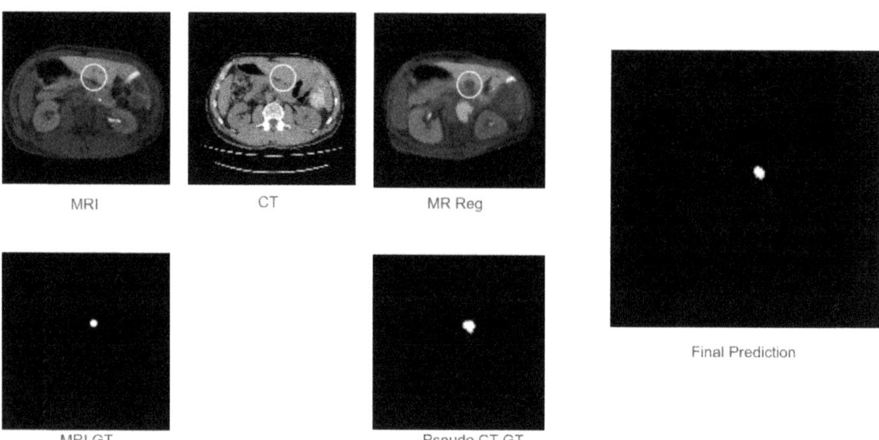

Fig. 5. Clinical Data Results: The tumour is visible in MRI (highlighted) but invisible in the corresponding CT region. The final prediction approximately localises the tumour despite poor Dice score.

3.6 Qualitative Analysis

Figure 5 illustrates the pipeline stages for clinical data and encapsulates the central finding of this research. The tumour is clearly visible in the MRI and MR_Reg images, highlighted by the annotation. Critically, the corresponding region in the CT image shows no visible tumour; the pathology is genuinely invisible in this modality.

The Pseudo CT_GT, generated by warping the MRI ground truth through the learned registration, correctly indicates the tumour location. The final prediction produces a segmentation that *approximately* identifies the tumour region but fails to capture the precise shape and extent. This observation is significant: the framework achieves *localisation* (finding the approximate tumour centre) even when precise *segmentation* (accurate boundary delineation) is not achievable. Whilst the Dice score is low due to the shape mismatch, the centre-point of the prediction falls within the true tumour margin, verifying successful localisation.

Whilst boundary delineation (Dice) was compromised by feature absence, the framework successfully recovered the tumour locus. The topological overlap is low, but the semantic localisation is preserved. This indicates that the registration successfully transferred the 'region of interest', even if the segmentation network could not refine the margins due to the lack of contrast. These findings demonstrate that spatial priors (registration) are insufficient without appearance cues (segmentation features) for precise boundary recovery, yet remain valuable for approximate tumour localisation.

For clinical applications such as surgical planning, localisation may provide meaningful value even when Dice scores are low. The Dice coefficient penalises boundary errors heavily, but for needle placement in ablation procedures, identifying the tumour centre with reasonable accuracy may be more clinically relevant than perfect boundary delineation.

4 Conclusions and Future Work

This work investigated the feasibility of cross-modality weak supervision for liver tumour segmentation, combining image registration and segmentation in an end-to-end framework. Two deep learning modules were developed and evaluated: MSCGUNet for inter-modal registration and UNet variants for segmentation.

The framework successfully demonstrates proof-of-concept on the CHAOS dataset, achieving Dice scores of 0.72 for healthy liver segmentation—acceptable performance considering the model never directly observes CT ground truth during training. This confirms that registration-assisted pseudo-label generation is viable when anatomical features are consistent across modalities.

However, application to clinical data containing liver tumours reveals fundamental limitations, with Dice scores dropping to 0.16. This performance degradation represents a significant scientific finding: when pathology is effectively invisible in the target modality (CT), registration-based label transfer cannot compensate for the absence of discriminative features. The network cannot segment what it cannot see; it can only propagate spatial information, which is insufficient for precise boundary delineation when visual confirmation is impossible.

The experimental comparison between UNet and UNet Deep Supervision models, using both Dice and Focal Tversky Loss functions, established that standard UNet with Dice Loss provides optimal performance for this application. Sequential training of registration and segmentation modules substantially outperforms end-to-end training.

These findings suggest that future research in invisible-tumour segmentation should move away from pure pixel-level transfer and focus on **uncertainty-aware localisation** or **multi-modal fusion** where the MRI remains available during inference.

Future research directions should address the fundamental "feature absence" problem identified in this work:

Multi-modal Fusion. If pre-operative registration quality permits, inputting both MRI and CT into the segmentation network simultaneously could provide the discriminative features from MRI whilst learning the spatial context from CT.

Uncertainty Quantification. Developing methods that allow the model to express confidence in its predictions would be clinically valuable. Rather than producing definitive segmentations in regions where the tumour is invisible, the model could indicate "I don't know where the tumour is" with associated uncertainty maps.

Clinical Evaluation. Systematic evaluation by medical professionals, particularly regarding the clinical utility of approximate localisation (as opposed to precise segmentation), would help establish the practical value of such frameworks in surgical planning.

Larger Clinical Datasets. Training on larger, more diverse clinical datasets with consistent acquisition protocols could improve generalisation and potentially reveal whether the method's limitations are intrinsic to the problem or partially attributable to data constraints.

References

1. Abraham, N., Khan, N.M.: A novel focal tversky loss function with improved attention u-net for lesion segmentation. In: 2019 IEEE 16th International Symposium on Biomedical Imaging (ISBI 2019), pp. 683–687. IEEE (2019)
2. Chatterjee, S., et al.: Micdir: multi-scale inverse-consistent deformable image registration using unetmss with self-constructing graph latent. Comput. Med. Imaging Graph. 102267 (2023)
3. Cheplygina, V., de Bruijne, M., Pluim, J.P.: Not-so-supervised: a survey of semi-supervised, multi-instance, and transfer learning in medical image analysis. Med. Image Anal. **54**, 280–296 (2019)
4. Ghafoorian, M., et al.: Transfer learning for domain adaptation in MRI: application in brain lesion segmentation. In: Descoteaux, M., et al. (eds.) MICCAI 2017. LNCS, vol. 10435, pp. 516–524. Springer, Cham (2017). https://doi.org/10.1007/978-3-319-66179-7_59
5. Kavur, A.E., et al.: Chaos challenge-combined (CT-MR) healthy abdominal organ segmentation. Med. Image Anal. **69**, 101950 (2021)
6. Lachinov, D.A.: Segmentation of thoracic organs using pixel shuffle. In: SegTHOR@ISBI (2019)
7. LeCun, Y., Bengio, Y., Hinton, G.: Deep learning. Nature **521**(7553), 436–444 (2015)
8. Litjens, G., et al.: A survey on deep learning in medical image analysis. Med. Image Anal. **42**, 60–88 (2017)
9. Ronneberger, O., Fischer, P., Brox, T.: U-net: convolutional networks for biomedical image segmentation. In: International Conference on Medical Image Computing and Computer-Assisted Intervention, pp. 234–241. Springer, Cham (2015)
10. Topol, E.J.: High-performance medicine: the convergence of human and artificial intelligence. Nat. Med. **25**(1), 44–56 (2019)
11. Zhen, S., et al.: Deep learning for accurate diagnosis of liver tumor based on magnetic resonance imaging and clinical data. Front. Oncol. **10**, 680 (2020)
12. Zhou, Z., Rahman Siddiquee, M.M., Tajbakhsh, N., Liang, J.: UNet++: a nested u-net architecture for medical image segmentation. In: Stoyanov, D., et al. (eds.) DLMIA/ML-CDS -2018. LNCS, vol. 11045, pp. 3–11. Springer, Cham (2018). https://doi.org/10.1007/978-3-030-00889-5_1

Transcending the Annotation Bottleneck: AI-Powered Discovery in Biology and Medicine

Soumick Chatterjee[1,2]($\boxtimes$) (iD)

[1] Human Technopole, Milan, Italy
contact@soumick.com
[2] Faculty of Computer Science, Otto von Guericke University Magdeburg,
Magdeburg, Germany

Abstract. The dependence on expert annotation has long constituted the primary rate-limiting step in the application of artificial intelligence to biomedicine. While supervised learning drove the initial wave of clinical algorithms, a paradigm shift towards unsupervised and self-supervised learning (SSL) is currently unlocking the latent potential of biobank-scale datasets. By learning directly from the intrinsic structure of data - whether pixels in a magnetic resonance image (MRI), voxels in a volumetric scan, or tokens in a genomic sequence - these methods facilitate the discovery of novel phenotypes, the linkage of morphology to genetics, and the detection of anomalies without human bias. This article synthesises seminal and recent advances in "learning without labels," highlighting how unsupervised frameworks can derive heritable cardiac traits, predict spatial gene expression in histology, and detect pathologies with performance that rivals or exceeds supervised counterparts.

Keywords: Unsupervised Learning · Medical Imaging · Phenotype Discovery · Anomaly Detection · Genomics

1 Introduction: The Annotation Bottleneck and the Unsupervised Solution

For the past decade, the standard workflow in biomedical data analysis has necessitated the curation of datasets, the manual annotation of regions of interest (e.g., tumours, lesions, or anatomical structures), and the training of supervised models to replicate these human labels. While effective for specific, narrow tasks, this approach is fundamentally constrained by the scarcity of high-quality labels, the inherent bias of human knowledge, and the high cost of expert time. Furthermore, supervised approaches typically discard the vast majority of information contained within high-dimensional data, focusing only on features relevant to the pre-defined label.

To overcome these limitations, the field has increasingly turned to unsupervised and self-supervised learning. A common critique of these methods is

C. Tommasino et al. (Eds.): AIBIO 2025, CCIS 2696, pp. 243–248, 2026.
https://doi.org/10.1007/978-3-032-17216-7_19

that they sacrifice accuracy for flexibility. However, recent evidence suggests this trade-off is vanishing. In an investigation of voxel-wise segmentation for additive manufacturing, Iuso et al. [11] compared sophisticated supervised models (such as UNet++) against unsupervised VAE-based approaches for porosity detection. Remarkably, they found that unsupervised models, particularly when post-processed, could achieve performance metrics (Average Precision 0.830) that rivalled or even exceeded their supervised counterparts (Average Precision 0.751) in challenging testing scenarios. This finding challenges the orthodoxy that supervised learning is invariably superior, suggesting that for complex, highly variable targets, a model that comprehends the fundamental data distribution may be more robust than one trained to mimic a limited set of human labels.

These techniques learn robust representations by solving "pretext" tasks—such as contrasting similar views of an image or reconstructing masked portions of data—rather than predicting extrinsic labels. Seminal works in computer vision established the efficacy of this approach: SimCLR [8] demonstrated that contrastive learning could produce visual representations comparable to supervised methods, while DINO [5] utilised self-distillation with Vision Transformers (ViT) to capture semantic segmentation properties without explicit supervision. In the medical domain, these principles were adapted to address data heterogeneity by Azizi et al. [1], paving the way for "foundation models" capable of discovering biological signals that may elude human observers.

2   Unsupervised Learning in Medical Imaging

The application of unsupervised learning in medical imaging has matured from simple dimensionality reduction to complex tasks involving phenotype discovery, anomaly detection, and image registration.

2.1   Phenotype Discovery and Genetic Linkage

A principal advantage of data-driven discovery is the capacity to define quantitative phenotypes that bridge the gap between macroscopic imaging and microscopic genetics. In the realm of multimodal learning, Taleb et al. [19] introduced the "ContIG" framework, demonstrating that self-supervised contrastive learning could effectively integrate medical imaging with genetic data to improve disease prediction.

Building upon this, Radhakrishnan et al. [17] utilised cross-modal autoencoders to learn holistic representations of the cardiovascular state. Expanding this frontier, Ometto et al. [16] recently developed a 3D diffusion autoencoder (3DDiffAE) to analyse temporal cardiac MRIs from the UK Biobank. Unlike traditional methods relying on fixed parameters such as ejection fraction, this unsupervised model learnt a "latent space" of 182 phenotypes describing complex cardiac wall motion and structure. Crucially, Ometto et al. demonstrated that these latent phenotypes shared a genetic architecture with established cardiac diseases, revealing 89 significant genomic loci.

This principle extends to the microscopic scale. In computational pathology, Cisternino et al. [9] utilised self-supervised Vision Transformers (ViT) trained on over 1.7 million histology tiles from the Genotype-Tissue Expression (GTEx) project. Their model, RNAPath, utilises these self-supervised features to predict spatial RNA expression levels directly from H&E-stained slides, effectively bridging the gap between tissue morphology and transcriptomics without the need for expensive spatial transcriptomics assays.

2.2 Robust Anomaly Detection

One of the most immediate clinical applications of learning without labels is anomaly detection—identifying pathology as a deviation from the normative distribution. StRegA [7] addressed this in neuroimaging, a pipeline utilising a context-encoding Variational Autoencoder (VAE). By learning the distribution of healthy brain anatomy, StRegA identifies regions that the model cannot accurately reconstruct, successfully localising brain tumours and other anomalies without ever observing a labelled tumour during training.

Building upon these foundational VAE-based approaches, recent advancements have introduced more sophisticated generative models. Li et al. [13] introduced Scale-Aware Contrastive Reverse Distillation (SCAD), a novel framework that enhances anomaly detection by leveraging multi-scale feature representations and contrastive learning. SCAD addresses the challenge of scale variance in medical anomalies by distilling knowledge from a pre-trained teacher network to a student network in a reverse manner, effectively capturing anomalies across different resolutions. Furthermore, Bercea et al. [4] critically evaluated normative representation learning in generative AI for robust anomaly detection in brain imaging. Their work highlights the importance of robust normative learning to ensure that generative models accurately capture the variability of healthy brain anatomy, thereby improving the sensitivity and specificity of anomaly detection. Addressing the limitations of standard diffusion models in preserving fine details, Beizaee et al. [3] introduced MAD-AD, a masked diffusion framework for unsupervised brain anomaly detection. By incorporating masking strategies into the diffusion process, MAD-AD effectively mitigates the issue of noise accumulation during image reconstruction, leading to more precise anomaly localisation compared to traditional diffusion-based methods.

The field continues to diversify with the emergence of State Space Models (SSMs) like Mamba, which have led to new architectures such as MAAT (Mamba Adaptive Anomaly Transformer) [20]. This model efficiently captures long-range dependencies in physiological data, offering a computationally efficient alternative to traditional Transformers. Furthermore, foundation models are being adapted for this task; Seeböck et al. [18] recently utilised self-supervised learning to guide segmentation in retinal OCT scans, effectively using anomaly detection as a weak supervision signal.

2.3 Image Registration

Deformable image registration has traditionally been computationally expensive. Unsupervised deep learning methods like VoxelMorph [2] learn to predict deformation fields by optimizing image similarity metrics, achieving state-of-the-art accuracy with significantly faster inference times. Building upon these foundations, MICDIR [6] introduced a multi-scale inverse-consistent framework incorporating a self-constructing graph latent. By explicitly encoding global dependencies and enforcing cycle consistency, MICDIR demonstrated statistically significant improvements over VoxelMorph in both intramodal and intermodal brain MRI registration tasks.

3 Deciphering the Molecular Code

Beyond imaging, unsupervised learning is revolutionising genomics and molecular biology by treating biological sequences as a "language" of life.

3.1 Genomic Sequence Modelling

Just as large language models learn the structure of text, genomic models can learn the grammar of regulatory elements and gene expression without explicit labels. Seminal works like DNABERT [12] applied the BERT architecture to k-mer sequences of DNA, demonstrating that attention mechanisms could capture global and local genomic context. More recently, the Nucleotide Transformer [10] scaled this approach to billions of parameters, training on multispecies genomes to predict molecular phenotypes and variant effects.

3.2 Single-Cell Analysis

The advent of single-cell RNA sequencing (scRNA-seq) has provided high-resolution views of cellular heterogeneity, but the data is inherently high-dimensional, sparse, and noisy. Deep generative models like scVI (Single-cell Variational Inference) [15] use variational inference to approximate the underlying probability distributions of gene expression. By learning a low-dimensional latent representation of each cell, scVI can correct for batch effects, impute missing values, and cluster cell types without reliance on pre-defined markers.

4 Clinical and Therapeutic Frontiers

The utility of unsupervised learning extends into the translation of biological insights into clinical practice and therapeutic development.

4.1   Computational Phenotyping from Electronic Health Records

Electronic Health Records (EHR) contain rich, longitudinal data on patient health. Unsupervised learning allows for "computational phenotyping"—the discovery of clinical patterns without manual cohort definition. Inspired by natural language processing, models like BEHRT [14] treat patient medical histories as sequences of events and use Transformer architectures to learn robust patient representations. These self-supervised embeddings can predict future disease risks and stratify patients into novel subtypes, effectively enabling precision medicine at the population scale.

5   Concluding Remarks

The transition from supervised to unsupervised learning marks a decisive maturation in biomedical AI, effectively circumventing the "annotation bottleneck" that has long stifled progress. No longer compromising on accuracy, these self-supervised frameworks now rival supervised counterparts and drive genuine discovery—from defining novel cardiac phenotypes to decoding the genomic "language" of life. By leveraging the intrinsic structure of data, the field is moving towards a holistic view of biology where insights are derived from the data itself rather than human bias.

Future research must focus on the convergence of these modalities into unified "foundation models" capable of reasoning across imaging, genomics, and electronic health records simultaneously. Additionally, the exploration of computationally efficient architectures, such as State Space Models (e.g. Mamba), offers a promising avenue for modelling long-range biological dependencies that traditional Transformers struggle to capture. Ultimately, the priority remains bridging the gap between these high-dimensional latent representations and interpretable, clinically actionable biomarkers.

References

1. Azizi, S., et al.: Big self-supervised models advance medical image classification. In: Proceedings of the IEEE/CVF International Conference on Computer Vision, pp. 3478–3488 (2021)
2. Balakrishnan, G., Zhao, A., Sabuncu, M.R., Guttag, J., Dalca, A.V.: Voxelmorph: a learning framework for deformable medical image registration. IEEE Trans. Med. Imaging **38**(8), 1788–1800 (2019)
3. Beizaee, F., Lodygensky, G., Desrosiers, C., Dolz, J.: Mad-ad: masked diffusion for unsupervised brain anomaly detection. In: International Conference on Information Processing in Medical Imaging, pp. 139–153. Springer, Cham (2025)
4. Bercea, C.I., Wiestler, B., Rueckert, D., Schnabel, J.A.: Evaluating normative representation learning in generative AI for robust anomaly detection in brain imaging. Nat. Commun. **16**(1), 1624 (2025)
5. Caron, M., et al.: Emerging properties in self-supervised vision transformers. In: Proceedings of the IEEE/CVF International Conference on Computer Vision, pp. 9650–9660 (2021)

6. Chatterjee, S., et al.: Micdir: multi-scale inverse-consistent deformable image registration using unetmss with self-constructing graph latent. Comput. Med. Imaging Graph. **108**, 102267 (2023)
7. Chatterjee, S., et al.: Strega: unsupervised anomaly detection in brain MRIs using a compact context-encoding variational autoencoder. Comput. Biol. Med. **149**, 106093 (2022)
8. Chen, T., Kornblith, S., Norouzi, M., Hinton, G.: A simple framework for contrastive learning of visual representations. In: International Conference on Machine Learning, pp. 1597–1607. PmLR (2020)
9. Cisternino, F., Ometto, S., Chatterjee, S., Giacopuzzi, E., Levine, A.P., Glastonbury, C.A.: Self-supervised learning for characterising histomorphological diversity and spatial RNA expression prediction across 23 human tissue types. Nat. Commun. **15**(1), 5906 (2024)
10. Dalla-Torre, H., et al.: Nucleotide transformer: building and evaluating robust foundation models for human genomics. Nat. Methods **22**(2), 287–297 (2025)
11. Iuso, D., Chatterjee, S., Cornelissen, S., Verhees, D., Beenhouwer, J.D., Sijbers, J.: Voxel-wise segmentation for porosity investigation of additive manufactured parts with 3D unsupervised and (deeply) supervised neural networks. Appl. Intell. **54**(24), 13160–13177 (2024)
12. Ji, Y., Zhou, Z., Liu, H., Davuluri, R.V.: Dnabert: pre-trained bidirectional encoder representations from transformers model for DNA-language in genome. Bioinformatics **37**(15), 2112–2120 (2021)
13. Li, C., Shi, Y., Hu, J., Zhu, X.X., Mou, L.: Scale-aware contrastive reverse distillation for unsupervised medical anomaly detection. In: The Thirteenth International Conference on Learning Representations (2025). https://openreview.net/forum?id=HNOo4UNPBF
14. Li, Y., et al.: Behrt: transformer for electronic health records. Sci. Rep. **10**(1), 7155 (2020)
15. Lopez, R., Regier, J., Cole, M.B., Jordan, M.I., Yosef, N.: Deep generative modeling for single-cell transcriptomics. Nat. Methods **15**(12), 1053–1058 (2018)
16. Ometto, S., et al.: Hundreds of cardiac MRI traits derived using 3D diffusion autoencoders share a common genetic architecture. medRxiv, pp. 2024–11 (2024)
17. Radhakrishnan, A., et al.: Cross-modal autoencoder framework learns holistic representations of cardiovascular state. Nat. Commun. **14**(1), 2436 (2023)
18. Seeböck, P., Orlando, J.I., Michl, M., Mai, J., Schmidt-Erfurth, U., Bogunović, H.: Anomaly guided segmentation: introducing semantic context for lesion segmentation in retinal oct using weak context supervision from anomaly detection. Med. Image Anal. **93**, 103104 (2024)
19. Taleb, A., Kirchler, M., Monti, R., Lippert, C.: Contig: self-supervised multimodal contrastive learning for medical imaging with genetics. In: Proceedings of the IEEE/CVF Conference on Computer Vision and Pattern Recognition, pp. 20908–20921 (2022)
20. Zakaria Sellam, A., Benaissa, I., Taleb-Ahmed, A., Patrono, L., Distante, C.: Maat: mamba adaptive anomaly transformer with association discrepancy for time series. arXiv e-prints, pp. arXiv–2502 (2025)

Increasing Data Availability Through Standardization: Unlocking AI in Digital Pathology

Francesco Martino[(✉)]

Dedalus HealthCare GmbH, Vienna, Austria
`francesco.martino@dedalus.com`

Abstract. As digital pathology enters a new era, the promise of AI-assisted diagnostics is often held back not by model performance, but by limited access to structured, interoperable data. The absence of standardized formats reduces the usability of whole slide images for machine learning, restricts multi-institutional collaborations, and complicates integration with clinical workflows. We explore how the lack of standardization in data formats remains a key obstacle to translating research models into clinical tools. We highlight the practical benefits of adopting the DICOM standard for digital pathology and demonstrate how standardization can improve data integration, enhance AI workflows, and support large-scale collaborations, ultimately accelerating the clinical impact of computational pathology.

1   Introduction

Digital pathology has undergone a rapid transformation driven by advances in whole slide imaging, storage architectures, and machine learning. As healthcare institutions increasingly adopt digital workflows, the volume of available image data has grown substantially [1]. These datasets are essential for training deep learning models capable of performing tasks such as tumor detection, grading, tissue segmentation, and biomarker quantification. Yet, despite their importance, the potential of these datasets remains only partially realized.

A key barrier is the fragmentation of data formats across vendors and institutions. Many scanners still produce proprietary formats that require specialized libraries or commercial software to open. These formats often lack standardized annotations, metadata fields, and consistent encoding of acquisition parameters. Such variability hinders reproducibility and limits the ability to merge datasets originating from different clinical sites [2].

The need for standardization becomes even more pronounced when considering clinical translation. AI tools deployed alongside pathologists must integrate with existing enterprise systems such as PACS, vendor-neutral archives, and hospital information systems [3]. Without a standard representation of digital pathology images, organizations are forced to implement custom integration

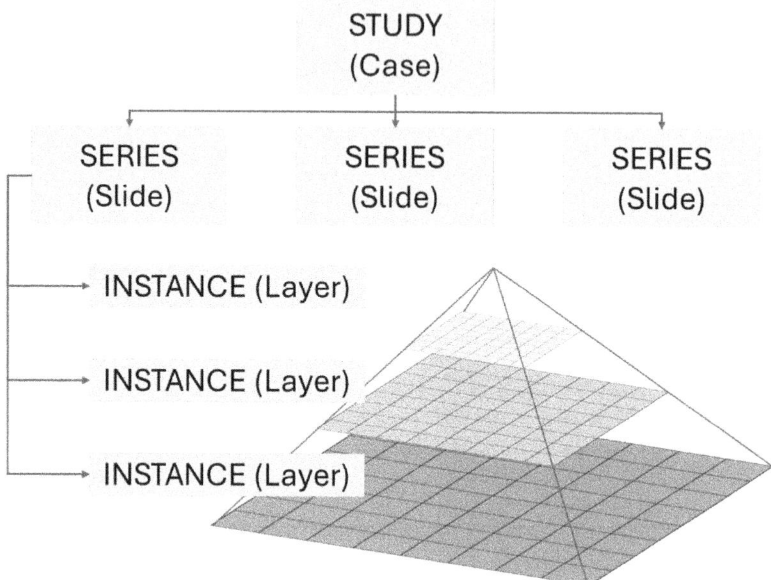

Fig. 1. Structure of a DICOM dataset, which contains study-information (a collection of images of a specific patient), series (each individual image generated by a slide scanner, therefore a single slide), and instances, each representing a resolution layer, including pixel data.

layers, increasing maintenance costs and slowing down adoption. Community standards, especially DICOM, offer a practical way to address these challenges [4]. By adopting a well-established medical imaging standard, digital pathology can benefit from decades of interoperability work already deployed in radiology.

Digital pathology is rapidly transforming the way laboratories, hospitals, and research institutions handle microscopic imaging, diagnostics, and data-driven workflows. As whole-slide imaging (WSI) becomes increasingly common and AI tools continue to expand, the need for a reliable, standardized, and interoperable method of managing and exchanging pathology data is more critical than ever. The Digital Imaging and Communications in Medicine (DICOM) standard has emerged as the cornerstone for enabling this transition [5]. Its role in digital pathology goes far beyond image formatting: DICOM provides a robust infrastructure for communication, interoperability, and structured data management.

2   DICOM as a Communication Standard

One of DICOM's foundational strengths is its design as a communication protocol [6]. It was created not just to define how images are stored, but how they are transmitted, queried, and retrieved across different systems and institutions.

In digital pathology, the ability to exchange whole-slide images and associated metadata reliably is essential. High-resolution pathology images can reach tens

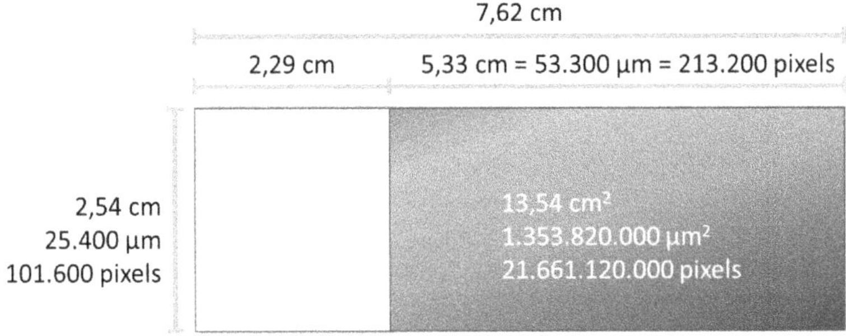

Fig. 2. Illustration of the physical and digital dimensions of a typical whole-slide image region. A physical slide has a 13.54 cm^2 area which corresponds to more than 1.3 billion µm^2 and over 21.6 billion pixels, demonstrating the extreme scale of whole-slide imaging, although not the entire area contains tissue so the real size is drastically reduced. Because anyhow such images cannot be retrieved or processed in their entirety at once, systems must access only the specific regions or frames required for visualization or analysis. This scale highlights the importance of a standardized method for accessing single frames to ensure efficient, interoperable, and reliable navigation of whole-slide images.

of gigabytes per slide, and managing their transfer requires a protocol capable of handling large, complex datasets, which are organized per study, series and instances, which for Digital Pathology are organized in a pyramid structure containing each a resolution layer [6], Fig. 1.

DICOM provides this capability through its standardized networking services, such as C-STORE for image transmission, C-FIND for querying, and C-MOVE or C-GET for retrieval. These services ensure that digital pathology systems can communicate efficiently regardless of the vendor or platform.

This communication framework is particularly important in distributed workflows, where slides can be scanned in one location, reviewed in another, and analyzed by AI tools hosted in the cloud. Without a standardized communication protocol, digital pathology would be fragmented, and laboratories would rely on proprietary file transfer mechanisms that hinder scalability and create bottlenecks.

3   Interoperability Across Vendors and Systems

Interoperability is one of the most significant challenges in digital pathology. Historically, each scanner vendor introduced its own image format, metadata representation, and software ecosystem. This lack of standardization made it difficult, or sometimes impossible to integrate systems from different manufacturers. It also forced laboratories to lock down vendors, limiting flexibility and increasing long-term costs [7].

DICOM addresses these issues by providing a vendor-neutral and universally recognized format for whole-slide images [6]. When scanners produce DICOM-compliant images, any viewer, PACS, or workflow system that supports the standard can ingest and display them. This approach decouples hardware from software and gives organizations the flexibility to select the tools that best suit their clinical and operational needs. This is particularly important given the size and resolution of whole-slide images, which make it impractical to retrieve the entire image at once Fig. 2. Instead, clinical systems must be able to access specific regions or frames of the slide on demand. A standardized protocol is therefore essential to ensure interoperability and consistent performance across devices and software platforms.

Interoperability also enables more sophisticated workflows. For example, integrating digital pathology images with radiology data, clinical laboratory systems, or electronic health records becomes much easier when all components speak the same language. This alignment is crucial to achieving the full promise of precision medicine, where cross-disciplinary data integration leads to more informed diagnoses and treatment decisions.

Furthermore, DICOM plays an essential role in enabling research and AI development. AI models trained on proprietary formats face compatibility hurdles and may struggle to generalize. DICOM's standardized structure ensures that data from different institutions can be aggregated, compared, and analyzed consistently; an essential requirement to build robust and high-quality machine learning pipelines [6].

DICOM in Digital Pathology does not only represent a theoretical possibility, but there are several examples of practical applications for it. In 2012, Amin et al. tested the possibility of integrating digital pathology images within an Enterprise PACS and proved its feasibility, provided that images are wrapped in a DICOM container [8]. Moreover, literature shows that there are several examples of the implementation of a DICOM-based digital pathology solution for collaborative approaches to Artificial Intelligence [9,10]. These studies reinforce the readiness of DICOM for Digital Pathology not only for PACS integration but also for enabling Artificial Intelligence within clinical workflows.

Despite the demonstrated feasibility and the maturity of the standard, real-world adoption remains limited. Many hospitals are cautious about moving away from proprietary formats that are deeply integrated into their existing diagnostic pathways. Vendors of digital pathology systems often resist fully adopting DICOM because doing so requires investment in redesigning image pipelines, optimizing performance for large whole-slide images, and reducing dependency on proprietary ecosystems that currently offer commercial advantages.

This reluctance contributes to a fragmented environment in which Medical Viewers retrieve patient and case information directly from AP-LIS systems. This approach separates clinical data from the image itself, even though such information should be embedded within the DICOM representation from the moment of acquisition [11]. The resulting inconsistency affects interoperability, limits multi-site collaboration, and restricts the ability to scale data-driven applications, all of which depend on high-quality and standardized metadata.

4   Structured Data for Consistency and Quality

Digital pathology is not just about images. It is equally about metadata: patient demographics, specimen descriptions, staining techniques, acquisition details, magnification levels, spatial mappings, and more. Proper capture and organizing of this information is essential for clinical quality, regulatory compliance, and data-driven analysis.

DICOM provides a rich and extensible data model that ensures that pathology information is structured and encoded consistently [12]. Instead of storing metadata in ad-hoc JSON files or proprietary header formats, DICOM embeds this information directly into the file using standardized data elements.

This structured approach offers several advantages:

- Standardized fields ensure that any DICOM-compliant system interprets metadata the same way, eliminating ambiguity and preventing data loss during cross-platform exchanges.

- Structured metadata allows laboratories to implement advanced search capabilities, e.g., find all slides stained with a specific protocol or all samples belonging to a certain anatomical site. It also supports automation, enabling systems to route cases, pre-populate reports, or trigger AI analysis pipelines.

- High-quality structured metadata is vital for quantitative pathology. Measurements, annotations, and algorithm outputs can be stored in a standardized format within the DICOM file itself, such as DICOM GSPS, or DICOM SR. This not only supports reproducibility but also creates a unified record that combines raw images, human interpretations, and machine-generated insights.

5   Conclusion

Digital pathology is entering a mature phase, where clinical adoption, AI integration, and cross-institutional collaboration are accelerating. However, these advances depend on a stable, interoperable, and richly structured foundation for managing data.

DICOM provides exactly that. As a communication standard, it enables the reliable and efficient exchange of large pathological images. As an interoperability framework, it breaks down barriers between vendors and systems, promoting flexibility and collaboration. And as a structured data model, it ensures consistency, quality, and scalability throughout the pathology workflow.

In short, DICOM is not only useful for digital pathology, it is indispensable. Its adoption is a critical step toward unlocking the full potential of digital transformation in pathology and ensuring that laboratories, clinicians, and researchers can work together using a common, powerful standard.

We conclude that standardization is a crucial step toward unlocking the full potential of AI in digital pathology. By improving interoperability, enabling multi-center collaboration, and reducing technical debt, standardized formats create a robust foundation for scalable and clinically meaningful AI solutions.

Adopting DICOM WSI not only enhances data availability but also supports the long-term sustainability and reproducibility of computational pathology research.

References

1. Mezei, T., et al.: Image analysis in histopathology and cytopathology: from early days to current perspectives. J. Imaging **10**(10), 252 (2024). https://doi.org/10.3390/jimaging10100252
2. Tizhoosh, H.R., Pantanowitz, L.: Artificial intelligence and digital pathology: challenges and opportunities. J. Pathol. Inform. **9**, 38 (2018). https://doi.org/10.4103/jpi.jpi_53_18
3. Caffery, L.J., et al.: The role of DICOM in artificial intelligence for skin disease. Front. Med. **7**, 619787 (2021). https://doi.org/10.3389/fmed.2020.619787
4. Singh, R., et al.: Standardization in digital pathology: supplement 145 of the DICOM standards. J. Pathol. Inform. **2**, 23 (2011). https://doi.org/10.4103/2153-3539.80719
5. DICOM Standards Committee. Digital Imaging and Communications in Medicine (DICOM). National Electrical Manufacturers Association (NEMA) (2023)
6. Herrmann, M.D., Clunie, D.A., Fedorov, A., et al.: Implementing the DICOM standard for digital pathology. J. Pathol. Inform. **9**, 37 (2018). https://doi.org/10.4103/jpi.jpi_42_18
7. Al-Janabi, S., Huisman, A., Van Diest, P.J.: Digital pathology: current status and future perspectives. Histopathology **61**(1), 1–9 (2012). https://doi.org/10.1111/j.1365-2559.2011.03814.x
8. Amin, M., et al.: Integration of digital gross pathology images for enterprise-wide access. J. Pathol. Inform. **3**(1), 10 (2012). https://doi.org/10.4103/2153-3539.93892. https://www.sciencedirect.com/science/article/pii/S2153353922005843. ISSN 2153-3539
9. Jesus, R., et al.: Personalizable AI platform for universal access to research and diagnosis in digital pathology. Comput. Methods Programs Biomedicine **242**, 107787 (2023). https://doi.org/10.1016/j.cmpb.2023.107787. https://www.sciencedirect.com/science/article/pii/S0169260723004534. ISSN 0169-2607
10. Hsu, C.-W., et al.: Mainecoon: implementing an open-source web viewer for DICOM whole slide images with AI-integrated PACS for digital pathology. J. Imaging Inform. Med. 1–15 (2025)
11. Clunie, D.A.: DICOM format and protocol standardization–a core requirement for digital pathology success. Toxicol. Pathol. **49**(4), 738–749 (2021)
12. Garcia-Rojo, M.: International clinical guidelines for the adoption of digital pathology: a review of technical aspects. Pathobiology **83**(2–3), 99–109 (2016). https://doi.org/10.1159/000441192

Why Accuracy Isn't Enough. Rethinking Model Evaluation in Clinical AI with a User-Centered Utility Metric

Federico Cabitza[⊠]

University of Milano-Bicocca, Viale Sarca 336, 20124 Milano, Italy
`federico.cabitza@unimib.it`

Abstract. Evaluating AI models in clinical decision support requires metrics that go beyond aggregate accuracy to reflect user needs, decision uncertainty, and real-world risk. Traditional metrics such as precision or AUC fail to capture these human-centered concerns, particularly in high-stakes and imbalanced settings. Current evaluation frameworks rarely integrate user hesitation, case relevance, or the asymmetry of error consequences. This abstract summarizes a keynote presented at the 1st Workshop on Artificial Intelligence for Biomedical Data (AIBio) 2025, co-located with ECAI 2025, where we aimed to fill this gap by introducing the weighted Utility (wU) metric–a user-centered evaluation method that incorporates rater-specific hesitation thresholds, relevance weights, and parameters for the asymmetric impact of model errors. The metric generalizes existing decision-theoretic measures such as the Standardized Net Benefit and operationalizes them in a case-dependent, psychometrically informed framework. In clinical case studies on knee MRI classification and ovarian cancer sonography, wU-optimized models improved overall AUC from 0.862 to 0.895 ($p < 0.05$), with the greatest gains on high-complexity cases (AUC from 0.85 to 0.92, $p < 0.05$). We also present two online tools, Metimeter and dAIagrams, which support the practical application of wU by enabling data upload, metric computation, and visual decision analysis. These findings suggest that wU offers a more clinically relevant evaluation lens, particularly in contexts where expert judgment is fragile. The metric supports the design and deployment of AI systems that align with human decision-making under uncertainty.

Keywords: Weighted Utility · Standardized net Benefit · AI evaluation

1 Background and Motivation

In the literature, several articles have warned against the practice of relying exclusively on accuracy metrics to evaluate the performance and skills of binary classifiers developed with machine learning techniques and methods [7]. For instance, it has been shown that accuracy and other common metrics such as

C. Tommasino et al. (Eds.): AIBIO 2025, CCIS 2696, pp. 255–264, 2026.
https://doi.org/10.1007/978-3-032-17216-7_21

recall, precision, and F1 score can be heavily influenced by class imbalance and prevalence, which often leads to misleading performance assessments, especially when the minority class is underrepresented [5].

A more fundamental critique, however, is that accuracy is often a poor proxy for the three main performance dimensions of any clinical AI system: *Robustness*, *Reliability*, and *Utility* [10].

- **Robustness** refers to the model's ability to maintain performance on naturally diverse data, ensuring it does not fail on complex cases despite being accurate on trivial ones [2,9,12].
- **Reliability** ensures the model has been trained on representative and truthful data, avoiding biases hidden by aggregate scores [1,6].
- **Utility** captures the actual positive impact on decisions and outcomes, distinguishing between statistically "correct" predictions and those that practically aid the decision-maker [4,13].

Having previously addressed how to better report on the reliability and robustness of machine learning models [3], in this work we focus specifically on the dimension of utility.

Traditional frameworks often fail to capture the real-world consequences of classification errors, urging for evaluation methods that consider decision-theoretic impacts beyond simplistic scores. As authors of [4], we believe that an example of these methods would be utility-based, and in this work we will discuss a user-centered extension of the most common utility metric, the net benefit [13]. To this aim, we will discuss the *weighted Utility* (wU) metric [4], which explicitly integrates the rater's hesitation, tolerance to false alarms, and the perceived importance of each case. This approach aims to measure not only how accurate a model is, but how useful it can be in assisting human experts under real decision uncertainty: thus, the weighted utility is proposed as an intrinsically user-centered way to capture the practical value of binary classification decisions by integrating user preferences and consequences into model evaluation.

2   From Usefulness to Weighted Utility

The *weighted Utility* (wU) quantifies the expected benefit of a model h as a function of three user-dependent factors:

1. The **hesitation threshold** $\tau_j(x_i)$: the confidence level at which the j-th rater would be uncertain about classifying case x_i. This threshold is pragmatically derived from the user's risk tolerance. Specifically, we can ask the rater to define K, the number of false alarms they are willing to tolerate to catch one additional true positive. The hesitation threshold is then analytically related to this ratio by the function $\tau = 1/(K+1)$ [13]. The model's probability $h(x_i)$ is compared to $\tau_j(x_i)$ to determine whether the model would issue a positive or negative recommendation for that specific rater and case context.

2. The **relevance weight** $r(x_i)$: a psychometric estimate of how important it is to classify case x_i correctly. Higher relevance may reflect higher perceived risk, clinical impact, or complexity. Each case thus contributes to the overall utility in proportion to its relevance.
3. The **impact parameters** α and β: scaling factors that reward the model when it corrects a human error ($\alpha > 1$) and penalize it when it induces one ($0 \leq \beta < 1$). These parameters capture, respectively, the model's corrective benefit and the potential cost of automation bias.

Intuitively, a decision support system is useful when it detects more real problems than false alarms. Yet, this intuition is incomplete: a truly supportive model should also help users avoid the *worst* kind of error, which for many decision makers will be missing a critical case; assist humans in correcting their own misjudgments (parameter α); prevent them from being misled by spurious model outputs (parameter β); express its recommendations with sufficient confidence to be considered trustworthy (hesitation threshold $\tau_j(x_i)$); and focus its assistance where it truly matters, i.e., on complex or high-stakes cases (relevance weight $r(x_i)$).

These five principles formalize the idea that the value of a decision support system cannot be captured by accuracy alone. Instead, it must be evaluated in terms of how it contributes to safer, more reliable, and context-sensitive decisions. The *weighted Utility* (wU) metric operationalizes precisely this perspective, aggregating the multiple ways in which an AI model can assist or harm human experts across heterogeneous and uncertain decision scenarios.

Formally, let I denote the set of test cases x_i and J the set of human raters d_j. Each rater is associated with an individual hesitation threshold τ_j, a tolerance to false alarms, and parameters α and β weighting the benefits and harms of modelhuman interaction. The overall *weighted Utility* of a model h is then defined as:

$$wU = \frac{1}{|J||I|} \sum_{j,i} r(x_i) \cdot U_j(x_i, \tau_j, \alpha, \beta)$$

where $r(x_i)$ is the *relevance weight* of case x_i, expressing how important it is to make a correct decision on that instance, and $U_j(x_i, \tau_j, \alpha, \beta)$ represents the case-level utility experienced by rater j when assisted by the model.

The individual utility term is defined analytically as:

$$U_j(x_i, \tau_j, \alpha, \beta) = \begin{cases} +\alpha, & \text{if } d_j(x_i) \neq y_i \text{ and } h(x_i) \geq \tau_j \text{ (model corrects a human error),} \\ +1, & \text{if } d_j(x_i) = y_i \text{ and } h(x_i) \geq \tau_j \text{ (model confirms a correct decision),} \\ -\beta, & \text{if } d_j(x_i) \neq y_i \text{ and } h(x_i) < \tau_j \text{ (model fails to correct an error),} \\ -1, & \text{if } d_j(x_i) = y_i \text{ and } h(x_i) \geq \tau_j \text{ but prediction is false positive,} \\ 0, & \text{otherwise.} \end{cases}$$

This formulation jointly accounts for (i) whether the model and the human agree or disagree, (ii) whether the model is correct or incorrect with respect to the true label y_i, and (iii) whether the model's confidence surpasses the user-specific hesitation threshold τ_j.

Positive utilities arise when the model either makes a correct autonomous decision or effectively assists the human in avoiding an error; negative utilities capture misleading recommendations or missed opportunities for correction. The scalar parameters α and β adjust the asymmetry between corrective benefits and misleading costs, allowing wU to reflect context-dependent risk preferences.

The metric ranges in $[-\infty, 1]$, where 0 marks the threshold between harmful and beneficial support. The formulation generalizes the well-known *Standardized Net Benefit* (sNB): when all cases are equally relevant ($r(x_i) = 1$) and all raters share the same threshold ($\tau_j(x_i) = \tilde{\tau}$), $wU(\tilde{\tau}) = sNB(\tilde{\tau})$. Hence, wU extends classical decision-analytic metrics into a user-centered, case-dependent space.

The practical computation of the weighted utility relies on retrospective human assessments rather than hypothetical preferences. A typical setup involves a set of approximately one hundred real cases, each independently evaluated by a small group of raters (usually between five and seven domain experts). For each case x_i, raters are asked to indicate their *maximum tolerable risk of failing to identify it as a positive instance*–that is, the number of false alarms they would be willing to accept rather than missing one true positive. This response determines their individual hesitation threshold $\tau_j(x_i)$.

Subsequently, raters classify each case, report their confidence in the correctness of their decision, and rate its perceived difficulty or complexity. These three inputs–confidence, threshold, and complexity–jointly allow for the estimation of $r(x_i)$, $\tau_j(x_i)$, and their interaction with model predictions. The resulting dataset thus encodes how humans perceive uncertainty and relevance, enabling the computation of wU as a genuinely user-centered evaluation metric that bridges psychometric and algorithmic perspectives.

The wU metric can be visualized as a three-dimensional surface defined by the model threshold τ, case relevance r, and overall utility (see Fig. 1). While standard decision-curve analysis (the sNB curve) corresponds to a single slice of this surface at fixed relevance (assuming all cases are equally important) and fixed global threshold, wU integrates across the entire volume. It weights each case by its specific relevance and adjusts for the rater's specific uncertainty. This multidimensional approach highlights that decisions are not all equal: a model exhibits positive weighted utility only when it provides a net benefit specifically in the cases where human experts are most uncertain or where errors are most consequential. Conversely, low or negative wU values indicate that the model fails to assist humans in relevant, high-stakes cases, even if its aggregate accuracy on trivial cases is high.

The wU metric was validated across theoretical analyses and real-world clinical case studies [4], confirming that it effectively generalizes utility-based metrics—such as the Net Benefit and Expected Maximum Profit—as well as standard error-based metrics like Balanced Accuracy and the Youden Index. Unlike traditional metrics that treat all errors equally, wU integrates case-wise raters' perceptions of "relevance" (e.g., case complexity) and "hesitation" (con-

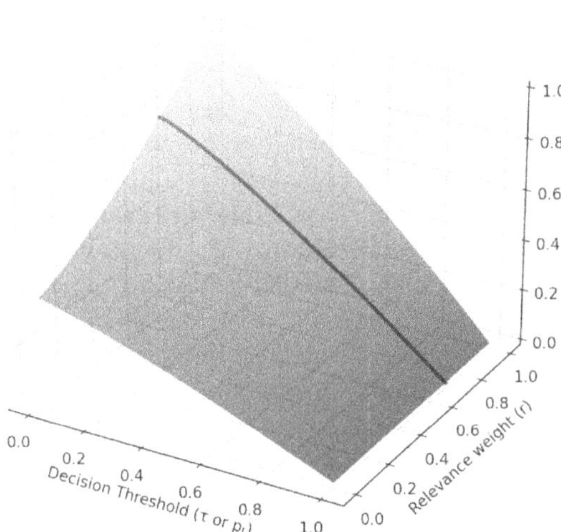

Fig. 1. The weighted Utility (wU) represented as a decision surface. Standard decision curves (sNB) appear as 2D slices of this surface where case relevance is assumed constant.

fidence). This formulation allows the metric to penalize automation bias and reward models that correct human errors on significant cases, providing a flexible framework for human-centered AI evaluation.

Empirical applications in knee MRI classification and ovarian cancer sonography demonstrated that optimizing models using wU yields superior results compared to standard AUC optimization. While the wU-optimized model showed improved global performance (AUC 0.862 vs. 0.895, $p < 0.05$), the gain was most pronounced on cases deemed complex by human annotators [4]. In this "hard-case region," the wU-optimized model increased the AUC from 0.85 to 0.92 ($p < 0.05$), indicating that utility-driven optimization successfully tunes model accuracy toward the specific instances where human decision-makers most require support.

3   Metric Implementation

We developed two complementary web-based tools to support the practical implementation of the wU metric (and other related metrics), once the average hesitation threshold—that is, the decision threshold—has been set. These tools are *Metimeter* and *dAIagrams*, which we describe in the following.

- The **Metimeter**[1] is a web-based suite of tools aimed at supporting interested researchers in evaluating the reliability of training data, the model's calibration, its robustness and utility.

---

[1] https://www.entechne.com/metimeter.

In particular, the utility evaluation tool[2] allows users to upload personalized prediction data and automatically derives a set of performance and utility metrics for binary classification models. Input must be provided as a comma-separated value file which, at minimum, must include a column `y_true`, encoding the ground-truth labels (0 = negative, 1 = positive), and a column `y_proba`, specifying the predicted probability for the positive class in the range $[0, 1]$. Two additional columns can be supplied to capture what makes computing the weigthed utility possible: `Relevance`, which specifies case-specific weights in $[0, 1]$, and `Threshold`, which specifies case-specific decision (or hesitation) thresholds (probabilities in $[0, 1]$) at which each instance is classified as positive. If no instance-wise threshold column is present, the tool accepts a single scalar threshold parameter, applied globally to all predictions. This scalar threshold corresponds to the probability at which the expected benefit of identifying a true positive equals the expected harm of a false positive; by default it is set to 0.5, representing an indifference point between benefit and harm. Based on the supplied data and threshold specification, the application computes and reports a set of primary utility metrics—weighted utility (`wU`) and standardized net benefit at several risk thresholds ($\tau = 0.25, 0.50, 0.75$)—together with standard performance measures, including sensitivity, specificity, accuracy, balanced accuracy, area under the ROC curve (AUC), and F1-score. These outputs are summarized numerically and through graphical displays (see Fig. 2), enabling users to assess both traditional discrimination/accuracy and decision-analytic consequences of using the model under different threshold and weighting regimes.

– **dAIagrams**[3] is an analytical and visualization platform for assessing model performance—in terms of discriminative power, classification accuracy, utility, and calibration—once a general (or average) decision threshold has been set. It enables a more fine-grained evaluation within the range of decision thresholds that are most representative of users' preferences and perceived risks.

In particular, also the **dAIagrams** evaluation tool accepts as input the predicted probabilities of a binary classification model together with the corresponding ground-truth labels for a test dataset. To this aim, users can either paste the vectors of true labels (`y_true`) and predicted probabilities (`y_prob`) directly into dedicated text fields or upload them from a file; a built-in demo dataset is also available for illustration. In addition to these data, the interface requires the specification of decision-analytic parameters that capture the preferences of the intended decision maker. Specifically, users may provide either (i) the decision threshold, expressed in terms of the maximum tolerable risk t of overlooking a true case (expressed as a percentage) or (ii) a value k describing how many false alarms they are willing to accept in order to detect one additional true case. Furthermore, they can indicate an uncertainty range SD around the chosen t, representing the interval of thresholds

---

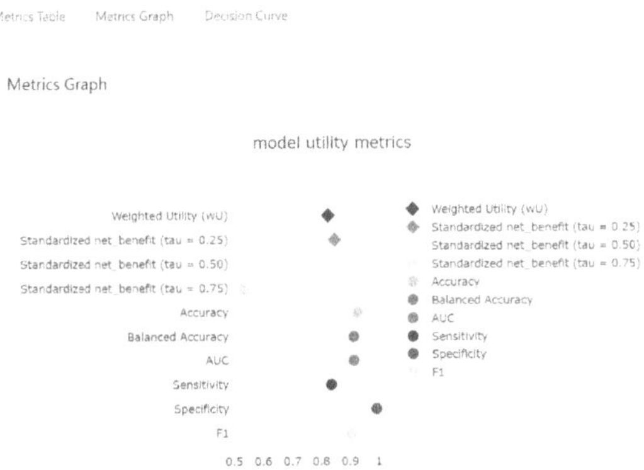

Fig. 2. Screenshot of the *Metrics Graph* panel of the web-based evaluation tool. Each point represents one performance or utility metric for the uploaded model: weighted utility (wU), standardized net benefit at three decision thresholds ($\tau = 0.25, 0.50, 0.75$), and standard performance measures (accuracy, balanced accuracy, AUC, sensitivity, specificity, and F1-score). All metrics are plotted on a common horizontal scale in $[0, 1]$, which facilitates visual comparison of the model's discriminatory performance and clinical utility.

that most decision makers would still find acceptable, and optionally supply an external prevalence P to be used in place of the prevalence observed in the test data. Given these inputs, the tool produces a set of coordinated graphical and numerical summaries that characterise both the statistical and decision-analytic performance of the model. The graphical output is shown in Fig. 3 includes (i) a receiver operating characteristic (ROC) curve with the region compatible with the specified decision preferences highlighted, (ii) a precision–recall curve, (iii) a decision curve that reports the standardised net benefit across the full range of decision thresholds, and (iv) a calibration plot comparing predicted risks with observed outcome frequencies. For a user-selected threshold t, the application also displays a comprehensive table of performance indices, including sensitivity, specificity, accuracy, positive and negative predictive values, F1-score, balanced accuracy, symmetric balanced accuracy, Matthews correlation coefficient, correlation distance, several variants of net benefit (treat-all, treat-none and model-based, in both raw and standardised form), Brier score and its decomposition (uncertainty, reliability, resolution) [11], likelihood ratios, post-test probabilities, global and local AUC, expected calibration error [8], and sharpness measures. Together, these outputs support the joint assessment of discrimination, calibration, and clinical utility of probabilistic prediction models under user-specified preferences.

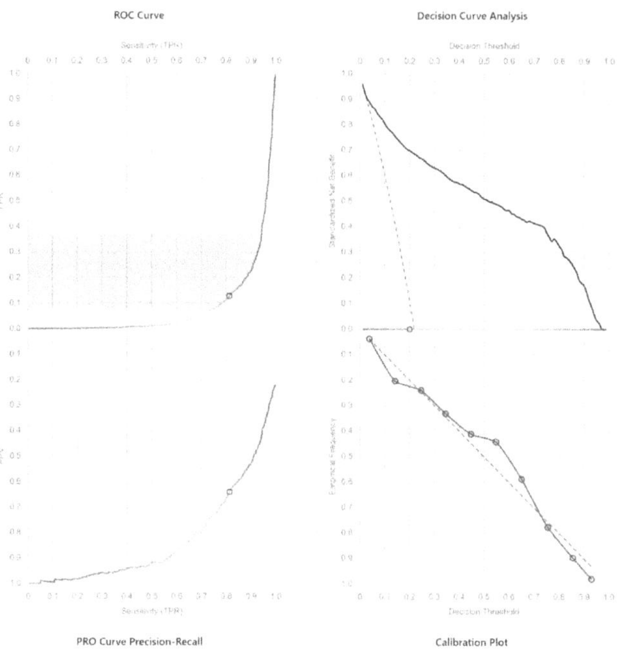

Fig. 3. Screenshot of the web-based model evaluation tool. The left-hand panels show the ROC curve and the PRO precision–recall curve, with the region compatible with the specified decision preferences shaded in grey. The right-hand panels display the decision curve (standardised net benefit as a function of the decision threshold) and the calibration plot (empirical outcome frequencies versus predicted probabilities). A detailed table below the plots reports threshold-specific performance, calibration, and decision-analytic metrics for the selected operating point.

4   Conclusion

Clinical AI systems demand evaluation frameworks that go beyond accuracy and consider the real-world consequences of model outputs. In the keynote summarized in this work, we have addressed this gap by proposing the weighted Utility (wU) metric, a user-centered evaluation method that integrates human uncertainty, contextual relevance, and asymmetric error costs into a unified analytic framework. Unlike conventional performance metrics, wU quantifies not only how often a model is correct, but how much its correctness matters–especially in high-risk, complex cases where human decision-making is most fragile.

Empirical applications demonstrate that models optimized with wU can outperform traditional AUC-based models precisely where support is most needed: in hard-case regions marked by expert uncertainty. By embedding rater-specific thresholds and relevance weights, wU operationalizes clinical intuitions about risk and utility into a formal evaluation tool that respects user subjectivity while maintaining analytical rigor.

While powerful, the approach does rest on the availability of rater-specific annotations and requires further validation across larger and more diverse clinical contexts. Nonetheless, these limitations do not undermine its core value: aligning AI evaluation with human-centered principles of safety, interpretability, and trust.

Future research should explore how wU extends to multi-class or temporal decision tasks, how best to elicit user thresholds at scale, and how model optimization can be directly informed by utility surfaces rather than post hoc analysis. Integrating such user-centered metrics into training and regulatory pipelines will be essential to ensure that clinical AI serves as a reliable partner–not just a predictive engine.

Ultimately, wU invites us to redefine what it means for AI to be "good": not merely accurate, but context-aware, user-aligned, and genuinely useful.

References

1. Cabitza, F., Campagner, A., Sconfienza, L.M.: As if sand were stone. new concepts and metrics to probe the ground on which to build trustable AI. BMC Med. Inform. Decis. Mak. **20**(1), 219 (2020)
2. Cabitza, F., et al.: The importance of being external. methodological insights for the external validation of machine learning models in medicine. Comput. Methods Programs Biomed. **208**, 106288 (2021)
3. Campagner, A., Angius, R., Cabitza, F.: A question of trust: old and new metrics for the reliable assessment of trustworthy AI. In: HEALTHINF, pp. 132–143 (2023)
4. Campagner, A., Sternini, F., Cabitza, F.: Decisions are not all equal-introducing a utility metric based on case-wise raters' perceptions. Comput. Methods Programs Biomed. **221**, 106930 (2022)
5. Chicco, D., Tötsch, N., Jurman, G.: Challenges in the real world use of classification accuracy metrics: from recall and precision to the matthews correlation coefficient. Briefings Bioinform. **24**(5), bbad345 (2023). https://doi.org/10.1093/bib/bbad345. https://pmc.ncbi.nlm.nih.gov/articles/PMC10550141/
6. Corso, A., Karamadian, D., Valentin, R., Cooper, M., Kochenderfer, M.J.: A holistic assessment of the reliability of machine learning systems. arXiv preprint arXiv:2307.10586 (2023)
7. Flach, P., et al.: Good classification measures and how to find them. Mach. Learn. (2022). https://arxiv.org/abs/2201.09044, preprint available as arXiv:2201.09044
8. Guo, C., Pleiss, G., Sun, Y., Weinberger, K.Q.: On calibration of modern neural networks. In: International Conference on Machine Learning, pp. 1321–1330. PMLR (2017)
9. Heim, E., Wright, O., Shriver, D.: A guide to failure in machine learning: reliability and robustness from foundations to practice. arXiv preprint arXiv:2503.00563 (2025)
10. Kelly, C.J., Karthikesalingam, A., Suleyman, M., Corrado, G., King, D.: Key challenges for delivering clinical impact with artificial intelligence. BMC Med. **17**(1), 195 (2019)

11. Murphy, A.H.: A new vector partition of the probability score. J. Appl. Meteorol. Climatol. **12**(4), 595–600 (1973)
12. Oakden-Rayner, L., Dunnmon, J., Carneiro, G., Ré, C.: Hidden stratification causes clinically meaningful failures in machine learning for medical imaging. In: Proceedings of the ACM Conference on Health, Inference, and Learning, pp. 151–159 (2020)
13. Vickers, A.J., Elkin, E.B.: Decision curve analysis: a novel method for evaluating prediction models. Med. Decis. Mak. **26**(6), 565–574 (2006)

Author Index